# THE
# PARAPSYCHOLOGY
# REVOLUTION

## A CONCISE ANTHOLOGY OF PARANORMAL AND PSYCHICAL RESEARCH

COMPILATION AND COMMENTARY BY

*Robert M. Schoch*, Ph.D.,

*and*

*Logan Yonavjak*

JEREMY P. TARCHER/PENGUIN
Published by the Penguin Group
Penguin Group (USA) Inc., 375 Hudson Street, New York, New York 10014, USA •
Penguin Group (Canada), 90 Eglinton Avenue East, Suite 700, Toronto, Ontario M4P 2Y3,
Canada (a division of Pearson Penguin Canada Inc.) • Penguin Books Ltd, 80 Strand,
London WC2R 0RL, England • Penguin Ireland, 25 St Stephen's Green, Dublin 2, Ireland
(a division of Penguin Books Ltd) • Penguin Group (Australia), 250 Camberwell Road,
Camberwell, Victoria 3124, Australia (a division of Pearson Australia Group Pty Ltd) •
Penguin Books India Pvt Ltd, 11 Community Centre, Panchsheel Park, New Delhi–110 017, India •
Penguin Group (NZ), 67 Apollo Drive, Rosedale, North Shore 0632, New Zealand (a division
of Pearson New Zealand Ltd) • Penguin Books (South Africa) (Pty) Ltd,
24 Sturdee Avenue, Rosebank, Johannesburg 2196, South Africa

Penguin Books Ltd, Registered Offices: 80 Strand, London WC2R 0RL, England

A list of permissions appears on pages 357–58, which are an extension of this copyright page.

Most Tarcher/Penguin books are available at special quantity discounts for bulk purchase for sales pro-
motions, premiums, fund-raising, and educational needs. Special books or book excerpts also can be created to fit specific needs. For details, write Penguin Group (USA) Inc. Special Markets, 375 Hudson
Street, New York, NY 10014.

Library of Congress Cataloging-in-Publication Data

The parapsychology revolution : a concise anthology of paranormal and psychical research /
compilation and commentary by Robert M. Schoch and Logan Yonavjak.
p.      cm.
Includes bibliographical references and index.
ISBN 978-1-58542-616-4
1. Parapsychology—Research   I. Schoch, Robert M.   II. Yonavjak, Logan.
BF1040.5P38      2008                   2007038615
130—dc22

Printed in the United States of America
1   3   5   7   9   10   8   6   4   2

BOOK DESIGN BY MEIGHAN CAVANAUGH

While the authors have made every effort to provide accurate telephone numbers and Internet addresses
at the time of publication, neither the publisher nor the authors assume any responsibility for errors, or
for changes that occur after publication. Further, the publisher does not have any control over and does
not assume any responsibility for author or third-party websites or their content.

# CONTENTS

## CONCLUDING REMARKS

*The more important fundamental laws and facts of physical science have all been discovered, and these are now so firmly established that the possibility of their ever being supplanted in consequence of new discoveries is exceedingly remote. . . . Future discoveries must be looked for in the sixth place of decimals.*

—ALBERT A. MICHELSON, NOBEL LAUREATE IN PHYSICS, 1907, speaking at the dedication of the Ryerson Physics Lab at the University of Chicago in 1894 before the elucidation of X-rays and the structure of the atom, and before the discovery of radioactivity and the development of quantum physics and relativity theory (quoted in Neil deGrasse Tyson, "The Beginning of Science," *Natural History*, 2001)

*It is one of the commonest of our mistakes to consider that the limit of our power of perception is also the limit of all that there is to perceive.*

—CHARLES WEBSTER LEADBEATER (*Man Visible and Invisible: Examples of Different Types of Men as Seen by Trained Clairvoyance*, second and revised edition, 1907, p. 19)

# INTRODUCTION:
# TAKING THE PARANORMAL
# SERIOUSLY

In many ways, given our materialistic and technological society, it is difficult to take the paranormal seriously. Can the thoughts in my consciousness really be transferred and mingled with the consciousness of another person at a distance without any information being passed by normal means of the senses? That is, does telepathy really occur? Can my mind alone influence the external material world without my exerting any muscular or mechanical action? That is, can psychokinesis really take place? The answer for many "rational" people is a resounding no, even if they have heard anecdotal stories from good friends, or had an odd experience firsthand. From a modern perspective, most people "know" and assume that such things cannot occur. Telepathy, clairvoyance, precognition, psychokinesis—these are examples that are beyond the "normal" laws of science and nature; they appear to break the rules of the everyday world: they are paranormal (the Greek *para* means "beyond" or "beside"). As far as we know, there is no known mechanism to explain such incidents, so according to conventional thought at best they must be chance-coincidence, or at worst deception. But then again, many people who are quick to say, "No, such things are impossible" have never taken the time to review any of the serious scientific literature recording the progress made in elucidating the paranormal over the last century and a half.

There are also the "true believers" who do not for a second doubt the reality of the paranormal, yet are unable to convince the rational doubter who demands clear-cut evidence that can withstand hard scrutiny. Too often, it seems, the evidence for paranormal phenomena is just "too soft" and easily explained away as coincidence, psychological tricks (where one may be easily fooled inadvertently, even by oneself), or active deception on the part of the unscrupulous. Furthermore, there is a slew of baggage that is inevitably associated with any serious attempt to critically evaluate the paranormal. Performing psychics and metal benders, healers and fortune-tellers, ghost hunters and UFO buffs, mediums and clairvoyants, astrologers and diviners, alien abductees and crop circle fanatics—to the layperson's eye all are included in the popular mind under the umbrella of the paranormal. Many persons of such ilk are viewed as simply charlatans preying on overanxious, aggrieved, naïve, and ill-informed persons.

The public face of science has reinforced such negative views of the paranormal. Psychical research, psi studies, parapsychology, extrasensory perception, and similar subjects have been widely misinterpreted and sometimes purposefully ignored by scientists who are leery of these topics, and in fact have no firsthand experience in the subject and have never pursued the serious scientific literature dealing with paranormal phenomena. There are many circumstances in history where an individual or individuals believed in something that ultimately was considered "wrong" from our modern point of view, but it still proved to be of heuristic scientific value, since it presented a step toward progress and led to new discoveries. Ideas at first dismissed as wrong or impossible, and openly joked about and disparaged, have proved to be both correct and groundbreaking; for instance, in the twentieth century such diverse theories as continental drift and the idea that useful energy could be extracted from the nucleus of an atom were initially dismissed as nonsense. The British mathematician and physicist Lord Kelvin (William Thomson, 1824–1907), one of the foremost scientists of his time, stated baldly that "X-rays will prove to be a hoax" (Youngson, 1998). Today many prominent scientists have the same opinion of psychical studies.

The British "stamp incident" is a good recent example of just how incredibly "charged" the topic of psychical studies remains to this day. In

2001 British Royal Mail issued six new stamps commemorating the centenary of the Nobel Prize. To accompany the new stamps, the Royal Mail published a booklet for which they invited various Nobel laureates to add contributions, including Brian Josephson, a professor at the University of Cambridge who won the Nobel Prize in Physics in 1973 for his work on superconductors. Josephson surprised the scientific community and the general public with a comment regarding "paranormal phenomena." For the booklet Josephson wrote that "a more detailed understanding of paranormal phenomena may emerge from a better understanding of quantum mechanics" and this "may lead to an explanation of processes still not understood within conventional science, such as telepathy—an area in which Britain is at the forefront of research" (Klarreich, 2001). This statement, even coming from a Nobel laureate, caused uproar among traditional physicists and other scientists in England and around the world. For example, the Oxford quantum physicist David Deutsch commented, "It is utter rubbish. . . . Telepathy simply does not exist. The Royal Mail has let itself be hoodwinked into supporting ideas that are complete nonsense" (McKie, 2001). So which is it? Does the paranormal exist and require scrutiny? Or is it utter rubbish? One of the purposes of this book is to present the subject so that readers can start to gain a better appreciation for what all the fuss is about.

# WHAT THIS BOOK IS AND IS NOT ABOUT: CIRCUMSCRIBING THE PARANORMAL

The topics addressed in this book are primarily those that are generally studied by practicing parapsychologists, namely extrasensory perception (encompassing telepathy and clairvoyance) and psychokinesis (mind over matter on the micro and macro level, such as movements of objects by thought or consciousness alone). These topics, and related matters, are discussed in more detail immediately below. What this book does not cover are certain topics that some people may think of as "paranormal," such as UFOs, ghost hunting (with the exception of "poltergeist activity," i.e., the unexplained, apparently paranormal, movement or breaking of inanimate objects, production of sounds, spontaneous setting of fires, and the like), Big Foot, pyramid power, the Loch Ness Monster, spontaneous human combustion, and so forth. Certain subjects that are related to the paranormal, such as altered states of consciousness (these may serve as a vehicle for the enhancement of paranormal experiences), out-of-body experiences, and near-death experiences are not covered in this volume due to space constraints and also because they are not necessarily central to the question of the paranormal (depending on the definition used for "paranormal"*). That is, paranormal experiences as discussed in this book (for instance, telepathy or clairvoyance) may or may not accompany an out-of-body experience or near-death experience. The question of survival beyond the grave is not a primary focus of this book, although we do touch on some of the scientific evidence that may support reincarnation.

The actual subject matter of psychical studies and parapsychology is difficult to define, other than to say it is the study of the paranormal,

---

\* In this work we use the term "paranormal" as essentially synonymous with the subject matter generally studied by serious researchers within parapsychology, as described in this book. The late parapsychologist Charles Honorton wrote: "I believe the concept of the 'paranormal' is an anachronism and should be abandoned. The term is usually used to imply that psi [a term covering both extrasensory perception and psychokinesis] interactions must necessarily, if real [and Honorton thought psi was real], represent an order of reality outside the natural realm. . . . A more empirically fruitful conceptualization is that parapsychology involves the study of currently anomalous communication and energetic processes. This approach guides the efforts of most parapsychological researchers I know, who work on the assumption that they are dealing with unexplained—anomalous, but not unexplainable—natural processes" (Honorton, 1994, pp. 210–11). Honorton did not suggest a replacement term for "paranormal." Note that often the term "paranormal" is used colloquially or popularly in a much broader sense, particularly to include unidentified flying objects (UFOs). Thus the television hypnotist Paul McKenna states, "The paranormal may be defined as those phenomena which can be proved to exist, but which science cannot yet explain" (McKenna with O'Bryen, 1997, p. vii).

and neither the range of subjects nor the definition of terms is necessarily consistent from one researcher to another. It is also generally defined in terms of negatives: for some people the paranormal is anything that cannot be explained by "normal" scientific theory, and thus as phenomena find explanations that fit traditional science, they are removed from the realm of the paranormal. As the term is now commonly applied, *parapsychology* is the study of extrasensory perception (ESP; including telepathy, clairvoyance, and precognition) and psychokinesis (PK, or "mind over matter"). One modern definition of parapsychology is "the scientific study of the capacity attributed to some individuals to interact with their environment by means other than the recognised sensorimotor channels" (Koestler Parapsychology Unit, 2006). The older term *psychical research* is often used synonymously with parapsychology, although some researchers consider parapsychology to focus primarily on laboratory experiments, and psychical research to refer primarily to non-laboratory work (such as investigating an alleged poltergeist incident "in the field"). Furthermore, the term psychical research was used more prominently in the earlier research, dating back to the Society for Psychical Research in the late nineteenth and early twentieth centuries.

Here we describe the subjects generally included within the field of parapsychology. These can be grouped under the four major categories of Extrasensory Perception, Psychokinesis, Materializations, and Survival Studies (which may involve aspects of ESP and PK).

# EXTRASENSORY PERCEPTION

§ 1. Mind-to-mind or person-to-person interactions and transmission of data (whether such data is expressed in terms of thoughts, feelings, emotions, physiological changes, or a sensory/pseudo-sensory stimulus, as for instance a "hallucination" or "apparition") through some means (as yet unknown) other than the normal senses such as vision, hearing, smell, taste, touch, balance, and so on. This includes phenomena that have been referred to by such terms as "mind-reading," "thought-reading," "thought-transference," "mental rapport," and so forth. The term we prefer for this class of phenomena is "telepathy."

§ 2. Clairvoyance ("clear vision"), the reception of information about objects, persons, and events (whether in the past, present, or future) by other than normal sensory means, also referred to as paragnosia (Rýzl, 1970, p. 2). Whereas telepathy involves mind-to-mind transmission, strict clairvoyance is a direct mental perception of objects, pictures, or events by other than normal sensory means without mind-to-mind communication. Clairvoyance is sometimes thought of as "second sight" or "seeing from a distance," such as when a person who is presumably clairvoyant can mentally "travel" and describe the contents of a room many miles away. In some cases, but not always, this may be associated with a so-called out-of-body experience, where one feels that one has actually left the physical body and traveled to the distant place, perhaps in "spirit form." An out-of-body experience need not involve distant travel, however; one may feel that one has left the physical body and simply looks down on the physical self from the ceiling of a room, for instance.

Here we are primarily concerned with clairvoyance in which the clairvoyant "sees" (or even feels or is aware of) objects and events at a distance mentally. This is now often referred to as remote viewing, although it is still unclear as to whether some or all remote viewing is actually a telepathic endeavor (the remote viewer gaining access to information in another person's mind—whether that mind observes the object or scene to be viewed in the present, past, or future—rather than directly from inanimate objects). The concept of clairvoyance in the most general sense goes back thousands of years and is apparently found in virtually all cultures (see Lang, 1894, 1898; De Vesme, 1931a, 1931b), and includes such concepts and practices as crystal-gazing and various forms of divination and prophecy. The term clairvoyance is sometimes used purposefully (see, for instance, Wyld, 1883) or inadvertently (colloquially) to include "reading" people's thoughts or mental states, or picking up other information from or about people, at a distance. Here we restrict the term clairvoyance to the reception of information about material objects, persons, and events by non-ordinary sensory and non-telepathic means. Psychometry (see the discussion by Roll on page 116; Buchanan, 1854, 1889; Denton and Denton, 1863), or the description of the circumstances and history of a material object by a sensitive using non-ordinary and non-telepathic means, should in our assessment be considered a form of clairvoyance. Clairvoyance is sometimes used colloquially to also include precognition.

§ 3. Precognition (also referred to as proscopy and premonition), the reception of information about future events. If telepathy and clairvoyance are not limited by time, then such information may be received telepathically and/or clairvoyantly.

§ 4. Retrocognition, the reception of information about past events other than by ordinary means. As for precognition, if telepathy and clairvoyance are not limited to the present, then such information may be received either telepathically and/or clairvoyantly. This category may include various supposed cases of reincarnation.

The above sorts of phenomena have been grouped together under the general label of extrasensory perception, or ESP (Rhine, 1934; originally the term was hyphenated as "extra-sensory"). This is a useful designation as it is in practice often difficult, if not impossible, to distinguish telepathy from clairvoyance as here defined. To illustrate one example, if a sitter or agent in one room focuses on a series of cards that in turn are detected and called correctly (or at least with a statistically significant positive result) by a percipient isolated in another room, or even in another building, is this clairvoyance (that is, the percipient gained the information directly from the cards) or telepathy (the information was transmitted from the agent's mind to the percipient's mind)? Whatever it is, it would be categorized as a form of ESP.

ESP involves the reception of information mentally, be it from another person and their mental thoughts and state, or directly from a non-living material object. We should point out that when we say "mental" and "person," this could also apply to other living organisms besides persons, and indeed there is evidence for ESP among animals (see section on Animal Psi below, page 47) and even plants and isolated cells (see below, page 50; Backster, 2003; Vogel, 1974; see also Swanson, 2003, pp. 77–83).

As more or less equivalents of the term ESP, phrases such as "extraordinary knowing," "anomalous communication," "anomalous knowing" (Mayer, 2007), and "anomalous cognition" (Cognitive Sciences Laboratory, 1999–2001) are sometimes used. Besides ESP, another branch of reputed paranormal phenomena includes physical effects on the material world by no known energetic or material means, but presumably by solely mental or consciousness means. For lack of a better term at the moment, we can refer to these as non-ESP paranormal phenomena. They include, but are not limited to, the following types of phenomena: Psychokinesis and Materializations.

# PSYCHOKINESIS

§ 5. Mind over matter effects, where apparently mental activity or consciousness alone (without any known or understood intervening material or energy) can move or manipulate material objects. This includes psychokinesis (PK for short), or the movement of objects, whether on a large (macro) scale (such as moving a spoon across a table or levitating a chair, perhaps with a person in it) or a small (micro) scale (such as statistically influencing the outcome of randomly rolled dice or causing an electronic random event generator to form a non-random pattern). PK is also known as telekinesis, which is an older term and originally referred to the movement of macroscopic objects during séances, for instance. Another term used for PK is "anomalous perturbation" (Cognitive Sciences Laboratory,

1999–2001). This general category may also include such reported phenomena as causing temperature changes, the production of sounds, and influencing chemical reactions solely by mental means. Poltergeist activities may also be included in the category of telekinesis or macro-PK.

§ 6. Mind over biological systems, sometimes referred to as DMILS (Direct Mental Interactions with Living Systems), where apparently mental activity or consciousness on the part of an agent affects another person or biological entity in a physical sense, such as promoting the healing of a sick patient or causing pain and suffering in a healthy person. This may include phenomena reported in conjunction with intercessory prayer studies. In our opinion, at least some such cases may be explained telepathically, where the intention of the "healer," is picked up by the mind of the "receiver," who then affects her or his own body. This can also include what is known as "intuitive healing" or "Medical Intuitive Diagnosis," which is the ability to diagnose medical illnesses, sometimes over distances, without the aid of any physical apparatus. This form of diagnosis is almost always used in conjunction with traditional medical care.

In the 1940s, the parapsychologists R. H. Thouless and B. P. Wiesner (1946, 1947) used the term "psi" (often used now in such phases as "psi phenomena") to include both ESP and PK. The term psi-research is often used as the equivalent of psychical research. The symbol $\Psi$ (psi) has long been used to represent the "general psychical world" (Lodge, 1908, p. 184) in contradistinction to the "general physical world" represented by $\Phi$ (phi; Lodge, 1908). Using the term psi, the parapsychologist Milan Rýzl (1970, p. 14) writes: "The possible existence of psychokinesis, however, suggests the possibility of hitherto unknown energetic relations among natural phenomena, in which a new type of energy takes part, the so-called PSI-energy propagating in a hypothetical PSI-field." Another way psi is used by professional parapsychologists is as follows: "The neutral term 'psi' is used to denote this hypothesised capacity ["attributed to some individuals to interact with their environment by means other than the recognised sensorimotor channels"] though no assumption is made as to the mechanisms underlying people's psi experiences" (Koestler Parapsychology Unit, 2006). "Anomalous mental phenomena" is sometimes used as an equivalent of "psi" (Cognitive Sciences Laboratory, 1999–2001).

# MATERIALIZATIONS

§ 7. The materialization and dematerialization of objects and other entities, such as potentially physical apparitions or "ghosts," that have a physical or energetic reality that can be recorded or detected by physical equipment (for instance, a camera), as opposed to hallucinations, even if veridical hallucinations. Materializations purportedly take many forms. They might appear out of "thin air" and disappear (dematerialize) once again. Or, amorphous substances might extrude or grow from a medium (often purportedly channeling the dead or spirits) during a séance and take the shape of objects, such as a hand, face, or even an entire human-like entity. In some instances it was suggested that as a spirit would materialize, the medium would dematerialize, in a way providing physical substance and sustenance for the spirit (and, perhaps a convenient rationale for why the medium and fully materialized spirit could not be viewed simultaneously). In other cases a fully formed spirit and the medium were presumably seen together.

When seemingly natural and normal objects suddenly appear during a séance-like situation, they are usually referred to as "apports." Apports can take the form of inanimate objects (such as coins, pottery, letters, and so on) or animate objects (various plants and animals). A typical interpretation of apports is that these objects are not paranormal per se, but have been transported paranormally from some other location; for instance, a plant in India might be paranormally dematerialized, transported, and rematerialized in an enclosed séance room in London. Thus, if true, an apport would also demonstrate the paranormal passage of matter through matter, or else how could the object have gotten into a completely enclosed and sealed room? The category of materialization includes the production of what have been referred to as paranormal objects, objects that cannot be produced by any known means or techniques. An example might be two totally solid (not in any way cut and reconnected) wooden rings that are linked together but of different species of trees. It has been suggested that a single such permanent paranormal object, which could be studied objectively, might satisfy at least some of the skeptics and reinvigorate the field of psychical studies and parapsychology (cf. Beloff, 1993, pp. 113, 229).

# SURVIVAL STUDIES

§ 8.  Another aspect of early psychical studies, but one that at least in an explicit sense has become increasingly divorced from parapsychology, is survival research. Do humans survive beyond the grave? Is there an afterlife? This of course is an ancient and fundamental question, one that has been central to many religious and philosophical systems, and certainly was on the minds of many early psychical researchers. It relates to other categories of paranormal phenomena, such as "ghosts," traditional séance manifestations, and includes the study of such phenomena as out-of-body experiences, near-death experiences, and suggestive evidence for reincarnation.

When it comes to so-called out-of-body experiences and near-death experiences, there is strong debate as to whether there are any genuine paranormal features involved, or if in fact these phenomena can be explained solely through standard (non-parapsychological) psychology and physiology, such as the effects of oxygen deprivation. For recent discussions and reviews of the literature on out-of-body and near-death experiences, see Alvarado (2000) and Greyson (2000) respectively.

Reincarnation is certainly a very ancient and hallowed belief, forming the mainstay of some of the world's great religions, including
Hinduism and Buddhism. Concerning recent interest and research in
the topic, there have been two major approaches: memories of past lives
induced by hypnotic past-life regression (see, for instance, the discussions in Cannon, 1953, and Edmunds, 1961) and the study of memories given spontaneously by very young children.

The modern past-life regression craze in Western culture, if it can
be called that, dates to the 1956 publication of *The Search for Bridey
Murphy* by the amateur hypnotist Morey Bernstein. Bernstein regressed Mrs. Virginia Tighe (known in the book by the pseudonym Ruth
Simmons, and she later remarried and was Mrs. Virginia Morrow)
and found that in a former life she was the Irish woman Bridget (Bridey)
Murphy, 1798–1864. After publication, controversy raged over the truth
to Bridey Murphy, and a reporter from the *Denver Post*, William J. Barker,
traveled to Ireland to search for a historical Bridey Murphy, something
that Bernstein had not done. Neither Bridey Murphy nor any of her family members, who had been named during the regressions, were actually
tracked down, but Barker did verify some details of the story, details that
one could argue it would be nearly impossible for Virginia Tighe to have
acquired other than paranormally.

For the 1965 edition of *The Search for Bridey Murphy*, Barker wrote
a chapter titled "Bridey's Debunkers Debunked" in which he exposed flaws in the critics' arguments against the reality of Bridey
Murphy, though ultimately the question remained open. In his chapter Barker included portions of an interview with Morey Bernstein
discussing the possible survival of consciousness after death. Bernstein
commented: "For at least two reasons the study of ESP is tied to the
question of survival after death. In the first place, the only kind of
perception possible in a discarnate state would be extrasensory. Second, death would seem a matter of coming to a halt in the space-time
world. But research already has proved that the mind has an area of
freedom from the limitations of space and time. Scientists like Dr.
J. B. Rhine of Duke University have not labored all these years in

parapsychology to prove merely that the human mind can correctly guess more than one out of five test cards. They know that the card experiments lead to bigger game. . . . It is noteworthy, therefore, that the parapsychology revolution has spread rapidly in the last decade" (Bernstein, 1965, pp. 310–311; it is from this quote that we took the title of this anthology).

One aspect of certain past-life regressions under hypnosis is purported xenoglossy, or the ability of the subject to speak a language that he or she has not, and perhaps could not, learn in this lifetime (Stevenson, 1974). A famous, if controversial, case is that of the young English medium Rosemary who, through the spirit of the ancient Egyptian woman Nona, supposedly spoke New Kingdom Egyptian (Wood and Hulme, 1936; Hulme and Wood, 1936–1938).

It is now understood that hypnosis does not always produce veridical memories when a hypnotized adult is regressed to her/his childhood in this life, much less to a time before the most recent birth, that is to a past life. One must be wary that any such recovered past life is simply a fiction (elaborated, perhaps, with cryptomnesia, hidden or unconscious memories, of relatively obscure things, originally obtained normally), although a meaningful fiction, in terms of the psyche of the patient involved. It is not inconceivable that even if such a "past life" is on the whole fictional, it may involve certain bits of information from another time, place, or person(s) that were in fact acquired paranormally. Without judging the actual veracity of the supposed past lives, psychotherapists have found that one can use past-life regression techniques to explore, and help heal, a patient. Likewise so-called future-life progressions have also been used for therapeutic purposes.

The late Dr. Ian Stevenson pioneered the evidence from young children for reincarnation (Stevenson, 1960a, 1960b, 1966, 1975, 1977, 1980, 1983b, 1987; see below, page 123). Stevenson, working with the children and the families involved, was in the best cases able to actually identify (at least to his satisfaction—skeptics would disagree) the former personality. Typically in the cases documented by Stevenson, the previous personality, or former incarnation, died no more than a few years before the child was born and lived not very far away. The young child would recount aspects or memories of the former life typically between the ages of two and five, but these would fade away in the ensuing years. In many cases the children showed behavioral traits that could be related to the previous personality, and in some cases where the former personality died violently, birthmarks were found on the child corresponding to wounds in the former personality (Stevenson, 1997a, 1997b).

Even if Stevenson's evidence is taken at face value, and it is accepted that something is transmitted from the former personality to the child, does this prove reincarnation in a traditional sense? Does it demonstrate that all beings are reincarnated? We think not. Minimally, it might only indicate the transmission of some data from one living being to another paranormally. Indeed, it has long been suggested that many paranormal phenomena that have been interpreted in some circles as evidence for survival beyond the grave could simply be the effects of psi in this life. Along these lines, a distinction has been made between so-called "theta psi" (a term introduced by William Roll, after the Greek word *thantos*, which means death and begins with theta [see Beloff, 1993, p. 296–297, note 89]), or the psi effects of discarnate entities, such as ghosts, and so-called "super-psi" (also known as super-ESP) effects that might produce similar phenomena without invoking the discarnate or any aspect of an afterlife. For instance, is a child who seems to remember a past life simply able to pick up this information and various trait characteristics from the deceased by super-psi rather than actually being the incarnation of the previous person? Or, again, could the child in question simply pick up the information from still living persons, that is telepathically, and also perhaps gather information clairvoyantly? To give another example, might a particular poltergeist phenomenon be the result of "ghosts" (theta psi) or the strong energy or field emanating from a living human (super-psi)? Ultimately, the super-psi hypothesis can be invoked to explain virtually any supposed communications or other evidence for spirits or discarnate entities.

# EARLY SCIENTIFIC STUDIES OF THE PARANORMAL: THE SOCIETY FOR PSYCHICAL RESEARCH

Until the last quarter of the nineteenth century, most of the evidence for paranormal phenomena consisted of hearsay and anecdotal accounts. With the rise of spiritualism (i.e., the belief in both survival after death and the ability to communicate with the deceased, for instance during séances) in particular, a prominent group of scientists, philosophers, and religious leaders came together to make a systematic study of psychical phenomena. The result was the founding of the Society for Psychical Research (SPR); for all intents and purposes, the first full-fledged scientific study of psychical phenomena had begun. The rationale and goals of this endeavor were succinctly summarized in the opening statement of the first volume of the society's published proceedings:

> It has been widely felt that the present is an opportune time for making an organised and systematic attempt to investigate that large group of debatable phenomena designated by such terms as mesmeric, psychical, and Spiritualistic.
>
> From the recorded testimony of many competent witnesses, past and present, including observations recently made by scientific men of eminence in various countries, there appears to be, amidst much illusion and deception, an important body of remarkable phenomena, which are *primâ facie* inexplicable on any generally recognised hypothesis, and which, if incontestably established, would be of the highest possible value. [*Proceedings of the Society for Psychical Research*, vol. 1, part 1, p. 3 (1883), italics in the original.]

The immediate origins of the SPR can be traced to January 6, 1882. On that date William F. Barrett, a professor of physics at the Royal College of Science in Dublin (Beloff, 1993, p. 70), organized and convened a conference in London on psychical matters, and the establishment of a scientific society for their investigation was discussed. The latter was achieved with the founding of the SPR in London on February 20, 1882 (*Proceedings of the Society for Psychical Research* 1, p. 3 [1883]). Barrett had a long-standing interest in psychical phenomena (see, for instance, his 1876 paper that includes a discussion of what later became known as telepathy, published in 1883) and spiritualistic matters, and in promoting the foundation of the SPR he worked with the journalist and spiritualist E. Dawson Rogers, the latter to whom is sometimes given credit for the initial idea for such a society (Beloff, 1993, p. 70), or it is suggested that the idea arose from a conversation between Rogers and Barrett (Haynes, 1982, p. 4).

Thus at the very beginning there was a close tie between certain spiritualists and the SPR, and undoubtedly the spiritualists associated with the society (Rogers was a member of the founding council of the society in 1882, as was the Reverend W. Stainton Moses, another leading spiritualist of the time) hoped that the society could scientifically vindicate their beliefs in survival beyond the grave. It quickly became clear, however, that the core members of the SPR would critically analyze all paranormal (to use a more modern term) phenomena that came under its scrutiny, and any detected deception or fraud would be exposed. In 1885 a long and damning report on supposed paranormal phenomena associated with the Theosophical Society was published by the SPR (in vol. 3 of the *Proceedings of the SPR*), and Madame H. P. Blavatsky (a cofounder of the movement) and her associates were charged with deliberate deception. There were also critical reports on spiritualist mediums and phenomena, with for instance the exposure of the highly regarded spiritualist medium William Eglinton (see *Proceedings of the SPR* 4 [1887]). As a result a number of members with spiritualistic tendencies resigned from the society (Beloff, 1993, p. 76). Since then, the SPR continues to be identified by certain spiritualists and their successors as a group of skeptics that are opposed to religion and the concept of survival after death (see, for instance, Bradley, 1931; Zammit, 2002).

Fast-forward a century and we find that many of the same questions, uncertainties, and tensions surrounding psychical research, now generally referred to as parapsychology, still dominate the field.

# THE CULTURAL CONTEXT OF MODERN PARAPSYCHOLOGY

Whether one even accepts that some supposed paranormal phenomena are "objectively real," the study of the paranormal is, or at least can be, a genuinely scholarly and scientific activity. This has been the case since at least 1882 with the founding of the Society for Psychical Research. Scholarly and scientific endeavors are human activities, and as such they fit into a cultural and historical framework. There is nothing purely and absolutely "objective" about scientific studies as carried out by real, living, human beings. The objectivity of science is either a myth or something to strive toward while recognizing that ultimately it is an unreachable goal. The best we can hope for is to understand any particular discipline, and thus its biases and influences, in a wider cultural and social context. Psychical studies and parapsychology are no exception. If anything, they may epitomize this rule to a greater degree than most other scientific fields, especially due to the fact that psychical studies have had such a bad reputation, their methodology has needed to be even more careful and systematic to gain any sort of recognition.

From a cultural point of view, the notion of paranormal phenomena is not insignificant (see Hansen, 2001, for an extended discussion of this and related topics). Paranormal phenomena play a role in our culture and many cultures around the world. Even in Western society, superstitious beliefs and the terminology of poltergeists and ghosts can still be found in everyday conversation and the mainstream media.

Cultural anthropologist David J. Hess, in his 1993 book *Science in the New Age: The Paranormal, Its Defenders and Debunkers, and American Culture*, made the case that in the 1980s parapsychology, skepticism, and the New Age movement were three components or cultures (we would call them subcultures) in the context of what Hess refers to as a "paraculture" within the broader framework of American culture, and we would argue Western (or at least English-speaking) culture more generally. In our opinion Hess's analysis is still broadly applicable and is worth considering further. In many respects modern parapsychology finds itself in a position between the remnants or successors of the New Age movement on the one hand and what we might refer to as the professional skeptics and debunkers on the other hand.

The New Age movement was essentially a loosely confederated quasi-religious movement that emerged in the 1970s and ran its course in the 1980s, although various aspects and offshoots linger in the early twenty-first century. It is difficult to define precisely what was and was not part of the New Age movement, since it was never centralized and systematically institutionalized. It involved, primarily, looking for alternative (alternative to the traditional materialistic approach) knowledge and realities, and reinvigorating a type of spirituality among its adherents. This reinvigoration combined non-traditional Western themes and orientations, such as aspects of Eastern religions (e.g., Hinduism, Buddhism, and Toa) and ancient cultures (especially Egypt, ancient Europe, Native American traditions, and the "lost civilizations" of Atlantis and Mu/Lemuria), with the occult, theosophy, various esoteric traditions, alchemy, shamanism, crystal healing, astrology, divination, naturopathic and homeopathic medicine, a return to Nature and the "mother goddess," channeling, astral projection, reincarnation and past-life regressions, shifts in the poles of Earth, and among some New Agers such phenomena as crop circles and UFOs. Into this hodgepodge of subjects was often stirred a healthy dose of the psychic, and invariably scientific studies of paranormal phenomena were seen as supporting and in a sense vindicating the movement. New Agers were not afraid of science and technology when it served their purposes, and many sought to integrate ancient metaphysical traditions with modern cutting-edge scientific knowledge and theory, such as quantum mechanics.

The epitome, and also the beginning of the decline in prestige, of the New Age movement may have been the Harmonic Convergence of August 16–17, 1987, when New Agers gathered at designated "sacred sites" around the world. Some believed that this would mark the beginning of a new epoch for humanity and a transformation of society, essentially renewal leading to a golden age. When this failed to happen, or at least happen quickly enough, the movement lost momentum and started to fray. Some adherents abandoned the concept, while others turned inward to personal transformation, self-understanding, and spiritual enlightenment, topics that had always been an important part of the movement. As the 1990s progressed the very term New Age was shunned by many persons who had once used it proudly.

Organized Skepticism (Skepticism with a capital S) can trace its origins back centuries, but was reified as a quasi-religious scientific fundamentalism in 1976 under the leadership of the humanist philosopher Paul Kurtz (see Hess, 1993, p. 11). In that year Kurtz and colleagues established the skeptical organization Committee for the Scientific Investigation of Claims of the Paranormal, commonly known as CSICOP (pronounced "psi cop," which probably intentionally alludes to policing and rooting out "psi" as in psychical studies; the original name of the organization was Committee to Scientifically Investigate Claims of Paranormal and Other Phenomena, which does not form such a telling acronym) and the popular "debunking" magazine *Skeptical Inquirer* was launched (the original publication of CSICOP was *The Zetetic*, founded by Marcello Truzzi, who later left CSICOP and established the *Zetetic Scholar*; see page 255 below and Hess, 1993, p. 33). The publishing house Prometheus Books, which Kurtz also helped to establish (Hess, 1993, p. 12), is another institutionalized branch of the Skepticism movement.

When it comes to the Skeptics, they are crusaders with a passion, initially going after components of the New Age movement and any studies, such as those of various parapsychologists, that might lend credence and support to New Age tenants. This passion and denial of anything that might be considered paranormal, versus a disinterested commitment to open-minded questioning, indicates that the Skeptics are in reality pseudo-skeptics. As the sociologist and student of the paranormal Marcello Truzzi stated: "Since 'skepticism' properly refers to doubt rather than denial—nonbelief rather than belief—critics who take the negative rather than an agnostic position but still call themselves 'skeptics' are actually *pseudo-skeptics* and have, I believe, gained a false advantage by usurping that label [the skeptic label]" (Truzzi, 1987). The publishing organ of the Skeptics, the *Skeptical Inquirer*, has earned a reputation for being anything but balanced, fair, and genuinely skeptical. As the late psychoanalyst and clinician Elizabeth Lloyd Mayer wrote, "Reading the *Skeptical Inquirer* was like reading a fundamentalist religious tract. I found the journal dismayingly snide, regularly punctuated by sarcasm, self-congratulation, and nastiness, all parading as reverence for true science" (Mayer, 2007, p. 93).

Since the collapse of the New Age movement, the Skeptics continue to find plenty of fodder in attacking anything they deem to be pseudo-science, including psychical and parapsychological studies. As Beloff (1990, p. 21) has pointed out, the Skeptics have failed to account for and discredit or invalidate paranormal phenomena and parapsychological experiments in general, for instance by developing some overarching mainstream scientific theory—be it even a theory of consistent hyper-aesthesia (extraordinary sensory acuteness, but still an acuteness of the known senses, not the paranormal or psychic), or perhaps a theory of mass delusion, or one of consistent statistical errors that make insignificant results appear significant (for a discussion of statistics as applied to parapsychology, see the article by Utts reprinted on page 163). Therefore, the Skeptics have had to resort to ad hoc attacks on each investigation that yields significant results, and (if all else fails) in some cases these attacks are essentially nothing more than accusations of either sloppy research methods or outright deception and fraud. Furthermore, as has been pointed out by the historian of the occult Robert Galbreath, this pattern of accusations against psychical researchers has been ongoing for a long time, and the critics sometimes appear to be guilty of the very charges leveled at their targets. "Many of these same pioneers [various founding members and early researchers of the SPR] have come under attack within the last decade for credulity, unreliable reporting, and even collusion in fraud. Some of the attacks seem open to the same charges, and the controversy has been a bitter one" (Galbreath, 1971, p. 743).

In 1955 the American chemist George Price, in an article in *Science* entitled "Science and the Supernatural" (discussed at length by Vasiliev, 2002, pp. 114–115; see also E. Bauer, 1984), explicitly said what many skeptics, both before and since, have suggested: supposed paranormal phenomena are "incompatible with modern science" and therefore should be rejected. Price continues, "If parapsychology and modern science are incompatible, why not renounce parapsychology? We do know that the hypothesis that some people lie and deceive themselves fits in well with the framework of science" (Price quotations from Vasiliev, 2002, p. 115). Price and others of a similar mind-set would explain all paranormal phenomena in terms of sloppy research, fraud, and self-deception, essentially disparaging the entire field and all researchers involved in the subject. By the same token, one might conclude that any radical or non-paradigmatic findings or ideas, be they in physics, chemistry, astronomy, biology, or any other scientific field, should simply be dismissed, yet it is just such anomalies and the theorizing that they incur that has the ability to revolutionize and advance science. Classic examples in physics are radioactivity, quantum theory, and relativity; in biology we can cite Darwinian evolutionary theory; in astronomy we can cite the even older revolutionary work of Copernicus, Kepler, and Galileo.

As Hess (1993, pp. 64–65) documents, Skeptics such as science and mathematics writer and arch-debunker Martin Gardner will resort to simple and unabashed ridicule in order to discredit parapsychologists and their research. Beloff (1990, p. 27) also notes that various individuals (examples that come to mind include Paul Kurtz, Martin Gardner, and the stage conjurer James Randi) have made their careers and reputations as "debunkers" of psychical and parapsychological claims, which begs the question of what they have contributed of their own and where they would be if it were not for psychical and parapsychological studies. The Skeptics, or more accurately pseudo-skeptics, have fully mortgaged their prestige to the object of their attention.

In the 1980s the serious study of psychical phenomena and parapsychology was caught in the middle between two quasi-religious, quasi-philosophical, quasi-ideological, and even quasi-scientific camps, namely the New Agers and the Skeptics. Essentially one could view the more rigorous parapsychologists as the true skeptics and genuine scientists straddling a sometimes-uncomfortable middle ground between diametrically opposed worldviews. This was nothing new to psychical researchers, but essentially a replay of a scenario that has occurred over and over since the 1880s and even earlier, and it continues in different forms to this day. It can be seen as successive attempts to have "science" support and vindicate what is essentially a religious perspective or philosophical worldview. Thus, to perhaps oversimplify to make the point, in the 1880s many spiritualists clearly hoped that science, and specifically the scientific studies carried out under the auspices of the Society for Psychical Research, would support and even prove their beliefs in spirits and the afterlife, thus putting their religion on a sound scientific footing. Likewise in other areas certain religious zealots sought a scientific confirmation of their beliefs, so for instance men like publisher John Taylor (1859–1860) and the well-known astronomer C. Piazzi Smyth (1864, 1880) sought confirmation of their brand of fundamentalist Christianity in the minute details and measurements of the Great Pyramid in Egypt (Schoch and McNally, 2005).

As noted earlier, spiritualists were disappointed and decried the psychical researchers when they failed to live up to expectations of confirming survival beyond the grave; rather the psychical researchers were not afraid to expose fraud, deception, and outright charlatans. But on the other side, materialistic scientists and philosophers ignored, dismissingly doubted, or outright attacked the psychical researchers and their evidence for some "minor" paranormal effects such as telepathic connections between human minds.

To us it appears that little has changed in the intervening years. Adherents of the New Age movement in the 1980s, and their spiritual successors, have always wanted to push parapsychology and psychical studies well beyond the limits of the solid empirical evidence (be it

laboratory experiments, field data, or collections of verifiable spontaneous psi occurrences) and sound theoretical analysis of that evidence.
The vanguard Skeptics have made it their profession to explain away,
debunk, rationalize, and otherwise dismiss any evidence whatsoever of
the "paranormal" that does not fit into their own self-styled scientific
and rationalistic conception of the universe. The serious psychical researchers and parapsychologists caught in the middle of this debate
often view themselves as the "true skeptics" (Hess, 1993, p. 190, note
8). Collectively, they have attempted to study and critically evaluate data
bearing on the paranormal independent of the preconceived notions of
the other camps. It is also the parapsychologists themselves who have
done the most to root out deception and fraud in their own field, exposing major scandals involving fraudulent manipulation of data and
unmasking charlatans (see, for instance, Beloff, 1990, p. 27, note c).

Perhaps it is inevitable that psychical studies, sometimes no matter
how boring on the surface of the often repetitive experiments (how
many times do we want to hear that a card-calling experiment got minor
but statistically significant results?), engender strong feelings when they
give positive results for paranormal effects. Of all scientific endeavors,
psychical studies impinge perhaps most directly on questions of religion
and spirituality: Is there mind and consciousness independent of the
matter in the human body? Is there something beyond the material
world? Is there a God, or gods? Do people have souls? Is there life after
death? Even "minor" instances of telepathy, on an occasional though
somewhat unpredictable basis, if they can be demonstrated beyond
doubt to actually occur, have profound philosophical and religious, and
even practical, implications for most people. Maybe we are not so isolated from each other as some would suggest. Maybe each person is not
that metaphorical island, but we are all entangled at some level, whether
we like it or want to admit it. Our culture has deeply ingrained a sense of
individual identity into all of us; to relax this idea, even just a little bit,
would mean changing the very foundation of our society. It would mean
focusing our desires not on self and immediate gratification but in a
deeper and more connected way, widening the extent of our wishes and

desires to include the implications on society and other living things. But in such speculations, perhaps we stray philosophically from the grounded empiricism of scientifically based psychical studies.

# THE PROBLEM OF FRAUD

It is clear that there have been irregularities, and downright fraud, in psychical research and parapsychology. Before speculating on the basis of "data" concerning the paranormal, psychical researchers must first root out fraudulent data. Fraudulent data takes several forms, such as explicit deception on the part of researchers and/or subjects (including fudging of data), and sloppy research and control techniques that can lead to easy or inadvertent fraud (perhaps on the part of a subject or assistant who is too eager to please, and so gives the results desired, even if not intentionally dishonestly). And there is also the potential problem of the genuinely honest experimenter who can fool him- or herself in a case of self-deception and self-delusion.

Since the late nineteenth century one method of studying the paranormal has been through experiments involving, for instance, card guessing, rolling of dice, and the like, in which one attempts to get more "hits" than would occur by chance (see Coover, 1917, for an early discussion). Such methods were formalized and applied scrupulously by Dr. Joseph Banks Rhine at Duke University, beginning in the 1930s (see page 129 for further discussion of J. B. Rhine and his parapsychology laboratory at Duke). Understandably, both parapsychologists and their critics were concerned about errors in statistical analysis. In the latter category we may say "presumed errors" in some cases, as statisticians and others may not always agree on what is and is not statistically significant among marginal results as different methods of analysis are utilized. It was even suggested at one point that the card-guessing experiments that seemed to show statistically significant results were not evidence of psi, but evidence of defects in probability theory and statistical analyses (Brown, 1953; see Krippner, 1977), a suggestion that has not so far been corroborated. During the early part of the Rhinean era in the early 1930s, after much dispute over J. B. Rhine's seminal monograph *Extra-Sensory Perception* (1934) in which he published the results of his early experiments supporting ESP, mathematicians such as R. A. Fisher, the dean of British statisticians, "conceded that Rhine's mathematics were valid. And Duke mathematician, Dr. Joseph Albert Greenwood, confirmed the theory of probability" (Brian, 1982, p. 116). It has also been charged that statistically significant results have been selectively published, whereas null results have been ignored (the "file drawer" error of not publishing negative results), and that in some cases statistically significant segments of data would be selected from larger sets of non-significant data, or that an experiment would be stopped once results had been achieved above the chance level rather than collecting more data to see if the results would remain at such a high level. For further discussion of these types of issues, see the selection by Utts (page 163) reprinted in this volume.

Given the controversial (and even abhorrent to some) nature of parapsychology, certain critics and debunkers have been quick to pick up on cases of fraud and other irregularities, or the possibility of fraud (even if undemonstrated), as a way to discount the entire subject. Despite widely publicized cases of impropriety (see next section, below), among serious parapsychologists, it is not clear that there is any more fraud than in other fields (Horne, 1996). But, parapsychology is classically associated with types of persons who are generally considered somewhat less than respectable and upstanding (with good reason, unfortunately; see below), such as mediums, occultists, and fortune-tellers (some of whom may even call themselves "parapsychologists"). A science that studies mediums is, in many an eye, tainted. Actually, it is not just that some parapsychologists study mediums and "psychics," for instance in the way that anthropologists or psychologists may study them, but some parapsychologists utilize mediums to produce the paranormal effects or events that are the real object of study. If the medium produces fraudulent events, which are then studied as if they were genuinely paranormal, what does that say about the particular parapsychologist, and by extension, the entire field? It is for this reason that at least some parapsychologists have shied away from the study of mediums—most notably the branch of laboratory research founded by J. B. Rhine, which avoided the use of mediums.

# EXAMPLES OF IRREGULARITIES IN EXPERIMENTAL STUDIES

The early members of the Society for Psychical Research were clearly duped on several occasions when they carried out experiments on "thought-transference" with apparently promising subjects. Two early cases of deception were the experiments with the Creery family (in particular the four daughters of Rev. A. M. Creery, his wife, and the family maid) and the Smith-Blackburn experiments.

The Creery experiments took various forms. One version can be summarized as follows. An experimenter (such as a member of the SPR) thought of an object, wrote it down, and showed the paper to all the family members in silence gathered in a sitting room except one who had left to act as the "percipient" (for instance, one of the sisters). Everyone would then concentrate on the name of the object, and the percipient would enter the room having fetched the object thought of (Gurney, Myers, and Podmore, 1886, vol. 1, p. 22). The Creery experiments came under severe criticism when they were first published. In 1887 during further tests of thought-transference using playing cards, two of the sisters (one was the agent and the other served as the percipient) were discovered using codes and a third one confessed signaling in some of the earlier experiments. This naturally led to doubts about all the Creery experiments, though some suggested that perhaps the better-controlled experiments still gave evidence of genuine telepathy. To the credit of the SPR, it was its own members who detected the deception and forthrightly published the exposure in both its *Journal* and *Proceedings*. The Creery case is discussed at length by Coover (1917).

The Smith–Blackburn experiments involved Douglas Blackburn and Mr. George A. Smith, both of Brighton on the south coast of England. Blackburn was the editor of the *Brightonian* (a local publication) and Smith was described as a "mesmerist" (in modern terms, probably the equivalent of a stage "hypnotist"). Smith and Blackburn came to the attention of the SPR through a letter penned by Blackburn that appeared in *Light*, a leading British spiritualist weekly journal of the time, describing how Smith could "read" Blackburn's thoughts.

In a typical simple experiment Smith would be blindfolded, Blackburn would hold Smith's hands (so that the two could be *en rapport*, as Blackburn described it), and a member of the SPR would write down a color, number, or name on a piece of paper and silently show it to Blackburn. Blackburn would then concentrate and "telepathically" transmit to Smith his thoughts. These types of experiments were described at length in the first volume of the *Proceedings* of the SPR (1883) and for many years were both attacked by critics and cited by advocates. In 1911 Blackburn, thinking he was the sole survivor of those involved in the experiments (he did not realize that his confederate, G. A. Smith, was also still very much alive, as well as Professor Barrett, who was present at some of the experiments), published a confession in which he detailed how he and Smith had used various codes to transmit information. Smith, who had since been working for and with the SPR, vehemently denied Blackburn's accusations. In hindsight, it seems clear that deception was involved in the Smith–Blackburn experiments, and Coover (1917, p. 491) implies that the leadership of the SPR may have suspected something was amiss early on. Coover notes that while the Smith–Blackburn experiments are featured prominently in SPR publications in 1883, by the time of the publication of *Phantasms of the Living* (Gurney, Myers, and Podmore) in 1886 they had apparently been dropped. Unlike the Creery experiments, the Smith–Blackburn experiments are not even mentioned in *Phantasms* or most of the later SPR publications.

The two examples given above of course do not invalidate the bulk of the early work of the SPR (in particular, they have no direct bearing on the compilation of spontaneous cases of psi; see page 61), but they certainly provide ammunition for the critics and detractors of psychical research, many of whom will point to one or two cases of clear fraud or even the possibility (though not actually demonstrated) of collusion and deception to damn the entire field (see, for instance, Hansel, 1966, 1980; and Randi, 1982).

Unfortunately questions, irregularities, and fraud have persisted among experimental parapsychologists up until the present day. Here we briefly discuss a few examples.

The results that J. B. Rhine published in his 1934 monograph *Extra-Sensory Perception* (see excerpt on page 131) struck many people as too good to be true, and almost immediately his experimental methods were attacked. For example, the cards used in the standard card–guessing experiments were criticized.

At a convention of the American Psychological Association in New York in April, 1938, Dr. Steuart Henderson Britt, of George Washington University, stated that the official ESP cards as sold to the public in America could be read from the backs, either by sight or touch, owing to too heavy printing or other defects. He proceeded to "read" correctly twenty-four cards out of a pack of twenty-five, with faces unseen. [H. Price, 1939, p. 180.]

Indeed, such poorly made cards would be a problem in face-to-face testing with minimal or no screening between the experimenter and the subject. But even if these were not the actual cards used in the tests reported by Rhine, that did not necessarily alleviate the situation. Early handmade cards could create even more problems, and used and reused cards might accumulate nicks, tears, folds, smudges, and other imperfections that would allow them to be identified (even if such identification was on a subconscious level rather than involving conscious deception). It was also suggested that a subject could pick up clues from a tester's facial expressions and subtle behaviors, and in some cases the faces of the cards might be reflected in the corneas or eyeglasses of the tester

(Wynn and Wiggins, 2001, p. 156). Such criticisms and speculations do not apply to cases where the agent and percipient were in different secured rooms or even different buildings, nor do they apply when cards are sealed in opaque envelopes or other precautions are taken, and they do not apply to experiments where cards are called down through a deck without even removing the cards. Pratt et al. (1940) addressed these criticisms and cited other experiments that had been carried out, both by the Rhine lab and elsewhere, that supported the ESP hypothesis. But there were still more problems to come.

In the 1930s Dr. Samuel G. Soal (1890–1975) of Queen Mary College, University of London, undertook to replicate Rhine's card-guessing results, but without success. Then it was suggested to him in November 1939 by psychical researcher Whateley Carrington that he should reanalyze his data, looking for displacement effects (that is, responses to unintended targets). Precognitive displacement, as defined by Soal (Soal and Bateman, 1954 [London edition], p. 377) refers to guessing correctly not the intended target (card) but the following card, whereas post-cognitive displacement refers to guessing correctly the preceding target. When he analyzed for displacement effects, Soal found apparent evidence of paranormal effects in his own data. Two of his subjects, Mrs. Gloria Stewart and Basil Shackleton, had demonstrated both precognitive and post-cognitive displacement. (As an aside, independent of Soal's fraud discussed immediately below, displacement is a controversial topic [see Milton, 1988], but it may genuinely occur in some data sets generated by competent investigators, and in fact it might even be real in Soal's early data sets assuming he was not committing fraud at that time.)

In the 1940s Soal carried out more experiments with Shackleton (the Soal-Goldney experiments as Mrs. K. M. Goldney of the Society for Psychical Research collaborated on the experiments), as well as with Mrs. Stewart. The experiments with Shackleton gave incredibly positive results and formed the core of Soal's 1954 book *Modern Experiments in Telepathy* (a photographic portrait of Shackleton serves as the frontispiece for the book). For decades, proponents pointed to these results as strong experimental evidence for telepathy. The critics, however, gnawed away at the experiments, suggesting problems with the experimental design and ways in which fraud might have occurred, particularly on the part of the subjects being tested (see Hansel, 1966). However, it was an agent (sender) involved in a 1941 experiment who raised serious warnings when, nearly twenty years later, she alleged that she had seen Soal tampering with the data (in particular target sheets for guesses after the guesses had been made). In the 1970s sophisticated analyses of the available data on the experiments (original target sheets were not available for inspection; Horne, 1996) demonstrated to the satisfaction of most people that Soal had actively committed fraud (see Hansel, 1980; Scott and Haskell, 1974; Markwick, 1978).

Unfortunately, fraud occurs in many scientific and academic fields, and an occasional fraudulent researcher should not be allowed to discredit the majority who are honest. The entire field must not be condemned because of the actions of those who are dishonest (although arch-skeptics such as Randi, 1982, effectively do take this approach of sweeping condemnation based on a few instances of fraud). We must face the problem of fraud forthrightly, identifying and eliminating fraud through critical examination of all research and data. Late in his career J. B. Rhine, a pioneer of modern laboratory research on psi, suffered the humility of fraud in his own laboratories. The director of the Institute of Parapsychology at Rhine's Foundation for Research on the Nature of Man (FRNM), Walter Jay Levy, was caught manipulating data in animal psi experiments (Hansel, 1980, p. 234). It is important to note that Rhine was quick to publicize the fraud, no matter how embarrassing it might be, and warned other scientists to disregard the questionable research and be wary of any other research associated with Levy (Rhine, 1974).

Even when fraud is not actually detected, merely the theoretical possibility of fraud is enough for some critics and skeptics to dismiss parapsychology and psychical research. A major proponent of this view is Hansel (1966, 1980), who devotes much of his book not to exposing fraud, per se, but arguing how conceivably fraud might have occurred in specific parapsychological experiments. Commenting on this line of thinking, parapsychologist Jeffery Mishlove wrote:

> Even C. E. M. Hansel (1966) . . . states, "It cannot be stated categorically that trickery was responsible for the results of these experiments, but so long as the possibility is present, the experiments cannot be regarded as satisfying the aims of their originators or as supplying conclusive evidence for ESP."
>
> Ransom [1971] points out that you simply cannot argue with this line of reasoning, "since the critic can always claim that everyone involved in the experiment in question was lying about any or all of the details. . . . Even if an experiment was repeated, it could be claimed that it is possible that all the experiments were fraudulent." This criticism could apply equally well to scientific experiments in every other field. Price (1955) argued in *Science* [a publication of the American Association for the Advancement of Science] that fraud, even experimenter fraud, must be involved in parapsychology because it was easier to believe that men are liars than that "miracles" could occur. In 1972, Price retracted his accusations. The criticism of fraud is partially answered when the skeptic deigns to conduct his or her own experiments—as has happened frequently in parapsychology—which accounts for the growth of the field beyond Rhine's own laboratory. [Mishlove, 1987.]

# DIFFICULTIES IN THE STUDY OF PSYCHICS AND MEDIUMS

A "psychic" is a colloquial term that is often applied to someone who is thought, or purports, to have relatively well-developed paranormal (psi) abilities, particularly of a mental nature, such as extrasensory perception, including clairvoyance and telepathy. The concept of a medium was originally that of a person who channeled or transmitted communications from the dead or other discarnate entities, such as spirits, whether or not such spirits were once living in a physical form. Mediums were a primary way that many spiritualists believed they could communicate with the beyond. Communications might flow directly from the mouth of the medium, or from the hand of the medium in the case of automatic writing or drawing. Sometimes a medium was considered "possessed" by a discarnate spirit or entity. Communications could also take the form of psychokinetic events, such as the movement of objects, the production of sounds, and the materialization of inanimate objects, plants, animals, human-like body parts, and in some cases entire "ghosts" or "spirit forms." Today the terms medium and psychic are sometimes used more or less interchangeably.

Historically, mediumship (the practices or actions of mediums, especially in séances and similar settings) has been quite important in the development of psychical research and parapsychology (see Gauld, 1983, and Heath, 2003, for reviews of various aspects of mediumship), both in a positive and a negative sense. William James and other early researchers were quite impressed by the medium Mrs. Piper (see page 94) and they were inspired to pursue further psychical research. Dr. J. B. Rhine and his wife and co-researcher Dr. Louisa E. Rhine were sorely disappointed with the fraud they detected at a sitting with the Boston, Massachusetts, medium "Margery" (Mina Stinson Crandon) in 1926 (Matlock, 1988). J. B. Rhine's early disillusionment with mediumship was probably a major factor in his subsequent emphasis on laboratory research and in turn played a fundamental role in shaping the nature of modern parapsychology.

As noted above, there are two types of mediums, or at least types of phenomena mediums may produce: mental phenomena (such as receiving knowledge telepathically or clairvoyantly, or speaking for possible discarnate personalities) and physical phenomena (such as movements of objects, productions of sounds, levitation, and materializations of substances and objects). Mrs. Piper, the medium who so impressed William James and other early psychical researchers, was strictly a mental medium. Mrs. Piper would go into a trance (a state of dissociation where the individual is relatively oblivious to her or his surroundings; Thalbourne, 2003, p. 127) and then speak. During a sitting she could name minute details concerning the lives and personal affairs of persons unknown or only vaguely familiar to her, details of which she apparently had no way of knowing through normal means (see further discussion beginning on page 94). "Margery," the medium that J. B. Rhine and L. E. Rhine condemned as a fraud, was a physical medium. "Margery" (Mina Crandon) was famous for her "ectoplasmic" phenomena (ecto-plasm, also known as teleplasm, was a material substance supposedly pro-duced from, or out of, the body of some mediums), such as a crude hand connected to her body by an umbilical-like cord or a "voice box" that seemed to extrude from her nose and settle on her chest or shoulder and through which a discarnate entity could presumably speak (see Crandon, 1927; Fodor, 1934; Chéroux et al., 2005). In some cases mental and physical phenomena may be combined or are manifested through the same medium, at least to varying degrees. Classic examples of such combinations are table tipping (ostensibly without the intervention of normal muscular action or other means) and raps being heard (without any normal source for the raps), and not only does the table tip or the raps occur, but through them questions might be answered (a table tipping to one side for "yes" and to the other side for "no," or raps counting out numbers or letters of the alphabet).

Whatever the source may be (telepathically acquired from living indi-viduals, true clairvoyance, or possibly acquired from spirits on the "other side"—note that we favor the telepathic explanation, at least in most cases, given that fraud is excluded), it seems that at least some mental mediums can produce information paranormally that has some degree of accuracy (Osty, 1923; Gauld, 1983; Mayer, 2007). Admittedly, there is a spectrum of possibilities: a mental medium may combine genuine ability with tricks and deception, while some are complete frauds. Why some mental mediums with genuine abilities may resort to fraud and trickery to supplement or enhance their performances is a difficult psychological conundrum that is beyond the scope of this discussion, but a number of researchers have noted that this seems to occur. Even in an experienced medium, paranormal phenomena may only occur quasi-spontaneously, and there may be a fear (conscious or unconscious) on the part of the medium that if paranormal phenomena do not come forth then their reality at other times will be doubted. Thus perhaps occasional trickery stems from a desire to "prove" that the paranormal abilities are real, despite the fact that being caught in deception will have just the opposite effect. Or perhaps trickery, in the absence of genuine paranormal phenomena, fulfills the need of the medium to "please" the audience. It may well be that in some cases trickery and deception on the part of a medium may not be premeditated, and indeed may not even be engaged in consciously but, for example, rather occurs at a subconscious level while the medium is in a trance or other altered state.

The late psychologist and Jungian analyst Marie-Louise von Franz suggests that a tendency toward deception, or at least a lack of awareness of typical moral codes of honesty, may be inherent in some mediums, as she pointed out in a lecture delivered in 1969.

> The unconscious *knows* things; it knows the past and future, it knows things about other people. We all from time to time have dreams which inform us about something which happens to another person. Most of you who analyse [von Franz was speaking to professionals, including other Jungian analysts] will know that prognostic and telepathic dreams occur quite frequently to practically everybody, and this knowledge of the unconscious Jung calls absolute knowledge. A medium is a person who has a closer relationship, one might say a gift, by which to relate to the absolute knowledge of the unconscious, generally by having a relatively low level of consciousness. This explains why mediums are very often very queer and often even morally odd people—not always, but often—or they are slightly criminal, or take to drink, and so on. They are generally very endangered personalities because they have that low threshold and are so near to the absolute knowledge of the unconscious. [von Franz, 1980, p. 39; italics in the original.]

Or, as the late parapsychologist John Beloff wrote concerning nineteenth-century séances, particularly as promoted by Spiritualists, ". . . by and large, psychic phenomena lack the one thing that is essential, from the religious point of view, a spiritual dimension. At best they may have practical importance for those concerned, like a telepathic distress signal or a premonition of disaster, at worst they may be malicious or destructive but, for the most part they are trivial, ridiculous or preposterous. . . . it soon became clear that some of the most powerful mediums were persons of low moral calibre when they were not outrightly immoral. One of the more confusing aspects of the search for good mediums was that a readiness to cheat could never be taken as a sign that the medium lacked genuine psychic abilities" (Beloff, 1990, p. 74). Despite all the issues of potential trickery and even fraud among mediums, there is good evidence that at least some paranormal phenomena associated with certain mental mediums are genuine (the classic example is Mrs. Piper; see page 94).

When it comes to physical phenomena, however, there is considerably more controversy over what percentage, if any, are real. Colonel Henry Steel Olcott, an early investigator and cofounder, with Madame H. P. Blavatsky and William Q. Judge, of the Theosophical Society in 1876, made the following comment relative to physical mediums in 1875.

> I am not, I am happy to say, of that class of pseudo-investigators which rejects the chance of finding truth in these marvels because mediums occasionally cheat. It has often, and justly, been said that the circulation of counterfeit coin is no proof that the genuine does not exist, but the reverse; and the reports of most intelligent writers agree in the statement that nearly all public mediums occasionally simulate their phenomena when, from any cause, they cannot produce the real ones. [Olcott, 1875, p. 20.]

Theodore Besterman, a former investigation officer for the Society for Psychical Research, had the opportunity to research and observe firsthand many of the prominent mediums of the first half of the twentieth century, in some ways the golden age of mediumship. Besterman, though inherently skeptical of all paranormal phenomena, accepted the mental mediumship of Mrs. Piper as absolutely genuine (Besterman,

1968, p. 156). For Besterman physical mediumship presented an entirely different situation, as evidenced by the following quotation, originally written in the 1930s.

Physical phenomena are much more easy to demonstrate, in the most rigorously scientific way, than mental phenomena. The mental phenomena are not things one can see or handle, whereas physical things are capable of being controlled. It is not possible to conceive of a phenomenon of a physical nature not controllable by physical instruments. If one has a medium who alleges herself able to produce supernormal movements and objects, this can be tested in the easiest possible way. One can have complete darkness or anything desired. One can arrange the séance room in the manner which seems most fitting. One can make certain tests, using instruments, and if one finds at the conclusion that the instrument has been altered and tampered with, one has absolute evidence which cannot be questioned. Again, one may have the medium enclosed in a cage and again carry out certain conclusive tests.

The reasons given by mediums for the nonproduction of the phenomena are very curious. I do not venture to say that the reasons are improper or that there is no foundation for them, but at first sight they do seem to be rather extraordinary. We find a medium saying that what he calls his ectoplasmic terminal cannot penetrate through a glass or a gauze partition, although it can lift heavy tables and can penetrate his clothing. It may be possible that supernormal substance is of such a nature that it can penetrate his clothing, but cannot penetrate a gauze netting, though on the face of it this is frankly difficult to conceive. One cannot conceive the nature of a substance which, with some mediums, must not be exposed to light, which, with other mediums, can be exposed to light, but cannot be photographed nor seen by the human eye, and with still other mediums cannot be exposed to light or to the human eye, but can be photographed with flashlight.

So far, then, we have these two points of view. Practically all the mediums known to us require to have next to them an acquaintance, or a friend. The mediums, unless they have a friend with them, say that they cannot get results. One cannot imagine any scientific analogy in which it would be necessary to have a second person present in these circumstances. Assuming the genuineness of the phenomena, it is a little difficult to see why this should be necessary. Many mediums produce physical phenomena very freely, and these phenomena decrease in number in the same ratio as the conditions of control increase. That is a thing of everyday observation. A medium goes to the séance room, and at the first sitting he does just as he likes and the phenomena are wonderful, chairs fall about, the banjo is played without apparently anyone touching it, and there are other mysterious occurrences. At the second sitting the medium is asked to have his hands held, whereupon the phenomena are reduced, and things out of the medium's reach no longer occur, but within his reach many things still take place. In the next sitting he is asked to allow his feet to be held, whereupon the phenomena which could have relation to his feet are discontinued. Eventually when one disables the medium's hands and feet, and also moves away his next friend, then generally—it is no exaggeration to say, always—the phenomena disappear.

All these circumstances taken together do tend to produce scepticism. You may reply very properly that there are in the literature phenomena recorded which occur, notwithstanding the strictest possible control. You can find phenomena recorded which could not have been produced fraudulently by the medium unless—and this "unless" must be emphasized—there is an error in the description of the conditions of the control given in the book. Here we find the real explanation of the facts. The discrepancies are sometimes of a perfectly childish kind—so childish that they are the best tribute one can possibly have to the honesty of the compiler of the book. Most of you will know a book called *The Phenomena of Materialisation*, by Schrenck-Notzing★. Although a large number of photographs are published in this book, showing these supernormal phenomena which are

---

★ The German physician, therapist, and psychical researcher Baron Albert von Schrenck-Notzing (1862–1929) published many photographs of supposed materializations produced by various physical mediums that he studied (Schrenck-Notzing, 1923a, 1923b).

quite incomprehensible, assuming that the test is correct, yet, after the death in 1924 of Gustave Geley (Paris), who was primarily responsible for certain experiments of his own, there were found in his papers a number of photographs in which the fraud carried out was quite apparent. These photographs, for some reason, no doubt quite satisfactory to the experimenters, had not been published.

Another point is that if you compare the illustrations in the book with the text, you will find curious discrepancies. One of the most striking bits of evidence for the reality of ectoplasm is certain experiments with a medium called Eva C. The medium sat behind some curtains, and in the text we read that during the whole of the sitting the hands and feet of the medium were continually visible. If that description is correct, then these phenomena must be accepted as supernormal, and they have, in fact, been so accepted by a large proportion of students of psychical research. Curiously enough, however, in a number of the photographs published, taken by flashlight, the hands of the medium are not visible, so that one is bound to conclude that there is a mistake in the record. Although the record says the medium's hands were continually visible, actually the hands were not continually visible. The flashlight photographs show, at least, that there was one moment when the hands were not visible.

I have given only a number of indications why it is I cannot accept personally any of the so-called physical phenomena so far alleged as genuine. We have, for example, the phenomenon of raps. All I can say about raps is that they are easily imitated. I have heard raps produced under most extraordinary conditions from different parts of the room, but, speaking for myself, I do not think these physical phenomena, or others, are at all conclusive. [Besterman, 1968, pp. 80–82.]

Price (1939) discusses at length various methods used by physical mediums to deceive investigators and the public alike. Backing up his claims, Price published a photograph of a chair seized from a medium containing a secret compartment and hidden paraphernalia used to create "materializations," as well as illustrations from a catalogue "privately circulated among professional mediums" advertising various items for sale, such as a table that produces raps, luminous paint for dark séance effects, a self-playing guitar, and "sealed" letters that can be read without disturbing the seal or envelope (Price, 1939, plate facing p. 209).

Baggally (1912) and Fodor (1959) also give interesting firsthand accounts of how physical mediums could produce their phenomena— for instance, apports (objects "materialized" during the séance) hidden in folds of skin, or strapped to the inner thighs, or concealed in the room or furniture prior to the séance. Reviewing reports of classic séances involving physical phenomena (e.g., Schrenck-Notzing, 1923a, who though a supporter of the reality of the phenomena provides some of the most damning evidence against them in his descriptions and photographs), it seems clear that even when precautions were taken prior to the séance, such as having the medium undress and checked, then sewn into a specially designed garment or even proceeding with the séance while the medium was naked or semi-naked (in the dark, of course), materializations from body cavities (regurgitation, extrusion from the vagina, and so forth) could occur. There was also a strong sexual flavor to many séances. A nude or semi-nude female medium might be positioned among male investigators trying to "control" her by physical restraint—often holding her hands and feet as she flays about in convulsive, spasmodic movements—so as to eliminate the possibility of fraud while materializations, levitations, and other phenomena occur. A male medium might feel he needs to cling to, clutch, or squeeze a female sitter in order to solicit the manifestation of phenomena to the fullest. In their catalogue of "occult photographs," Chéroux et al. (2005, p. 197) include a 1913 photograph of the French medium "Eva C." (Marthe Beraud) naked with a materialized "ghost" as well as a 1925 photograph of the hand of the male investigator E. J. Dingwall held over the exposed genital area, only partially covered by a handkerchief-like cloth, of the American medium "Margery" (Mina Crandon) as an "ectoplasm hand" supposedly extrudes from her navel (p. 220).

Fodor (1959, pp. 180–185) strongly expresses his opinion, and cites other opinions in support, that there is a strong connection between physical mediumship and sex, and between sex and poltergeist activity for that matter (see Price, 1945). While it might consist of nothing more than sexual innuendos at times, it is explicit in certain cases described by Fodor that both mediums and attendees received some form of sexual gratification during séances, perhaps occasionally of the most extreme form on the part of a participant. For example, in the late nineteenth century a male séance attendee physically seized "Yolande," the "spirit" of a young Arab woman allegedly materialized through the English medium Mme. d'Espérance (also known as Elizabeth Hope, 1855–1919). The male attendee claimed that Yolande and the medium were one and the same entity, a contention that d'Espérance adamantly denied. Whatever the truth is, the medium herself recounts experiencing excruciating pain, violence, anguish, and horror. As a result of the incident, she suffered severe illness and did not fully regain her health for several years (d'Espérance, 1897, pp. 298–302). Based on d'Espérance's couched description of the incident, it would seem that Yolande and/or the medium was raped in the dark of the séance setting, as bluntly suggested by Fodor (1959, p. 183; see also Fodor, 1934, pp. 83–85; Tromp, 2006, pp. 94–95).

Returning to the subject of deception and fraud in physical mediumship, it appears that all of this sexual baggage would in many cases only detract from careful analysis of the veracity of the material phenomena. Indeed, in such heightened or "altered" states, both the mediums and the sitters might temporally lose their critical faculties and conscious or unconscious deception on the part of the medium, and an ineffable willingness to believe on the part of the sitters might occur. Delusion, deception (conscious or unconscious), and self-delusion might run wild, resulting in such a "masterpiece" as the thick, well-illustrated (with many photographs taken during séances showing supposed materializations) book of Schrenck-Notzing (1923a, 1923b). Classic séances featuring physical phenomena seem to illustrate the trickster aspect of the paranormal (or reputed paranormal) so deftly discussed by Hansen (2001). As an aside, it might be noted that Baron von Schrenck-Notzing (1862–1929) was a physician and therapist who, besides his psychical studies, took a special interest in hypnosis and sexual disorders (see Schrenck-Notzing, 1895).

Despite all the clear deception and fraud that has, and continues to be, an inextricable part of physical mediumship, might there be anything real or genuine to it at all? Many eminent scientists of the past, such as the English chemist and physicist Sir William Crookes (1831–1919) and Nobel Prize winner Charles Richet (see Tymn, 2002; see page 87 for comments on Richet), have testified as to their belief in the authenticity of at least *some* physical séance phenomena. In line with the trickster aspect of mediums and psychics (Hansen, 2001), it is often repeated that many a medium combined fraud, deception, and genuine phenomena in a career, and even during a single séance sitting (see summaries and discussions in Holms, 1925, 1969, who was an advocate of the reality of at least some of the phenomena). The typical medium, it can be suggested, may have (or had) some genuine paranormal abilities, but when these fail, deception may be used. Such deception might occur consciously on the part of the medium, constituting downright fraud. Alternatively, the deception may occur unconsciously, as when the medium is in a trance, and the deception may be unknown to the medium when in a conscious, waking state. Thus, the issue of deception among mediums is not clear-cut; deception may be obscure even to the deceiving medium.

So, might there be anything legitimate or genuine about any aspect or any form or instance of purported physical mediumship? If psychokinetic effects, no matter how small, have indeed been genuinely demonstrated in the laboratory (see pages 137 and 144) and are perhaps possible according to some physical theories (see page 300), doesn't that leave the door open for genuine manifestations of such phenomena during séances and other settings? Is there an inherent human ability that is manifesting itself under different states of consciousness? Perhaps even more telling, if at least some so-called poltergeist incidents are genuine manifestations of the paranormal (see page 103), then perhaps we should not be surprised to find similar phenomena occasionally occurring in a séance type of setting. Furthermore, in some instances poltergeist activities apparently include dematerializations and materializations of objects, as has been claimed in séances. In her overview of physical paranormal phenomena, parapsychologist, hypnotherapist, and physician Pamela Rae Heath (2003, p. 64) notes that several famous physical mediums, including the nineteenth-century Scottish medium D. D. Home, were also the focus of poltergeist activities as adolescents. This correlation might be expected if some of the mediumistic and poltergeist phenomena are genuine. Of course, the skeptic can argue that it is also to be expected that a child faking poltergeist phenomena might mature to an adult faking mediumistic phenomena.

# INNATE FEAR OF PSI?

Complicating the whole issue of fraud in parapsychological research, it was suggested by the late British psychologist Kenneth Batcheldor (1983, 1984; Beloff, 1990, p. 198; Beloff, 1993, p. 232) that the best way to elicit paranormal phenomena, whether in a laboratory setting or otherwise, is to be intentionally ambiguous and not take standard safeguards against deceit and so forth. Batcheldor's method even allowed for minor cheating, and in many ways was a throwback or reenactment of Victorian-style séances during which presumed psi phenomena were manifested in abundance. The underlying theory to this approach is that every person, whether a researcher, skeptic, or "true believer," has an innate and deep-seated fear of psi and the paranormal, especially and particularly if emanating from ourselves. No matter how hard we might desire and try to elicit psi phenomena, unconsciously we will sabotage ourselves. (Likewise, it can be suggested that some people may not want other people to know about them; they are afraid or not open, so they subconsciously block psi.) In the ambiguous settings suggested by Batcheldor, such as a darkened séance room with plenty of opportunities for "tricks," he suggests that genuine paranormal phenomena can occur even as our unconscious concerns can be put to rest by assuming that it is all just chicanery. The problem, of course, is that in such situations it becomes perhaps impossible to distinguish the tricks and non-paranormal phenomena from the genuinely (if any) paranormal. If psi effects are time independent (that is, psi can travel both forward and backward in time, such that our intentions, desires, and fears in the present may paranormally affect both the past and the future), and Batcheldor's basic theory has some merit, even attempting to determine after the fact which phenomena of a sitting are truly paranormal may destroy their paranormal aspects and cause them to collapse into non-paranormal fraud or at least mistaken identity (a normal phenomenon is mistaken for a paranormal phenomenon, or vice versa).

The Batcheldorean theory does suggest, however, that in a few exceptional cases certain individuals may have simply lacked the generally innate fear of psi and thus such individuals could become exceptional mediums. Further, one might argue that in modern technological society the fear of psi has increased, whereas in so-called primitive societies, or even in "eastern" societies of today, there is less fear of psi. With less fear of psi, increased psi phenomena and ability are manifested among the population. By the Batcheldorean theory one might also expect the strongest psi phenomena among the general population (versus among the exceptional people who lack the fear of psi) under conditions of spontaneity when such phenomena are not expected, thus the importance of documenting spontaneous cases of telepathy and other paranormal phenomena, as recognized by the founders of the Society for Psychical Research in the 1880s and exemplified by the case collection of over fifteen thousand classified reports by Louisa Rhine beginning in the late 1940s. Batcheldorean theory might also explain the widely noted decline effect observed in experimental situations of psi (the decline effect refers to the often observed tendency of paranormal phenomena, or psi effects, such as high scores on an ESP test, to decrease during an experimental run, during a sequence of runs, or even during the career or lifetime of an individual). Given the fear of psi, as one demonstrated psi ability one might unconsciously block it or sabotage it so that the psi phenomena occur to a lesser and lesser extent. One way that many mediums may be able to create situations conducive to the production of paranormal phenomena, and connect with information paranormally, is through mental disassociation. The subconscious or unconscious mind is allowed to take over while the "conscious" self or personality of the medium is actually set aside. This may in fact be a psychological phenomenon (Barnard, 1933; von Franz, 1980). Many classic divination techniques and oracle mechanisms depend on a way to separate the conscious from the unconscious, allowing knowledge, including paranormal knowledge, to be manifested, as described by Jungian analyst Marie-Louise von Franz.

> One stares at a chaotic pattern [such as tea leaves, sticks thrown on the ground, or the flickering light reflected in a crystal] and then gets a fantasy, and the complete disorder in the pattern confuses one's conscious mind. We could all be mediums, and all have absolute knowledge, if the bright light of our ego consciousness would not dim it. That is why the medium needs an *abaissement du niveau mental* [lowering of the mental age] and has to go into a trance, a sleep-like state, to pull up his or her knowledge. I have myself observed that in states of extreme fatigue, when I am really dangerously physically exhausted, I suddenly get absolute knowledge; I am much closer to it then, but as soon as I have slept well for a few nights then this wonderful gift is gone again. Why? Absolute knowledge is like candlelight, and if the electric light of ego consciousness is burning, then one cannot see the candlelight. [von Franz, 1980, pp. 39–40, italics in the original.]

Various forms of dowsing (the popular image being the use of a forked stick, a divining rod, to find water, but there are many other forms of dowsing for many different purposes) may also have as their basis the separation of the conscious from the unconscious or subconscious. Dowsing may be another technique of bringing to the conscious mind that which is below the conscious level, including in some cases paranormal knowledge (Barrett and Besterman, 1926).

# PSYCHIC PERFORMERS

Since the first half of the twentieth century, classic séance room mediumship has generally fallen out of favor as a topic of serious psychical research (however, see G. Schwartz with Simon, 2002; G. Schwartz,

2003, and Hyman, 2003a, 2003b, for discussions of recent work with "mediums"), but investigations of so-called "psychics," persons who seem to demonstrate exceptional psi abilities in the mental and/or physical realm, continue. In many cases, such psychics are performers of one kind or another, whether stage performers (closely akin to magicians in the sense of conjurors versus magicians in an occult or indigenous/anthropological sense, though the two types of magicians are often found in the same person), radio or television personalities, fortune-tellers and psychic consultants, or newspaper columnists, Web bloggers, or book authors. Just as some skeptics have made a career of attacking parapsychology and debunking supposed paranormal phenomena, some psychics have made their careers performing and working with researchers to have their "powers" experimentally validated.

"Even if one wishes to disregard the relatively weaker testimony, the overwhelming majority of most widely known psychic performers have a reputation for trickery. This is simply a cultural fact" (Hansen, 2001, p. 129). Backing up this statement, the widely respected parapsychologist George P. Hansen (2001, p. 120) presents a table of psychics/mediums/performers who have been reported to engage in trickery and fraud, along with the references to the reports of trickery. Among this list are the Fox sisters (Kate and Margaret Fox of Hydesville, New York, who are often credited with starting the Spiritualist movement when in 1848 they "discovered" that rapping sounds were producing messages from the dead), Daniel Dunglas Home (1833–1886, a world-renown Scottish physical medium), the cofounder of the Theosophical Society Helena Petrovna Blavatsky (1831–1891), Eusapia Palladino (1854–1918, a famous Italian physical medium), "Margery [the Medium]" (Mina Crandon, 1888–1941, a Boston, Massachusetts, physical medium active in the 1920s), as well as Uri Geller (born 1946, the Israeli performer of "paranormal feats," most famously bending spoons), Sathya Sai Baba (born late 1920s, the Indian religious leader and guru), and Don Juan Matus.

Don Juan Matus, a Yaqui (indigenous people from the area of Sonora, Mexico, and Arizona, U.S.) shaman/sorcerer, is of particular contemporary interest in that he was, and continues to be, extremely influential as an introduction for many people to the world of the paranormal, yet he may well be an entirely fictional character created by his "student" Carlos Castaneda (1925?–1998). One view is that Castaneda essentially pulled off an incredible hoax, convincing the University of California Press to initially publish his works, becoming a best-selling author (Castaneda, 1968, 1971, 1972, 1987), and even receiving a Ph.D. in anthropology from the University of California at Los Angeles for his "research" and "fieldwork" (De Mille, 1976, 1980; Hansen, 2001, p. 127; Moehringer, 1998). However, this may not be the full story. Even if Castaneda's Don Juan was not a literal character, Castaneda tapped into a deep undercurrent of potent spiritual thought systems that should not be lightly dismissed. Fiction at a literal level and authenticity on the spiritual level appear to be combined in Castaneda. Perhaps this is the riddle and the trickery of Castaneda.

Even though a number of prominent psychics have been caught using deception at one time or another, parapychological researchers may continue to study them (see Hansen, 1990), searching for ostensibly genuine paranormal phenomena. If a psychic has committed fraud, why keep studying the individual? As already discussed, fraud and apparently genuine paranormal phenomena are all too often found manifested by the same individual, and so some parapsychologists continue to feel it is worthwhile to expend their resources experimenting with such individuals. From a strictly public relations point of view, such studies of psychics (whether or not the particular individual has ever been accused of fraud) have not enhanced the image of the field of parapsychology in general, in the eyes of either other scientists or the public at large. Indeed some parapsychologists, such as the late J. B. Rhine (see page 131) at Duke University, eschewed the study of professional psychics and emphasized the study of "ordinary," yet psychically "talented," individuals in strictly controlled laboratory settings.

Returning to the topic of the study of "exceptional" individuals—or "psychics"—it is clearly critical for scientific purposes to determine why such individuals are "exceptional." Is it due to genuine paranormal abilities and phenomena, in which case the individual may merit serious study? Or is it simply a ruse? Or, possibly, some combination of both?

These are extremely important questions that have not always been adequately addressed by researchers who, at least in some cases, are perhaps a bit naïve and gullible when it comes to both the motivations and the means involved in deception (Hansen, 1990; see also Hansen, 2001, who has discussed this topic at length). It has been suggested that in some cases scientists are inherently gullible in that they are trained to observe and study natural phenomena, and nature does not have the habit of cheating and lying as some people do. To avoid these weaknesses that attend relying upon human subjects, some investigators have turned to the investigation of paranormal phenomena among non-human organisms.

# ANIMAL PSI: THE QUESTION OF THE EXTENSION OF PSI BEYOND HUMANS

Clearly the serious investigator of potential paranormal phenomena must always be on the lookout for trickery, deception, and fraud, especially with apparently "exceptional" or "gifted" individuals. To minimize or eliminate the possibility of deception, some researchers have turned to controlled laboratory studies using "normal" individuals, and not just single individuals, but groups of individuals such that no single person can overly skew the data, following the aphorism of "Don't put all your eggs in one basket." Another approach is to avoid using human subjects altogether and focus on animals. Presumably animals will not actively engage in cheating and deception as some human subjects may.

Historically, and in modern times, there have been many anecdotal reports of animals exhibiting paranormal behavior. The term animal-psi or anpsi refers to the psychic interactions between animals and humans, and animals with each other and the environment. Some examples are dogs that know when their owners are coming home or animals that can navigate home from tremendous distances and over unfamiliar territory (called psi-trailing). Other reports allude to animals being able to sense impending danger or even the threat of death or serious harm to a human or other animal. One modern example of mass animal escape from danger is the 2004 tsunami that hit Southeast Asia. Many animals were able to escape and sensed the impending danger before humans, and some parapsychology researchers like Rupert Sheldrake do not believe that this can all be attributed to the animals picking up slight tremors from seismic activity or other normal cues (Sheldrake, 2005). This poses the question: Since many animals have conventional senses that far surpass those of humans in acuity (smell in a variety of animals, for example), or even include senses that humans apparently lack (such as detection of subtle electric and magnetic fields, and echolocation), could these also include psi-mediated "senses"? The full range of animal senses are often very difficult to evaluate; there seem to be multifaceted avenues for information exchange and flow that differ from species to species (Morris, 1977, p. 694). But is psi part of the spectrum of senses?

Our evolutionary history is intertwined closely with the animal kingdom. Therefore, the potential of animal psi is profoundly important to the understanding of psi phenomena more generally. Animal psi also has implications for our understanding of the evolutionary significance of psi as well as our ability to interact with other species. Animals may also offer an interesting mechanism for studying psi, since it has been speculated that animals do not have the same defense to psi and do not have the conflicting means of communicating that humans do (language) and therefore may be easier to study.

Although most of the research on the paranormal has related to humans, there have also been a number of reports indicating that animals can exhibit paranormal abilities (e.g., see De Vesme, 1931a, pp. 78–95). For the most part these reports have not been empirically tested, but some empirical research has been done. J. B. Rhine undertook research in 1952–1953 in collaboration with the U.S. Army. Essentially, the goal was to see if German shepherds, using ESP, could locate land mines buried too deeply underwater for the dogs to use their "normal" senses. Even though the dogs did fairly well at the tests, it was difficult to determine with certainty whether olfactory or other clues were adequately controlled for (Brian, 1982).

More recently, Rupert Sheldrake has conducted extensive research with animals. In one study he found significant telepathic abilities in a male African Grey parrot named N'kisi who could apparently pick up the thoughts of its owner (Sheldrake and Morgana, 2003). Sheldrake and Pamela Smart also performed more than two hundred trial experiments to test if a dog, a male terrier named Jaytee, knew when its owner was coming home and found statistically significant evidence that the dog knew in advance that its owner was coming home (Sheldrake and Smart, 1998, 2000a). Studies with another dog, Kane, produced similarly significant results (Sheldrake and Smart, 2000b). Interestingly, Radin (2002b) found that in the studies with Jaytee, the dog's anticipatory behavior was affected by geomagnetic factors (higher global geomagnetic flux correlated with lowered anticipatory performance). This is in keeping with other findings that indicate psi phenomena correlate with geomagnetic fluctuations (see discussion below, page 64).

Researchers have used surveys in England and California to test the rates of pet owners who have had psychic experiences with their domesticated animals. Three surveys found significant results in the category of "telepathy" and also found that dogs were more receptive than cats with regards to thoughts, silent commands, and telepathic rapport with their owners (see Sheldrake, 1999).

Not only do animal studies help validate the reality of psi, but they also shed light on the biological context of psi. Sheldrake, Lawlor, and Turney (1998) summarize the importance of animal psi studies as follows:

> If some pets do turn out to have unexplained powers, there would be several far-reaching implications. First, the boundaries of scientific explanation would have to be widened, for example by hypothesizing a new kind of field connecting pets and owners, or another kind of interaction at present unknown to physics, or by extending the idea of non-locality and non-separability already present in quantum physics (Sheldrake [1994]; Sermonti [1996]; and Sheldrake [1996]). An extensive discussion of these possibilities has recently been published in German (Dürr and Gottwald [1997]).

Second, if present in pets, similar forms of perceptiveness may play an important role in communication between animals in the wild, and on farms.

Third, if animals have a "sixth sense" or telepathic powers, then the evidence for such phenomena in human beings (e.g. Radin [1997a]) would take on a new significance. These phenomena would no longer be seen as peculiarly human, but as rooted in our biological heritage. They may be widespread and better-developed in many species of animals than they are in people. And perhaps civilized people have lost them more than most. [Sheldrake, Lawlor, and Turney, 1998.]

Animal psi studies, in conjunction with human psi studies, strengthen the case for the reality of psi and enhance our understanding of the paranormal.

# THE BACKSTER EFFECT, PRIMARY PERCEPTION, AND BIOCOMMUNICATION

Backster Effect: The ability of simpler life forms, such as plants and single cells, to respond to the thoughts, intentions and actions of humans, as evidenced by electrical response and other objective measurements. [Physicist Claude Swanson, 2003, p. 77.]

Not only do psi phenomena extend to non-human animals, but also there is evidence for apparent psi among plants and even single cells. The polygraph (lie detector) expert Cleve Backster has spearheaded such studies. This research began for Backster at about 7 A.M. on the morning of February 2, 1966, when he attached electrodes used to measure galvanic skin responses (GSR) to the leaf of a dracaena plant in his office. He did this not in a search for psi, but out of curiosity to see if there would be a response on watering the plant as the water rose through the stem and into the leaves. Backster did not get the response he expected from water rising through the plant, so he began to experiment with other ways to generate a response from the plant. A human typically shows a polygraph response when his or her well-being is threatened, such as being asked about a crime that in fact he or she committed. Backster decided to use the same approach with the plant. Here is his description of that portentous morning:

I decided to figure out how I could threaten the well-being of the plant. I wasn't into talking to plants, not at that time. So as a substitute threat, I immersed the end of a leaf, that was neighboring the electroded leaf, into a cup of hot coffee. There was no noticeable chart reaction, and there was a continuing downward tracing trend [in the recording on the chart]. With a human, this downward trend would indicate fatigue or boredom. Then, after about fourteen minutes of elapsed chart time, I had this thought: As the ultimate plant threat, I would get a match and burn the plant's electroded leaf.

At that time the plant was about fifteen feet away from where I was standing and the polygraph equipment was about five feet away. The only new thing that occurred was this thought. It was early in the morning and no other person was in the laboratory. My thought and intent was: "I'm going to burn that leaf!" The very moment the imagery of burning the leaf entered my mind, the polygraph recording pen moved rapidly to the top of the chart! No words were spoken, no touching the plant, no lighting of matches, just my clear intention to burn the leaf. The plant recording showed dramatic excitation. To me this was a powerful, high-quality observation.

I must state that, on February 2, 1966 at 13 minutes, 55 seconds into that chart recording, my whole consciousness changed. I then thought, "Gee, it's as though this plant read my mind!" I left the room and went to my secretary's desk to get some matches, as she smoked. When I returned the plant was still showing highly visible reactions. I then reconsidered burning the electroded leaf, as I probably would not be able to recognize any additional tracing changes. Instead, I made a feeble pass at another leaf with a lighted match, but by then I was not really into harming the plant. I thought the best thing for me to do was to remove the threat, and see if the plant would calm down. After returning the matches to my secretary's desk, the tracing returned to the calmness displayed prior to the original decision to burn the electroded leaf. [Backster, 2003, pp. 24–25.]

In his book, from which the above quote is taken, Backster includes reproductions of the sections of the actual chart showing the response of the plant (Backster, 2003, p. 25).

Backster went on to study biocommunication ("[t]he general field of study of communication between different biological life forms" [Backster Website, 2007]) among not just plants and humans, but a variety of organisms and parts of organisms, including, for instance, between plants and brine shrimp (the plants gave strong reactions when the brine shrimp were killed by being dumped into boiling water), between live bacteria that are not in physical contact, and through monitoring live animal and human cells which, *in vitro* and far removed from the donor, continued to respond to events, emotions, and intentions in the life of the donor. For a full and very readable discussion of Backster's experiments and findings, see his book *Primary Perception* (2003).

Backster's incredible, and controversial, experiments and data have been repeated and verified by other laboratories (Vogel, 1974; Swanson, 2003; see discussion in Backster, 2003; see also Tompkins and Bird, 1973, and Stone, 1989). Clearly Backster's work extends the paranormal well beyond the realm of humans or even "higher" animals and is of profound significance for understanding psi. Backster coined the term "primary perception" and distinguishes it from ESP, at least as often conceived in reference to humans.

Primary Perception: The vehicle of communication, the invisible, unrecognized field that interconnects all species and life forms, whereby *biocommunication* can occur. Coined by Cleve Backster, primary perception is distinct from extra sensory perception (ESP) in that it occurs before the human specialized senses of taste, touch, hearing, sight and smell. It is likely going on all the time. [Backster Website, 2007.]

Other researchers, such as the research chemist Marcel Vogel, who successfully replicated Backster-type experiments with plants, consider "primary perception" and ESP to be essentially synonymous. "The term [primary perception] is a synonym for 'extrasensory perception,' except in Backster's view there is nothing 'extra' about it" (Vogel, 1974, p. 289). Independent of where one decides to draw the line between primary perception and ESP, clearly the two concepts are related to one another and one might hypothesize that primary perception is the fundamental underlying basis for ESP as generally recognized.

# FUNDING THE STUDY OF THE PARANORMAL

As we hope will be clear from perusing the contents of this volume, despite the admonitions of the naysayers and skeptics, there is solid evidence for at least some paranormal phenomena. Certain types of experiments have found statistically significant evidence for anomalous effects, and rigorous analyses of spontaneous cases of apparent psi have supported the notion of genuine paranormal experiences. These accomplishments are significant and have come despite an overall lack of funding for parapsychological research. In 1993, the late parapsychologist Charles Honorton wrote, "Throughout its history, research in parapsychology has been sustained through extremely meager resources. Utrecht University psychologist Sybo Schouten . . . compared funding patterns in parapsychology with those of American psychology; he found that the total human and financial resources devoted to parapsychology since 1882 might, at best, equal the expenditures for *two months* of conventional psychological research in the United States in the year 1983!" (Honorton, 1994, p. 193; originally published in 1993; italics in the original).

Little has changed since the early 1990s in terms of funding available to parapsychologists. As the well-respected parapsychologist George P. Hansen points out, "Parapsychology is a tiny field; in the U.S. fewer than 50 people could be said to be professionally conversant with the scientific findings. Only two laboratories in the U.S. employ more than two full-time researchers, and there are probably no more than 10 full-time professional parapsychologists in the U.S. who conduct research and report it in refereed journals. In addition, a few professors and independent scholars conduct research. Despite the small size, there has been more than a century of continuous, professional, published research on these topics" (Hansen, 2001, p. 15). Since these words were written, the Princeton Engineering Anomalies Research (PEAR) laboratories, perhaps the largest facility actively engaged in parapsychological research in the last thirty years, has closed its doors (see discussion, page 144) and the Rhine Research Center struggles to make ends meet. Hansen (p. 198) also notes "Unlike other areas of science, it is not institutions (e.g., corporations, government agencies, philanthropic foundations), but rather individuals, who have provided the primary financial backing for psychical research." Furthermore, Hansen (pp. 197–198) points out that various wealthy individuals in the past have "established foundations to support parapsychology, but after their deaths, professional philanthropists took control, changed the focus of the foundations, and eliminated support for parapsychology."

Given the paucity of resources, and the small number of serious researchers in the field, it is a wonder that parapsychologists have accomplished as much as they have.

# THE STIGMA OF THE PARANORMAL

In current Western culture a definite stigma surrounds the paranormal. This stigma attaches to those who experience paranormal phenomena as well as those who study such phenomena. Indeed, the stigma extends even to the skeptics and debunkers, who attack parapsychology and psychical studies, with the attitude in some quarters: "Why waste time on such nonsense?"

Psi-related experiences (PREs), described by E. Targ et al. (2000, p. 220) as an experience where the experient feels or believes that a paranormal event occurred without judging whether or not such is objectively the case (i.e., it is the experience per se that is important), may be used as a criterion to diagnose psychopathology. "Within the Western medical model . . . reports of PREs are usually presumed to be linked to mental illness and emotional instability. . . . The diagnostic criteria for several psychotic, personality, and dissociative disorders contain items that are similar to those endorsed by people reporting spontaneous PREs" (Targ et al., 2000, p. 230). These authors go on to point out that the fourth edition of the standard *Diagnostic and Statistical Manual of Mental Disorders* explicitly includes "belief in clairvoyance, telepathy, or 'six sense' " as one of the diagnostic criteria for Schizotypal Personality Disorder (American Psychiatric Association, 1994, p. 645; note that to be competently diagnosed with this disorder, one must fit additional criteria beyond simply such a belief). (For those unfamiliar with Schizotypal Personality Disorder, "the essential feature . . . is a pervasive pattern of social and interpersonal deficits marked by acute discomfort with, and reduced capacity for, close relationships as well as cognitive and perceptual distortions and eccentricities of behavior" [American Psychiatric Association, 1994, p. 641].) Such an approach can do a grave injustice to the experient of the PRE (especially, one might add, if the PRE was a genuine paranormal experience).

However, PREs are certainly not uncommon. Surveys taken in various countries around the world consistently indicate that more than half the population reports having had a PRE (see references in Targ et al., 2000). There is plenty of evidence that otherwise normal and healthy persons may experience PREs; that is, PREs alone do not necessarily imply psychopathology (Cardeña et al., 2000; Targ et al., 2000). Cardeña, et al. (2000, p. 17) optimistically wrote concerning their volume titled *Varieties of Anomalous Experience* (which contains the Targ et al., 2000, contribution): "In the future, we expect that the clinician will consult this, or a similar volume, along with the *Diagnostic and Statistical Manual of Mental Disorders* . . . to help clarify the extent to which an experience [such as a PRE] does or does not imply pathology." In a similar vein, Roll (1987) has suggested that "clinical parapsychologists" be available to counsel persons disturbed by PREs, or we suggest, such clinical parapsychologists might work in conjunction with psychologists, psychiatrists, and other professionals to address patient needs.

To this day, persons experiencing PREs have been treated as pathological. Those actively involved in studying the paranormal have been accused of being immoral, as discussed by the philosopher and Anglican priest James R. Horne (1996) and summarized in the following quotation:

> I find that the moral charges against parapsychology are of three distinct kinds. The first states that parapsychology is wrong because it is a waste of human resources. The second says that parapsychologists not only make intellectual errors, but should be morally condemned for doing so. That is, parapsychologists are not only fools, but culpable fools. The third holds that parapsychology is an activity such that one engaging in it as experimenter or subject is exceptionally liable to moral corruption. This third accusation occurs in two variations: a scientific one contending that requirements for success in the field predispose both subjects and experimenters to carelessness or fraud, and a religious variation saying that paranormal powers themselves place subjects and experimenters in grievous moral danger. The religious accusation again branches into a traditional interpretation of the dangers as demonic and a liberal interpretation of them as psychological. [Horne, 1996, pp. 198–199.]

For those who accept the proposition that the study of psi phenomena is immoral at some level (and note that Horne, 1996, does not), perhaps the entire field of parapsychology and psychical research is best avoided. We strongly disagree with this proposition. For us, psychical studies are not only inherently interesting from numerous perspectives, but also absolutely critical to a full understanding of what it means to be human.

The implications of psi studies, even if only a "little bit true," are far-reaching and worldview-shifting.

Parapsychology draws elements from many subjects, and asks questions that are inherently philosophical in nature. One of the principal concerns of many religious leaders, ethicists, researchers, scientists, and ordinary human beings is the fundamental nature of the human personality and what determines our boundaries and our role in the natural world—a major topic, perhaps the central concern, of psychical studies. Parapsychology addresses those most primordial questions: Who am I? How do I fit into the world at large? Despite the difficulties encountered in researching psi, which appears by its very nature often to be obscure and non-amenable to easy experimental and observational study, we must press forward. Parapsychologists are cartographers of the hidden inner realms of the human psyche. Their mission is to frame points of reference, establish strong footholds on firm territory, and then press on in the continuing quest to understand the true capacities of our species.

# PART I

SPONTANEOUS INSTANCES
OF THE PARANORMAL

P arapsychology owes much of its sustenance to the wide-ranging, interesting, and sometimes peculiar spontaneous experiences that many individuals have outside the laboratory. Historically spontaneous phenomena were, and largely still are, a subject that draws interest to the field. Some researchers go so far as to say that spontaneous cases are the "natural subject matter" (Rush, 1986, p. 51) of parapsychology. Most of the early psychical research and much of the contemporary research has sprung from an effort to categorize and understand these anomalous, and occasionally inexplicable, phenomena. According to one categorization, spontaneous experiences include: "dreams that contain verifiable information not otherwise known to the dreamer; waking visions, voices, or intuitive impressions that include such information; movements of objects and other physical effects without normal explanation; 'miraculous' recoveries from disease or injuries; and some other effects" (Rush, 1986, p. 47). Many researchers believe that spontaneous cases are an excellent tool for understanding and hypothesizing about psi phenomena as well as developing laboratory tests. Certainly, the undertaking of parapsychology and psychical studies would never have occurred had it not been for spontaneous cases.

Both of us (RMS and LY) are ultimately more impressed, that is convinced of the authenticity or reality of paranormal events, by spontaneous cases than by experimental laboratory studies (see Stokes, 1997, and Alvarado, 2002, for recent discussions of the use of spontaneous cases in parapsychology). I, RMS, am impressed perhaps because I am a trained and practicing field scientist (versus a laboratory scientist) and natural historian (Ph.D. in geology and geophysics, with a specialization in vertebrate paleontology and also a B.A. in anthropology), and thus I place more value on spontaneous cases and field studies than some might. It strikes me that psi is a natural phenomenon and is best studied in its natural setting. To try to artificially replicate a setting inductive to psi production in a laboratory may be difficult, and lack of laboratory replicability is not necessarily evidence for the non-existence of psi (although, of course, it does not add to the evidence for psi, either). I, LY, believe that psi is very difficult to bring into "controlled" conditions, and the more natural form of psi is spontaneous. Perhaps it is not necessarily practical to attempt to apply reductionistic methods to paranormal events; one must look at them contextually and in a more gestalt-like fashion.

There are many aspects of nature that are not reducible to laboratory settings—volcanoes, lithosphere plates, meteorites, quasars, planetary nebulae, etc.—although perhaps some components of them can be analyzed in a laboratory (we can study the mineralogy of a volcanic rock or meteorite in the lab once we have acquired a sample from the field, and we can model planetary nebulae theoretically). We cannot simply command a meteorite to drop from the sky, or a volcano to erupt. We must wait patiently until such an event occurs, and if we want to observe it in action we must hope to be at the right place at the right time. Many a meteorite expert has never actually collected a meteorite that was directly observed by him or her to drop from the sky. Rather, rocks are collected and analyzed that are apparently of extraterrestrial origin, meteors (shooting stars) are observed in Earth's atmosphere (but are generally volatilized before ever reaching the surface), accounts are investigated of rocks by chance being observed falling from the sky, and all the evidence is put together to conclude that extraterrestrial objects do occasionally make it from outer space to the surface of Earth. To give a biological example, there are some organisms that have yet to be bred successfully or consistently under artificial conditions (laboratory, zoo, or botanical garden); still, they exist in nature and no one doubts that they successfully breed under natural conditions—or else they would go extinct. Evolutionary processes, such as natural selection and speciation, remain difficult to fully replicate in a laboratory situation. Likewise, glimpses or aspects of psi may sometimes be obtainable in a lab, but for a fuller view one must look at spontaneous cases. Lightning occurs in nature. Artificial lightning can be produced to some extent in the lab, but not to the same degree as found in nature. Poltergeist activity may be to laboratory micro-PK what lightning is to laboratory discharges of static electricity.

An objection often raised to taking spontaneous cases of the paranormal too seriously is that, being spontaneous, they are rarely observed directly by a serious investigator or researcher (the exception being poltergeist-type activity that may last long enough for investigators to arrive on the scene while incidents are still occurring). While undoubtedly there are memory lapses, mistakes, and even downright fraud among reputed cases of spontaneous psi, this does not mean that all such cases are spurious. Indeed, there has been fraud in the laboratory also (see above, page 24). Among the first generation of researchers at the Society for Psychical Research were three men in particular—Edmund Gurney (1847–1888), Frederic W. H. Myers (1843–1901), and Frank Podmore (1856–1910)—who dedicated considerable time to critically analyzing all presumed cases of the paranormal, separating the wheat from the chaff. In their classic *Phantasms of the Living* (1886; see page 65), the authors undertook heroic efforts to examine the cases they included and weed out fraud, as other investigators have done before and since. Another approach (used, for instance, by L. E. Rhine, 1981, and Green and McCreery, 1975) is to collect spontaneous cases with somewhat less initial discrimination (i.e., trust in the honesty and good faith of those reporting the cases, and do not investigate each one individually), and determine if patterns occur among the cases collected. Over a period of thirty-five years, starting in 1948, L. E. Rhine collected more than thirty thousand unsolicited cases from individuals across the globe regardless of age, gender, and socioeconomic backgrounds, and classified more than fifteen thousand of these cases (Drewes, 2002). Her case collection remains the most extensive case collection in history (Rao, 1986; see also L. E. Rhine, 1981, and Feather and Schmicker, 2005). Consistent patterns and types of phenomena, not necessarily predicted by an analysis of modern folklore or "ghost stories," it may be concluded, will occur among genuine cases. Spurious cases will fall outside the patterns established by the majority of cases (presuming the majority in a large sample are genuine), and can thus be eliminated from the study of psi.

A third approach that may help establish the overall authenticity of spontaneous cases of apparent psi is if they show relationships and correlations with other phenomena that would not be expected if they were simply fabrications or well-intentioned but non-veridical stories. An impressive example of such a correlation is that spontaneous cases of telepathy appear to correlate negatively with geomagnetic activity whereas poltergeist activity correlates positively with geomagnetic activity (see, for instance, Persinger, 1987; Persinger and Schaut, 1987; Roll and Gearhart, 1974; and the review in Stokes, 1997, pp. 59–62). In a paper titled "Geomagnetism and Anomalous Experiences, 1868–1980," Wilkinson and Gauld summarized their findings:

> . . . in the end we were left with a residuum of positive findings: (a) There is a weak but persistent statistical relationship between lowish absolute levels of geomagnetic activity and the occurrence of spontaneous cases of apparent telepathy/clairvoyance. (b) There is a small tendency for the days of onset of cases of poltergeists and hauntings to be days of higher-than-usual geomagnetic activity. What underlies these observed relationships remains to be determined. [Wilkinson and Gauld, 1993, p. 276.]

These findings strongly support the notion that the overall data set of spontaneous psi cases is genuine. If most or all were fraudulent, there seems little chance that they would correlate with geomagnetic activity, unless one wants to suggest that hoaxes of telepathy are more likely to take place on days of low levels of geomagnetic activity whereas days of high geomagnetic activity tend to inspire poltergeist hoaxes. But remember, in some cases it has been demonstrated that animal psi also correlates with geomagnetic fluctuations (see Radin, 2002b, for the case of the dog Jaytee), and it is unlikely that an animal will know to "fake" psi in conjunction with changes in geomagnetic activity. A more parsimonious explanation seems to be that such paranormal phenomena have a basis in reality and somehow psi (or the expression of psi phenomena) is either influenced by geomagnetic activity, or correlates with phenomena that are affected by geomagnetic activity (see pages 280 in the Burns article and 308, Electromagnetic Theories in the article by Stevens). Indeed, there is increasing evidence that psi is influenced by, or at least somehow correlates with, other physical variables besides geomagnetic activity, such as Local Sidereal Time (see Bremseth, 2001, and page 248; May, 2001). This is further evidence for the reality of psi and associated paranormal phenomena.

# TELEPATHY AND MONITIONS

## ARTICLE 1. CRISIS APPARITIONS AND THE THEORY OF CHANCE-COINCIDENCE, *by Edmund Gurney, 1886.*

[Source: Excerpts from Edmund Gurney, Frederic W. H. Myers, and Frank Podmore. *Phantasms of the Living*. London: Society for Psychical Research and Trübner and Co., 1886. Vol. 2, pp. 54–55, "An Example of a Crisis Apparition"; and Edmund Gurney, in *Phantasms of the Living*. Vol. 2, pp. 1–18, "The Theory of Chance-Coincidence."]

*Editors' Comments*

Published in 1886, just four years after the founding of the Society for Psychical Research, *Phantasms of the Living* summarized the early work of the Literary Committee of the SPR. To this day this thick, two-volume work remains a crowning achievement and testament to the industry of its authors, particularly Edmund Gurney, and other early members of the SPR. *Phantasms* certainly did not end the work of the SPR. Following Gurney's premature death in 1888, a "Census of Hallucinations" was compiled based on the responses of some seventeen thousand people (Sidgwick et al., 1894), which supplemented and supported the findings of *Phantasms* (see Gauld, 1968, for a history of *Phantasms* and the "Census of Hallucinations").

The core of *Phantasms* is a collection of "crisis apparitions" or "crisis hallucinations" (sometimes referred to as cases of "crisis telepathy") that occur to a "receiver" or "percipient" in conjunction with a crisis situation, often death or near death, on the part of the "agent" or "sender." The authors of *Phantasms* interpreted such apparitions to be veridical hallucinations formed in the mind of the percipient based on information telepathically communicated from the agent, often at the approximate moment of death (although the telepathic message might be received in the subconscious of the agent, remain dormant or latent for a period of time, before being brought to the conscious realm). The title of the work, *Phantasms of the Living*, stresses this notion that a still living person transmitted such telepathic messages.

Here it is worth pointing out that as used by the authors of *Phantasms* and other early members of the SPR, the term "hallucination" (and "apparition," for that matter) could refer to a visual hallucination, an auditory hallucination, an olfactory hallucination, a tactile hallucination (such as the feeling of being punched or brushed against), or even what might be called emotional or ideational hallucinations and impressions (suddenly feeling sad, or the idea enters one's head that a friend or family member is in trouble or just died). The word "phantasm," while etymologically related to phantom, referred to any such apparitions or hallucinations. The authors of *Phantasms* included telepathic dreams in their collection and discussion, as well as "borderland" cases where hallucinations were experienced at the transition state between sleeping and waking. "The subject of this book is one which a brief title is hardly sufficient to explain. For under our heading of 'Phantasms of the Living,' we propose, in fact, to deal with all classes of cases where there is reason to suppose that the mind of one human being has affected the mind of another, without speech uttered, or word written, or sign made;—has affected it, that is to say, by other means than through the recognised channels of sense" (F. W. H. Myers, Introduction to *Phantasms*, vol. 1, p. xxxv).

Generally the term "hallucination" was understood in terms of a sensory hallucination as opposed to a non-sensory hallucination (e.g., a person who "hallucinates" that the entire world is plotting against him). Furthermore, and most important, despite what popular notions might be, not all hallucinations are simply false. Hallucinations may carry true information; that is, they may be veridical. If you have a visual hallucination of your mother (who is a thousand miles away) standing at the end of your bed one night, and learn the next morning that she died at the approximate time you "saw" her, such might be considered a veridical hallucination.

*Phantasms* is an important collection of spontaneous cases that remains valuable raw data for analyses and hypothesizing on the nature of telepathy. The authors of the work did not simply accept cases on face value or with relatively minimal verification, as have other compilers of spontaneous cases of the paranormal (such as Flammarion, 1902, 1907, 1922a, 1922b, 1923, 1924; and L. Rhine, 1981). Rather, they did their best to examine, cross-examine, analyze, and verify the authenticity of each case included in the work (note that Flammarion and L. Rhine did not simply accept all cases indiscriminately as true, but their standards were much lower than those applied by the authors of *Phantasms*). These cases were collected in the nineteenth century, and in hindsight that perhaps lends an advantage, and means that a similar set of case studies could not be duplicated. The cases in *Phantasms* predate the widespread use of telephones and even telegraphs, so when a soldier stationed in India hallucinated one night that his grandmother, who was in England, was standing at the foot of his bed, he had plenty of opportunity to mention this hallucination to friends (who could then independently verify his story) before receiving a letter, perhaps a week or two or a month later, announcing that his grandmother had died that night. In our day and age of instant communication, anyone claiming to have a hallucination prior to learning of the grandmother's death is immediately suspect. Even if such a story is given in good faith, it can easily be argued that the "percipient" is "confused" as to the timing of the hallucination and the time when the news of the death was received.

In the selection from *Phantasms* reprinted here, we first give an example from the 702 cases included in the original work. We then reprint a portion of Gurney's analysis of whether or not simple chance coincidence can explain the hundreds of reported occurrences of apparently veridical hallucinations.

## CRISIS APPARITIONS AND THE THEORY OF CHANCE-COINCIDENCE, *by Edmund Gurney, 1886.*

"May 20th, 1884.

(237) [Case Number assigned to this case by the authors of *Phantasms*] "I sat one evening reading, when on looking up from my book, I distinctly saw a school-friend of mine, to whom I was very much attached, standing near the door. I was about to exclaim at the strangeness of her visit, when, to my horror, there were no signs of anyone in the room but my mother. I related what I had seen to her, knowing she could not have seen, as she was sitting with her back towards the door, nor did she hear anything unusual, and was greatly amused at my scare, suggesting I had read too much or been dreaming.

"A day or so after this strange event, I had news to say my friend was no more. The strange part was I did not even know she was ill, much less in danger, so could not have felt anxious at the time on her account, but may have been thinking of her; that I cannot testify. Her illness was short, and death very unexpected. Her mother told me she spoke of me not long before she died, and wondered I had not been to see her, thinking, of course, I had some knowledge of her illness, which was not the case. It may be as well to mention she left a small box she prized rather, to be given to me in remembrance of her. She died the same evening and about the same time that I saw her vision, which was the end of October, 1874.

"ELLEN M. GREANY."

In answer to an inquiry, Ellen Greany adds that this hallucination is the only one she has ever experienced. She tells Miss Porter that she went to see her dead friend before the funeral, which accords with her statement that she heard the news of the death very soon after it occurred; and there is no reason to doubt that, at the time when she heard the news, she was able correctly to identify the day of her vision.

Her mother corroborates as follows:

"Acton, July, 1884.

"I can well remember the instance my daughter speaks of. I know she was not anxious at the time, not knowing her friend was ill. I took no notice of it at the time, as I do not believe in ghosts, but thought it strange the next day, when we heard she was dead, and died about the same time that my daughter saw her.

"MARGARET GREANY."

[(Note by Edmund Gurney) I have seen Ellen Greany, who is a superior and intelligent person. She went over her story without prompting, giving an entirely clear and consistent account, and standing cross-examination perfectly. But the favourable effect of such an interview on one's own mind cannot, of course, be conveyed to others.]

[. . .]

## THE THEORY OF CHANCE-COINCIDENCE.

§ 1. An issue has now to be seriously considered which I have several times referred to as a fundamental one, but which could not be treated without a preliminary study of the subject of sensory hallucinations. *That,* as I have tried to show, is the order of natural phenomena to which "phantasms of the living" in general belong; they are to be regarded as projections of the percipient's brain by which his senses are deceived. We have further found that in a certain number of cases—which may be taken as representing the still larger number to be cited in the following chapters—a phantasm of this kind is alleged to have coincided very closely in time with the death, or some serious crisis in the life, of the person whose presence it suggested. The question for us now is whether these coincidences can, or cannot, be explained as accidental. If they *can,* then the theory of telepathy—so far as applied to apparitions—falls to the ground. If they *cannot,* then the existence of telepathy as a fact in Nature is proved on the evidence; and the proof could only be resisted by the assumption that the evidence, or a very large part of it, is in its main features untrustworthy. It is very necessary to distinguish these two questions—whether the evidence may be trusted; and if trusted, what it proves. It is the latter question that is now before us. The character of the evidence was discussed at some length in the fourth chapter, and is to be judged of by the narratives quoted throughout the book. In the present chapter it is assumed that these narratives are in the main trustworthy; that in a large proportion of them the essential features of the case—i.e., two marked experiences and a time-relation between them—are correctly recorded.

Here, then, is the issue. A certain number of coincidences of a particular sort have occurred: did they or did they not occur by chance? Now there are doubtless some who do not perceive that this question demands a reasoned examination at all. They settle it *a priori.* "One is constantly coming across very startling coincidences," they observe, "which no one thinks of ascribing to anything but chance; why should not these, which are no more startling than many others, be of the number?" This idea need hardly detain us: the point in our cases is, of course, not that the coincidence is *startling*—that alone would be insignificant—but that the *same sort* of startling coincidence is again and again repeated. That is clearly a fact which demands treatment by a particular method, often vaguely appealed to as "the doctrine of chances." The actual application of that doctrine, however, even to simple cases, seems to require more care than is always bestowed upon it.

Especially is care required in the simple preliminary matter of deciding, before one begins to calculate, what the subject-matter of the calculation is to be—what precise class of phenomena it is to which the doctrine of chances is to be applied. I need only recall Lord Brougham's treatment of his own case (vol. I., pp. 396–7). His attempted explanation, as we say, entirely depended on his miscalling his experience, and referring it to the class of dreams—a class numerous enough, as he rightly perceived, to afford scope for numbers of startling coincidences. And his remarks illustrate what is really a very common outside view of psychical research. Dreams, and hallucinations, and impressions, and warnings, and presentiments—it is held—are the "psychical" stock-in-trade; and these phenomena are all much on a par, and may all be shown by the same arguments to be undeserving of serious attention. There has been the more excuse for this view, in that those who have claimed objective validity for what others dismiss as purely subjective experiences have often themselves been equally undiscriminating. Even this book might lead a critic who confined his perusal to the headings of the chapters to imagine that dreams form a corner-stone of the argument; and in admitting that topic at all, we have so far laid ourselves open to misunderstanding. Thus a distinguished foreign critic of our efforts thought the subjective nature of what we regard as telepathic incidents sufficiently proved by the suggestion that "any physician will consider it quite within the bounds of probability that one per cent. of the population of the country are subject to remarkably vivid *dreams, illusions, visions, &c.*," and that each of these persons is "subject to a *dream or vision* once a week." It is obvious enough that in circles whose members have "spectral illusions" of their friends as often as once a week, the approximate coincidence of one of these experiences with the death of the corresponding person will be an insignificant accident. But we have not ourselves met with any specimen of this class; and the present collection comprises first-hand accounts of recognised apparitions, closely coinciding with the death of the original, from 109 percipients, of whom only a small minority can recall having experienced even a single other visual hallucination than the apparition in question. Once again, then, let me repeat that, though this work connects the sleeping and the waking phenomena in their *theoretic and psychological* aspects, it carefully and expressly separates them in their *demonstrational* aspect. The extent to which either class demonstrates the reality of telepathy can only be known through the application of the doctrine of chances; but the application must be made to them separately, not together; we must not, like Lord Brougham, argue to one class from the data of the other. I have already applied the doctrine to a particular class of dreams, with results which, though numerically striking, left room for doubt, owing to the peculiar untrustworthiness of memory in dream-matters. It remains to apply it to the waking phantasms; and here I think that the results may fairly be held to be decisive.

§ 2. It is clear that the points to be settled are two:—the frequency of the phantasms which have markedly corresponded with real events; and the frequency of phantasms which have had no such correspondence, and have been obviously and wholly subjective in character. These points are absolutely essential to any conclusion on the question before us; and if not settled in any other way, they must be settled by guesses or tacit assumptions. The theory of chance-coincidence, as opposed to that of telepathy, has so far depended on two such assumptions. The first is that the coincidences themselves are *extremely rare*. They can then be accounted for as accidental. For we know that there are such things as hallucinations representing human forms, which do not correspond with any objective fact whatever outside the organism of the percipient; and it would be rash to deny that the death of the person represented may now and then, in the world's history, have fallen on the same day as the hallucination. The second assumption is that these purely subjective apparitions of forms are *extremely common*. It can then be argued that even a considerable number of them might fall on the same day as the death of the corresponding human being. Supposing that we could each of us recall the occasional experience of gazing at friends or relatives in places which were really empty, then—since people are perpetually dying who are the friends and relatives of some of us—every year might yield a certain crop of the coincidences.

But as soon as we make these assumptions explicit and look at them, we see how baseless and arbitrary they are. Why should either of them be admitted without challenge? The second one especially seems opposed to what we may call the common-sense view of ordinary intelligent men. The question whether or not a very large proportion of the population have had experience of morbid or purely subjective hallucinations is one, I submit, where the opponents of the chance-theory might fairly take their stand on the ordinary observation of educated persons, and have thrown on others the *onus* of proving them wrong. On this point a broad view, based on one's general knowledge of oneself and one's fellows, does exist; and according to it, "spectral illusions"—distinct hallucinations of the sense of vision—are very far from the everyday occurrences which they would have to be if we are to suppose that, whenever they coincide in time with the death of the person seen, they do so by accident. Nay, if we take even one of our critics, and bring him fairly face to face with the question, "If *you* all at once saw in your room a brother whom you had believed to be a hundred miles away; if he disappeared without the door opening; and if an hour later you received a telegram announcing his sudden death—how should you explain the occurrence"? he does not as a rule reply, *"His* day and hour for dying happened also to be *my* day and hour for a spectral illusion, which is natural enough, considering how common the latter experience is." The line that he takes is, "The supposition is absurd; there are no really authentic cases of that sort." Under the immediate pressure of the supposed facts, he instinctively feels that the argument of chance-coincidence would not seem effective.

Still "common-sense"—though it would support what I say—is not here the true court of appeal. And, moreover, it is not unanimous. On the second point, as on the first, I have received the most divergent replies from persons whom I have casually asked to give a guess on the subject; and some have guessed the frequency of the purely subjective hallucinations as very much *below* what it actually is. The moral—that we cannot advance a step without statistics—seems pretty obvious, though the student of the subject may read every word that has ever been published on both sides of the argument without encountering a hint of the need. There is plenty of assertion, but no figures; and a single instance, one way or the other, seems often to be thought decisive. To A, who has himself seen a friend's form at the time of his death at a distance, the connection between the two facts seems obvious; B, having heard of a phantasm of a living person which raised apprehensions as to his safety, but which "came to nothing," is at once sure that A's case was "a chance." I have even seen this view expanded, and a leading review gravely urging that the coincidences must be regarded as accidental, if against every hallucination which *has* markedly corresponded with a real event we can set another which has *not*. This is certainly a statistical argument—of a sort—and might be represented as follows:—At the end of an hour's rifle-practice at a long-distance range, the record shows that for every shot that has hit the bull's-eye another has missed the target: therefore the shots that hit the bull's-eye did so by accident.

§ 3. Perhaps the neglect of statistics has in part been due to an apparent hopelessness of attaining a sufficient quantity of reliable facts on which to found an argument—to an idea that any census on which a conclusion could be founded would have to be carried out on a scale so vast as to be practically impossible. "Do you intend," I have been sometimes asked, "to ask every man and woman in England whether he or she has experienced any subjective hallucination during, say, the last twenty years, and also to get a complete record of all the alleged coincidences within the same period, and then to compare the two lists?" Happily nothing at all approaching this is required. We shall find that approximately accurate figures are necessary only on one point—the frequency of the subjective hallucinations; and this can be ascertained by making inquiries of any fraction of the population which is large and varied enough to serve as a fair sample of the whole. Even this smaller task, however, is a very tedious one, consisting, as it does for the most part, in carefully registering *negative* information. The believer in telepathy may feel that he is doing much more to advance his belief by narrating a striking positive instance at a dinner party than by ascertaining, for instance, from twenty of his acquaintance the dull fact that they have never experienced a distinct visual hallucination. Just in the same way a scientific lecturer may win more regard at the moment by a sensational experiment with pretty colours and loud explosions than by laborious quantitative work in his laboratory. But it must be persistently impressed on the friends of "psychical research" that the laborious quantitative work has to be done; and it is some satisfaction to think that the facts themselves may stand as material for others to deal with, even if the conclusions here drawn from them are incorrect.

Nor has the dulness of the work been by any means the only difficulty: its purpose has been widely misconceived, and its scope has thereby been much curtailed. The proposal for a numerical estimate was introduced in a circular letter, every word of which might have been penned by a zealous sceptic, anxious above all things to prove that, in cases where the phantasm of a distant person has appeared simultaneously with the person's death, the coincidence has been an accidental one. Not a syllable was used implying that the authors of the letter had themselves any opinion as to whether phantasms to which no real event corresponds *are* or are *not* common things; it was simply pointed out that it is necessary to have some idea *how* common they are, before deciding whether phantasms to which real events *do* correspond are or are not to be fairly accounted for by chance. And since sensory hallucinations, whatever their frequency, are at any rate phenomena as completely admitted as measles or colour-blindness, it did not occur to us that the following question could possibly be misunderstood:—

*Since January 1, 1874, have you—when in good health, free from anxiety, and completely awake—had a vivid impression of seeing or being touched by a human being, or of hearing a voice or sound which suggested a human presence, when no one was there? Yes or no?*

Clearly, the more *yeses* are received to this question—i.e., the *commoner* the purely subjective hallucinations prove to be—the stronger is the argument for *chance* as an adequate explanation of the instances of coincidence; the more *noes*—the *rarer* the purely subjective hallucinations prove to be—the stronger the argument that the death or other crisis which *coincides* with the apparition is in some way the *cause* of the apparition. We should have expected, if any injustice was to be done us, that it would have taken the form of attributing to us an inordinate desire for *noes*. To our amazement we found that we *were* supposed to be aiming exclusively at *yeses*—and not only at *yeses,* but at *yeses* expanded into orthodox "ghost-stories"—to be anxious, in fact, that every one in and out of Bedlam who had ever imagined something that was not there, or mistaken one object for another, should tell us his experience, with a view that we might immediately interpret it as due to the intervention of a bogey. A more singular instance of the power of *expectancy*—of the power of gathering from words any meaning that a critic comes predisposed to find there—can hardly be conceived. A statistical question on a perfectly well-recognised point in the natural history of the senses was treated, in scientific and unscientific quarters alike, as a manifesto of faith in "supernatural" agencies; and we found ourselves solemnly rebuked for ignoring the morbid and subjective character of many hallucinations—that is to say, for ignoring the fact which we had set forth as the very basis of our appeal, and from which its whole and sole point was derived.

§ 4. If I have dwelt thus on difficulties and misconceptions, it is not that I may boast of having altogether triumphed over them. On the contrary, they have made it impossible to attain more than a fraction of what I once hoped. I began with the idea that the census might be extended to 50,000 persons; the group actually included numbers only

5705. Still, though this is certainly not a showy number, anyone who is familiar with work in averages will, I think, admit that it is adequate for the purpose; and the friends who have assisted in the collection of the answers (to whom I take this opportunity of offering my grateful thanks) need certainly not feel that their labour has been in vain. It is possible for a *small* group to be quite fairly *representative*. Thus, if 50 males were taken at random from the inhabitants of London, if the heights of their respective owners were measured, and added together, and if the total were divided by 50, the result might be taken as representing, within extremely small limits of error, the average height of adult male Londoners; we should not get a much more correct result by taking the mean of 500, or 500,000 heights. This is the simplest sort of case. When it is a question of what proportion of the population have had a certain experience which many of them have *not* had, we must take a larger specimen-number, adjusting it to some extent by our rough previous knowledge. For instance, if we want to know what proportion of the inhabitants of London have had typhoid fever, it would not be safe to take 50 of them at random, and then, if we found that 10 of these had had the illness, to argue that one-fifth of the inhabitants of London had had it. Our rough knowledge is that a great many have not had it, and that a good many have; and in such circumstances we should probably get a very appreciably more certain result by enlarging our representative group to 500. If, again, the experience was of extraordinary rarity, such as leprosy, the number of our specimen-group would have to be again increased; even if we took as many as 500,000 people at random, that is about one-ninth of the population, and ascertained that one of them was a leper, it would not be safe to conclude that there were nine lepers in London. Now our rough knowledge as to hallucinations would place them in this regard very much more on a par with typhoid fever than with leprosy. We realise that a great many people have not had experience of them; but we realise also that they are in no way marvellous or prodigious events. And if a group of 5705 persons seems a somewhat arbitrary number by which to test their frequency, the view that it is *too small* and that 50,000 would be greatly preferable, is one that can at any rate hardly be held with consistency by advocates of the theory of chance-coincidence. For the main prop of that theory, as we have seen, is the assumption that purely subjective hallucinations are *tolerably common* experiences; whereas it is only of *decidedly rare* experiences that the frequency, in relation to the whole population, would be much more correctly estimated from the proportion of *fifty* thousand people that have had them than from the proportion of *five* thousand people that have had them. However, the adequacy of the latter number approves itself most clearly in the course of the census itself. We find as we go on that hallucinations are sufficiently uncommon to force us to take our specimen-group of persons in thousands, not in hundreds, but not so uncommon as to force us to take very many thousands; after the first thousand is reached the proportion of "yeses" to "noes" keeps pretty uniformly steady—as would, no doubt, be the case if the question asked related not to hallucinations but to typhoid fever.

As regards the sort of persons from whom the answers have been collected—if there have been any answers from persons whose deficiencies of education or intelligence rendered them unfit subjects for a simple inquiry bearing on their personal experience, they form, I may confidently say, an inappreciable fraction of the whole. Perhaps a fourth of the persons canvassed have been in the position of shopkeepers and artisans or *employés* of various sorts; but the large majority have belonged to what would be known as the educated class, being relatives and friends of the various collectors. It is, no doubt, safest to assume that a certain degree of education is a pre-requisite to even the simplest form of participation in scientific work; and this condition, it will be observed, in no way detracts from the *representative* character of the group. A few thousand educated persons, taken at random, present an abundantly sufficient variety of types; and, indeed, for the purpose in view, the group is the more truly representative for belonging mainly to the educated class, inasmuch as it is from that class that the majority of the cases which are presented in this work as probably telepathic are also drawn.

§ 5. To say, however, that the answers came in the main from an educated class, is not, of course, a guarantee of the accuracy of the census; and before giving the actual results it may be well to forestall some possible objections.

It may be said, to begin with, that people may have had the experience inquired about, but may have forgotten the fact. This is the objection which was considered above in respect of dreams of death, and which there seemed to have decided force. In respect of waking hallucinations of the senses, its force is very much less. No doubt hallucinations may exhibit all degrees of vagueness; and it is very possible that extremely slight and momentary specimens may make little impression, and may rapidly be forgotten; but for the purposes of the census it would not in the least matter that persons whose experience had been of this slight and momentary kind should answer *no* instead of *yes*. It would have been unwise to complicate the question asked by an attempt to define the extent of vividness that the hallucination must have reached, to be reckoned as an item in our census; but clearly the only subjective hallucinations of which it really concerns us to ascertain the frequency are those which are in themselves *as distinct and impressive* as the hallucinations that we represent as telepathic; and any that fall below this point of distinctness and impressiveness have no bearing on the argument. And, *per contra,* it will be seen that by not limiting the wording of the question to distinct and impressive hallucinations, the collector exposes himself to receiving the answer "yes" from persons whose hallucination actually was very vague and momentary, but who do, as it happens, remember its occurrence. In point of fact, this has occurred a good many times; and the swelling of the list of *yeses* by this means probably outweighs any losses of what should have been genuine *yeses* through failure of memory. For consider what such failure of memory would imply. A fact of sight, hearing, or touch, as clear and unequivocal as most of the sensory impressions which we adduce as evidence for telepathy, must be very clear and unequivocal indeed. And the absence of the normal external cause of such an impression, when recognised, can hardly fail to give rise to genuine surprise—the surprise that follows a novel and unaccountable experience: this has been the result of almost all the "telepathic" phantasms, quite independently of the news which afterwards seemed to connect them with reality. Now, can it be a common thing for an experience as unusual and surprising as this to be, within a dozen years or any shorter period, so utterly obliterated from a person's mind that his memory remains a blank, even when he is pointedly asked to try and recall whether he has had such an experience or not?

A second objection is this. It has been suggested that untrue answers may be given by persons wishing to amuse themselves at our expense. Now I cannot deny that persons may exist who would be glad to thwart us, and amuse themselves, even at the cost of untruth. But when the question is put, "Do you remember having ever distinctly seen the face or form of a person known to you, when that person was not really there?" it is not at once obvious whether the *amusing* untruth would be "Yes" or "No." In neither case would the joke seem to be of a very exhilarating quality; but, on the whole, I should say that "Yes" would be the favourite, as at any rate representing the rarer and less commonplace experience. "Yes" is, moreover, the answer, which (as I have explained) it has been very generally thought that we ourselves preferred; so that to give it might produce a piquant sense of fooling us to the top of our bent. But the reader has seen that, so far as the census might be thus affected, it would be affected in a direction *adverse* to the telepathic argument; for the commoner the purely casual hallucinations are reckoned to be, the stronger is the argument that the visions which correspond with real events do so *by chance*. And if the number of these coincident visions makes the chance-argument untenable, even when the basis of estimation is affected in the way supposed, *a fortiori* would this be the case if the *yeses* were reduced to their true number.

Yet another objection is that persons who have had hallucinations may sometimes be disinclined to admit the fact, and may say "No" instead of "Yes" in self-defence. This source of error must be frankly admitted; but I feel tolerably confident that it has not affected the results to a really detrimental extent. Any reluctance to give the true answer is, as a rule, observable at the moment; and in most cases it disappears when the purpose of the census is explained, and careful suppression of names is guaranteed. And against this tendency to swell the *noes* may be set several reasons why, quite apart from untruth, a census like this is sure to produce an unfair number of *yeses*. Quite apart from any wish to deceive, the very general impression that *yeses* were what was specially wanted could not but affect some of the answers given, at any rate to the extent of causing indistinct impressions to be represented as vivid sensory experiences; and it has also led some of those who have aided in the collection to put the questions to persons of whom it was *known beforehand* that their answer would be *yes*. Moreover, when question-forms to be filled up are distributed on a large scale, it is impossible to bring it home to the minds of many of the persons whose answer would be "No" that there is *any use* in recording that answer. They probably have a vague idea that they have heard "negative evidence" disparaged, and fail to see that every percentage in the world involves it—that we cannot know that one man in 100 is six feet high without evidence that 99 men in 100 are *not* six feet high. This difficulty has been encountered again and again; and on the whole I have no doubt that the proportion of *yeses* is decidedly larger than it ought to be. Fortunately, incorrectness on this side need not trouble us—its only effect being that the telepathic argument, if it prevail, will prevail though based on distinctly unfavourable assumptions.

§ 6. And now to proceed to the actual results of the census, and to the calculations based thereon. I will begin with auditory cases. Of the 5705 persons who have been asked the question, it appears that 96 have, within the last 12 years, when awake, experienced an auditory hallucination of a voice. The voice is alleged to have been unrecognised in 48 cases, and recognised in 44, in 13 of which latter cases the person whose voice seemed to be heard was known to have been dead for some time. In the remaining 4 cases it has been impossible to discover whether the voice was recognised or not; the numbers being so even, I shall perhaps be justified in assigning 2 of these to one class, and 2 to the other. The computation will be clearer if we consider only the cases in which the voice was recognised, and the person whom it suggested was living; these, then may be taken as 33. But, out of the 33 persons, 10 profess to have had the experience more than once. Such cases of repetition, or at any rate most of them, might fairly have been disregarded; for since the large majority of the persons who have had one of the coincidental hallucinations, which appear later in the calculation, can recall no other hallucination besides that one, I might in the same proportion confine the present list, which consists wholly of non-coincidental or purely subjective hallucinations, to similarly *unique* experiences, and leave out of account those occurring to people who seem rather more pre-disposed to such affections. However, in order to make ample allowance for the possibility that the witnesses in the coincidental cases may have had subjective hallucinations which they have forgotten, let us take the repetitions into account; and let us suppose each of the 10 persons just mentioned to have had 4 experiences of the sort within the specified 12 years. The most convenient way of making this allowance will be to add 30 to the former total of 33—*i.e.,* to take the number of persons who have had the experience under the given conditions as 63. This amounts to 1 in every 90 of the group of 5705 persons named, or (if that group be accepted as fairly representative of the population of this country) 1 in every 90 of the population.

Let us now see what the proportion of the population who have had such an experience ought to be, on the hypothesis that the similar impressions of recognised voices presented in this book as telepathic were really chance-coincidences. *As* before in the case of dreams (Vol. I., pp. 303–7), I take cases where the coincidence of the hallucination was with *death*—the reasons for this selection being (1) that death is the prominent event in our telepathic cases; and (2) that for the purpose of an accurate numerical estimate it is important to select an event of a very definite and unmistakeable kind, such as only happens once to each individual. Again also, in accordance with the official returns which give 22/1000 as the annual death-rate, the proportion of anyone's relatives and acquaintances who die in the course of 12 years is taken as 264/1000; and as we have seen (Vol. I., pp. 305–6), it will make no appreciable difference to the calculation whether a person's circle of relatives and acquaintances, the voice of anyone of whom his hallucination may represent, is large or small. The probability, then, that a person hallucinated in the way supposed will, by accident, have his hallucination within 12 hours on either side of the death of the relative or acquaintance whose voice it represents is 1 in (12 × 365 × 1000)/264, or 1/16,591 [Note by editors: That is, "within 12 hours on either side of death" is a day, and the proportion of 264/1000 must be divided by 365 days per year times 12 years to calculate the probability that the death of a relative or acquaintance will occur on any particular day during that 12-year period. $(264/1000)/(12 \times 365) = 1$ in $(12 \times 365 \times 1000)/264 = 1/16,591$. Actually, using this reasoning, the probability of accidental coincidence on any particular day independent of a specified time period, twelve years or otherwise, is $(22/1000)/365 = 1/16,591$.]. That is to say, each coincidental hallucination of the sort in question implies 16,590 purely subjective cases of the same type [Note by editors: That is, according to Gurney, the probability of a purely subjective hallucination that is not coincidental is 16,590/16,591.]. Now our collection may be reckoned to include 13 first-hand and well-attested coincidental cases of this kind, which have occurred in this country within the specified time. On the hypothesis, therefore, that these cases were accidental, the circle of persons from whom they are drawn ought to supply altogether, in the specified 12 years, 215,670 examples [of such hallucinations].

The next point to decide is the size of the circle from which our coincidental cases are drawn. The number here is not one that it is possible to estimate accurately: what must be done, therefore, is to make sure that our margin is on the side adverse to the telepathic argument, *i.e.*, to take a number clearly in excess of the true one. Our chief means of obtaining information has been by occasional requests in newspapers. A million-and-a-half would probably be an outside estimate of the circulation of the papers which have contained our appeals; but it by no means follows that every paragraph in a paper is studied by every person, or by a tenth of the persons, whom the paper reaches. However, I will make the extreme assumption that as many as a quarter of a million of people have by this means become aware of the kind of evidence that was being sought—an assumption which probably arrogates to us who sought it many times as much fame as we really possess; and I will allow another 50,000 for those who have become aware of the object of our work through private channels. This would raise the number of the circle from whom our evidence is drawn to 300,000, or about 1/80 of the adult population. No one, I think, will maintain on reflection, that I am taking too low an estimate. Would anyone, for instance, suppose that if he canvassed the first 1000 adults whom he met in the streets of any large town, he would find that 12 or 13 of them had, within the last three years, been aware of what we wanted, and of the address to which information might be sent? and for rural districts such a supposition would be even more violent. But I am further supposing that this area of 300,000 persons has been drained dry—again an extravagant concession; for though it is easily assumed that anyone who has ever had a "psychical" experience is desirous to publish it abroad, as a matter of fact people do not usually take the trouble to write a letter about family and personal matters to perfect strangers, on the ground of a newspaper appeal; and I have already mentioned that we ourselves know of much evidence which the reluctance or indifference of the parties concerned has made unavailable for our collection; we cannot, therefore, doubt that much more remains unelicited even among those whom our appeal has reached. A further strong argument for the existence of these unelicited facts is the very large proportion of our actual cases that has been drawn from a circle of our own, unconnected with "psychical" inquiry—from the friends, or the friends' friends, of a group of some half-dozen persons who have had no such experiences themselves, and who have no reason to suppose their friends or their friends' friends better supplied with them than anybody else's.

Here, then, is the conclusion to which we shall be driven, if our coincidental cases were really purely subjective hallucinations, and the coincidence was an accident:—that in a circle of 300,000, within 12 years, 215,670 subjective hallucinations of the type in question have taken place; that is that, on an average, 7 persons in every 10 have had such an experience within the time. But the result of the census above described showed the proportion to be 1 person in every 90 only. Thus the theory of chance-coincidence, as applied to this class of cases, would require that the proportion of those who have not had, to those who have had, a subjective hallucination of a recognised voice should be 63 times as large as it has been shown to be; that is, would require either that the subjective hallucinations should be 63 times as numerous as they actually are, or else that the circle from whom our coincidental cases are drawn should amount to 63 times the assumed size—in other words, that our existence and objects should have been prominently before the minds of more than three-fourths of the adult population of the country!

Another form of the estimate is as follows. The probability that a person, taken at random, will, in the course of 12 years, have the form of hallucination in question is 1/90; the probability that any assigned member of the general population, and therefore any particular person whose phantasmal voice is heard, will die within 12 hours of an assigned point of time is $22/1000 \times 1/365$; hence the probability that, in the course of 12 years, a hallucination of this form *and* the death of the person whose voice seems to be heard will fall within 12 hours of one another is $1/90 \times 22/1000 \times 1/365$, or almost exactly 1 in 1,500,000. And the circle from which our coincidental cases are drawn is assumed to be 300,000. From these data it may be calculated that the odds against the occurrence, by accident, of as many coincidences of the type in question as that circle produced, are *more than a trillion to 1.*

§ 7. But the *reductio ad absurdum* becomes far more striking when we apply the doctrine of chances to *visual* cases. Out of the 5705 persons taken at random, of whom the above question was asked, only 21 could recall having, in the conditions named and within the specified 12 years, experienced a visual hallucination representing a living person known to them. But two of the 21 had had 2 experiences of the sort; so let us take the total as 23. That is, the experience has fallen to the lot of one 248th of the group of persons asked, or, if that group be fairly representative, to 1 person in every 248 of the population. Now, just as before, each coincidental hallucination of the sort in question supposing it to have been purely subjective and the coincidence to have been accidental, should stand for 16,590 purely subjective hallucinations. But our collection includes 31 first-hand and well-attested coincidental cases of this type, which have occurred in this country within the specified time; and the circle of persons from whom they were drawn—liberally supposed, as before, to number 300,000—ought, therefore, to supply altogether, in the specified 12 years, 514,290 examples. That is to say, it ought to have happened on an average to everybody once, and to most people twice, within the given time, distinctly to see an absent relation or acquaintance in a part of space that was actually vacant. But the census has shown that, within the given time, only about 1 in every 248 persons has had such an experience even once. Thus the group of visual coincidental cases now in question, if ascribed to accident, would require either that the subjective hallucinations should be more than 396 times as numerous as they actually are; or else that the circle from whom our coincidental cases are drawn should amount to more than 396 times the assumed size—in other words, that our existence and objects should have been prominently before the minds of every adult member of a population 5 times as large as the existing one.

The second form of estimate in the last section applied to visual cases, will give as the probability that the hallucination and the death will fall within 12 hours of one another, $1/248 \times 22/1000 \times 1/365$, or 1 in 4,114,545. And the circle from which our coincidental cases are drawn is assumed to be 300,000. From these data it may be calculated that the odds against the occurrence, by accident, of as many coincidences of the type in question as the 31 which that circle produced, are about *a thousand billion trillion trillion trillions to* 1. Or, to put it in yet another way—the theory of chances, which gives 1 as the most probable number of coincidences of the type in question for every 4,114,545 of the population to yield, will give 6 as the most probable number for the whole adult population to yield, within the given period. Yet we draw more than 5 times that number from a fraction of the adult population which can only by an extravagantly liberal estimate be assumed to amount to an 80th part of the whole, and which has been very inadequately canvassed.

[. . .]

## ARTICLE 2. ON THE FREQUENCY OF MONITIONS,
*by Charles Richet, 1923.*

---

[Source: Excerpt from Charles Richet, *Thirty Years of Psychical Research, being a Treatise on Metapsychics* (translated by Stanley De Brath). New York: Macmillan, 1923, pp. 267–270, 278–282.]

### Editors' Comments

An influential psychical researcher in France during the late nineteenth and early twentieth centuries was the Nobel Prize (physiology/medicine, 1913) winner Charles Richet (1850–1935). A man of many talents and interests (including early aerodynamics and flight in addition to his work in medicine, physiology, and psychical studies), Richet performed very early telepathy/clairvoyance experiments with playing cards, he studied mediums, and as seen in the selection included here, he collected cases of spontaneous psi. Richet applied statistical methods to psychical studies as early as 1884 (see discussion in Rhine, 1934), following up on his suggestion that "feeble thought-reading powers or slight mental reverberations may possibly be detected in most persons by applying the laws of probability to a great number of guesses made by them at a limited series of objects" (translated from the French; quoted from Haynes, 1982, p. 188). Richet served as president of the Society for Psychical Research in 1905.

As Richet points out, experiences that may be viewed as spontaneous cases of psi are not uncommon, and many readers of this book probably have incidents they can recount. Both of us (LY and RMS) have had experiences that might be considered spontaneous instances of apparent telepathy. Here we give an example that occurred recently to RMS. There is nothing particularly "extraordinary" about it, but it may make one stop and wonder.

A spider bit me one Saturday. The spider had the appearance of a hairy little tarantula with large green "eyes" that I found very striking (the anatomical structures I thought of as green eyes may not have actually been eyes; I am not an expert on spiders). I was worried about the incident as my thumb hurt where I had been bitten, and I had heard of people getting very sick or even dying from certain spider bites. I did not know what kind of spider it was, as I had never seen its kind before, so before letting it go (I could not bear to kill it, it was so beautiful) I took photographs of the spider in order to later identify the species in case it proved poisonous. That night or early the next morning a friend of mine dreamed or hallucinated (her description—she described it as both a dream and a hallucination) concerning a tarantula-like spider, and also dreamed of a baby with "beautiful large green eyes" (quoting from her email to me). Furthermore, I was in her dreams that night and she felt a need to tell me about the spider, and so sent me an email about her dream (she does not write to me that often, and certainly does not normally tell me her dreams). I should mention that I live in Massachusetts and she lives in Texas, and there have been other instances where she seemed to have picked things up from me telepathically.

Is this a true paranormal event in that thoughts or ideas were transmitted from one mind to another (telepathy), or did one person pick up glimpses of the happenings taking place thousands of miles away (clairvoyance), or was it simply a chance-coincidence? We make no claims for this incident one way or the other, but simply offer it as an example for consideration.

In the following selection Richet offers a sampling of cases of spontaneous psi (which he refers to as monitions).

## ON THE FREQUENCY OF MONITIONS, *by Charles Richet, 1923.*

[Editors' note: Richet (1923; see his p. 245) uses the term "monition" in a general sense to refer to spontaneous cases of "things" that are "known," but "known" through some means other than the normal sensory channels. Monitions in this sense include what others sometimes refer to as "veridical hallucinations" (which may be visual, auditory, the sense of touch, or simply a feeling), and are commonly attributed to telepathy and/or clairvoyance.]

Monitions are much more frequent than is commonly thought. When speaking to a sceptic on this point, he often replies, "I could tell you a very singular fact of this kind that happened to me personally": and this "singular fact" which seems to him evidential he will accept and recount with simple-minded satisfaction, while rejecting with infantile inconsequence other facts perhaps more evidential because they did not happen to himself.

I do not hesitate to say that some instances of telepathy, more or less evidential, could be gathered from nearly all families. If they are not made public it is from a praiseworthy feeling they are not sufficiently evidential, or from fear of ridicule, but chiefly from reluctance to make the effort to confirm them by exact dates, official certificates, and other data without which a mere story has no great value. They seem nearly independent of age and sex; they occur in the daytime rather less frequently than at night on going to sleep or in dreams. [Editors' note: Louisa Rhine's categorization of spontaneous cases of apparent psi includes a distinction between waking cases and dreaming instances. The waking versus dreaming versions, Rhine (1953) suggests, may involve different levels of ease in bringing an impression received by the unconscious to a conscious state of awareness. Perhaps considerable motivation (even if the motivation is below the conscious level) is necessary to bring psi into conscious awareness during the waking time. Dreams are on the border between conscious and unconscious states, and therefore could allow a greater facilitation of psi.]

We may be confident that this psychological phenomenon is much more common than is supposed, and when a person who has received a monition is no longer branded as a visionary, instances will be multiplied. It is sheer idiocy to refer them to a colossal fraud repeated for fifty years in all lands, or to a series of gross illusions. It is equally unreasonable to think them due to chance; the mass of precise and unlikely details given precludes this supposition.

We are, then, in presence of a known but unexplained phenomenon: and is not this the character of most of the facts with which science is concerned? When a new case of monition is reported it is almost always possible to find analogous cases, just as a botanist can always refer a new plant to known species. This is characteristic of scientific knowledge. Experiment has given indubitable proofs of cryptesthesia [a general term used by Richet, 1923, p. 64, to cover various cases of "lucidity," "clairvoyance," and "telepathy." The Greek etymology is "a hidden sensibility"]. Observation has confirmed this proof by different but equally sure methods.

To show how interesting these monitions are, I have collected in the following pages a considerable number. They may be monotonous reading, but in a scientific work it is necessary to present a large number of duly attested facts. Their value appears by their quantity as well as by their quality. It is not possible, and it would be absurd to suppose, that *all* these facts authenticated by laborious cross-examination and investigation should be false or erroneous. Every unbiassed [unbiased; spelling incorrect in the original] person who reads the evidence will acquire the certainty that neither lying nor exaggeration nor chance can account for *all* these monitions.

[. . .]

The aggregate is a weighty mass of documentary evidence. Considering each case separately, we find some imperfect and only vaguely demonstrative; but that is inseparable from all observational science. Observations can never give the same certitude as experiment, and to warrant any conclusion a very large number must be compared.

If, after carefully reading the instances here adduced, the reader cannot decide that monitions exist, i.e., that there is a relation, the working of which remains a mystery, between an external event and its cognition which neither our sense nor our reason can account for, if, I say, this conclusion is not accepted, then all observational and historical science must be rejected, and we must doubt the existence of aërolites [meteorites] or that Charlemagne ever lived. Monitions (sporadic lucidity) confirm experimental lucidity, and the latter corroborates the former.

[Below is just a sampling of the more than fifty pages of examples of monitions that Richet (1923) recounts. Those reprinted below (from Richet, 1923, pp. 278–282) include some that Richet collected, and a few that occurred to him personally.]

The next story (from the unpublished enquiry through the *Bulletin des Armées*) is so evidential that I give *in extenso* the letter received from Captain V., January 14, 1917:

"On September 3, 1916, during the attack on the Chemin-Creux, between Maulpas and Cléry, Second Lieutenant D., of the 13th battalion of the Alpine chasseurs, was wounded by a bullet in both arms, and left the line to have his wounds dressed. That evening and for fifteen days he was missing at roll-call, and was sought in vain in the dressing-stations. On September 18th the 13th battalion returned to the same sector, the front line having been advanced three kilometres. During the night of September 18th–19th Second Lieutenant V., an intimate friend of D.'s, saw in a dream his friend D. dying in a shell-hole at the edge of the Chemin-Creux, under a willow tree, reproaching him vehemently for letting his best friend die unassisted.

"V., a cool-headed and sceptical officer, was nevertheless obsessed by his dream, and went to his commandant, S., who at first did not take the matter seriously, but in the end, in kindness, and to finish with the affair, gave V. a short leave to search the place. V. came to the Chemin-Creux and there found the surroundings as seen in his dream. At the foot of a willow was a stick with the label, 'Here lie two French soldiers.' There was nothing to connect this with D., but on opening the grave, D.'s body was found, which had been buried about fifteen days before. This strange fact could be attested by the officers of the 13th, but they have other things to do."

Dr. Ollivier, at Huelgoat (Finistère) went on horseback at 8 P.M. on a dark night to visit a patient in the country, and was thrown from his horse, breaking his collar-bone. At nine o'clock, his wife on retiring to rest was seized with violent trembling, called the servant, and said, "My husband has met with an accident and is killed or hurt." It may have been a monition, but chance coincidence is possible, or even likely, in this case.

A soldier, a peasant of La Creuse, told M. Raymond Mialaret, in very simple words, that one morning his little girl of seven had seen him in a dream lying on the ground bleeding from the left arm. She told the dream to her mother, who said it was a nightmare. That same night the soldier was wounded in the left arm (Enquiry through the *Bull. des Armées*).

Mr. Fraser Harris, who had gone from London to lecture at St. Andrews, went on Sunday to a small family hotel, and suddenly saw the front of his house in London. His wife was on the doorstep speaking to a workman who was holding a large broom. She seemed troubled, and Mr. Harris made out that this poor man was asking for help. At that very time Mrs. Harris was speaking to a poor man seeking work, who offered to sweep the snow from the steps and said he had nothing for himself or his children to eat. On returning to London, Mr. Harris found the man just as he had seen him in vision.

Lieutenant G., at the front near Reims, had not heard from his wife for three days. One night he dreamed that he saw her pale as death on her bed. He woke up sobbing and waited impatiently for news. Three days later he learned that on the night of his dream she had a narrow escape from suffocation by fire in her room, which scorched all the bedding. Mme. G. felt the result of the semi-suffocation for a long while (Enquiry through the *Bull. des Armées*).

A little girl of ten, in a dream, sees her father, Lieutenant D., coming home on leave from the front, and added that he had a rubber cape, which no one knew of his having. Next day the lieutenant arrived, a month before he was expected, wearing a waterproof that he had bought on his way home (Enquiry through the *Bull. des Armées*).

Professor S. Venturi, in charge of the lunatic asylum at Garofalo, left home for Pozzuoli, but under a strong presentiment, determined, in spite of difficulties, to return to his house at Nocera. He found his wife in great agitation. Their little girl had a dangerous attack of croup [a bad cough caused by inflammation of the upper airway], and Mme. Venturi had cried out for her husband in her distress.

[. . .]

One winter evening in 1899 I was working in my library in the Rue de l'Université. My wife was at the opera that evening with my daughter Louise. Suddenly, about 10.30, I thought for the first time in my life, and without there being any smoke at all in the room to suggest the idea, that there was a fire at the opera. The impression was so strong that I wrote down "Fire! Fire!" and a few minutes later, thinking this not enough, I wrote "Att," meaning "attention." Not much disturbed I returned to my work. Towards midnight, when my wife and daughter returned, I at once asked them, to their great surprise, "Was there a fire?" My wife answered, "No, there was no conflagration, but we were much frightened. Between the acts some smoke rose from the orchestra; there was a rumour of fire; I left the box quickly to learn what was the matter, telling my daughter, 'When I come back leave at once without waiting for anything.' They reassured me and the performance went on without incident."

This is not all. At the moment when I wrote "Fire" in my notes, my sister, Mme. Ch. Buloz, whose room opens off mine, fancied that mine was on fire. She went to the door, but feeling that her fears were groundless, stopped, saying to herself, "No, I will not disturb my brother for such a silly fancy."

Therefore my sister and I had an impression of fire at the same moment; that is how I can best describe the vague notion that came to me while my wife and daughter were at the opera nearly a mile distant at which a real danger from fire arose. Is this a coincidence? Was there at my house an odour of smoke too faint to be consciously perceived?

# MEDIUMSHIP: QUASI-SPONTANEOUS PSI

## ARTICLE 3. ON TRANCE PHENOMENA OF MRS. PIPER, by *William James, 1890.*

[Source: Excerpts from William James, "On Trance Phenomena of Mrs. Piper." *Proceedings of the Society for Psychical Research* 6, pp. 651–659 (1890).]

### Editors' Comments

A professor of psychology at Harvard University, and well known for his contributions to that field (his works include *The Varieties of Religious Experience* and *The Will to Believe*), William James (1842–1910) also took an active interest in psychical research, beginning with his 1869 review of a book by Epes Sargent, summarizing contemporary spiritualism, titled *Planchette; or the Despair of Science* (see Murphy and Ballou, 1969). James helped to found the American Society for Psychical Research (1884–1885; reinstituted and reorganized in 1906–1907), and he served a term as president of the Society for Psychical Research (1894–1895). James is credited with the discovery of Mrs. Piper as a medium in 1885.

Mrs. Leonore E. Piper (1859–1950) was a famous, if sometimes reluctant, medium from Boston who first came to attention when she was "discovered" by William James and subsequently studied by him and various members of both the American and English Society for Psychical Research for a number of decades. She reputedly manifested or channeled spirits and departed souls via verbal speech while in a trance during séances and through automatic writing. Like any medium, she was condemned as a fraud by some, and made mistakes at times. Still, as a result of her feats, many persons were converted to the belief in survival after death. It is not clear what Mrs. Piper's own view was. She was quoted in the October 20, 1901, edition of the *New York Herald* as saying, "The theory of telepathy strongly appeals to me as the most plausible and genuinely scientific solution of the problem [Editors' note: of where the information she expressed came from] . . . I do not believe that spirits of the dead have spoken through me when I have been in the trance state . . . It may be that they have, but I do not affirm it." In the October 25, 1901, edition of *The Boston Advertiser* she stated, "I did not make any such statement as that published in the *New York Herald* to the effect that spirits of the departed do not control me . . . My opinion is to-day as it was eighteen years ago. Spirits of the departed may have controlled me and they may not. I confess that I do not know. I have not changed . . . I make no change in my relations" (quotations from Shepard, 1980, vol. 2, p. 712).

## ON TRANCE PHENOMENA OF MRS. PIPER,
*by William James, 1890.*

[. . .]

I made Mrs. Piper's acquaintance in the autumn of 1885. My wife's mother, Mrs. Gibbens, had been told of her by a friend, during the previous summer, and never having seen a medium before, had paid her a visit out of curiosity. She returned with the statement that Mrs. P. had given her a long string of names of members of the family, mostly

Christian names, together with facts about the persons mentioned and their relations to each other, the knowledge of which on her part was incomprehensible without supernormal powers. My sister-in-law went the next day, with still better results, as she related them. Amongst other things, the medium had accurately described the circumstances of the writer of a letter which she held against her forehead, after Miss G. had given it to her. The letter was in Italian, and its writer was known to but two persons in this country.

(I may add that on a later occasion my wife and I took another letter from this same person to Mrs. P., who went on to speak of him in a way which identified him unmistakably again. On a third occasion, two years later, my sister-in-law and I being again with Mrs. P., she reverted in her trance to these letters, and then gave us the writer's name, which she said she had not been able to get on the former occasion.)

But to revert to the beginning. I remember playing the *esprit fort* on that occasion before my feminine relatives, and seeking to explain by simple considerations the marvelous character of the facts which they brought back. This did not, however, prevent me from going myself a few days later, in company with my wife, to get a direct personal impression. The names of none of us up to this meeting had been announced to Mrs. P., and Mrs. J. and I were, of course, careful to make no reference to our relatives who had preceded. The medium, however, when entranced, repeated most of the names of "spirits" whom she had announced on the two former occasions and added others. The names came with difficulty, and were only gradually made perfect. My wife's father's name of Gibbens was announced first as Niblin, then as Giblin. A child Herman (whom we had lost the previous year) had his name spelled out as Herrin. I think that in no case were both Christian and surnames given on this visit. But the *facts predicated* of the persons named made it in many instances impossible not to recognize the particular individuals who were talked about. We took particular pains on this occasion to give the Phinuit control [a discarnate entity who supposedly spoke through Mrs. Piper] no help over his difficulties and to ask no leading questions. In the light of subsequent experience I believe this not to be the best policy. For it often happens, if you give this trance personage a name or some small fact for the lack of which he is brought to a standstill, that he will then start off with a copious flow of additional talk, containing in itself an abundance of "tests."

My impression after this first visit was that Mrs. P. was either possessed of supernormal powers, or knew the members of my wife's family by sight and had by some lucky coincidence become acquainted with such a multitude of their domestic circumstances as to produce the startling impression which she did. My later knowledge of her sittings and personal acquaintance with her has led me absolutely to reject the latter explanation, and to believe that she has supernormal powers.

I visited her a dozen times that winter, sometimes alone, sometimes with my wife, once in company with the Rev. M. J. Savage. I sent a large number of persons to her, wishing to get the results of as many *first* sittings as possible. I made appointments myself for most of these people, whose names were in no instance announced to the medium. In the spring of 1886 I published a brief "Report of the Committee on Mediumistic Phenomena" in the *Proceedings* of the American Society for Psychical Research, of which this is an extract:—

"To turn to the much simpler and more satisfactory case of Mrs. P. This lady can at will pass into a trance condition, in which she is 'controlled' by a power purporting to be the spirit of a French doctor ["Phinuit"], who serves as intermediary between the sitter and deceased friends. This is the ordinary type of trance-mediumship at the present day. I have myself witnessed a dozen of her trances, and have testimony at first hand from twenty-five sitters, all but one of whom were virtually introduced to Mrs. P. by myself. Of five of the sittings we have *verbatim* stenographic reports. Twelve of the sitters, who in most cases sat singly, got nothing from the medium but unknown names or trivial talk. Four of these were members of the society, and of their sittings *verbatim* reports were taken. Fifteen of the sitters were surprised at the communications they received, names and facts being mentioned at the first interview which it seemed improbable should have been known to the medium in a normal way. The probability that she possessed no clue as to the sitter's identity was, I believe, in each and all of these fifteen cases, sufficient. But of only one of them is there a stenographic report; so that, unfortunately for the medium, the evidence in her favor is, although more abundant, less exact in quality than some of that which will be counted against her. Of these fifteen sitters, five, all ladies, were blood relatives, and two (I myself being one) were men connected by marriage with the family to which they belonged. Two other connections of this family are included in the twelve who got nothing. The medium showed a most startling intimacy with this family's affairs, talking of many matters known to no one outside, and which *gossip* could not possibly have conveyed to her ears. The details would prove nothing to the reader, unless printed *in extenso,* with full notes by the sitters. It reverts, after all, to personal conviction. My own conviction is not evidence, but it seems fitting to record it. I am persuaded of the medium's honesty, and of the genuineness of her trance; and although at first disposed to think that the 'hits' she made were either lucky coincidences, or the result of knowledge on her part of who the sitter was and of his or her family affairs, I now believe her to be in possession of a power as yet unexplained."

I also made during the winter an attempt to see whether Mrs. Piper's medium-trance had any community of nature with ordinary hypnotic trance. I wrote in the report:—

"My first two attempts to hypnotize her were unsuccessful. Between the second time and the third, I suggested to her 'control' in the medium-trance that he should make her a mesmeric subject for me. He agreed. (A suggestion of this sort made by the operator in one hypnotic trance would probably have some effect on the next.) She became partially hypnotized on the third trial; but the effect was so slight that I ascribe it rather to the effect of repetition than to the suggestion made. By the fifth trial she had become a pretty good hypnotic subject, as far as muscular phenomena and automatic imitations of speech and gesture go; but I could not affect her consciousness, or otherwise get her beyond this point. Her condition in this semi-hypnosis is very different from her medium-trance. The latter is characterized by great muscular unrest, even her ears moving vigorously in a way impossible to her in her waking state. But in hypnosis her muscular relaxation and weakness are extreme. She often makes several efforts to speak ere her voice becomes audible; and to get a strong contraction of the hand, for example, express manipulation and suggestion must be practiced. The automatic imitations I spoke of are in the first instance very weak, and only become strong after repetition. Her pupils contract in the medium-trance. Suggestions to the 'control' that he should make her recollect after the trance what she had been saying were accepted, but had no result. In the hypnotic trance such a suggestion will often make the patient remember all that has happened.

"No sign of thought-transference—as tested by card- and diagram-guessing—has been found in her, either in the hypnotic condition just described; or immediately after it; although her 'control' in the medium-trance has said that he would bring them about. So far as tried (only twice), no right guessing of cards in the medium-trance. She was twice tried with epistolary letters in the medium-trance—once indicating the contents in a way rather surprising to the sitter; once failing. In her normal waking state she made one hundred and twenty-seven guesses at playing-cards looked at by me—I sometimes touching her, sometimes not. Suit right (first guess) thirty-eight times—an excess of only six over the 'probable' number of thirty-two—obviously affording no distinct evidence of thought-transference. Trials of the 'willing game,' and attempts at automatic writing, gave similarly negative results. So far as the evidence goes, then, her medium-trance seems an isolated feature in her psychology. This would of itself be an important result if it could be established and generalized, but the record is obviously too imperfect for confident conclusions to be drawn from it in any direction."

Here I dropped my inquiries into Mrs. Piper's mediumship for a period of about two years, having satisfied myself that there was a genuine mystery there, but being over-freighted with time-consuming duties, and feeling that any adequate circumnavigation of the phenomena would be too protracted a task for me to aspire just then to undertake. I saw her once, half accidentally, however, during that interval, and in the spring of 1889 saw her four times again. In the fall of 1889 she paid us a visit of a week at our country house in New Hampshire, and I then learned to know her personally better than ever before, and had confirmed in me the belief that she is an absolutely simple and genuine person. No one, when challenged, can give "evidence" to others for such beliefs as this. Yet we all live by them from day to day, and practically I should be willing now to stake as much money on Mrs. Piper's honesty as on that of anyone I know, and am quite satisfied to leave my reputation for wisdom or folly, so far as human nature is concerned, to stand or fall by this declaration.

[. . .]

The skeptical theory of her successes is that she keeps a sort of detective bureau open upon the world at large, so that whoever may call is pretty sure to find her prepared with facts about his life. Few things could have been easier, in Boston, than for Mrs. Piper to collect facts about my own father's family for use in my sittings with her. But although my father, my mother, and a deceased brother were repeatedly announced as present, nothing but their bare names ever came out, except a hearty message of thanks from my father that I had "published the book." I *had* published his *Literary Remains;* but when Phinuit was asked "what book?" all he could do was to spell the letters L, I, and say no more. If it be suggested that all this was but a refinement of cunning, for that such skillfully distributed reticences are what bring most credit in to a medium, I must deny the proposition *in toto.* I have seen and heard enough of sittings to be sure that a medium's trump cards are promptitude and completeness in her revelations. It is a mistake in general (however it may occasionally, as now, be cited in her favor) to keep back anything she knows. Phinuit's stumbling, spelling, and otherwise imperfect ways of bringing out his facts is a great drawback with most sitters, and yet it is habitual with him.

[. . .]

My mother-in-law, on her return from Europe, spent a morning vainly seeking for her bankbook. Mrs. Piper, on being shortly afterwards asked where this book was, described the place so exactly that it was instantly found. I was told by her that the spirit of a boy named Robert F. was the companion of my lost infant. The F.'s were cousins of my wife living in a distant city. On my return home I mentioned the incident to my wife, saying, "Your cousin did lose a baby, didn't she? but Mrs. Piper was wrong about its sex, name, and age." I then learned that Mrs. Piper had been quite right in all those particulars, and that mine was the wrong impression. But, obviously, for the source of revelations such as these, one need not go behind the sitter's own storehouse of forgotten or unnoticed experiences. Miss X.'s experiments in crystal-gazing prove how strangely these survive. If thought-transference be the clue to be followed in interpreting Mrs. Piper's trance utterances (and that, as far as my experience goes, is what, far more than any supra-mundane instillations, the phenomena *seem* on their face to be) we must admit that the "transference" need not be of the conscious or even the unconscious thought of the sitter, but must often be of the thought of some person far away. Thus, on my mother-in-law's second visit to the medium she was told that one of her daughters was suffering from a severe pain in her back on that day. This altogether unusual occurrence, unknown to the sitter, proved to be true. The announcement to my wife and brother of my aunt's death in New York before we had received the telegram . . . may, on the other hand, have been occasioned by the sitters' conscious apprehension of the event. This particular incident is a "test" of the sort which one readily quotes; but to my mind it was far less convincing than the innumerable small domestic matters of which Mrs. Piper incessantly talked in her sittings with members of my family. With the affairs of my wife's maternal kinsfolk in particular her acquaintance in trance was most intimate. Some of them were dead, some in California, some in the State of Maine. She characterized them all, living as well as deceased, spoke of their relations to each other, of their likes and dislikes, of their as yet unpublished practical plans, and hardly ever made a mistake, though, as usual, there was very little system or continuity in anything that came out. A *normal* person, unacquainted with the family, could not possibly have said as much; one acquainted with it could hardly have avoided saying more.

The most convincing things said about my own immediate household were either very intimate or very trivial. Unfortunately the former things cannot well be published. Of the trivial things, I have forgotten the greater number, but the following, *rarae nantes,* may serve as samples of their class: She said that we had lost recently a rug, and I a waistcoat. (She wrongly accused a person of stealing the rug, which was afterwards found in the house.) She told of my killing a gray-and-white cat, with ether, and described how it had "spun round and round" before dying. She told how my New York aunt had written a letter to my wife, warning her against all mediums, and then went off on a most amusing criticism, full of *traits vifs* [sharp features or comments], of the excellent woman's character. (Of course no one but my wife and I knew the existence of the letter in question.) She was strong on the events in our nursery, and gave striking advice during our first visit to her about the way to deal with certain "tantrums" of our second child, "little Billy-boy," as she called him, reproducing his nursery name. She told how the crib creaked at night, how a certain rocking chair creaked mysteriously, how my wife had heard footsteps on the stairs, etc., etc. Insignificant as these things sound when read, the accumulation of a large number of them has an irresistible effect. And I repeat again what I said before, that, taking everything that I know of Mrs. P. into account, the result is to make me feel as absolutely certain as I am of any personal fact in the world that she knows things in her trances which she cannot possibly have heard in her waking state, and that the definitive philosophy of her trances is yet to be found. The limitations of her trance information, its discontinuity and fitfulness, and its apparent inability to develop beyond a certain point, although they end by rousing one's moral and human impatience with the phenomenon, yet are, from a scientific point of view, amongst its most interesting peculiarities, since where there are limits there are conditions, and the discovery of these is always the beginning of explanation.

# POLTERGEISTS:
# SPONTANEOUS PSYCHOKINESIS

Poltergeists have been known for centuries, as here described by Sir William Barrett, one of the founding members of the Society for Psychical Research.

There was [is] no exact English equivalent for Poltergeist, but as the German word *polterer* meant a boisterous fellow, so *poltergeist* was a boisterous ghost. It is a convenient term to express those apparently meaningless noises, disturbances, movements of objects and ringings of bells (even when the wires are severed) for which no assignable cause can be found. [Editors' note: The breaking out of fires is also sometimes associated with poltergeist incidents.] The phenomena are sporadic, breaking out unexpectedly, lasting a few days or months and terminating as suddenly. They differ from hauntings, inasmuch as ghostly forms are not seen, and are associated not so much with a particular locality as with a particular (and usually young) person in a particular room. They appear to have some intelligence behind them, as response to a definite number of raps, or other sounds, asked for by the investigator, can usually be obtained. The phenomena take place equally well in broad daylight, under the searching gaze of investigators, or at night time. Of the genuineness and inexplicable nature of the phenomena there can be no manner of doubt, in spite of occasional attempts at their fraudulent imitation. This latter . . . sometimes occurs after the original phenomena have passed away, and usually when the psychic has been taken to a new locality. [Barrett, 1911, p. 37.]

Are poltergeist manifestations real? That is, are genuinely paranormal effects involved in at least some cases, or are they nothing more than hoaxes and frauds? Initially both of us were extremely skeptical of the entire concept of poltergeists as evidence of the paranormal. However, after intensely studying the literature and RMS witnessing what might be considered a very mild "poltergeist incident" (a book falling off a shelf for no apparent normal physical reason; this occurred in the presence of a person who has been the target of other minor poltergeist activity and the book's topic had personal significance and meaning relative to the context of the situation), we are not so sure.

If poltergeist activities are real, then what is their meaning and significance? In the twenty-first century increasing evidence supports the contention that poltergeist manifestations are genuine. Furthermore, they are generally focused on a single individual (who may be causing the manifestations, even if not consciously and not by normal means), and the physical objects and actions involved in poltergeist manifestations often have meaning and significance for the person in the center of the activity (in the minor incident recounted in the last paragraph, not just any book fell off the shelf, but one with a topic pertinent to the context of emotionally charged issues being discussed at that moment). Some researchers suggest that poltergeist activity results from deep-seated emotional and psychological issues. Parapsychologist and physicist Joseph H. Rush has succinctly summarized the work of Layard and Fodor along these lines:

John Layard (1944), a Jungian psychologist in Britain, proposed that poltergeists resemble other psychological phenomena in that they serve a curative function or purpose by providing relief of psychological conflicts. The two clinical cases he offered in support of this interpretation admittedly were weak, but Layard emphasized that he was merely offering a hypothesis that ought to be investigated further. His insightful paper was denounced by most of the writers who responded.

Meanwhile Nandor Fodor, psychic investigator and psychoanalyst, had been developing a similar concept through practical experience. In a succession of cases that came to his attention (Fodor, 1948, 1958, 1959, 1964), he repeatedly found evidence that unresolved emotional tensions may be expressed in poltergeist phenomena. Sometimes he witnessed paranormal events; more often he had to rely upon testimony of others. However, he found enough evidence to convince him that at least a substantial portion of such reports was reliable, and he was more concerned with their psychiatric implications.

Fodor's cases exhibit a common pattern. Deeply repressed drives or conflicts in persons with hysteric tendencies sometimes became so intense that they produced various "conversion" symptoms, including externalization as PK phenomena. Usually these repressions concealed deep guilt or fear. Whenever he was able to take the tormented person into analytic treatment, both the paranormal and the clinical hysterical symptoms subsided as repressed material was acknowledged. In one case (Fodor, 1964, p. 177), spontaneous PK effects developed around an adolescent boy who, Fodor learned, was a potentially creative writer, but was oppressed by lack of recognition among even family and friends. When his frustration was relieved by an opportunity to write for publication, the phenomena stopped. [Rush, 1977, p. 41.]

Please keep these ideas in mind as you read the following article on poltergeists (in modern terminology dubbed "recurrent spontaneous psychokinesis" or RSPK) by William G. Roll.

## ARTICLE 4. POLTERGEISTS, ELECTROMAGNETISM AND CONSCIOUSNESS, *by William G. Roll, 2003.*

[Source: William G. Roll, "Poltergeists, Electromagnetism and Consciousness." *Journal of Scientific Exploration* 17, no. 1, pp. 75–86 (2003).]

### Editors' Comments

Dr. William G. Roll, a noted psychologist and parapsychologist, has worked in the field for more than half a century. In the early 1950s he undertook research in parapsychology at Oxford University, and subsequently worked in Rhine's Parapsychology Laboratory (1957–1964). In 1986 Dr. Roll joined the psychology department of the State University of West Georgia (at the time called West Georgia College). Roll received his Ph.D. in 1989 from Lund University, Sweden, and lived in Lund before returning to West Georgia. Though now retired, he maintains an affiliation with the State University of West Georgia. Roll is best known for his work on poltergeists, a topic he has consistently explored throughout his career. In this selection Roll discusses poltergeists from a modern perspective, including a theory to help explain the occurrence of such phenomena.

## POLTERGEISTS, ELECTROMAGNETISM AND CONSCIOUSNESS[1],
*by William G. Roll, 2003.*

ABSTRACT

Poltergeist occurrences are displays of energy that induce the movement of common household objects which ordinarily are held in place by inertia and gravity. At the same time the events reflect psychological tension between the central person and others, including investigators. Thus, the phenomenon combines physical and psychological processes. It is commonly referred to as recurrent spontaneous psychokinesis or RSPK.

INTRODUCTION

I became interested in poltergeists or recurrent, spontaneous psychokinesis (RSPK) because it was the only convincing psi phenomenon I had witnessed at the time. I did not expect to learn anything profound about human nature or the cosmos. I have since changed my mind. First, I will provide a summary of some cases.

Psi is divided into ESP or receptive psi and PK or expressive psi. PK is further divided into micro-PK, where the target is the output of a random event generator, and macro-PK, where large-scale objects

---

1 This is the Tim Dinsdale Memorial Award essay for 2002. Thanks to Gary L. Owens for supporting the writing of this article.

levitate. RSPK is a form of macro-PK. I hoped to understand the energy that brings this about.

The first case I looked into (Pratt & Roll, 1958), "the house of flying objects," took place in Seaford, Long Island. Detective Tozzi, who was in charge of the police investigation, suspected Jimmy, the 12-year-old son in the family, of trickery because he was usually at home and awake when things moved. But then an officer witnessed an incident he could not explain away. Pratt and I spent several days in the home and were present when a laundry bottle in the basement fell over and spilled when we were with the family upstairs.

Pratt and I thought the phenomena were probably genuine, but could not be certain since there had only been one incident when we were present, and that took place in another part of the house. Assuming the occurrences were real, I examined the factors on which they seemed to depend (Roll, 1968). Most of the disturbed things belonged to the parents and the events often happened in their living space. For instance, a male and a female figurine moved several feet and broke in the sitting room, which was reserved for the parents. Psychological studies suggested that the boy had strong feelings of anger towards his father. Bottle incidents were common, indicating a focusing effect. The bottles were mostly associated with the mother, and the disturbances may also have reflected unmet dependency needs.

To explore the physical aspects of the incidents, I measured the distances of the objects from the boy. I found that the number of movements showed a statistically significant decline with distance, which suggested that the force was energetic at the same time it was psychological.

Three of the other cases we investigated were more convincing, the Miami case, the Olive Hill case, and the Tina Resch case.

### The Miami Case (Roll & Pratt, 1971)

When Pratt and I arrived at Tropication Arts, a warehouse for novelty items in Miami, Florida, we noticed that there were certain shelves from which things were more likely to take off. This suggested an experiment where we placed things from the warehouse on the special shelves. We asked Julio, the 18-year-old shipping clerk who was the center of the activity, and the other employees to stay away from these sites.

One time I watched Julio place a ceramic alligator on a shelf when a glass four feet behind him fell to the floor and shattered. Both his hands were occupied; in the right he held the alligator, in the left his clipboard. The two other workers in the room were more than 15 feet from the glass. They could not have picked it up previously and then thrown it because we had placed the glass on the shelf ourselves and no one had been near it since then. The glass was among ten targets we had set out that moved when one or both of us had the area under surveillance and when we were the first to enter the area after the incident. The incident was also among seven when Pratt or I had Julio in direct view at the time. We could not account for these events except by RSPK. The clustering of events in certain areas and on certain types of objects suggested area and object focusing. There was a significant reduction of occurrences with distance from the agent.

Mischo (1968) has suggested that objects affected by RSPK are "substitute objects" that represent people associated with the objects. Gertrude Schmeidler, who analyzed Julio's responses to the thematic apperception test (TAT) and Rorschach pictures (in this study as in most of our others) said that Julio experienced the owner as "phoney and cheating" (Roll, 1972, p. 171). The events caused the breakage of merchandise and the disruption in business. There was a subtle change during our investigation. Pratt and I hoped to witness the occurrences, and after a few days objects moved in our presence, seven of these when we had Julio in direct view. It seemed as if he was rewarding our attention. The breakages would probably have continued whether we were there or not but they would not have involved the objects we set out. The meaning of the events had changed and thereby the course they took, but the intensity of the energy seemed the same. There were no incidents when Julio was absent. However, a reporter who stayed alone in the warehouse overnight claimed there was an object movement of several feet.

### The Olive Hill Case (Roll & Stump, 1969; Roll, 1972, Ch. 11)

John and Ora Callihan had seen most of their ceramic lamps and figurines carried out as buckets of shards from their home in rural Kentucky. Their 12-year-old grandson, Roger, who regularly assisted his grandparents, helped with this chore as well.

The movements had been confined to the grandparents' home, but changed to the boy's when John Stump and I were there. At one point, I was following Roger into the kitchen, when the kitchen table flew up, rotated 45 degrees and fell down on the backs of the chairs that stood around it, its four legs off the floor. Roger and the table were in full view when this happened. Later, when I was standing in the doorway between the living room and the children's bedroom, I saw a bottle fly off the dresser and land four feet away. It did not slide off and roll into the room but was clearly airborne. When this took place, Roger was in my peripheral vision on my right in the living room, walking away. His sister was standing slightly behind me on my left; there was no one else in the room. I could discover no way in which the event could have been faked. Altogether there were 10 occurrences when Stump or I were watching Roger and the disturbed object when he had no tangible contact with it. The family described about 184 incidents in the grandparents' home before we arrived, of which 21 apparently occurred when Roger was away.

I speculated that the boy was frustrated at spending time with the grandparents and that this was part of the explanation for the breakages in their home. The inclusion of Roger's own home when we were there, I thought, was due to the attention we paid the boy. As in Miami, the presence of investigators seemed to change the incidents. Here too there were significantly fewer events as the distance from Roger increased.

The family members were Jehovah's Witnesses and attributed the events to a demon. When the incidents started up in their own home after John and I arrived, Roger's mother concluded that we had brought the demon along from the grandparents' and asked us to leave, hoping the demon would follow. This unfortunately did not happen. We had to depart while the occurrences were still going on.

## Tina Resch at Spring Creek Institute (Baumann, 1995)

Dr. Stephen Baumann, who was then at the University of North Carolina, Chapel Hill, was setting up tests for micro-PK at Spring Creek Institute. When the equipment was ready, in October 1984, Tina Resch was invited to be a subject. The previous March, the 14-year-old had been the center of disturbances in her home in Columbus, Ohio (Roll, 1993). That case had not seemed promising at first. Before I arrived at the home, a TV news crew had filmed Tina pulling over a lamp, and the incidents that took place the first three days I was present could have been staged. But then there was a string of occurrences in my presence that I could not dismiss. Tina and her parents, John and Joan Resch, agreed to my bringing her to North Carolina for research and counseling.

By the time Baumann was ready, the activity around the girl had died down. To bring the incidents back, a psychotherapist, Jeannie Stewart, who was counseling Tina, suggested that hypnosis might evoke the bodily sensations that had been associated with the events and thereby the events themselves (Stewart, Roll & Baumann, 1987). This led to a resumption of occurrences.

The question at the back of my mind when I brought Tina to Spring Creek was whether PK could be used as an adjunct to medical treatment. Baumann (1995) did two tests with Tina. In one she tried to influence electric discharges from the nerve cell of a sea slug, in the other from a piezoelectric crystal. This material is found in teeth, bone and connective tissue. The results were promising but there were problems in the test protocol that made them difficult to evaluate.

The RSPK occurred during breaks in the tests when Tina was not trying to use PK. To study the incidents under controlled conditions, we set up a table with PK targets. If any moved, we would know where it came from. Tina was not allowed near the table; otherwise her movements during the rest periods were not restricted. The heaviest target to move was a 12-inch socket wrench. When Stewart and Baumann were standing between Tina and the target table and facing her, there was a loud noise from the hallway behind the girl. The wrench had moved 18 feet, passed the two experimenters and Tina without notice, and hit the door to a storage room. In all, there were 21 movements of objects when Tina was under observation, of which eight came from the target table. The incidents showed a significant decrease with distance.

Nearly all the events took place when Tina was present. The single exception was in her home after John had taken her to church and Joan was home alone with their four young foster children. She said she was downstairs with the children when there were rumbling noises from the empty rooms. When John returned, they found that the mattresses had come off the two beds in Tina's room and her dresser had moved out from the wall. The furniture in her brother's room and in the sitting room had also moved. Tina was still in church and the front door was locked.

The original incidents seemed to reflect Tina's negative feelings about her family and herself (Carpenter, 1993). But when she came to North Carolina, the incidents were wanted. From being destructive to others, the RSPK had become desirable.

## THE ELECTROMAGNETIC FIELD OF SPACE
*Physics is a way to talk about psychic phenomena in a respectable manner.*

I have suggested that psi effects may be understood in terms of "psi fields" that have psychological and physical characteristics and surround and connect physical objects (Roll, 1964). William Joines (1975) suggests more specifically that RSPK is due to "psi waves" that manifest as wave motion like physical waves and interact with the objects to generate their movements. As in the case of physical waves, there should be a decline of incidents with distance from the source, that is, the RSPK agent. This was seen in the three selected cases and in other cases as well.

Object and area focusing would also be consistent with the physical wave analogy. This too was seen in all studies. It was harder to explain how the actual movement of objects could be accomplished. The most likely scenario, we thought, was a suspension of gravity at the site, but we did not know how this could come about (Roll & Joines, 2001).

Hal Puthoff (private communication, Feb. 8, 2001) has proposed that an object may be freed from gravity/inertia if the RSPK agent affects the zero-point energy (ZPE), a sea of random electromagnetic fluctuations that fills all of space. The agent would not generate the energy for object-movements, but would cause the ZPE to cohere and thereby loosen the hold of gravity/inertia that ordinarily keeps things in place. Gravity is closely related to inertia, the effect that causes stationary objects to remain at rest and moving objects to remain in motion. Puthoff gives an example: If you stand on a train at a station and it leaves with a jerk, inertia may cause you to topple backwards (and lurch forward if the train suddenly stops). Inertia, it is thought, is due to pressure from the ZPE. The electromagnetic fluctuations of the ZPE have been detected in the lab (e.g., Chan et al., 2001).

In the light of the ZPE theory, Joines analyzed the decline of occurrences with distance in the Miami, Olive Hill, and Tina Resch cases. The best fit was a product of an inverse distance curve and an exponential decay curve. This was consistent with the ZPE theory. The electromagnetic aspect of psi waves should be attenuated by dispersal in space, and the waves should be converted to some other form of energy as they penetrate the ZPE. In previous analyses of the Miami and Olive Hill cases (Roll, Burdick & Joines, 1973, 1974), where we plotted the data against the inverse and exponential curves, the latter gave the better fit. The exponential effect is seen when energy passes through a "lossy" medium. Sunlight going through water and being converted to kinetic energy (i.e., heat) is an example. We thought that in RSPK psi waves were converted to the kinetic energy seen in the movement of objects.

If RSPK involves transient reductions of the gravity/inertia of the moving objects, the reductions should be reflected in a lowering of the weights of the objects. I do not know of any work where weight measurements were made of the objects or areas in RSPK, but Hasted, Robertson, and Spinelli (1983) reported two sudden increases of the body weight of J. H., the agent for the Enfield RSPK (which had ceased by then). The increases were about one kilo and each lasted five seconds. Just before the two episodes J. H. had been asked to rock slowly back and forth, but there were no weight anomalies during this activity. Two other subjects, presumably inactive, showed four transient increases of up to 0.8 kilo, each taking less than a second. The three subjects were the only ones in a group of about 20 to show weight anomalies.

RSPK may be an extreme form of normal processes within the body. Strenuous physical exertion, such as running and weightlifting, is sometimes associated with feelings of lightness. In sports such as golf and baseball, players who enter the "zone" claim that the ball moves more forcefully and accurately than in ordinary states of consciousness (Murphy, 1993, p. 444; Murphy & White, 1978). According to Japanese practitioners of martial arts, *ki* (in China, *chi*) operates within the body in "internal *ki*" and between body and environment in "external *ki*," the equivalent of PK. In a summary of martial arts lore, Murphy (1993, p. 452) notes that adepts are said to mass *ki* in the body to increase its weight or to dissipate *ki* to make the body lighter. Some adepts reportedly knock down opponents or break physical objects by *ki*.

A weightlifting program called "gravitational gymnastics" is used by Vladimir Chubinsky (Kicklighter, 2000) to alleviate the physical or mental problems of clients. By lifting increasingly heavier weights in the course of weekly sessions, the problems are reportedly reduced and energy increases. It is not known whether the procedure results in actual weight anomalies.

If PK is involved in the workings of the skeletal muscles, the body should weigh less during physical activity and more during rest (but note that the rocking motions of J. H. were not associated with weight gains). Death, the ultimate rest, should result in weight gains. Lewis Hollander (2001) reports transient weight gains in seven dying sheep (but not with three lambs and a goat) that were to be slaughtered. The gains ranged from 18 to 780 grams and lasted one to six seconds. On the other hand MacDougall (1907) found weight losses of between three-eighths to one-and-a-half ounces in four persons at the moment of death. He attributed the losses to the weight of the departing soul. MacDougall used mechanical gauges, Hasted and Hollander used electronic systems.

## OBSERVER PARTICIPANCY
*The world is a structure and the architects are us.*

Physics is considered the bedrock on which the other sciences rest and to which they can ultimately be reduced. This bedrock is not as solid as it once seemed. The change is epitomized by John Wheeler's (1990) concept of "observer participancy." Wheeler says, "Observer participancy gives rise to information; and information gives rise to physics" (quoted by Frieden, 1998, p. 1). The idea that perception affects the physical world is not new (Berkeley, 1713, 1988; Russell, 1926). What is new is that the ideas of Wheeler and others like him are based on experiment. In the famous two-slit experiment photons behave like waves or like particles according to how the process is being observed.

A radical formulation of observer participancy is due to Roy Frieden (1998): "The 'request' for data creates the law that, ultimately, gives rise to the data. The observer creates his or her local reality" (p. i). Frieden goes beyond quantum mechanics when he derives statistical mechanics, thermodynamics and the Einstein field equations from a theory where the observer is part of the phenomena that are measured. He describes all physical processes in terms of differential equations. (The theory is an outgrowth of the work of the British statistician, A. R. Fisher.) According to Frieden, observation injects information into its object. Information thereby interacts with the energy and matter within the object and between this and other objects. Information is "a physical entity" that can "flow" from one object to another (p. 106).

Evan Walker (1974, 1985) has noted that tests in psychokinesis and quantum mechanics both imply that human operators affect physical systems. "This must lie at the heart of the solution to the problem of psi phenomena; and indeed an understanding of psi phenomena and of consciousness must provide the basis of an improved understanding of [quantum mechanics]" (1985, p. 26). Walker brings in the Bell theorem as another instance where quantum mechanics and parapsychology may overlap. Tests of the Bell theorem have shown that the two halves of a subatomic system interact instantaneously across kilometer distances, in other words that objects connected in the past remain connected when separated, and this without the benefit of light or other electromagnetic signals.

Walker's theory of psi is restricted to statistical effects that are allowed by the Heisenberg uncertainty principle. Macro-PK, where movements of large-scale objects are observed, he says may require an outside source of energy (1974, p. 564). RSPK researchers George Owen (1964) and Hans Bender (1969, p. 100) have reached similar conclusions. The zero-point energy could be the source. F. W. H. Myers (1903), a leading light in early parapsychology, postulated a "metetherial environment" where life and thought are carried on apart from matter (pp. 215–218). The metetherial environment is equivalent to the "subliminal self" where the self extends beyond the borders of its waking, "supraliminal" counterpart. Myers suggested that the metetherial environment is continuous with the ether that was thought to permeate space. The ether has since been replaced by the ZPE.

## PSYCHOLOGICAL ASPECTS OF OBSERVER PARTICIPANCY

Puthoff (private communication, February 8, 2001) suggests that if the ZPE is involved in RSPK, this shows that the ZPE has a consciousness component. It seems clear that psychological factors, especially emotion, are involved in RSPK (Carpenter, 1993; Mischo, 1968; Roll, 1968, 1972, 1977). But for most agents, the phenomena seem to be no more conscious than muscle spasms. On the other hand there are anecdotal reports that some RSPK agents have learnt to bring the phenomena on at will (Roll, 1977). If these reports can be trusted, they suggest that the process may become conscious.

Psychologists have shown that perception and behavior are molded by physiology, intention, needs, memories and other cognitive and conative factors that are likely to be different for each person. Physics on the other hand does not predict that differences between observers are associated with different experimental results. From the usual physics perspective the effect of observation is the same for all observers. This is not true for psi research. In their micro-PK experiments with random event generators, Jahn and Dunne (1987) report deviations above or below chance expectancy according to the intentions of their subjects. Similar results have been reported by others. The principal difference between this work and the tests in physics is the focus on motivation in PK. In RSPK, the link between motivation and event seems obvious as well.

Observation and its emotional concomitants are known to affect the way people perceive and act on the environment. It would be surprising if the same were not true for physicists and their experiments. It is suggestive that results in tests conducted by believers in a certain effect (cold fusion comes to mind) support their belief while skeptics get null results. It should be part of the experimental protocols in physics that the intentions and beliefs of the researchers be recorded to determine if there is a correlation with the results (psi tests suggest that researchers may affect results even though they are not present at the test).

Frieden (1998) is the only physicist I know of who proposes that observation is affected by ". . . *the meaning* of the acquired data to the observer" [his italics] (p. 235). Observation is "knowledge based" as well as physical. Frieden does not continue this train of thought, but it leads to the expectation that there will be different results in tests by physicists to whom the results have different meanings. Frieden's theory has another consequence. If observation leaves an imprint on the observed object, this should affect subsequent observations by others. The practice of psychometry may be a case in point. In psychometry the subject is said to obtain information about a distant individual solely by handling an object, such as a personal belonging, that is associated with the individual (Duncan & Roll, 1995, chap. 10). The same reportedly occurs if the subject enters the home of the person. If the person is deceased, and the impression takes the form of a visual image, this may lead to the belief that the departed haunts the home. Reports of haunting apparitions of living people are at least as frequent (e.g., Roll et al., 1996).

Psychometry tests are out of style, but psychometrists are often asked to locate a criminal or a missing person by means of an object with which the person has been in contact, such as a piece of clothing. Explorations in the early days of parapsychology suggest that the phenomenon may be real (Osty, 1923; Roll, 1967, 1975).

H. H. Price (1940) has advanced the concept of "place memories" to account for psychometry and veridical haunting apparitions (i.e., apparitions that resemble people who occupied the area and are unknown to the percipient). According to Frieden's version of observer participancy, it makes sense that interaction with an object or area should affect later observations by others.

Price's concept of place memory should not be confused with the conventional meaning of the term, the tendency to remember events by revisiting the place where they took place. In Price's sense of the term, you "remember" events experienced by others. Like familiar memories, events that are recent, frequent and emotionally significant (to the earlier observer) may be more likely to be brought to mind by the later observer than others (Osty, 1923; Roll, 1967, 1975).

To understand how emotion may bring on actual movements of objects, the concept of observer participancy may be combined with the ZPE and psi wave theories. By interacting with the ZPE, the electromagnetic component of psi waves would be expected to bring on a transient attenuation of the gravity/inertia that ordinarily keeps things in place. If an emotionally charged object has been freed of gravity/inertia, the object may levitate. The role of the RSPK agent would be twofold, to cause a brief cancellation of the gravity/inertia of the object by cohering the ZPE and to direct energy to the object for it to move. Because the object is now free to move, the intensity of the energy from the agent would be relatively minor.

The ZPE theory of RSPK says that an object may move when its weight is reduced. Object focusing, where the same object is repeatedly affected, may suggest that some reduction of weight persists so that the object is more likely to move again than others (the objects must be equidistant from the agent to rule out the effect of proximity). The type of object focusing where similar objects move may be a resonance effect. Area focusing, where the same location is the center of repeated movements, may indicate that prior events leave a modification of the local gravitational/inertial field that persists for some time. These possibilities can be explored by comparing the weight of an RSPK object immediately after the event with its weight after a period of time. According to the ZPE theory, weight losses of RSPK objects result from cohesion of the electromagnetic field of the vacuum. This leads to the further expectation that anomalous electromagnetic readings may be obtained near RSPK objects or areas. I know of only one relevant study, an investigation by Joines (1975) where he detected an emission of 146 MHz in an RSPK area. The emission lasted about a minute and was about two feet in diameter, which is consistent with a frequency of 146 MHz.

There are other indications that electromagnetism may be at work in RSPK. Several agents show symptoms of complex partial seizure (CPS); in other words their brains are subject to sudden electromagnetic discharges (Roll, 1977). It has also been found that the onset of RSPK is associated with geomagnetic perturbations (Gearhart and Persinger, 1986; Roll and Gearhart, 1974).

Frieden spells out the interaction of observer and object when he defines an object as composed of two types of information, information acquired by observing the object, which he designates $I$, and information that the object is yet to reveal, designated $J$. The purpose of science is to reduce $J$ in favor of $I$. From a psychological perspective, $I$ is conscious information, $J$ is unconscious information. Conscious information represents the object as it is known to science; unconscious information represents its unknown properties. Psychometric information, usually unconscious, may be accessed by people who are skilled in this form of perception.

In studies of micro-PK where the subject's task was to affect random physical processes, Jahn and associates (Jahn et al., 1997) have found that subjects who were at a distance from the machines were as successful as when in the same room. Similar findings have been reported by others. What seems important is not the physical proximity of the machine but its proximity in terms of meaning. The successful subjects mentioned ". . . a sense of 'resonance' or 'bond' with the machine; . . . of 'falling in love' with it; of 'having fun' with it."

Is it possible to develop macro-PK abilities? It is sometimes reported that practitioners of yoga and meditation develop psychokinetic abilities. This may suggest that the ZPE can be manipulated without technical tools. The Buddhist concept of reality as *sunyata,* a plentitude of no-things with which you may unite if your mind is emptied of particulars, is not unlike the idea of the vacuum as an infinite field of energy and consciousness. (An anonymous Zen Buddhist has called Zen "the vacuum cleaner of the mind.")

We may see the same process at work in these practices as in RSPK, but in a voluntary rather than involuntary form. Yogic or meditative practices would add a dimension of personal exploration to the enterprise.

## Concluding Remarks

The goal of science is no longer the observation of immutable reality but the realization of one possibility over others. Which possibility will become manifest would depend on the intention of the observer. Observer participancy weaves ethics into the fabric of science.

Observer participancy has arrived in the public forum with an article in *Discover* magazine (Folger, 2002) about Wheeler and others who share his perspective. Folger quotes Stanford University physicist, Andrei Linde, as saying that conscious observers are an essential component of the universe. In the words of Jahn and Dunne (1997): "Consciousness . . . defines itself only in its interactions with its physical surround. Conversely, just as physical detectors respond only to external stimuli, the 'objective' properties of the universe are, without exception, only defined by some inquiring, ordering consciousness. This recognition, in turn, opens the door to admittance of the most powerful, but most difficult to represent, family of subjective parameters, those of the teleological genre that comprise conscious (and very possibly unconscious) intention, desire, will, need, or purpose. These are demonstrably primary correlates of empirical consciousness-related anomalies of all ranks, from laboratory-based microscopic human/machine effects, to macroscopic poltergeist phenomena, to creativity of all forms."

REFERENCES

Baumann, S. B. (1995). "An Overview with Examples Including a Case Study of an RSPK Subject." *Proceedings of Presented Papers: The 38th Annual Convention of the Parapsychological Association*, pp. 11–19.

Bender, H. (1969). "Presidential Address: New Developments in Poltergeist Research." *Proceedings of Presented Papers: The Parapsychological Association* 6, pp. 81–102.

Berkeley, G. (1713, 1988). *Principles of Human Knowledge and Three Dialogues between Hylas and Philonous.* London: Penguin.

Carpenter, J. (1993). *Projective Testing on Tina Resch, October, 1984. Proceedings of Presented Papers: The 36th Annual Convention of the Parapsychological Association*, pp. 492–499.

Chan, H. B., V. A. Aksyuk, R. N. Kleiman, D. J. Bishop, and F. Capasso (2001). "Quantum Mechanical Actuation of Microelectromechanical Systems by the Casimir Force." *Science* 191, pp. 1941–1944.

Duncan, L., and W. G. Roll (1995). *Psychic Connections.* New York: Delacorte.

Folger, T. (June 2002). "Does the Universe Exist If We're Not Looking?" *Discover*, pp. 44–48.

Frieden, B. R. (1998). *Physics from Fisher Information: A Unification.* Cambridge, UK: Cambridge University Press.

Gearhart, L., and M. A. Persinger (1986). "Geophysical Variables and Behavior: XXXIII. Onsets of Historical and Contemporary Poltergeist Episodes Occurred with Sudden Increases in Geomagnetic Activity." *Perceptual and Motor Skills* 62, pp. 463–466.

Hasted, J. B., D. Robertson, and E. Spinelli (1983). "Recording of Sudden Paranormal Changes of Body Weight." *Research in Parapsychology, 1982*, pp. 105–106.

Hollander, L. E. (2001). "Unexplained Weight Gain Transients at the Moment of Death." *Journal of Scientific Exploration* 15, pp. 495–500.

Jahn, R. G., and B. J. Dunne (1987). *Margins of Reality.* New York: Harcourt Brace.

———— (1997). "Science of the Subjective." *Journal of Scientific Exploration* 11, pp. 201–224.

Jahn, R. G., B. J. Dunne, R. D. Nelson, Y. H. Dobyns, and G. J. Bradish (1997). "Correlations of Random Binary Sequences with Pre-stated Operator Intentions: A Review of a 12-Year Program." *Journal of Scientific Exploration* 11, pp. 345–367.

Joines, W. (1975). "A Wave Theory of Psi Energy." *Research in Parapsychology, 1974*, pp. 147–149.

Kicklighter, K. (2000). "Weighty Issues." *Atlanta Journal-Constitution*, August 30, pp. 1E and 4E.

MacDougall, D. (1907). "Hypothesis Concerning Soul Substance Together with Experimental Evidence of the Existence of Such Substance." *Journal of the American Society for Psychical Research* 1, pp. 237–244.

Mischo, J. (1968). "Personality Structure of Psychokinetic Mediums." *Proceedings of the Parapsychological Association* 5, *1968*, pp. 35–37.

Murphy, M. (1993). *The Future of the Body: Explorations into the Further Evolution of Human Nature.* New York: Putnam.

Murphy, M., and R. White (1978). *The Psychic Side of Sport.* New York: Addison-Wesley.

Myers, F. W. H. (1903). *Human Personality and Its Survival of Bodily Death.* Vol. I. New York: Longman, Green.

Osty, E. (1923). *Supernormal Faculties in Man.* London: Methuen.

Owen, A. R. G. (1964). *Can We Explain the Poltergeist?* New York: Garrett.

Pratt, J. G., and W. G. Roll (1958). "The Seaford Disturbances." *Journal of Parapsychology* 22, pp. 79–124.

Price, H. H. (1940). "Some Philosophical Questions About Telepathy and Clairvoyance." *Philosophy* 15, pp. 363–374.

Roll, W. G. (1964). "The Psi Field." Paper presented at the proceedings of the Parapsychological Association. Vol. 1: 1957–1964, pp. 32–65.

———— (1967). "Pagenstecher's Contribution to Parapsychology." *Journal of the American Society for Psychical Research* 61, pp. 219–240.

———— (1968). "Some Physical and Psychological Aspects of a Series of Poltergeist Phenomena." *Journal of the American Society for Psychical Research* 62, pp. 263–308.

—— (1972). *The Poltergeist.* New York: Doubleday.

—— (1975). *Theory and Experiment in Psychical Research.* New York: Arno Press.

—— (1977). "Poltergeists." In B. B. Wolman, editor. *Handbook of Parapsychology.* New York: Van Nostrand Reinhold, pp. 382–413.

—— (1993). "The Question of RSPK vs. Fraud in the Case of Tina Resch." Paper presented at the proceedings of the Parapsychological Association, 36th Annual Convention, pp. 456–482.

Roll, W. G., D. Burdick, and W. T. Joines (1973). "Radial and Tangential Forces in the Miami Poltergeist." *Journal of the American Society for Psychical Research* 67, pp. 267–281.

—— (1974). "The Rotating Beam Theory and the Olive Hill Poltergeist." In W. G. Roll, R. L. Morris, and J. Morris, editors. *Research in Parapsychology, 1973.* Metuchen, N.J.: Scarecrow Press, pp. 64–67.

Roll, W. G., and L. Gearhart (1974). "Geomagnetic Perturbations and RSPK." In W. G. Roll et al. *Research in Parapsychology, 1973,* pp. 44–46.

Roll, W. G., and W. T. Joines (2001). "RSPK and Consciousness." Paper presented at the proceedings of the Parapsychological Association, 44th Annual Convention, pp. 267–284.

Roll, W. G., and J. G. Pratt (1971). "The Miami Disturbances." *Journal of the American Society for Psychical Research* 65, pp. 409–454.

Roll, W. G., L. C. Sheehan, M. A. Persinger, and A. Y. Glass (1996). "The Haunting of White Ranch." Paper presented at the proceedings of the Parapsychological Association, 39th Annual Convention, pp. 279–294.

Roll, W. G., and J. Stump (1969). "The Olive Hill Poltergeist." Paper presented at the proceedings of the Parapsychological Association. Vol. 6, pp. 57–58.

Russell, B. (1926). *Our Knowledge of the External World.* London: Allen and Unwin.

Stewart, J. L., W. G. Roll, and S. Baumann (1987). "Hypnotic Suggestion and RSPK." In D. H. Weiner and R. D. Nelson, editors. *Research in Parapsychology, 1986.* Metuchen, N.J.: Scarecrow Press, pp. 30–35.

Walker, E. H. (1974). "Consciousness and Quantum Theory." In J. White, editor. *Psychic Exploration.* New York: Putnam.

Walker, E. H. (1985). "Quantum Mechanics and Parapsychology." *Journal of Indian Psychology,* 4, 21–26.

Wheeler, J. A. (1990). "Information, Physics, Quanta: The Search for Links." In S. Kobayashi, H. Ezawa, Y. Murayama, and S. Nomura, editors. Paper presented at the proceedings of the 3rd International Symposium on Quantum Mechanics in the Light of New Technology, Tokyo, 1989. Tokyo: Physical Society of Japan, pp. 354–368. Quoted by Frieden (1998, p. 1).

# NOTES ON REINCARNATION

Though many people are attracted to psychical research and parapsychology because of their questions concerning survival beyond the grave, this is not a topic that we have elected to focus on in this anthology. However, we do want to take note of a large body of data bearing on the survival question: the evidence compiled by the late Dr. Ian Stevenson (1918–2007). A psychiatrist associated with the University of Virginia (Charlottesville) for nearly half a century, Dr. Stevenson collected, scrutinized, verified, and analyzed literally thousands of cases of individuals who apparently have memories of former lives. His work involved literature searches and field studies around the world (see, for instance, Stevenson, 1960a, 1960b, 1966, 1975, 1977, 1980, 1983b, 1987).

Besides claimed memories of individuals (mostly children) that can be correlated with verifiable facts relating to the life of a deceased person, Stevenson also documented both behavioral patterns and physical characteristics shared between the living individual and the deceased (Stevenson, 1997a, 1997b). Such similarities are not limited to characteristics that the deceased had during most of life, but can include wounds traumatically inflicted near or at the time of death, such as the areas of gunshot wounds in the deceased appearing as birthmarks in the presumed incarnation.

In these same works, Stevenson gives examples of bodily changes that apparently correspond to mental images, both mental images in the person affected and also mental images of another person. In the former category, Stevenson includes psychosomatic manifestations, such as aches and pains or even visible changes on the skin brought about by suggestion or impressionability. Stigmata imitating the supposed wounds of Jesus on the cross would fall into this category.

Mental images affecting another person may be part of the more general spectrum of telepathic impressions. A wife may feel a sharp pain when her husband at a remote location suddenly receives an injury. Or a person may feel sick, or even develop welts or blemishes on the skin, in possible telepathic sympathy to disease or injury in a distant loved one (it can also be suggested that such phenomena, sometimes referred to as DMILS [Direct Mental Interactions with Living Systems], are a form of psychokinesis rather than telepathy; see Delanoy, 2001). As an extreme example of such possibilities, Stevenson (1997a, pp. 23–24) cites the case of Olga Kahl, a Russian living in France in the 1920s. A person could write a name or draw a design on a small piece of paper (without showing it to Olga), then roll the paper in a ball and hold it in his or her hand. The letters or design would then appear in red on Olga's skin (usually on her arm or upper chest), apparently due to localized changes in superficial blood vessels according to Stevenson.

Maternal impressions are an additional form of mental images affecting another person. Here we summarize two examples given by Stevenson (1997a, pp. 24–27). A pregnant woman sees a man with partially amputated feet; she worries that her baby might be born with similar defects, and unfortunately it is. In another case, a woman's brother had to have his penis amputated due to cancer; while she was pregnant, the woman looked at the site of her brother's amputation, and afterwards gave birth to a baby boy lacking a penis. After analyzing several hundred cases of maternal impression, Stevenson found that the causative impression more often occurred in the first trimester than in the second or third. This makes sense, as it is understood that the embryo is more susceptible to other factors, such as drugs or disease, at earlier stages of development.

The work of Stevenson discussed in the preceding paragraphs may have major implications for biology and medicine. One might even speculate that psi and paranormal phenomena may influence evolution, especially if by psi one generation can affect the next. Another thought-provoking finding on Stevenson's part is that marks made on the body of a person after the person died apparently may appear on the body of a presumed incarnation of the deceased person. Here are a couple of examples from Stevenson (1997a, pp. 79–80), both from Burma: (1) A deceased child was marked with grease around the sole of the foot and the presumed incarnation had a large, dark birthmark in the same area.

(2) A young woman with congenital heart disease died during open-heart surgery. During the preparation of her body for burial a mark was placed on the back of her neck with red lipstick. The woman's presumed incarnation, born thirteen months later, had a prominent red birthmark at the back of her neck, a line of diminished pigment corresponding to the incision in her abdomen and chest made during the surgery, and when the baby began to speak she seemed to have knowledge of the previous life that she could not have acquired by normal means. Stevenson also points out that the mother of the baby did not know about the marking of the young woman's body, so the corresponding birthmark cannot be attributed to maternal impression.

If Stevenson's data on birthmarks in subsequent presumed incarnations caused by marking or mutilation of a cadaver after death of the previous person stands up to scrutiny, it could have far-reaching implications. It is one thing to hypothesize that fragments or portions or even the totality of a personality might be transmitted from a dying person (perhaps telepathically, whatever telepathy really is), including aspects of that person's death (compare this notion to the concepts of *Phantasms of the Living* and crisis apparitions discussed above, page 65), but to suggest that somehow a lingering discarnate personality is aware of what happens to its former physical body and incorporates marks or mutilations to the body in the next incarnation raises many theoretical and philosophical issues. Is this evidence for the existence of "ethereal beings," "spiritual entities," or "soul-components"?

# PART II

EXPERIMENTAL AND
LABORATORY WORK
ON THE PARANORMAL

M odern experimental parapsychology owes an incredible debt to one man: Joseph Banks Rhine (1895–1980). J. B. Rhine was a classically trained scientist. He received both his M.A. and his Ph.D. from the University of Chicago in botany, but early on in his career turned to psychical research. In the late 1920s and early 1930s J. B. Rhine, with his wife and fellow parapsychologist Louisa Ella Rhine (1891–1983, who also received her doctorate from the University of Chicago in botany, but turned to psychical research), ultimately settled at Duke University (Durham, North Carolina) under the tutelage of the psychologist William McDougall (1871–1938). At Duke, the Rhines established their basic procedures and protocols for parapsychological experiments in a laboratory setting. J. B. Rhine created a stir with his 1934 monograph *Extra-Sensory Perception* (see selection from this work, page 131) and was a dominant figure in the field for the next several decades. Incidentally, it was J. B. Rhine who popularized the term "parapsychology" (anglicized from the German term "parapsychologie") to refer to the study of the paranormal. This term came to supplant the older term "psychical research" in many quarters, although some researchers use parapsychology in a restricted sense to refer to experimental or laboratory research (Rhine, 1934; Dessoir, 1889; Thalbourne, 2003, pp. 84–85).

When Rhine entered the field of psychical research he had three main objectives (Beloff, 1993). The first was to introduce progressive, experimental research methodology into the study of the paranormal, and the second, which was more overarching than the first, was to establish parapsychology as a respected academic field of science. Although these ideas were not necessarily "new," Rhine was involved with the first long-term university laboratory devoted solely to parapsychology research in the United States. And finally, the third objective was to potentially demonstrate that psi abilities are not just present in a small percentage of the population, but may be a more widespread ability. Unfortunately, none of these objectives has totally been fulfilled. Although there has been progress in establishing experimental phenomena, parapsychology research remains extremely difficult to replicate in the lab. As far as credibly establishing parapsychology as a respected academic science, this has occurred in some circles, but for the most part it is still widely ignored by mainstream science (although, with quantum physics research, more attention has been paid to it in some circles). And finally, it has still yet to be established whether measurable levels of psi are present in the majority of the population.

Here we need to point out a major theoretical issue that complicates the study of psi in the laboratory, as well as in the field. This is the problem of "unintentional psi," or the "source-of-psi" problem (Weiner, 1987, p. 206). It has been suggested that even when psi is demonstrated, it can be very difficult or impossible to know the true source of the psi. Could it be from the subject being tested, could it be from the experimenter, or could it be from an assistant, a data checker, or even a casual observer who, ostensibly, is not taking part in the experiment? It has been noted that some experimental parapsychologists consistently seem to get better results than other experimental parapsychologists, even when using exactly the same methodologies (sometimes referred to as the experimenter effect). One explanation might be that the experimenter who gets better results, more psi-positive results, simply puts the subjects at ease and elicits from them their peak psi abilities. But what if it is actually the experimenter who is using psi, unintentionally, to get psi-positive results?

Another complicating factor is often referred to as the sheep-goat effect, a concept introduced by Gertrude Schmeidler (City College, New York) in conjunction with her studies of psi (such as card-guessing) during the 1940s and 1950s (see Schmeidler and McConnell, 1958). She found that "believers" in the paranormal (whom she labeled "sheep") scored significantly above chance expectations while "disbelievers" ("goats") under identical experimental conditions generally scored worse, including below chance expectation. This strongly suggests that attitude toward psi and its reality affects the manifestation of psi phenomena. If true, this of course makes controlled experimentation all the more difficult in this field, and it has been suggested that as a result of these types of effects, skeptical experimenters may produce negative or insignificant results when experimenting with psi, whereas experimenters who are more open and favorable to psi manifestations will produce genuinely significant results; this is sometimes referred to as an "experimenter effect." Differences in results, therefore, between experimenters and laboratories are not simply a matter of "pure objectivity" on the part of "skeptics" and "wishful thinking" or "self-delusion" on the part of positive-attitude psi researchers. There are also cases of parapsychologists who are ostensibly and consciously very open toward, and "believing in," psi phenomena, but for whatever reason they cannot personally produce good results in their own labs, or in some cases their very presence even seems to "sabotage" other investigators' experiments.

In the following selections we reprint portions from two classic Rhine papers: the first from *Extra-Sensory Perception* (1934) and the second from the initial report of the first experiments by the Rhines on psychokinesis. Following these is a paper on mind-matter interactions, especially using the techniques pioneered at Princeton, and a review of statistical meta-analyses of experimental results in parapsychology.

## ARTICLE 5. EXTRA-SENSORY PERCEPTION,
*by J. B. Rhine, 1934.*

[Source: Excerpts from J. B. Rhine, *Extra-Sensory Perception*. With a foreword by Professor William McDougall and an introduction by Walter Franklin Prince. Boston, Mass.: Boston Society for Psychic Research, 1934, pp. 35–41.]

*Editors' Comments*

Here we include an excerpt from J. B. Rhine's 1934 monograph on ESP, one of the most influential books ever published on parapsychology.

Note that in the following selection "p.e." stands for "probable error," or "that deviation from the mean (chance) expectation at which the odds are even (1:1) as to whether pure chance alone is operating or not" (Rhine, 1934, p. 32).

## EXTRA-SENSORY PERCEPTION, *by J. B. Rhine, 1934.*

THE EXPERIMENTAL RESULTS: A GENERAL SURVEY

The investigation of extra-sensory perception at Duke University has now been going on for more than three years, and has come to include well over 90,000 trials. To give a comprehensive report of these trials, with a proper account of procedure, conditions and results, would make a large volume. Much summarizing must, therefore, be done in order to present the results in a reasonably readable form. It seems best to present first merely a narrative sketch of the main lines of the research and to state the general results . . .

Following upon our experimental interest in the telepathic horse, Lady, during 1928 and 1929, considerable effort was made to find other infra-human telepathic subjects but this was in vain. In the summer of 1930, then, I turned to the task of trying to find human subjects. I began by giving "guessing contests" to some groups of children in summer recreation camps. The tests consisted simply in having each child guess the numeral (0 to 9) which was stamped on a card that I held concealed from him in my hand and looked at. Each child had a pencil and card, and noted down his guesses silently. From the thousand (approximately) trials thus made, no one individual stood out well enough to seem to warrant further investigation.

During the fall semester following my colleague, Dr. K. E. Zener, proposed that we try sealed envelope guessing tests on our own college classes. We accordingly prepared envelopes with numerals (or, in some classes, with letters of the alphabet) effectively concealed and sealed within. These were passed out to the students with instructions to guess the number (or letter) stamped inside, under certain conditions of quiet and relaxation. Of these trials 1,600 were carried out, also with quite insignificant results. The results of the five series as a whole were very close to the chance expectation, three of the groups coming out above chance and two below that figure. This, too, was then given up, partly because it was quite laborious, and partly because of indications of failure. [. . .]

The objective had been partly to measure the ability of the group and partly to discover individuals with special ability to perceive without the senses. The latter goal was achieved, since we did discover one able subject through these tests, Mr. A. J. Linzmayer. In the two group tests in which he took part he was the highest scorer. In the better of these, on envelopes containing figures chosen from 0 to 9, giving a probability of being right of 1/10 per trial, he got three correct in five trials. In the other, with a probability of 1/5 for correctness on each one, he scored four correct in five trials. From these results it was thought worth while to try further tests with Mr. Linzmayer. These I will describe later.

At about the same time, the fall of 1930, another colleague in our Department of Psychology, Dr. Helge Lundholm, kindly offered to co-operate in an attempt to measure "telepathic" perception (clairvoyance was not excluded) in the state of hypnotic trance. He assumed responsibility for providing the trance and we worked with, in all, 30 subjects, who made a total of 1,115 trials. These fall into three groups; they have a different probability basis in each and cannot therefore be thrown together. All are somewhat above the chance expectation but only slightly. The best groups, in which numbers from 0 to 9 were used as symbols, totalled 530 trials and yielded 65 right as against 53 expected on chance. This positive deviation of 12 is only 2.6 times the probable error ($+/-$ 4.66). It might be said that, had we continued these tests for as many more trials with equal results, the data would have approximated the point of significance. But the procedure was slow and we discovered that such slight deviations as we got could be had as well in the waking condition. So we discontinued the series. [. . .]

A few tests in simple "card-guessing" made now and then upon individuals by Dr. Zener and myself during the year 1930–31 seemed to give promising results. They were never high but seemed to favor the positive side to an interesting degree. These were mostly carried out on the basis of symbols suggested chiefly by Dr. Zener, five in number; namely: circle, rectangle [or square], plus [plus sign], star and wavy lines . . . [these cards became known as "Zener Cards"; see Stuart and Pratt, 1937]. We early began to use them in packs of five each, 25 in all. The subject usually called the top card, as the pack lay face down on the table before him. A series of 25 trials without any extra-sensory perception would yield, on the average, about 5 correct hits. But these odd tests we were making yielded around 6, on an average. And, keeping track of those of my own observation alone, I found after a while that they were becoming fairly meaningful statistically. From a total of 800 trials carried out during the academic year, 207 hits were recorded, which is a positive deviation of 47 and is more than 6 times the probable error. But this yield (around an average of 6.5 correct in 25 trials) was low in comparison with what was in store for us just ahead in the work of Linzmayer.

[. . .]

Now we return to Linzmayer. Late in May, 1931, he was given 45 card-guessing trials in very light hypnosis (which was as deep as he could go) and called 21 correct as against chance expectation of 9. In the few days we could work with him after this and before his leaving the campus with the close of the year, he brought his total trials up to 600, run for the regular test, with another 900 for a special test. The 600 regular trials yielded 238 hits, a positive gain over chance of 118; this is about 18 times the probable error. This figure can leave no intelligent question of the operation of a significant principle. In the average number of successes per 25 trials this rises to the unprecedented figure of approximately 10. In one series of 25 Linzmayer got 21 hits, 15 of them being successive. In this series he did not see the cards as they were dealt and called. But (and alas!), after three most exciting days of experimentation with Linzmayer, he had to leave.

[. . .]

In the month of October, 1931, we were able to get Mr. Linzmayer for a short period again and made 945 tests on clairvoyant card-guessing as before. But this time he ran at a much lower rate. His yield was 246, which is 57 above chance expectation; this is about 7 times the p.e. The rate per 25 was 6.5. This is, however, still quite significant even though it was low in contrast with his first 600 trials.

[. . .]

In March of 1932 we again had a short visit from Mr. Linzmayer and obtained 960 regular trials with him, as well as some more special tests. The 960 trials yielded 259 (a still lower rate than the last time) which has a positive deviation of 67, and this is 8.0 times the p.e.; the average per 25 is 6.75. (In the preceding fall, it had been 6.9.) One of the special experiments was made at this time by giving the subject 15 grams of the narcotic drug, sodium amytal. By an hour after the ingestion Linzmayer was quite sleepy and dull-witted. He was "thick-tongued," jolly and talkative. I kept him awake for 275 trials but he could not score appreciably above chance. The average per 25 was 5.1, having gotten a total of 56 (as against 55). Before and after this experiment Linzmayer ran at an average of 6.75 in 25, as reported above.

Mr. J. G. Pratt, an assistant in our Department, was engaged during the year to help in the necessary prospecting for more good subjects. He carried out on 15 students 10,035 tests with a yield of only 144 above the chance expectation; this is, however, still more than 5 times the probable error. His tests on himself numbered 2,885 and yielded a deviation above that is 3.9 times the p.e. But his main contribution lay in the discovery of Mr. Hubert Pearce, Jr., a young ministerial student whom I had asked to submit to the tests, on learning that his mother was reported to have possessed parapsychological ability. Mr. Pearce ran low for a few series of 25 each, but soon picked up and then held fairly steadily at about double the chance figure (of 5 per 25). Pearce, too, was discovered at about the close of the school year, but he was able to stay over for a time and 2,250 witnessed trials were made in clairvoyant card-guessing. The yield was 869 or 419 above chance. This means an average of 9.7 per 25. The huge deviation from chance expectation is 32.75 times the p.e., a figure of reassurance against the chance hypothesis that simply leaves no question of significance. The experiments were then interrupted by Pearce's appointment to ministerial service for the summer.

One of the characteristics of Pearce's work was the relative smoothness of the results from day to day. He would average around 10 per 25. He did not at this time seem to be helped by having the observer look at the cards. Curiously enough, he would drop in his scoring under this condition. However, almost any change whatever, unless he himself proposed it, seemed to throw him off his rate of scoring. Visitors disturbed him for a while but he would always get back to his level if they remained for a time. Also he would become adjusted to the changes in procedure in the course of time, so far as we tried to make him. But we did not want to induce too much strain and often yielded on a desired innovation. Certain changes were introduced by talking about their possibility indifferently and allowing Pearce to say if he wanted to attempt them. In this way we started the calling for low score; *i.e.,* trying to make wrong calls. In 225 low-score trials made under this condition he scored only 17, which is 28 below the chance expectation, and this is 6.9 times the p.e. Highly significantly *low!* This averaged below 2 hits per 25 calls. He produced, for example, when asked to score "high," a 10 in 25, then for "low," a 1 in 25, then a 9 in 25 for "high," and another 1 in 25 for a "low." It seemed purely a matter of choice!

Another new feature introduced into Pearce's work in a half-playful way, and which was also successful immediately, was calling cards down through the pack without removing the cards until the finish of the run. This started off with scores of 8, 8, 12, 6, etc., per 25 for the beginning runs. The first 275 trials yielded 87 hits, a gain of 32 or over

7 times the p.e., and an average of 7.9 per 25. The value of these data is enormous, as we will emphasize later, first in connection with alternate theories of hyperacute sense perception and second in connection with theories of the physical basis of the process of extra-sensory perception; *i.e.,* the subject reads the cards under conditions to which no radiation theory seems applicable and no sensory perception seems adequate.

We repeated on Pearce the sodium amytal experiment made on Linzmayer, using only 6 gr. this time. This would be equal to about half what Linzmayer had taken, allowing for weight differences. Pearce was not incoherent and irrational, but was quite sleepy. He could, however, keep himself awake and could converse intelligently. He made effort several times to re-integrate himself, once even washing his face with cold water. At the beginning his scoring fell off at once, yielding 5, 4, 3 for the first three runs of 25 each. Then he "pulled himself together" and got 10 on the next. The average for 325 trials is 6.1 in 25, as against 9.7 for his regular scoring. This is a very significant drop. This ended the series for the summer, leaving the young minister barely time to "sober up" for his first sermon.

[. . .]

## ARTICLE 6. THE PSYCHOKINETIC EFFECT, *by Louisa E. Rhine and J. B. Rhine, 1943.*

[Source: Excerpts from Louisa E. Rhine and J. B. Rhine. "The Psychokinetic Effect: I. The First Experiment." *Journal of Parapsychology* 7, pp. 20–43 (1943); excerpts from pp. 20–23, 39–41.]

### Editors' Comments

In this selection L. E. Rhine and J. B. Rhine formally report, for the first time, the experiments that had been carried out at Duke on psychokinesis

(PK), or "mind over matter." They also tentatively suggest a connection between ESP and PK.

## THE PSYCHOKINETIC EFFECT, *by Louisa E. Rhine and J. B. Rhine, 1943.*

ABSTRACT

This is the first of a long series of research reports describing experiments on what is called the "psychokinetic" or "PK" effect. The PK effect is colloquially called "mind over matter," and means the direct influencing of a physical system by the action of a subject's effort, without any known intermediate energy or instrumentation.

The test procedure consisted of dice-throwing, in which a pair of common dice was thrown either by hand or by a semi-mechanical method. The objective was to cause them to come up as "high dice," i.e., with faces totaling 8 or above. A "run" consisted of 12 throws of the pair and the expectation for each run was 5 successes (8 or above); the average score obtained for the 562 runs that were made was actually 5.53. This represents a total score that is 300 hits above the total expectation from chance, and it gives a critical ratio [deviation divided by standard deviation, a measure of significance; see Pratt et al., 1940, p. 24] of 7.40, which represents extremely high odds against the likelihood of such results occurring by chance.

The possible weaknesses of the test and of its interpretation are considered. The possibility of "tricky throwing" as an explanation is ruled out by the use of a semi-mechanical test procedure, and the hypothesis that the extra-chance character of the results might be caused by defects in the dice may be dismissed since there are significant differences between various sections of the data. Other alternatives are considered and the tentative conclusion is reached that the PK hypothesis is the best available explanation of the results.

A definite relation between ESP and PK is suggested, one in which each complements the other much as in the analogous relation between sensory perception and the motor abilities; but this, like the case for the PK effect itself, is stated as best held in suspended judgment until more of the main body of the experimentation is published. The importance of extensive repetition of the PK experiments in the meantime is stressed.

## INTRODUCTION

In the nine years that have elapsed since February, 1934, a great quantity of data has been accumulated, in this laboratory and elsewhere, on a problem of investigation which goes by the title of the Psychokinetic Effect, or more briefly, the PK Effect. This effect was encountered in the course of the research in extra-sensory perception going on here at the time and the two lines of investigation have since proceeded side by side. However, up to the present, nothing has been published on the topic of the PK effect and it has scarcely been mentioned publicly.

Now, however, there are reasons for going ahead with the task of reporting the findings. There have been, during the years since 1934, a long time for careful consideration of the results and for many repetitions of the experiments. The findings have been confirmed again and again by many careful experimenters working independently. It therefore appears reasonable to hope that altogether we have taken most of the risk of error out of the research before it is offered to a wider audience.

Furthermore, the ESP research itself, which in its very nature was difficult of acceptance by many people, now seems to be fairly well established. Research in ESP has been opened up in a number of university laboratories and its future topic of inquiry is probably secure.

The central program in this laboratory in the past has emphasized the study of the effect of distance upon ESP performance as the first main sequel to the establishment of ESP; and, following the distance test program, there came investigation of ESP of the future, precognition. This now has reached a point where the cumulative results and numerous confirmations afford a moderately strong case. The time is ripe, then, so far as the ESP work is concerned for a new step to be taken. [Footnote by Rhine and Rhine: Those readers who have not followed the literature of ESP will find it surveyed up to 1940 in *Extra-Sensory Perception after Sixty Years* (Pratt, J. G., J. B. Rhine, B. M. Smith, C. E. Stuart, and J. A. Greenwood, *Extra-Sensory Perception After Sixty Years: A Critical Appraisal of the Research in Extra-Sensory Perception*. 1940. New York: Holt). Most of it in recent years has appeared, either in the original or in reprint or review, in this *Journal*.] The war, too, has played a part in the decision to publish the PK work at this time, for in the very uncertainties it raises about the future of research, it impels one to bring into the comparative safety of the printed page all work that may have value for the field.

## The Problem and Its Setting

Students of ESP research have probably often asked, in some form, such questions as these: If *extra-sensory perception* occurs, is there not perhaps a corresponding *extra-motor ability*, on the analogy of the normal sensory-motor relation? If the individual has a capacity to orient himself (i.e. to perceive) beyond the limits of the known *sensory* processes, may he not have the complementary capacity to determine events (i.e., behave) effectively beyond the limits of the known *motor* functions; that is, to exert some influence on the physical environment without the use of his muscular system?

There is, we recognize, nothing new about the hypothesis that there is a PK effect any more than there is that ESP occurs. For that matter, the same source materials that led to the investigation of ESP, the spontaneous ("psychic") experiences of unexplainable character that seem to show evidence of extra-normal knowledge, likewise frequently appear to show some kind of direct psychophysical action such as that which we are calling the PK effect. The same medium or medicine man or saint who claimed powers of extra-sensory perception has frequently also claimed capacity to transcend normal laws with regard to physical effects as well. This is not to say that we must therefore believe these claims to be true. They help to explain, however, how natural it is for the ESP explorer to be open-minded to the PK hypothesis and to be ready to seize whatever opportunity is offered to put it to experimental test. [Footnote to this paragraph by Rhine and Rhine: There is even a name for the unexplainable mediumistic phenomena of physical nature—"telekinesis." But to those who are familiar with this word it connotes "ectoplasm," mediums, dark room séances, and other associations which it has accumulated and which we do not deal with in these experiments. We believe we are legitimately avoiding unnecessary difficulties by not adopting the name, telekinesis. And there is another reason: It may be that the thought-brain relation is similar to—perhaps the same as—that found in the PK tests. Psychokinesis seems better for a general term to cover both effects than telekinesis, which leaves out the psychical and emphasizes distance. In any case it will be long before the terminology is very important.]

None of the anecdotal material just referred to would meet the requirements of scientific proof. Its spontaneous character tends to rule it out, for a degree of control and repeatability is very important in scientific work. We can seldom wait for rare occurrences to supply the evidence on a highly debatable issue such as this. The search among mediums and primitive medicine men may in time get around the difficulties involved in the lack of adequate control; but progress has been slow, and reliable interpretation very difficult. Patient laboratory experiment, simply designed and often repeated, is of course the surest method of investigation, provided the occurrences in question can be induced to occur under the conditions desired and with the subjects available.

As it happened, accident—at least incident—played a part in the choice of experimental procedure for research on the PK hypothesis, as it has at so many strategic points in scientific inquiry. Early in 1934, a young amateur gambler visited this laboratory to discuss ESP and its role in gambling and quite casually expressed the view that many gamblers (himself included) believed they could mentally influence the fall of dice, apart from any use of methods of trickery. Dice throwing as the basis of a test of the PK effect! It struck us at once as being, methodologically, a simple, direct way of getting at the old question of a direct psychophysical effect. It combined a game like procedure with easy experimental control and ready statistical evaluation of the results and scores.

[. . .]

# Discussion

[. . .]

## Relation of PK to ESP

The general bearing of the PK effect can more profitably be discussed when more is known about it, but its relation to ESP is probably clear enough already to warrant at least a brief discussion. In this relationship may constitute one of the most significant features of the newer line of research.

As we stated in the introduction, the same types of human experience which led to the belief in powers akin to what is called extra-sensory perception also frequently involved aspects that seemed more like the PK effect. Reports in the annals of psychical research, in the legends and histories of the different religions, and in the reports of anthropologists concerning primitive magic have often touched upon both issues at the same time. The two are, in their pre-scientific history, very often associated. This is at least suggestive.

But while this is true and while, on the analogy of the sensor-motor system, we should more or less anticipate an extra-motor effect, having found an extra-sensory one, nevertheless we need more positive grounds for relating the two phenomena. To a certain extent, these seem to us to be provided in the logical interpretation of the test results pointing to a necessary connection between the processes of PK and ESP. For example, in PK there is an obvious need for some *intelligently* directed effect on the dice as they roll. And certainly no sensory guidance would be adequate to keep track of two rapidly rolling, bounding dice. No one can even watch their faces. The scores reported, we think, therefore *require* the assumption of an extra-sensory mode of perception. And were there no evidence of such an ability, it would forthwith have to be assumed with the establishment of PK. The PK research, then, confirms the case for ESP.

Conversely, the argument may be made that ESP requires at least some predisposition toward the PK effect; for perception, as we know it in the sensory range, is an interactive process. When we touch, we do something to the object; in smelling and tasting, we absorb some of the chemical substance and it interacts with the sense organs. Of course we interact, as in light, sound, and smell, with radiant, vibratory, or vaporous effects or "indicators" of the objects seen, heard, or smelled, and these latter we have learned to identify by the intermediary physical determinants. So all sensory perception is interactive. Indeed, what causal action is not?

In ESP we get some kind of orienting experience of an object; and from what we know of perception via the senses, then, we would expect it to be interactive, not necessarily directly *with* the object, it may be with some physical emanate or reflection of the object, some-what analogous to vision. And if there is *any* interaction in ESP, the subject presumably does something to the object or to an intermediate physical system. That, if true, would be a little bit—a trace—of psychophysical interaction. Hence, it would be, in principle, the PK effect.

These logical efforts are not important to the *establishment* of either ESP or PK. But if such possible interrelationships do exist, then we have the clear beginnings of an organizable system of these unrecognized capacities where otherwise only isolated processes would obtain. If there is a relation between ESP and PK, there will likely be found in the research of the future many common properties and reactions. Indeed, we might point with considerable reason to the decline effect which is reported in this paper as a case in point, for decline effects in ESP have been reported in many instances [. . .]. But this is not the place or time yet to stress this similarity. It will be better first to present the further evidence of declines in the PK research and even to bring out a more complete study than could now be pointed to, of the various decline effects in the ESP research. Other evidence suggesting a relation between

ESP and PK will appear in future papers and eventually the decision as to how closely interrelated these two effects actually are will be easier to make than it would be now.

[. . .]

## ARTICLE 7. INFORMATION, CONSCIOUSNESS, AND HEALTH, *by Robert G. Jahn, 1996.*

[Source: Excerpts from Robert G. Jahn, "Information, Consciousness, and Health." *Alternative Therapies* 2, no. 3, pp. 32–38 (1996).]

### Editors' Comments

Dr. Robert G. Jahn, an aerospace scientist and the former dean of Princeton University's School of Engineering and Applied Science, became interested in psychical research and parapsychology in the 1970s. In 1979 Jahn established the legendary Princeton Engineering Anomalies Research [PEAR] program at Princeton University. Jahn and Dr. Brenda J. Dunne, a developmental psychologist from the University of Chicago who came to PEAR as laboratory manager, developed PEAR into a leading center of parapsychological research globally. One of the main goals of PEAR was "to study the potential vulnerability of engineering devices and information processing systems to the anomalous influence of the consciousness of their human operators" (PEAR, 2007). As we write this in 2007, however, the PEAR lab has closed down (Carey, 2007; PEAR, 2007).

As described by Jahn in the selection reprinted here, the PEAR labs were a major force in researching various aspects of the paranormal, and in particular PEAR refined the use of random event generators (REGs; also referred to as random number generators, RNGs) as a way to test for mind-matter interactions, or psychokinesis, on a very small scale (micro-PK).

Essentially the method is to produce very large sets of binary data, typically encoded as + and −, or 0 and 1, using an electronic random event (number) generator where, all other things being equal, the distribution of 0s and 1s or pluses and minuses should be 50/50. Over a quarter of a century of research and data accumulation, the PEAR labs have made a strong case that there is a genuine human mind–machine interaction. That is, an operator or subject can influence the sequence of information bits to deviate from a random pattern (Jahn and Dunne, 1987). The magnitude of the effects detected by the PEAR researchers is typically very small (the equivalent of one bit per 10,000 being influenced), but given the large number of experiments run and huge databases involved, they are statistically significant (see Radin and Nelson, 2000). Radin (2006a, p. 157) has recently recalculated an updated meta-analysis incorporating the latest data, and found the odds against chance as an explanation for the data to be between 50,000 to 1 and 3,050 to 1, depending on the assumptions made concerning possible selective reporting. This corroborates the earlier findings of statistical significance among these studies (see the selection from Utts, page 163).

This research methodology has been adopted by The Global Consciousness Project (Nelson, no date) as a set of experiments designed to test for mass human "psi" during global events. Data collection began in August 1998, and there are now dozens of "testing sites" all over the world. These "randomicity detectors" are constantly running, twenty-four hours a day, seven days a week, around the year, and have shown certain "spikes" or changes in fluctuation of the binary code, which means that the data is no longer "random," just before and/or during an event of global significance, such as the September 11, 2001, terrorist attacks on the World Trade Center in New York and the Pentagon near Washington, D.C. (see Radin, 2002a). Indeed, the data begins to show anomalies a couple of hours before the actual event, suggesting perhaps a collective premonition of what would transpire (see discussion in Swanson, 2003, pp. 95–99). The Global Consciousness Project is sometimes referred to as the EGG project, in reference to the network of electronic detectors set up around the world (EGG is an acronym for "Electrogaiagram," taking readings on Earth [Gaia] in analogy to a standard Electroencephalogram, EEG, that is used to measure the electrical activity of the brain).

Not everyone agrees with the importance or significance of the random event generator data. One prominent critic is Jeffers (2003, 2006), who has run his own experiments and found no statistically significant anomalous effects. Furthermore, Jeffers does not find the PEAR and related micro-PK data convincing. In particular, Jeffers (2006) points out that the PEAR random number generator baseline data (data collected when the operator is purposefully not trying to influence the machine) is sometimes "too good" (that is, it hovers around the 50/50 line more closely than would be expected statistically), but in at least one compilation of PEAR studies the baseline data actually deviates positively above the 50/50 mark to achieve "statistical significance" at the p = .05 (1 chance in 20) level. Jeffers suggests that this indicates nonrandom behavior of the "random" generators, thus invalidating the data and analyses based on the data.

Indeed, Jahn and Dunne (1987, pp. 116–119) discuss the "baseline bind"—the issue of the baseline data being "too good" (not showing the expected variance, and not conforming to the variance seen in calibration data). They suggest that the baseline bind may be due to "some conscious or unconscious motivation on the part of the operators to achieve a 'good' baseline" (Jahn and Dunne, 1987, p. 118). Jeffers (2003, p. 148) points out that the baseline bind apparently occurs when the operator is trying to not influence the machine and the operator is relatively close to the machine (for instance, in the same room), but baseline bind does not seem to occur when the operator is at a distance from the machine. If this is the case, then according to Jeffers, this violates the contention of Jahn and Dunne that the influence of the mind or consciousness on the machine is independent of distance. However, we would point out that there is indeed evidence that mind–matter influences are to at least some extent distance-dependent. In genuine poltergeist activity, for instance, there is evidence that the physical phenomena seem to drop off dramatically with distance from the person who is the center of the activity (see the article by Roll on poltergeist activity reprinted in this volume, page 105).

## INFORMATION, CONSCIOUSNESS, AND HEALTH,
*by Robert G. Jahn, 1996.*

*A 16-year empirical assessment of anomalous human/machine interactions provides strong evidence that consciousness can add information to otherwise random digital strings. A parallel program of remote perception studies establishes the inverse process: the anomalous acquisition of information about distant physical targets. Remarkably, neither of these extraordinary capabilities shows any dependence on either the distance or the time separating the participant from the target. The relevance of these consciousness abilities to human health follows from recognition that physiology entails myriad subtle information processes, all of which involve some degree of randomicity in their normal functions, and thus may be similarly influenced by conscious volition.*

[. . .]

## PEAR Program

The Princeton Engineering Anomalies Research (PEAR) program was formally established in the University's School of Engineering and Applied Science in 1979, for the sole purpose of rigorous scientific study of the interaction of human consciousness with random physical processes. The present laboratory staff comprises a compatible mixture of theoretical and experimental physicists, psychologists, and engineers, each complementing particular scientific expertise with appropriate humanistic interests. Financial support has been provided by a number of institutional and private philanthropic sources, which also have underwritten the program's efforts to stimulate broader collaborative research on consciousness-related topics within the University and around the world via such organizations as the Princeton Human Information

Processing Group, the International Consciousness Research Laboratories, the Academy of Consciousness Studies, the Society for Scientific Exploration, and other less formal enterprises.

The research agenda of the PEAR laboratory itself has focused on three major areas: anomalous human/machine interactions, remote perception, and theoretical modeling of consciousness/environment interactions. Considerable technical literature on each of these programs has been published,[2] and a comprehensive review of the research, its contemporary relevance, and its broader cultural implications are presented in the book *Margins of Reality*.[3] Here we can only offer a brief sampler of these efforts and their major results.

### Human/Machine Interactions

The basic protocol of these experiments requires human operators to attempt by anomalous means to influence the output of various simple machines, each of which involves some sort of random physical process. These devices are electrical, mechanical, fluid dynamical, optical, or acoustical in character; macroscopic or microscopic in scale; and digital or analog in their information processing and feedback displays. They generate data over a broad range of rates, in formats that are theoretically, or at least empirically, predictable. All are equipped with numerous fail-safe features to guarantee the integrity of the data and their freedom from artifact, and all can be precisely calibrated to establish their unattended statistical output distributions.

In all benchmark experiments the operators, seated in front of these machines (but in no physical contact with them) and using whatever personal strategies they wish, endeavor to produce statistically higher output values, lower output values, and baseline or unaltered output values over interspersed periods of pre-stated intentions. Great care is taken in the experimental design and data acquisition to preclude any form of spurious interference with the machine operation. Therefore, any systematic deviation of these three data streams from one another can only indicate the existence and scale of the sought anomalous effect.

Over the 17-year history of the program, more than 100 operators have performed such experiments. These participants have varied greatly in personality, background, intellectual sophistication, and style of operation, but all have remained anonymous, untrained, and uncompensated for their work, and none has claimed extraordinary abilities before or after their efforts. Throughout, we have regarded these operators as research colleagues rather than subjects of study, and no psychological or physiological tests have been attempted.

Variants of the benchmark protocols that have been explored include whether the intended direction of effort is chosen by the operator or assigned by some random indicator; whether the machine runs continuously or is initiated at intervals imposed by the operator; the pace and size of the data blocks; the presence or absence of feedback, and its character; the number of operators addressing the machine; the distance of the operator from the machine; and the time of machine operation relative to the time of operator effort. As of this writing, some 50 million experimental trials have been performed, containing more than 3 billion bits of binary information. From this large body of results, the following salient features may be extracted:[4]

1. Anomalous correlations of the machine outputs with prestated operator intentions are clearly evident. These take the form of shifts of the distribution means that are statistically replicable, and quantifiable in the range of a few parts in 10,000 deviation from chance expectation, on the average. Over the total database, the composite anomaly is unlikely by chance to about one part in a billion.

2. The output mean shifts achieved by the entire group of operators range smoothly over distributions that would be expected by chance, except that the composite mean values are shifted as specified above. No outlying values, indicative of "superstar" performance, are found.

3. Several of the individual operator databases are sufficiently distinctive and replicable in their relative effectiveness of high, low, and

baseline intentions, and in their responses to particular protocol variations, to constitute characteristic "signatures" of achievement.

4. Both individually and collectively, the interior structures of the distributions of anomalous mean shifts are consistent with a model wherein the elemental binary probability intrinsic in each experiment has been altered from its design value of precisely one half to slightly higher or lower values, depending on the operator, intention, and protocol.

5. The scale and character of the results are relatively insensitive to the particular random device employed. In some cases, the characteristic operator signatures are quite similar from one device to another.

6. Although few psychological or physiological correlates have been attempted, significant differences in male and female performance have been identified.

7. Two operators addressing a given experiment together do not simply combine their individual achievement signatures; rather, their "co-operator" results are characteristic of the pair. Co-operators of the same sex are less effective than male/female pairs. "Bonded" male/female pairs produce the highest scores of any operator subsets.

8. No learning or experience benefits are observed. To the contrary, operators tend to perform best over their first major experimental sets, then decline in performance over the next one or two sets, after which they recover better performance that stabilizes to their individual values over subsequent sets. These sequential patterns, termed "series position effects," are reminiscent of switching transients occurring in many physical and biological situations.

9. No dependence of individual or collective effect sizes on the distance of the operators from the machine appears in the data. Operators addressing the machines from thousands of miles away produce effect sizes and characteristic signatures similar

to those that they achieve seated next to the machines in the laboratory.

10. Experiments performed "off-time" (i.e., with operators exerting their intentions several hours before or after the machines actually produce their data strings) show similar effect sizes and internal characteristics to those performed "on-time" (i.e., with machine operation concurrent with the operators' periods of effort).

11. Subjective reports from the most successful operators speak of a sense of resonance or bond with the machine, of surrendering their sense of identity to merge with the machine into a unified system, of exchanging roles with the machine, of "falling in love" with it, or of having "fun" with it.

From this huge array of empirical indications, it seems unavoidable to conclude that operator consciousness is capable of inserting information in its most rudimentary *objective* form—namely, binary bits—into these random physical systems by some anomalous means, independent of space and time.

Human/machine experiments similar to these have been conducted at many other laboratories, with anomalous results commensurate with our own.[5] Of particular interest to the human health arena are those few studies that have demonstrated responses from biological substances or living organisms employed as the random targets of the operators' intentions. Equally relevant are a small body of experiments in which the role of the operators has been played by other than human species (e.g., chicks, rabbits, mice, etc.), all of which seem capable of influencing random electronic processors to respond to some biological or emotional needs.[6] These results, combined with further studies in our own program that demonstrate anomalous responses of portable random event generator units unobtrusively placed in various human group environments—such as religious services, sporting events, professional meetings, medical counseling sessions, or other convocations entailing some collective emotional potential[7]—confirm the ubiquitous character of these information anomalies, and broaden their potential importance to our individual and cultural welfare.

## Remote Perception

In this complementary class of experiment, the "target" is not a physical device or process in a laboratory environment, but a physical scene at some remote geographical location. The goal of the human participant is not to insert information into the target, but to extract information from it by anomalous means. In the usual protocol, two participants are involved in any given experiment. One, the "agent," is physically present at the target location, which has been selected by some random process, and there immerses himself emotionally and cognitively in the scene, records its characteristics on a standard check sheet, and takes photographs of it. The other, the "percipient," located many miles from the scene and with no prior knowledge of it, attempts to perceive aspects of its ambiance and detail, then records those impressions on the same standard check sheet in some less structured narrative or sketch. The agent and percipient check sheets are subsequently digitized, and their degree of consonance is scored numerically by a variety of algorithms. The results, indicative of the amount of objective information acquired by the percipient, can then be arrayed in quantitative statistical formats similar to those used in the human/machine experiments.

Several hundred such remote perception experiments have been performed and scored, with results quite similar to those of the human/ machine experiments.[8] The overall anomalous effect size is actually somewhat larger, but the interior statistical details are qualitatively much the same, and participant-specific characteristics are again evident. Most importantly, the effect sizes are again statistically independent of the distance between the percipient and the target, up to ranges of several thousand miles. They, too, are independent of the time interval between the perception effort and the agent's immersion in the target, up to several days, both positive and negative.

Studies such as these also have been performed elsewhere, albeit with somewhat different protocols and scoring methods, and similar anomalous yields have been obtained.[9] Unfortunately, there have been few controlled studies reported that employ biological systems or physiological features as targets, although some psychic practitioners will claim such abilities. Nevertheless, from our extensive body of rigorous remote perception experiments we must draw a second basic conclusion: human consciousness is able to extract information from physical aspects of its environment by some anomalous means that is independent of space and time. Although the information acquired by the percipient is originally subjective in character, it nevertheless survives the transposition to an objective, digital information form imposed by the scoring methods.

## Theoretical Models

Any attempt to set forth a theoretical model to complement such experimental data in a traditional scientific dialog is an awesome epistemological task. Not only are the empirical effects keenly anomalous in the present scientific framework, but in their demonstrably participant-specific characteristics they involve important subjective parameters not readily accommodated by scientific language, let alone by scientific formalism. Beyond this, the results are inescapably hyperstatistical, i.e., they involve a folding of the personal and collective statistical variations in participants' performances with the normal statistical behavior of the physical systems. Also, the series position sensitivity of the results, along with the lack of superposability of individual operator effects in co-operator experiments, imply strong nonlinearities in the underlying mechanisms. On the psychological side, a number of the empirical results indicate that unconscious as well as conscious processes may be involved, and very little theoretical framework for the former is available. Finally, the demonstrated lack of dependence of the phenomena on distance and time will strain any model rooted in classical physical theory.

Given all of this, it is essential to approach the modeling task at a rudimentary level. To begin, we might reiterate the four generic ingredients that pervade all of the research outlined above:

- *a random process or system* such as a machine driven by some random physical process, or an array of physical details embodied in a randomly selected geographical target
- *consciousness* of the operators, percipients, and agents, acting under some intention, volition, or desire
- *information*, coded in binary form, being added to, or extracted from, the random system
- *a resonance*, or bond, or sharing of identity between operator and machine, percipient and agent, percipient and target, or two operators that facilitates the information transfer between the consciousness and the random system in some lighthearted, game-like context.

It also may be useful to note that these are just special cases of the more general ingredients that characterize virtually any form of creative human experience:

- *an environment or context* that provides raw material for the creation
- *a consciousness* driven by some intention, purpose, or desire
- *information* flowing between the consciousness and the pertinent environment
- *a resonance* between the consciousness and the environment that nurtures the creative task, be it artistic achievement, athletic performance, or simple creative rumination on any subject.

In other words, the narrow range of consciousness-related anomalous phenomena we have been studying may be an indicative microcosm of a much broader genre of human capacity—the capacity to create, to order, or to heal. Thus, in attempting to model our empirical data, we may in fact be modeling the essence of human creative experience.

On the basis of our earlier crude catalog of the science of information, it follows that any model we erect to represent consciousness must encompass all four quadrants of its active and proactive, objective and subjective interactions with the physical world. Substantial bodies of established theory addressing some elements of this matrix exist, but unfortunately they do not communicate well with one another, and they leave major gaps in the coverage. For example, modern science is replete with objective, reactive models of the physical world, most of which have been well confirmed empirically. For our purposes, the formalisms of statistical mechanics, information theory, and quantum mechanics seem most apt, and we indeed invoke them heavily in our model. Objective models of consciousness also abound in the regimes of cognitive psychology and neuroscience, albeit in less precise formats than their physical counterparts, and some reference to these also can prove useful. But on the subjective side of the matrix our reservoirs of established models stand very shallow. Physical science has virtually nothing to say about subjective experience and, with the possible exception of the observational interpretations of quantum mechanics, acknowledges no proactive role for human participants. The situation is little better in the psychological and neurophysiological sectors, where subjective and proactive aspects of the psyche have seldom been treated in other than vague qualitative terms. One might hope that the troubled history of scholarly parapsychology or the clinical practice of psychiatry might contain some useful empirical experience, conceptualization, and nomenclature, but quantitative modeling has rarely been attempted in either field. Thus, our theoretical task becomes much more than redeployment of established models; major increments in concept, as well as in structure, will be required.

Very briefly, our strategy has been to appropriate the one form of existing physical theory that acknowledges human observation, however obliquely—namely, the so-called "Copenhagen" interpretation of quantum mechanics—and to extend its concepts and formalisms to include consciousness much more broadly and explicitly. We thereby attempt to extend what has been termed the "physics of observation" into a "physics of experience." The main postulates of this model, which are developed in detail in the references,[3,10] may be summarized:

1. Like elementary particles (a form of matter) and physical light (a form of energy), consciousness (a form of information) enjoys a wave/particle duality that allows it to circumvent and penetrate barriers and to resonate with other consciousnesses and with appropriate aspects of its environment. Thereby it can both acquire and insert information, both objective and subjective, from and to its resonant partners, in a manner that would be anomalous to its "particulate" representation.

2. The celebrated quantum mechanical principles of "uncertainty," "exclusion," "correspondence," "complementarity," "superposition," "indistinguishability," etc.—all of which are inexplicable in classical scientific terms—are at least as characteristic of the consciousness as of the physical systems and processes with which consciousness interacts. Manifestations of these transposed "consciousness principles" can readily be noted in a broad range of human activities and relationships.

3. The traditional objective properties and coordinates of physical theory—distance, time, mass, charge, momentum, energy, and so on—can be generalized to encompass corresponding subjective concepts, of which the objective versions are just special cases, more rigidly defined for analytical purposes.

4. The composite theory is not a model of consciousness per se, nor of the physical world; rather, it is a model of the experiential products of the interpenetration of an otherwise ineffable consciousness into an equally ineffable environmental surround.

Using such a perspective and vocabulary, it is possible to erect various consciousness "structures" and interactions, using essentially the same formalistic approach as does quantum physics. For example, consciousness "atoms" may be assembled wherein the experiences of an individual are represented by patterns of standing waves, akin to the bound electronic configurations of the hydrogen atom. With these conscious-ness atoms thus defined, their combination into consciousness molecules may also be undertaken. This bonding process, which is classically inex-plicable even in physical situations, is a particularly illuminating format for representation of the anomalous operator/machine and percipient/target interactions described earlier, and for broader comprehension of many other consciousness-related phenomena as well. For example, in the physical regime, when the wave patterns of the valence electrons of two atoms come into close interaction, they cannot be distinguished in any observable sense. This loss of identity or information, when properly acknowledged in the quantum mechanical formalism, leads to an "ex-change energy" that is the basis of the molecular bond. (This process is an excellent example of the equivalence of energy and information mentioned earlier.) Our metaphor would thus predict that an individual consciousness immersed in a given environmental situation would sus-tain a set of characteristic experiences.

A second individual, exposed to the same situation, would manifest a different set of experiences. However, if these two consciousnesses were strongly interacting, their experiential wave patterns would become res-onantly intertwined, resulting in a new pattern of standing waves in their common environment. As demonstrated in the co-operator exper-iments described earlier, these "molecular" experiences may be quite different from the simple sum of their "atomic" behaviors, and if we in-sist on comparing them with such, they will appear anomalous. In their own properly constituted molecular context, however, they are quite normal and, in principle, predictable.

Even our individual operator/machine effects may be addressed in this fashion if we are willing to concede some form of "consciousness" to the machine—in the sense that it, too, is a system capable of exchanging information with its environment. Thus, a bonded opera-tor/machine system should not be expected to conform to the isolated operator and isolated machine behaviors, but to establish its own char-acteristic behavior. Viewed as an influence of one system (the operator) upon another (the machine), the empirical results are inexplicable within the canonical behaviors of the isolated systems; viewed as a process of wave-mechanical resonance between two components of a single interactive system, they behave quite appropriately. Otherwise put, the surrender of subjective identity implicit in the human/machine bond is manifested in the appearance of objective information on the digital output string; the entropy of that string has literally been reduced by its involvement with a human consciousness.

Such a model can also be applied to the remote perception effects in terms of a resonant bond between the percipient and the agent that enables the "anomalous" acquisition of information about the prevailing physical target environment in which both are emotionally immersed. Alternatively, one might pose the "molecular bond" between the percipient and the target scene, with the agent assigned the role of establishing a facilitating environment for the anomalous communication between the two. In either representation, the merging of subjective identities again enables the transfer of objective information, in this case manifesting as a coherence between the agent and percipient response forms.

This concept of resonance as a mechanism for introducing order into random physical processes may also be a viable model for comprehending other equally "anomalous," if somewhat less provocative, processes such as artistic, intellectual, or biological creativity; or human trust, hope, or affection. That is, the essential mechanisms of these processes may devolve from the same principle of indistinguishability, whereby the surrender of information distinguishing the two interacting subsystems within a single complex system translates into an increment in the structural strength of the bonded system. Thus, when the perceived boundary between consciousness and its environment is permeated via subjective merging of the "I" with the "Not I," the resultant bonded system may manifest alterations in both the physical environment and the consciousness in some consequential way. If this resonance entails a volitional or intentional component, be it conscious or unconscious, the bonded system will reflect that intention in a manner unique to the particular "molecule." Our experimental results suggest that, whereas the scales of these effects may be marginally small and impossible to identify on a trial-by-trial basis, they nevertheless can manifest in significant probabilistic trends accumulated over large bodies of experience.

From all of this emerges the intriguing possibility that what we denote as "chance" behavior in any context, rather than deriving from some ultimately predictable, fully mechanistic behavior of a deterministic physical world, is actually some immense subsumption of a broad distribution of potentialities reflective of all possible resonances and intentions of consciousness with respect to the system or process in question. Sir Arthur Eddington[11] proposed the possibility in only slightly different terms:

> It seems that we must attribute to the mind power not only to decide the behaviour of atoms individually but to affect systematically large groups—in fact to tamper with the odds on atomic behaviour . . . Unless it belies its name, probability can be modified in ways in which ordinary physical entities would not admit of. There can be no unique probability attached to any event or behaviour; we can only speak of "probability in the light of certain given information," and the probability alters according to the extent of the information.

## IMPLICATIONS FOR HEALTH

What has all this to do with the third element in our title—human health? Without question, the most magnificent of all information acquisition, processing, and generation systems is the human consciousness. It handles both objective and subjective information with an elegance and sophistication that no contemporary data processor or controller can approach. Likewise, the most magnificent of all communication and response systems is the human physiology. From its most basic atomic and molecular structure, through its DNA and RNA macromolecules, to its proliferate physical, chemical, and biological networks, it handles all manner of objective and subjective information via a plethora of processes that invariably involve certain random components. Many physiological malfunctions and diseases including allergies, the HIV spectrum, cancer, and various neurological aberrations are directly attributable to some "disorder" of such simple and complex information processors. When functioning properly, however, both the consciousness and the physiological corpus are past masters at exchanging information with their external environments, allowing themselves to learn from, and adjust to, the latter.

But doubtless the most intimate of all systemic resonances is that between the physical body and its associated consciousness, given how heavily each is committed to the other for sustenance, safety, and challenge. Through an amazing array of hard-wired, soft-wired, and—in all likelihood—wireless connections and activators, the mind and body have elaborate options for guiding, protecting, and providing for each other to the higher welfare of the whole. The most primordial of needs—to eat, sleep, survive, and procreate—dominate the limbic brain and propagate throughout the basic organism. But also various subtler health aspirations—to be strong, attractive, alert, and intelligent—are physiological drivers imposed by conscious or subconscious volition on its compatriot corpus.

If, as we have demonstrated, consciousness, via its own expressed desire, can bring some degree of order into a simple random string of ones and zeros emerging from a rudimentary electronic machine, is it so unreasonable to suspect that it can invoke similar, or subtler, processes to influence the far more elaborate, relevant, and precious information processing systems that underlie its own health?

If we accept this proposition, what then are the requisite strategies for activation of the process? Once again, the four critical ingredients are available to us: (1) the consciousness, now addressing, with volition, (2) its own physical body, or that of another partner, into which it instills (3) some form of beneficial information or order via (4) an appropriate resonant bond. It thus remains only to specify and achieve this last criterion, the appropriate resonant bond, that enables the anomalous information transfer. This issue was debated at some length in *Margins of Reality*, converging onto the following recipe:

> To achieve such bonds, whether in physical or consciousness space, it is first necessary to acknowledge that there are distinct partners. That distinction

established, however, the individual identities must then be at least partially surrendered to a bonded state if the exchange energy is to be activated. Thus, successful strategy for anomalies experimentation involves some blurring of identities between operator and machine, or between percipient and agent. And, of course, this is also the recipe for any form of *love*: the surrender of self-centered interests of the partners in favor of the pair[3] (p. 343).

*Love!* Even by the most rigorous scientific experimentation and analytical logic, it appears that we have come upon nothing less than the driving force of life and of the physical universe: Love, with a capital L—the same overarching force of creative existence long recognized in virtually every other scholarly discipline and in every other cultural age; the same force heralded by the philosopher Rollo May[12] ("For in every act of love and will—and in the long run they are both present in each genuine act—we mold ourselves and our world simultaneously") and by the incomparable theologian Teilhard de Chardin[13] ("Someday, after we have mastered the winds, the waves, the tides and gravity, we shall harness for God the energies of love. Then for the second time in the history of the world, man will have discovered fire"). It is the same force that St. John names in his first Letter: "God is Love"[14] (which, in our scientific context, appears to be equally valid when stated in the reverse order).

The entry of this fourth currency of Love into the scientific exchequer may at first seem radical and revolutionary, but even here we find some rare earlier hints of the same universal insight, none better than that of Prince Louis de Broglie,[15] consummate scientist, renaissance man, and patriarch of modern physics:

If we wish to give philosophic expression to the profound connection between thought and action in all fields of human endeavor, particularly in science, we shall undoubtedly have to seek its sources in the unfathomable depths of the human soul. Perhaps philosophers might call it "love" in a very general sense—that force which directs all our actions, which is the source of all our delights and all our pursuits. Indissolubly linked with thought and with action, love is their common mainspring and, hence, their common bond. The engineers of the future have an essential part to play in cementing this bond.

I doubt that de Broglie would have hesitated to apply this exhortation to the healing professions as well, or to each of us individually who yearns for greater physical, mental, and spiritual health. Careful application of scientific knowledge and rigor of method, within a permeating atmosphere of "love in a very general sense," is a powerful plan for relating thought to action in any technical arena, not least of all the arena of health. In essence, then, the scientific message is this:

> In loving ourselves, we can heal
> ourselves. In loving the world, we
> can heal the world.

ACKNOWLEDGMENTS

The Princeton Engineering Anomalies Research program is indebted to the McDonnell Foundation, the Fetzer Institute, Mr. Laurance S. Rockefeller, Mr. D. C. Webster, and the Ohrstrom Foundation for their support of this research. The author is also deeply appreciative of the enormous contributions of time and energy by the various operators who have contributed to the databases, and to those staff members who helped with the preparation of this paper.

REFERENCES

[. . .]

2. *Princeton Engineering Anomalies Research*. Publication Summaries, August 1995.

3. Jahn, R. G., and B. J. Dunne. *Margins of Reality: The Role of Consciousness in the Physical World*. New York: Harcourt Brace Jovanovich, 1987.

4. ———. *Consciousness and Anomalous Physical Phenomena*. Technical note PEAR 95004. Princeton Engineering Anomalies Research, School of Engineering/ Applied Science, Princeton University, 1995.

5. Radin, D. I., and R. D. Nelson. "Evidence for Consciousness-Related Anomalies in Random Physical Systems." *Foundations of Physics* 19 (1989), pp. 1499–1514.

6. Peoc'h, R. "Psychokinetic Action of Young Chicks on the Path of an Illuminated Source." *Journal of Scientific Exploration* 9 (1995), pp. 223–229.

7. Nelson, R. D., G. J. Bradish, Y. H. Dobyns, B. J. Dunne, and R. G. Jahn. *Field REG: Random Event Generator Response to Group Dynamics.* Technical note PEAR 95003. Princeton Engineering Anomalies Research, School of Engineering/Applied Science, Princeton University, 1995.

8. Dunne, B. J., R. G. Jahn, and R. D. Nelson. *Precognitive Remote Perception.* Technical note PEAR 83003. Princeton Engineering Anomalies Research, School of Engineering/Applied Science, Princeton University, 1983.

9. Puthoff, H. E., and R. Targ. "A Perceptual Channel for Information Transfer Over Kilometer Distances: Historical Perspective and Recent Research." *Proceedings, Institute of Electrical and Electronic Engineers* 64 (1976), pp. 329–354.

10. Jahn, R. G. and B. J. Dunne. "On the Quantum Mechanics of Consciousness, with Application to Anomalous Phenomena." *Foundations of Physics* 16 (1986), pp. 721–772.

11. Eddington A. *The Nature of the Physical World.* Ann Arbor: University of Michigan Press, 1978, pp. 313–315.

12. May, R. *Love and Will.* New York: Dell, 1969, p. 325.

13. Teilhard de Chardin, P. "The Evolution of Chastity." *On Love.* New York: Harper and Row, 1967, pp. 33–34.

14. I John 4:8 (King James Version).

15. de Broglie, L. "The Role of the Engineer in the Age of Science." In A. J. Pomerans, translator. *New Perspectives in Physics.* New York: Basic Books, 1962, p. 213.

## ARTICLE 8. REPLICATION AND META-ANALYSIS IN PARAPSYCHOLOGY, *by Jessica Utts, 1991.*

[Source: Jessica Utts, "Replication and Meta-Analysis in Parapsychology." *Statistical Science* 6, no. 4, pp. 363–403 (1991). Available from: http://anson.ucdavis.edu/~utts/91rmp.html. Accessed 21 June 2006. Permission to reprint was granted by the Institute of Mathematical Statistics.]

*Editors' Comments*

Since so much of laboratory research in parapsychology depends on apparently small or weak statistical deviations from chance, it has been easy for some critics to dismiss such deviations as essentially meaningless; perhaps they are not significant, or are due to such factors as poor experimental design, poor or inappropriate statistical analysis, or downright fraud.

Dr. Jessica Utts, a professor in the Department of Statistics at the University of California, Davis, has long taken an interest in the use of statistics in parapsychology (see Utts, 1999; Utts and Josephson, 1996). In this selection Dr. Utts analyzes collectively, from a statistical point of view, the laboratory research carried out on psi phenomena over the decades. Her conclusion is that there is indeed an anomalous effect that remains even when taking other factors into account.

A Note: Some details of this article might be difficult to follow for those not well versed in mathematics and statistics, but those sections can be skimmed, and the author makes her major points in very readable prose. We decided to leave the details for those readers who are interested in studying them closely and also to maintain the integrity of the article.


# REPLICATION AND META-ANALYSIS IN PARAPSYCHOLOGY,
*by Jessica Utts, 1991.*


## ABSTRACT

Parapsychology, the laboratory study of psychic phenomena, has had its history interwoven with that of statistics. Many of the controversies in parapsychology have focused on statistical issues, and statistical models have played an integral role in the experimental work. Recently, parapsychologists have been using meta-analysis as a tool for synthesizing large bodies of work. This paper presents an overview of the use of statistics in parapsychology and offers a summary of the meta-analyses that have been conducted. It begins with some anecdotal information about the involvement of statistics and statisticians with the early history of parapsychology. Next, it is argued that most nonstatisticians do not appreciate the connection between power and "successful" replication of experimental effects. Returning to parapsychology, a particular experimental regime is examined by summarizing an extended debate over the interpretation of the results. A new set of experiments designed to resolve the debate is then reviewed. Finally, meta-analyses from several areas of parapsychology are summarized. It is concluded that the overall evidence indicates that there is an anomalous effect in need of an explanation.

## 1. INTRODUCTION

In a June 1990 Gallup Poll, 49% of the 1236 respondents claimed to believe in extrasensory perception (ESP), and one in four claimed to have had a personal experience involving telepathy (Gallup and Newport, 1991). Other surveys have shown even higher percentages; the University of Chicago's National Opinion Research Center recently surveyed 1473 adults, of which 67% claimed that they had experienced ESP (Greeley, 1987).

Public opinion is a poor arbiter of science, however, and experience is a poor substitute for the scientific method. For more than a century, small numbers of scientists have been conducting laboratory experiments to study phenomena such as telepathy, clairvoyance and precognition, collectively known as "psi" abilities. This paper will example some of that work, as well as some of the statistical controversies it has generated.

Parapsychology, as this field is called, has been a source of controversy throughout its history. Strong beliefs tend to be resistant to change even in the face of data, and many people, scientists included, seem to have made up their minds on the question without examining any empirical data at all. A critic of parapsychology recently acknowledged that "The level of the debate during the past 130 years has been an embarrassment for anyone who would like to believe that scholars and scientists adhere to standards of rationality and fair play" (Hyman, 1985a, p. 89). While much of the controversy has focused on poor experimental design and potential fraud, there have been attacks and defenses of the statistical methods as well, sometimes calling into question the very foundations of probability and statistical inference.

Most of the criticisms have been leveled by psychologists. For example, a 1987 report of the U.S. National Academy of Sciences concluded that "The committee finds no scientific justification from research conducted over a period of 130 years for the existence of parapsychological phenomena" (Druckman and Swets, 1988, p. 22). The chapter on parapsychology was written by a subcommittee chaired by a psychologist who had published a similar conclusion prior to his appointment to the committee (Hyman, 1985a, p. 7). There were no parapsychologists involved with the writing of the report. Resulting accusations of bias (Palmer, Honorton and Utts, 1989) led U.S. Senator Claiborne Pell to request that the Congressional Office of Technology Assessment (OTA) conduct an investigation with a more balanced group. A one-day workshop was held on September 30, 1988, bringing together parapsychologists, critics and experts in some related fields (including the author of this paper). The report concluded that parapsychology needs "a fairer hearing across a broader spectrum of the scientific community, so that emotionality does not impede objective assessment of experimental results" (Office of Technology Assessment, 1989).

It is in the spirit of the OTA report that this article is written. After Section 2, which offers an anecdotal account of the role of statisticians and statistics in parapsychology, the discussion turns to the more general question of replication of experimental results. Section 3 illustrates how replication has been (mis)interpreted by scientists in many fields. Returning to parapsychology in Section 4, a particular experimental regime called the "ganzfeld" is described, and an extended debate about the interpretation of the experimental results is discussed. Section 5 examines a meta-analysis of recent ganzfeld experiments designed to resolve the debate. Finally, Section 6 contains a brief account of meta-analyses that have been conducted in other areas of parapsychology, and conclusions are given in Section 7.


## 2. STATISTICS AND PARAPSYCHOLOGY

Parapsychology had its beginnings in the investigation of purported mediums and other anecdotal claims in the late 19th century. The Society for Psychical Research was founded in Britain in 1882, and its American counterpart was founded in Boston in 1884. While these organizations and their members were primarily involved with investigating anecdotal material, a few of the early researchers were already conducting "forced-choice" experiments such as card-guessing. (Forced-choice experiments are like multiple choice tests; on each trial the subject must guess from a small, known set of possibilities.) Notable among these was Nobel laureate Charles Richet, who is generally credited with being the first to recognize that probability theory could be applied to card-guessing experiments (Rhine, 1977, p. 26; Richet, 1884).

F. Y. Edgeworth, partly in response to what he considered to be incorrect analyses of these experiments, offered one of the earliest treatises on the statistical evaluation of forced-choice experiments in two articles published in the *Proceedings of the Society for Psychical Research* (Edgeworth, 1885, 1886). Unfortunately, as noted by Mauskopf and McVaugh (1979) in their historical account of the period, Edgeworth's papers were "perhaps too difficult for their immediate audience" (p. 105).

Edgeworth began his analysis by using Bayes' theorem to derive the formula for the posterior probability that chance was operating, given the data. He then continued with an argument "savouring more of Bernoulli than Bayes" in which "it is consonant, I submit, to experience, to put $1/2$ both for $\alpha$ and $\beta$," that is, for both the prior probability that chance alone was operating, and the prior probability that "there should have been some additional agency." He then reasoned (using a Taylor series expansion of the posterior probability formula) that if there were a large probability of observing the data given that some additional agency was at work, and a small objective probability of the data under chance, then the latter (binomial) probability "may be taken as a rough measure of the sought *a posteriori* probability in favour of mere chance" (p. 195). Edgeworth concluded his article by applying his method to some data published previously in the same journal. He found the probability against chance to be 0.99996, which he said "may fairly be regarded as physical certainty" (p. 199). He concluded:

> Such is the evidence which the calculus of probabilities affords as to the existence of an agency other than mere chance. The calculus is silent as to the nature of that agency—whether it is more likely to be vulgar illusion or extraordinary law. That is a question to be decided, not by formulae and figures, but by general philosophy and common sense [p. 199].

Both the statistical arguments and the experimental controls in these early experiments were somewhat loose. For example, Edgeworth treated as binomial an experiment in which one person chose a string of eight letters and another attempted to guess the string. Since it has long been understood that people are poor random number (or letter) generators, there is no statistical basis for analyzing such an experiment. Nonetheless, Edgeworth and his contemporaries set the stage for the use of controlled experiments with statistical evaluation in laboratory parapsychology. An interesting historical account of Edgeworth's involvement and the role telepathy experiments played in the early history of randomization and experimental design is provided by Hacking (1988).

One of the first American researchers to use statistical methods in parapsychology was John Edgar Coover, who was the Thomas Welton Stanford Psychical Research Fellow in the Psychology Department at Stanford University from 1912 to 1937 (Dommeyer, 1975). In 1917, Coover published a large volume summarizing his work (Coover, 1917). Coover believed that his results were consistent with chance, but others have argued that Coover's definition of significance was too strict

(Dommeyer, 1975). For example, in one evaluation of his telepathy experiments, Coover found a two-tailed $p$-value of 0.0062 [Editors' note: That is, odds against chance of approximately 160 to 1]. He concluded, "Since this value, then, lies within the field of chance deviation, although the probability of its occurrence by chance is fairly low, it cannot be accepted as a decisive indication of some case beyond chance which operated in favor of success in guessing" (Coover, 1917, p. 82). On the next page, he made it explicit that he would require a $p$-value of 0.0000221 [Editors' note: That is, odds against chance of approximately 45,000 to 1] to declare that something other than chance was operating.

It was during the summer of 1930, with the card-guessing experiments of J. B. Rhine at Duke University, that parapsychology began to take hold as a laboratory science. Rhine's laboratory still exists under the name of the Foundation for Research on the Nature of Man, housed at the edge of the Duke University campus [Editors' note: Its successor is the Rhine Research Center, Durham, North Carolina].

It wasn't long after Rhine published his first book, *Extrasensory Perception* in 1934, that the attacks on his methodology began. Since his claims were wholly based on statistical analyses of his experiments, the statistical methods were closely scrutinized by critics anxious to find a conventional explanation for Rhine's positive results.

The most persistent critic was a psychologist from McGill University named Chester Kellogg (Mauskopf and McVaugh, 1979). Kellogg's main argument was that Rhine was using the binomial distribution (and normal approximation) on a series of trials that were not independent. The experiments in question consisted of having a subject guess the order of a deck of 25 cards, with five each of five symbols, so technically Kellogg was correct.

By 1937 several mathematicians and statisticians had come to Rhine's aid. Mauskopf and McVaugh (1979) speculated that since statistics was itself a young discipline, "a number of statisticians were equally outraged by Kellogg, whose arguments they saw as discrediting *their* profession" (p. 258). The major technical work, which acknowledged that Kellogg's criticisms were accurate but did little to change the significance of the results, was conducted by Charles Stuart and Joseph A. Greenwood and published in the first volume of the *Journal of Parapsychology* (Stuart and Greenwood, 1937). Stuart, who had been an undergraduate in mathematics at Duke, was one of Rhine's early subjects and continued to work with him as a researcher until Stuart's death in 1947. Greenwood was a Duke mathematician, who apparently converted to a statistician at the urging of Rhine.

Another prominent figure who was distressed with Kellogg's attack was E. V. Huntington, a mathematician at Harvard. After corresponding with Rhine, Huntington decided that, rather than further confuse the public with a technical reply to Kellogg's arguments, a simple statement should be made to the effect that the mathematical issues in Rhine's work had been resolved. Huntington must have successfully convinced his former student, Burton Camp of Wesleyan, that this was a wise approach. Camp was the 1937 President of IMS [Institute of Mathematical Statistics]. When the annual meetings were held in December of 1937 (jointly with AMS [American Mathematical Society] and AAAS [American Association for the Advancement of Science]), Camp released a statement to the press that read:

> Dr. Rhine's investigations have two aspects: experimental and statistical. On the experimental side mathematicians, of course, have nothing to say. On the statistical side, however, recent mathematical work has established the fact that, assuming that the experiments have been properly performed, the statistical analysis is essentially valid. If the Rhine investigation is to be fairly attacked, it must be on other than mathematical grounds. [Camp, 1937.]

One statistician who did emerge as a critic was William Feller. In a talk at the Duke Mathematical Seminar on April 24, 1940, Feller raised three criticisms to Rhine's work (Feller, 1940). They had been raised before by others (and continue to be raised even today). The first was that inadequate shuffling of the cards resulted in additional information from one series to the next. The second was what is now known as the "file-drawer effect," namely, that if one combines the results of published studies only, there is sure to be a bias in favor of successful studies. The third was that the results were enhanced by the use of optional stopping, that is, by not specifying the number of trials in advance. All three of these criticisms were addressed in a rejoinder by Greenwood and Stuart (1940), but Feller was never convinced. Even in its third edition published in 1968, his book *An Introduction to Probability Theory and Its Applications* still contains his conclusion about Greenwood and Stuart: "Both their arithmetic and their experiments have a distinct tinge of the supernatural" (Feller, 1968, p. 407). In his discussion of Feller's position, Diaconis (1978) remarked, "I believe Feller was confused . . . he seemed to have decided the opposition was wrong and that was that."

Several statisticians have contributed to the literature in parapsychology to greater or lesser degrees. T.N.E. Greville developed applicable statistical methods for many of the experiments in parapsychology and was Statistical Editor of the *Journal of Parapsychology* (with J. A. Greenwood) from its start in 1937 through Volume 31 in 1967; Fisher (1924, 1929) addressed some specific problems in card-guessing experiments; Wilks (1965a, b) described various statistical methods for parapsychology; Lindley (1957) presented a Bayesian analysis of some parapsychology data; and Diaconis (1978) pointed out some problems with certain experiments and presented a method for analyzing experiments when feedback is given.

Occasionally, attacks on parapsychology have taken the form of attacks on statistical inference in general, at least as it is applied to real data. Spencer-Brown (1957) attempted to show that true randomness is impossible, at least in finite sequences, and that this could be the explanation for the results in parapsychology. That argument re-emerged in a recent debate on the role of randomness in parapsychology, initiated by psychologist J. Barnard Gilmore (Gilmore, 1989, 1990; Utts, 1989; Palmer, 1989,

1990). Gilmore stated that "The agnostic statistician, advising on research in psi, should take account of the possible inappropriateness of classical inferential statistics" (1989, p. 338). In his second paper, Gilmore reviewed several non-psi studies showing purportedly random systems that do not behave as they should under randomness (e.g., Iversen, Longcor, Mosteller, Gilbert and Youtz, 1971; Spencer-Brown, 1957). Gilmore concluded that "Anomalous data . . . should not be found nearly so often if classical statistics offers a valid model of reality" (1990, p. 54), thus rejecting the use of classical statistical inference for real-world applications in general.

## 3. REPLICATION

Implicit and explicit in the literature on parapsychology is the assumption that, in order to truly establish itself, the field needs to find a repeatable experiment. For example, Diaconis (1978) started the summary of his article in *Science* with the words "In search of repeatable ESP experiments, modern investigators . . ." (p. 131). On October 28–29, 1983, the 33rd International Conference of the Parapsychology Foundation was held in San Antonio, Texas, to address "The Repeatability Problem in Parapsychology." The Conference Proceedings (Shapin and Coly, 1985) reflect the diverse views among parapsychologists on the nature of the problem. Honorton (1985a) and Rao (1985), for example, both argued that strict replication is uncommon in *most* branches of science and that parapsychology should not be singled out as unique in this regard. Other authors expressed disappointment in the lack of a single repeatable experiment in parapsychology, with titles such as "Unrepeatability: Parapsychology's Only Finding" (Blackmore, 1985) and "Research Strategies for Dealing with Unstable Phenomena" (Beloff, 1985).

It has never been clear, however, just exactly what would constitute acceptable evidence of a repeatable experiment. In the early days of investigation, the major critics "insisted that it would be sufficient for

Rhine and Soal to convince them of ESP if a parapsychologist could perform successfully a single 'fraud-proof' experiment" (Hyman, 1985a, p. 71). However, as soon as well-designed experiments showing statistical significance emerged, the critics realized that a single experiment could be statistically significant just by chance. British psychologist C. E. M. Hansel quantified the new expectation, that the experiment should be repeated a few times, as follows:

> If a result is significant at the .01 level and this result is not due to chance but to information reaching the subject, it may be expected that by making two further sets of trials the antichance odds of one hundred to one will be increased to around a million to one, thus enabling the effects of ESP—or whatever is responsible for the original result—to manifest itself to such an extent that there will be little doubt that the result is not due to chance. [Hansel, 1980, p. 298.]

In other words, three consecutive experiments at $p \leq 0.01$ would convince Hansel that something other than chance was at work.

This argument implies that if a particular experiment produces a statistically significant result, but subsequent replications fail to attain significance, then the original result was probably due to chance, or at least remains unconvincing. The problem with this line of reasoning is that there is no consideration given to sample size or power. Only an experiment with extremely high power should be expected to be "successful" three times in a succession.

It is perhaps a failure of the way statistics is taught that many scientists do not understand the importance of power in defining successful replication. To illustrate this point, psychologists Tversky and Kahneman (1982) distributed a questionnaire to their colleagues at a professional meeting, with the question:

> An investigator has reported a result that you consider implausible. He ran 15 subjects, and reported a significant value, $t = 2.46$. Another

investigator has attempted to duplicate his procedure, and he obtained a nonsignificant value of $t$ with the same number of subjects. The direction was the same in both sets of data. You are reviewing the literature. What is the highest value of $t$ in the second set of data that you would describe as a failure to replicate? [1982, p. 28.]

In reporting their results, Tversky and Kahneman stated:

The majority of our respondents regarded $t = 1.70$ as a failure to replicate. If the data of two such studies ($t = 2.46$ and $t = 1.70$) are pooled, the value of $t$ for the combined data is about 3.00 (assuming equal variances). Thus, we are faced with a paradoxical state of affairs, in which the same data that would increase our confidence in the finding when viewed as part of the original study, shake our confidence when viewed as an independent study. [1982, p. 28.]

At a recent presentation to the History and Philosophy of Science Seminar at the University of California at Davis, I asked the following question. Two scientists, Professors A and B, each have a theory they would like to demonstrate. Each plans to run a fixed number of Bernoulli trials and then test $H_0$: $p = 0.25$ versus $H_a$: p > 0.25. Professor A has access to large numbers of students each semester to use as subjects. In his first experiment, he runs 100 subjects, and there are 33 successes ($p = 0.04$, one-tailed). Knowing the importance of replication, Professor A then runs an additional 100 subjects as a second experiment. He finds 36 successes ($p = 0.009$, one-tailed).

Professor B only teaches small classes. Each quarter, she runs an experiment on her students to test her theory. She carries out ten studies this way, with the results in Table 1.

I asked the audience by a show of hands to indicate whether or not they felt the scientists had successfully demonstrated their theories. Professor A's theory received overwhelming support, with approximately 20 votes, while Professor B's theory received only one vote.

If you aggregate the results of the experiment for each professor, you will notice that each conducted 200 trials, and Professor B actually demonstrated a *higher* level of success than Professor A, with 71 as opposed to 69 successful trials. The one-tailed *p*-values for the combined trials are 0.0017 for Professor A and 0.0006 for Professor B.

## TABLE 1

### ATTEMPTED REPLICATIONS FOR PROFESSOR B

| *n* | Number of successes | One-tailed *p*-value |
|-----|---------------------|----------------------|
| 10  | 4                   | 0.22                 |
| 15  | 6                   | 0.15                 |
| 17  | 6                   | 0.23                 |
| 25  | 8                   | 0.17                 |
| 30  | 10                  | 0.20                 |
| 40  | 13                  | 0.18                 |
| 18  | 7                   | 0.14                 |
| 10  | 5                   | 0.08                 |
| 15  | 5                   | 0.31                 |
| 20  | 7                   | 0.21                 |

To address the question of replication more explicitly, I also posed the following scenario. In December of 1987, it was decided to prematurely terminate a study on the effects of aspirin in reducing heart attacks because the data were so convincing (see, e.g., Greenhouse and Greenhouse, 1988; Rosenthal, 1990a). The physician-subjects had been randomly assigned to take either aspirin or a placebo. There were 104 heart attacks among the 11,037 subjects in the aspirin group, and 189 heart attacks among the 11,034 subjects in the placebo group (chi-square = 25.01, $p < 0.00001$).

After showing the results of that study, I presented the audience with two hypothetical experiments conducted to try to replicate the original result, with outcomes in Table 2.

## TABLE 2

### HYPOTHETICAL REPLICATIONS OF THE
### ASPIRIN / HEART ATTACK STUDY

|  | Replication #1 | | Replication #2 | |
| --- | --- | --- | --- | --- |
|  | Heart attack | | Heart attack | |
|  | Yes | No | Yes | No |
| Aspirin | 11 | 1156 | 20 | 2314 |
| Placebo | 19 | 1090 | 48 | 2170 |
| Chi–square | 2.596, | $p = 0.11$ | 13.206, | $p = 0.0003$ |

I asked the audience to indicate which one they thought was a more successful replication. The audience chose the second one, as would most journal editors, because of the "significant $p$-value." In fact, the *first* replication has almost exactly the same proportion of heart attacks in the two groups as the original study and is thus a very close replication of that result. The second replication has very *different* proportions, and in fact the relative risk from the second study is not even contained in a 95% confidence interval for relative risk from the original study. The *magnitude* of the effect has been much more closely matched by the "nonsignificant" replication.

Fortunately, psychologists are beginning to notice that replication is not as straightforward as they were originally led to believe. A special issue of the *Journal of Social Behavior and Personality* was entirely devoted to the question of replication (Neuliep, 1990). In one of the articles, Rosenthal cautioned his colleagues: "Given the levels of statistical power at which we normally operate, we have no right to expect the proportion of significant results that we typically do expect, even if in nature there is a very real and very important effect" (Rosenthal, 1990b, p. 16).

Jacob Cohen, in his insightful article titled "Things I Have Learned (So Far)," identified another misconception common among social scientists: "Despite widespread misconceptions to the contrary, the rejection of a given null hypothesis gives us no basis for estimating the probability that a replication of the research will again result in rejecting that null hypothesis" (Cohen, 1990, p. 1307).

Cohen and Rosenthal both advocate the use of effect sizes as opposed to significance levels when defining the strength of an experimental effect. In general, effect sizes measure the amount by which the data deviate from the null hypothesis in terms of standardized units. For instance, the effect size for a two-sample $t$-test is usually defined to be the difference in the two means, divided by the standard deviation for the control group. This measure can be compared across studies without the dependence on sample size inherent in significance levels. (Of course there will still be variability in the sample effect sizes, decreasing as a function of sample size.) Comparison of effect sizes across studies is one of the major components of meta-analysis.

Similar arguments have recently been made in the medical literature. For example, Gardner and Altman (1986) stated that the use of $p$-values "to define two alternative outcomes—significant and not significant—is not helpful and encourages lazy thinking" (p. 746). They advocated the use of confidence intervals instead.

As discussed in the next section, the arguments used to conclude that parapsychology has failed to demonstrate a replicable effect hinge on these misconceptions of replication and failure to examine power. A more appropriate analysis would compare the effect sizes for similar experiments across experimenters and across time to see if there have been consistent effects of the same magnitude. Rosenthal also advocates this view of replication:

> The traditional view of replication focuses on significance level as the relevant summary statistic of a study and evaluates the success of a replication in a dichotomous fashion. The newer, more useful view of replication focuses on effect size as the more important summary statistic of a study and evaluates the success of a replication not in a dichotomous but in a continuous fashion. [Rosenthal, 1990b, p. 28.]

The dichotomous view of replication has been used throughout the history of parapsychology, by both parapsychologists and critics (Utts, 1988). For example, the National Academy of Sciences report critically evaluated "significant" experiments, but entirely ignored "nonsignificant" experiments.

In the next three sections, we will examine some of the results in parapsychology using the broader, more appropriate definition of replication. In doing so, we will show that the results are far more interesting than the critics would have us believe.

## 4. The Ganzfeld Debate in Parapsychology

An extensive debate took place in the mid-1980's between a parapsychologist and critic, questioning whether or not a particular body of parapsychological data had demonstrated psi abilities. The experiments in question were all conducted using the ganzfeld setting (described below). Several authors were invited to write commentaries on the debate. As a result, this data base has been more thoroughly analyzed by both critics and proponents than any other and provides a good source for studying replication in parapsychology.

The debate concluded with a detailed series of recommendations for further experiments, and left open the question of whether or not psi abilities had been demonstrated. A new series of experiments that followed the recommendations were conducted over the next few years. The results of the new experiments will be presented in Section 5.

## 4.1 Free-Response Experiments

Recent experiments in parapsychology tend to use more complex target material than the cards and dice used in the early investigations, partially to alleviate boredom on the part of the subjects and partially because they are thought to "more nearly resemble the conditions of spontaneous psi occurrences" (Burdick and Kelly, 1977, p. 109). These experiments fall under the general heading of "free-response" experiments, because the subject is asked to give a verbal or written description of the target, rather than being forced to make a choice from a small discrete set of possibilities. Various types of target material have been used, including pictures, short segments of movies on video tapes, actual locations and small objects.

Despite the more complex target material, the statistical methods used to analyze these experiments are similar to those for forced-choice experiments. A typical experiment proceeds as follows. Before conducting any trials, a large pool of potential targets is assembled, usually in packets of four. Similarity of targets within a packet is kept to a minimum, for reasons made clear below. At the start of an experimental session, after the subject is sequestered in an isolated room, a target is selected at random from the pool. A sender is placed in another room with the target. The subject is asked to provide a verbal or written description of what he or she thinks is in the target, knowing only that it is a photograph, an object, etc.

After the subject's description has been recorded and secured against the potential for later alteration, a judge (who may or may not be the subject) is given a copy of the subject's description and the four possible targets that were in the packet with the correct target. A properly conducted experiment either uses video tapes or has two identical sets of target material and uses the duplicate set for this part of the process, to ensure that clues such as fingerprints don't give away the answer. Based on the subject's description, and of course on a blind basis, the judge is asked to either rank the four choices from most to least likely to have been the target, or to select the one from the four that seems to best match the subject's description. If ranks are used, the statistical analysis proceeds by summing the ranks over a series of trials and comparing the sum to what would be expected by chance. If the selection method is used, a "direct hit" occurs if the correct target is chosen, and the number of direct hits over a series of trials is compared to the number expected in a binomial experiment with $p = 0.25$.

Note that the subjects' *responses* cannot be considered to be "random" in any sense, so probability assessments are based on the random selection of the target and decoys. In a correctly designed experiment, the probability of a direct hit by chance is 0.25 on each trial, regardless of the response, and the trials are independent. These and other issues related to analyzing free-response experiments are discussed by Utts (1991).

## 4.2 *The Psi Ganzfeld Experiments*

The ganzfeld procedure is a particular kind of free-response experiment utilizing a perceptual isolation technique originally developed by Gestalt psychologists for other purposes. Evidence from spontaneous case studies and experimental work had led parapsychologists to a model proposing that psychic function may be masked by sensory input and by inattention to internal states (Honorton, 1977). The ganzfeld procedure was specifically designed to test whether or not reduction of external "noise" would enhance psi performance.

In these experiments, the subject is placed in a comfortable reclining chair in an acoustically shielded room. To create a mild form of sensory deprivation, the subject wears headphones through which white noise is played, and stares into a constant field of red light. This is achieved by taping halved translucent ping-pong balls over the eyes and then illuminating the room with red light. In the psi ganzfeld experiments, the subject speaks into a microphone and attempts to describe the target material being observed by the sender in a distant room.

At the 1982 Annual Meeting of the Parapsychological Association, a debate took place over the degree to which the results of the psi ganzfeld experiments constituted evidence of psi abilities. Psychologist and critic Ray Hyman and parapsychologist Charles Honorton each analyzed the results of all known psi ganzfeld experiments to date, and they reached strikingly different conclusions (Honorton, 1985b; Hyman, 1985b). The debate continued with the publication of their arguments in separate articles in the March 1985 issue of the *Journal of Parapsychology*. Finally, in the December 1986 issue of the *Journal of Parapsychology*, Hyman and Honorton (1986) wrote a joint article in which they highlighted their agreements and disagreements and outlined detailed criteria for future experiments. That same issue contained commentaries on the debate by 10 other authors.

The data base analyzed by Hyman and Honorton (1986) consisted of results taken from 34 reports written by a total of 47 authors. Honorton counted 42 separate experiments described in the reports, of which 28 reported enough information to determine the number of direct hits achieved. Twenty three of the studies (55%) were classified by Honorton as having achieved statistical significance at 0.05.

## 4.3 The Vote-Counting Debate

Vote-counting is the term commonly used for the technique of drawing inferences about an experimental effect by counting the number of significant versus nonsignificant studies of the effect. Hedges and Olkin (1985) give a detailed analysis of the inadequacy of this method, showing that it is more and more likely to make the wrong decision as the number of studies increases. While Hyman acknowledged that "vote-counting raises many problems" (Hyman, 1985b, p. 8), he nonetheless spent half of his critique of the ganzfeld studies showing why Honorton's count of 55% was wrong.

Hyman's first complaint was that several of the studies contained multiple conditions, each of which should be considered as a separate study. Using this definition he counted 80 studies (thus further reducing the sample sizes of the individual studies), of which 25 (31%) were "successful." Honorton's response to this was to invite readers to examine the studies and decide for themselves if the varying conditions constituted separate experiments.

Hyman next postulated that there was selection bias, so that significant studies were more likely to be reported. He raised some important issues about how pilot studies may be terminated and not reported if they don't show significant results, or may at least be subject to optional stopping, allowing the experimenter to determine the number of trials. He also presented a chi-square analysis that "suggests a tendency to report studies with a small sample only if they have signficant results" (Hyman, 1985b, p. 14), but I have questioned his analysis elsewhere (Utts, 1986, p. 397).

Honorton refuted Hyman's argument with four rejoinders (Honorton, 1985b, p. 66). In addition to reinterpreting Hyman's chi-square analysis, Honorton pointed out that the Parapsychological Association has an official policy encouraging the publication of nonsignificant results in its journals and proceedings, that a large number of reported ganzfeld studies did not achieve statistical significance and that there would have to be 15 studies in the "file-drawer" for every one reported to cancel out the observed significant results.

The remainder of Hyman's vote-counting analysis consisted of showing that the effective error rate for each study was actually much higher than the nominal 5%. For example, each study could have been analyzed using the direct hit measure, the sum of ranks measure or one of two other measures used for free-response analyses. Hyman carried out a simulation study that showed the true error rate would be 0.22 if "significance" was defined by requiring at least one of these four measures to achieve the 0.05 level. He suggested several other ways in which multiple testing could occur and concluded that the effective error rate in each experiment was not the nominal 0.05, but rather was probably close to the 31% he had determined to be the actual success rate in his vote-count.

Honorton acknowledged that there was a multiple testing problem, but he had a two-fold response. First, he applied a Bonferroni correction and found that the number of significant studies (using his definition of a study) only dropped from 55% to 45%. Next, he proposed that a uniform index of success be applied to all studies. He used the number of direct hits, since it was by far the most commonly reported measure and was the measure used in the first published psi ganzfeld study. He then conducted a detailed analysis of the 28 studies reporting direct hits and found that 43% were significant at 0.05 on that measure alone. Further, he showed that significant effects were reported by six of the 10 independent investigators and thus were not due to just one or two investigators or laboratories. He also noted that success rates were very similar for reports published in refereed journals and those published in unrefereed monographs and abstracts.

While Hyman's arguments identified issues such as selective reporting and optional stopping that should be considered in any meta-analysis, the dependence of significance levels on sample size makes the vote-counting technique almost useless for assessing the magnitude of the effect. Consider, for example, the 24 studies where the direct hit measure was reported and the chance probability of a direct hit was 0.25, the most common type of study in the data base. (There were four direct hit studies with other chance probabilities and 14 that did not report direct hits.) Of the 24 studies, 13 (54%) were "nonsignificant" at $\alpha = 0.05$, one-tailed. But if the 367 trials in these "failed replications" are combined, there are 106 direct hits, $z = 1.66$, and $p = 0.0485$, one-tailed. This is reminiscent of the dilemma of Professor B in Section 3.

Power is typically very low for these studies. The median sample size for the studies reporting direct hits was 28. If there is a real effect and it increases the success probability from the chance 0.25 to an actual 0.33 (a value whose rationale will be made clear below), the power for a study with 28 trials is only 0.181 (Utts, 1986). It should be no surprise that there is a "repeatability" problem in parapsychology.

## 4.4 Flaw Analysis and Future Recommendations

The second half of Hyman's paper consisted of a "Meta-Analysis of Flaws and Successful Outcomes" (1985b, p. 30), designed to explore whether or not various measures of success were related to specific flaws in the experiments. While many critics have argued that the results in parapsychology can be explained by experimental flaws, Hyman's analysis was the first to attempt to quantify the relationship between flaws and significant results.

Hyman identified 12 potential flaws in the ganzfeld experiments, such as inadequate randomization, multiple tests used without adjusting the significance level (thus inflating the significance from the nominal 5%) and failure to use a duplicate set of targets for the judging process (thus allowing possible clues such as fingerprints). Using cluster and factor analyses, the 12 binary flaw variables were combined in three new variables, which Hyman named General Security, Statistics and Controls.

Several analyses were then conducted. The one reported with the most detail is a factor analysis utilizing 17 variables for each of 36 studies. Four factors emerged from the analysis. From these, Hyman concluded that security had increased over the years, that the significance level tended to be inflated the most for the most complex studies and that both effect size and level of significance were correlated with the existence of flaws.

Following his factor analysis, Hyman picked the three flaws that seemed to be most highly correlated with success, which were inadequate attention to both randomization and documentation and the potential for ordinary communication between the sender and receiver. A regression equation was then computed using each of the three flaws as dummy variables, and the effect size for the experiment as the dependent variable. From this equation, Hyman concluded that a study without these three flaws would be predicted to have a hit rate of 27%. He concluded that this is "well within the statistical neighborhood of the 25% chance rate" (1985b, p. 37), and thus "the ganzfeld psi data base, despite initial impressions, is inadequate either to support the contention of a repeatable study or to demonstrate the reality of psi" (p. 38).

Honorton discounted both Hyman's flaw classification and his analysis. He did not deny that flaws existed, but he objected that Hyman's analysis was faulty and impossible to interpret. Honorton asked psychometrician David Saunders to write an Appendix to his article, evaluating Hyman's use of a factor analysis. Saunders first criticized Hyman's use of a factor analysis with 17 variables (many of which were dichotomous) and only 36 cases and concluded that "the entire analysis is meaningless" (Saunders, 1985, p. 87). He then noted that Hyman's choice of the three flaws to include in his regression analysis constituted a clear case of multiple analysis, since there were 84 possible sets of three that could have been selected (out of nine potential flaws), and Hyman chose the set most highly correlated with effect size. Again, Saunders concluded that "any interpretation drawn from [the regression analysis] must be regarded as meaningless" (1985, p. 88).

Hyman's results were also contradicted by Harris and Rosenthal (1988b) in an analysis requested by Hyman in his capacity as Chair of the National Academy of Sciences' Subcommittee on Parapsychology. Using Hyman's flaw classifications and a multivariate analysis, Harris and Rosenthal concluded that "our analysis of the effects of flaws on study outcome lends no support to the hypothesis that ganzfeld research results are a significant function of the set of flaw variables" (1988b, p. 3).

Hyman and Honorton were in the process of preparing papers for a second round of debate when they were invited to lunch together at the 1986 Meeting of the Parapsychological Association. They discovered that they were in general agreement on several major issues, and they decided to coauthor a "Joint Communiqué" (Hyman and Honorton, 1986). It is clear from their paper that they both thought it was more important to set the stage for future experimentation than to continue the technical arguments over the current data base. In the abstract to their paper, they wrote:

> We agree that there is an overall significant effect in this data base that cannot reasonably be explained by selective reporting or multiple analysis. We continue to differ over the degree to which the effect constitutes evidence for psi, but we agree that the final verdict awaits the outcome of future experiments conducted by a broader range of investigators and according to more stringent standards [p. 351].

The paper then outlined what these standards should be. They included controls against any kind of sensory leakage, thorough testing and documentation of randomization methods used, better reporting of judging and feedback protocols, control for multiple analyses and advance specification of number of trials and type of experiment. Indeed, any area of research could benefit from such a careful list of procedural recommendations.

### 4.5 Rosenthal's Meta-Analysis

The same issue of the *Journal of Parapsychology* in which the Joint Communiqué appeared also carried commentaries on the debate by 10 separate authors. In his commentary, psychologist Robert Rosenthal, one of the pioneers of meta-analysis in psychology, summarized the aspects of Hyman's and Honorton's work that would typically be included in a meta-analysis (Rosenthal, 1986). It is worth reviewing Rosenthal's results so that they can be used as a basis of comparison for the more recent psi ganzfeld studies reported in Section 5.

Rosenthal, like Hyman and Honorton, focused only on the 28 studies for which direct hits were known. He chose to use an effect size measure called Cohen's $h$, which is the difference between the arcsin transformed proportions of direct hits that were observed and expected:

$$h = 2(\arcsin /\sqrt{\hat{p}} - \arcsin /\sqrt{p} ).$$

One advantage of this measure over the difference in raw proportions is that it can be used to compare experiments with different chance hit rates. If the observed and expected numbers of hits were identical, the effect size would be zero. Of the 28 studies, 23 (82%) had effect sizes greater than zero, with a median effect size of 0.32 and a mean of 0.28. These correspond to direct hit rates of 0.40 and 0.38 respectively, when 0.25 is expected by chance. A 95% confidence interval for the true effect size is from 0.11 to 0.45, corresponding to direct hit rates of from 0.30 to 0.46 when chance is 0.25.

A common technique in meta-analysis is to calculate a "combined $z$," found by summing the individual $z$ scores and dividing by the square root of the number of studies. The result should have a standard normal distribution if each $z$ score has a standard normal distribution. For the ganzfeld studies, Rosenthal reported a combined $z$ of 6.60 with a $p$-value of $3.37 \times 10^{-11}$. He also reiterated Honorton's file-drawer assessment by calculating that there would have to be 423 studies unreported to negate the significant effect in the 28 direct hit studies.

Finally, Rosenthal acknowledged that, because of the flaws in the data base and the potential for at least a small file-drawer effect, the true average effect size was probably closer to 0.18 than 0.28. He concluded, "Thus, when the accuracy rate expected under the null is 1/4, we might estimate the obtained accuracy rate to be about 1/3" (1986, p. 333). This is the value used for earlier power calculation.

It is worth mentioning that Rosenthal was commissioned by the National Academy of Sciences to prepare a background paper to accompany its 1988 report on parapsychology. That paper (Harris and Rosenthal, 1988a) contained much of the same analysis as the commentary summarized above. Ironically, the discussion of the ganzfeld work in the National Academy Report focused on Hyman's 1985 analysis, but never mentioned the work it had commissioned Rosenthal to perform, which contradicted the final conclusion in the report.

## 5. A Meta-Analysis of Recent Ganzfeld Experiments

After the initial exchange with Hyman at the 1982 Parapsychological Association Meeting, Honorton and his colleagues developed an automated ganzfeld experiment that was designed to eliminate the methodological flaws identified by Hyman. The execution and reporting of the experiments followed the detailed guidelines agreed upon by Hyman and Honorton.

Using this "autoganzfeld" experiment, 11 experimental series were conducted by eight experimenters between February 1983 and September 1989, when the equipment had to be dismantled due to lack of funding. In this section, the results of these experiments are summarized and compared to the earlier ganzfeld studies. Much of the information is derived from Honorton et al. (1990).

## 5.1 *The Automated Ganzfeld Procedure*

Like earlier ganzfeld studies, the "autoganzfeld" experiments require four participants. The first is the Receiver (R), who attempts to identify the target material being observed by the Sender (S). The Experimenter (E) prepares R for the task, elicits the response from R and supervises R's judging of the response against the four potential targets. (Judging is double blind; E does not know which is the correct target.) The fourth participant is the lab assistant (LA) whose only task is to instruct the computer to randomly select the target. No one involved in the experiment knows the identity of the target.

Both R and S are sequestered in sound–isolated, electrically shielded rooms. R is prepared as in earlier ganzfeld studies, with white noise and a field of red light. In a nonadjacent room, S watches the target mate-rial on a television and can hear R's target description ("mentation") as it is being given. The mentation is also tape recorded.

The judging process takes place immediately after the 30–minute sending period. On a TV monitor from the isolated room, R views the four choices from the target pack that contains the actual target. R is asked to rate each one according to how closely it matches the ganzfield mentation. The ratings are converted to ranks and, if the correct target is ranked first, a direct hit is scored. The entire process is automatically recorded by the computer. The computer then displays the correct choice to R as feedback.

There were 160 preselected targets, used with replacement, in 10 of the 11 series. They were arranged in packets of four, and the decoys for a given target were always the remaining three in the same set. Thus, even if a particular target in a set were consistently favored by Rs, the probability of a direct hit under the null hypothesis would remain at 1/4. Popular targets should be no more likely to be selected by the com-puter's random number generator than any of the others in the set. The selection of the target by the computer is the only course of random-ness in these experiments. This is an important point, and one that is often misunderstood. (See Utts, 1991, for elucidation.)

Eighty of the targets were "dynamic," consisting of scenes from movies, documentaries and cartoons; 80 were "static," consisting of photographs, art prints and advertisements. The four targets within each set were all of the same type. Earlier studies indicated that dynamic targets were more likely to produce successful results, and one of the goals of the new experiments was to test that theory.

The randomization procedure used to select the target and the order of presentation for judging was thoroughly tested before and during the experiments. A detailed description is given by Honorton et al. (1990, pp. 118–120).

Three of the 11 series were pilot series, five were formal series with novice receivers, and three were formal series with experienced receivers. The last series with experienced receivers was the only one that did not use the 160 targets. Instead, it used only one set of four dynamic targets in which one target had previously received several first place ranks and one had never received a first place rank. The receivers, none of whom had had prior exposure to that target pack, were not aware that only one target pack was being used. They each contributed one session only to the series. This will be called the "special series" in what follows.

Except for two of the pilot series, numbers of trials were planned in advance for each series. Unfortunately, three of the formal series were not yet completed when the funding ran out, including the special series, and one pilot study with advance planning was terminated early when the experimenter relocated. There were no unreported trials during the 6-year period under review, so there was no "file drawer."

Overall, there were 183 Rs who contributed only one trial and 58 who contributed more than one, for a total of 241 participants and 355 trials. Only 23 Rs had previously participated in ganzfeld experiements, and 194 Rs (81%) had never participated in any parapsychological research.

## 5.2 Results

While acknowledging that no probabilistic conclusions can be drawn from qualitative data, Honorton et al. (1990) included several examples of session excerpts that Rs identified as providing the basis for their target rating. To give a flavor for the dream-like quality of the mentation and the amount of information that can be lost by only assigning a rank, the first example is reproduced here. The target was a painting by Salvador Dali called "Christ Crucified." The correct target received a first place rank. The part of the mentation R used to make this assessment read:

> . . . I think of guides, like spirit guides, leading me and I come into a court with a king. It's quiet . . . It's like heaven. The king is something like Jesus. Woman. Now I'm just sort of summersaulting through heaven . . . Brooding . . . Aztecs, the Sun God . . . High priest . . . Fear . . . Graves. Woman. Prayer . . . Funeral . . . Dark. Death . . . Souls . . . Ten Commandments. Moses . . . [Honorton et al., 1990.]

Over all 11 series, there were 122 direct hits in the 355 trials, for a hit rate of 34.4% (exact binomial $p$-value = 0.00005) when 25% were expected by chance. Cohen's $h$ is 0.20, and a 95% confidence interval for the overall hit rate is from 0.30 to 0.39. This calculation assumes, of course, that the probability of a direct hit is constant and independent across trials, an assumption that may be questionable except under the null hypothesis of no psi abilities.

Honorton et al. (1990) also calculated effect sizes for each of the 11 series and each of the eight experimenters. All but one of the series (the first novice series) had positive effect sizes, as did all of the experimenters.

The special series with experienced Rs had an exceptionally high effect size with $h = 0.81$, corresponding to 16 direct hits out of 25 trials (64%), but the remaining series and the experimenters had relatively homogeneous effect sizes given the amount of variability expected by chance. If the special series is removed, the overall hit rate is 32.1%, $h = 0.16$. Thus, the positive effects are not due to just one series or one experimenter.

Of the 218 trials contributed by novices, 71 were direct hits (32.5%, $h = 0.17$), compared with 51 hits in the 137 trials by those with prior ganzfeld experience (37%, $h = 0.26$). The hit rates and effect sizes were 31% ($h = 0.14$) for the combined pilot series, 32.5% ($h = 0.17$) for the combined formal novice series, and 41.5% ($h = 0.35$) for the combined experienced series. The last figure drops to 31.6% if the outlier series is removed. Finally, without the outlier series the hit rate for the combined series where all of the planned trials were completed was 31.2% ($h = 0.14$), while it was 35% ($h = 0.22$) for the combined series that were terminated early. Thus, optional stopping cannot account for the positive effect.

There were two interesting comparisons that had been suggested by earlier work and were preplanned in these experiments. The first was to compare results for trials with dynamic targets with those for static targets. In the 190 dynamic target sessions there were 77 direct hits (40%, $h = 0.32$) and for the static targets there were 45 hits in 165 trials (27%, $h = 0.05$), thus indicating that dynamic targets produced far more successful results.

The second comparison of interest was whether or not the sender was a friend of the receiver. This was a choice the receiver could make. If he or she did not bring a friend, a lab member acted as sender. There were 211 trials with friends as senders (some of whom were also lab staff), resulting in 76 direct hits (36%, $h = 0.24$). Four trials used no sender. The remaining 140 trials used nonfriend lab staff as senders and resulted in 46 direct hits (33%, $h = 0.18$). Thus, trials with friends as senders were slightly more successful than those without.

Consonant with the definition of replication based on consistent effect sizes, it is informative to compare the autoganzfeld experiments with the direct hit studies in the previous data base. The overall success rates are extremely similar. The overall direct hit rate was 34.4% for the autoganzfeld studies and was 28% for the comparable direct hit studies in the earlier meta-analysis. Rosenthal's (1986) adjustment for flaws had placed a more conservative estimate at 33%, very close to the observed 34.4% in the new studies.

One limitation of this work is that the autoganzfeld studies, while conducted by eight experimenters, all used the same equipment in the same laboratory. Unfortunately, the level of funding available in parapsychology and the cost in time and equipment to conduct proper experiments make it difficult to amass large amounts of data across laboratories. Another autoganzfeld laboratory is currently being constructed at the University of Edinburgh in Scotland, so interlaboratory comparisons may be possible in the near future.

Based on the effect size observed to date, large samples are needed to achieve reasonable power. If there is a constant effect across all trials, resulting in 33% direct hits when 25% are expected by chance, to achieve a one-tailed significance level of 0.05 with 95% probability would require 345 sessions.

We end this section by returning to the aspirin and the heart attack example in Section 3 and expanding a comparison noted by Atkinson, Atkinson, Smith and Bem (1990, p. 237). Computing the equivalent of Cohen's $h$ for comparing observed heart attack rates in the aspirin and placebo groups resulted in $h = 0.068$. Thus, the effect size observed in the ganzfeld data base is triple the much publicized effect of aspirin on heart attacks.

## 6. Other Meta-Analyses in Parapsychology

Four additional meta-analyses have been conducted in various areas of parapsychology since the original ganzfeld meta-analyses were reported. Three of the four analyses focused on evidence of psi abilities, while the fourth examined the relationship between extroversion and psychic functioning. In this section, each of the four analyses will be briefly summarized.

There are only a handful of English-language journals and proceedings in parapsychology, so retrieval of the relevant studies in each of the four cases was simple to accomplish by searching those sources in detail and by searching other bibliographic data bases for keywords.

Each analysis included an overall summary, an analysis of the quality of the studies versus the size of the effect and a "file-drawer" analysis to determine the possible number of unreported studies. Three of the four also contained comparisons across various conditions.

## 6.1 Forced-Choice Precognition Experiments

Honorton and Ferrari (1989) analyzed forced-choice experiments conducted from 1935 to 1987, in which the target material was randomly selected *after* the subject had attempted to predict what it would be. The time delay in selecting the target ranged from under a second to one year. Target material included items as diverse as ESP cards and automated random number generators. Two investigators, S. G. Soal and Walter J. Levy, were not included because some of their work has been suspected to be fraudulent.

**Overall Results.** There were 309 studies reported by 62 senior authors, including more than 50,000 subjects and nearly two million individual trials. Honorton and Ferrari used $z / \sqrt{n}$ as the measure of effect size ($ES$) for each study, where $n$ was the number of Bernoulli trials in the study. They reported a mean $ES$ of 0.020, and a mean $z$-score of 0.65 over all studies. They also reported a combined $z$ of 11.41, $p = 6.3 \times 10^{-25}$. Some 30% (92) of the studies were statistically significant at $\alpha = 0.05$. The mean $ES$ per investigator was 0.033, and the significant results were not due to just a few investigators.

**Quality.** Eight dichotomous quality measures were assigned to each study, resulting in possible scores from zero for the lowest quality, to eight for the highest. They included features such as adequate randomization, preplanned analysis and automated recording of the results. The correlation between study quality and effect size was 0.081, indicating a slight tendency for higher quality studies to be more successful, contrary to claims by critics that the opposite would be true. There was a clear relationship between quality and year of publication, presumably because over the years experimenters in parapsychology have responded to suggestions from critics for improving their methodology.

**File Drawer.** Following Rosenthal (1984), the authors calculated the "fail-safe $N$" indicating the number of unreported studies that would have to be sitting in file drawers in order to negate the significant effect. They found $N = 14,268$, or a ratio of 46 unreported studies for each one reported. They also followed a suggestion by Dawes, Landman and Williams (1984) and computed the mean $z$ for all studies with

$z > 1.65$. If such studies were a random sample from the upper 5% tail of a $N(0,1)$ distribution, the mean $z$ would be 2.06. In this case it was 3.61. They concluded that selective reporting could not explain these results.

**Comparisons.** Four variables were identified that appeared to have a systematic relationship to study outcome. The first was that the 25 studies using subjects selected on the basis of good past performance were more successful than the 223 using unselected subjects, with mean effect sizes of 0.051 and 0.008, respectively. Second, the 97 studies testing subjects individually were more successful than the 105 studies that used group testing; mean effect sizes were 0.021 and 0.004, respectively. Timing of feedback was the third moderating variable, but information was only available for 104 studies. The 15 studies that never told the subjects what the targets were had a mean effect size of 0.001. Feedback after each trial produced the best results, the mean *ES* for the 47 studies was 0.035. Feedback after each set of trials resulted in mean *ES* of 0.023 (21 studies), while delayed feedback (also 21 studies) yielded a mean ES of only 0.009. There is a clear ordering; as the gap between time of feedback and time of the actual guesses decreased, effect sizes increased.

The fourth variable was the time interval between the subject's guess and the actual target selection, available for 144 studies. The best results were for the 31 studies that generated targets less than a second after the guess (mean $ES = 0.045$), while the worst were for the seven studies that delayed target selection by at least a month (mean $ES = 0.001$). The mean effect sizes showed a clear trend, decreasing in order as the time interval increased from minutes to hours to days to weeks to months.

## 6.2 *Attempts to Influence Random Physical Systems*

Radin and Nelson (1989) examined studies designed to test the hypothesis that "The statistical output of an electronic RNG [random number generator] is correlated with observer intention in accordance with pre-specified instructions" (p. 1502). These experiments typically involved RNGs based on radioactive decay, electronic noise or pseudorandom number sequences seeded with true random sources. Usually the subject is instructed to try to influence the results of a string of binary trials by mental intention alone. A typical protocol would ask a subject to press a button (thus starting the collection of a fixed-length sequence of bits), and then try to influence the random source to produce more zeroes or more ones. A run might consist of three successive button presses, one each in which the desired result was more zeroes or more ones, and one as a control with no conscious intention. A z score would then be computed for each button press.

The 832 studies in the analysis were conducted from 1959 to 1987 and included 235 "control" studies, in which the output of the RNGs were recorded but there was no conscious intention involved. These were usually conducted before and during the experimental series, as part of the RNGs.

**Results.** The effect size measure used was again $z / \sqrt{n}$ where $z$ was positive if more bits of the specified type were achieved. The mean effect size for control studies was not significantly different from zero ($-1.0 \times 10^{-5}$). The mean effect size for the experimental studies was also very small, $3.2 \times 10^{-4}$, but it was significantly higher than the mean $ES$ for the control studies ($z = 4.1$).

**Quality.** Sixteen quality measures were defined and assigned to each study, under the four general categories of procedures, statistics, data and the RNG device. A score of 16 reflected the highest quality. The authors regressed mean effect size on mean quality for each investigator and found a slop of $2.5 \times 10^{-5}$ with standard error of $3.2 \times 10^{-5}$, indicating little relationship between quality and outcome. They also calculated a weighted mean effect size, using quality scores as weights, and found that it was very similar to the unweighted mean $ES$. They concluded that "differences in methodological quality are not significant predictors of effect size" (p. 1507).

**File Drawer.** Radin and Nelson used several methods for estimating the number of unreported studies (pp. 1508–1510). Their estimates ranged from 200 to 1000 based on models assuming that all significant studies were to be reported. They calculated the fail-safe $N$ to be 54,000.

## 6.3 Attempts to Influence Dice

Radin and Ferrari (1991) examined 148 studies, published from 1935 to 1987, designed to test whether or not consciousness can influence the results of tossing dice. They also found 31 "control" studies in which no conscious intention was involved.

**Results.** The effect size measure used was $z / \sqrt{n}$, where $z$ was based on the number of throws in which the die landed with the desired face (or faces) up, in $n$ throws. The weighted mean *ES* for the experimental studies was 0.0122 with a standard error of 0.00062; for the control studies the mean and standard error were 0.00093 and 0.00255, respectively. Weights for each study were determined by quality, giving more weight to high-quality studies. Combined $z$ scores for the experimental and control studies were reported by Radin and Ferrari to be 18.2 and 0.18, respectively.

**Quality.** Eleven dichotomous quality measures were assigned, ranging from automated recording to whether or not control studies were interspersed with the experimental studies. The final quality score for each study combined these with information on method of tossing the dice, and with source of subject (defined below). A regression of quality score versus effect size resulted in a slope of −0.002, with a standard error of 0.001. However, when effect sizes were weighted by sample size, there was a significant relationship between quality and effect size, leading Radin and Ferrari to conclude that higher-quality studies produced lower weighted effect sizes.

**File Drawer.** Radin and Ferrari calculated Rosenthal's fail-safe $N$ for this analysis to be 17,974. Using the assumption that all significant studies were reported, they estimated the number of unreported studies to be 1152. As a final assessment, they compared studies published before and after 1975, when the *Journal of Parapsychology* adopted an official policy of publishing nonsignificant results. They concluded, based on that analysis, that more nonsignificant studies were published after 1975, and thus "We must consider the overall (1935−1987) data base as suspect with respect to the file-drawer problem."

**Comparisons.** Radin and Ferrari noted that there was bias in both the experimental and control studies across die face. Six was the most likely to come up, consistent with the observation that it has the least mass. Therefore, they examined results for the subset of 69 studies in which targets were evenly balanced among the six faces. They still found a significant effect, with mean and standard error for effect size of 8.6 $\times$ $10^{-3}$ and 1.1 $\times$ $10^{-3}$, respectively. The combined $z$ was 7.617 for these studies. They also compared effect sizes across types of subjects used in the studies, categorizing them as unselected, experimenter and other subjects, experimenter as sole subject, and specially selected subjects. Like Honorton and Ferrari (1989), they found the highest mean $ES$ for studies with selected subjects; it was approximately 0.02, more than twice that for unselected subjects.

### 6.4 Extroversion and ESP Performance

Honorton, Ferrari and Bem (1991) conducted a meta-analysis to examine the relationship between scores on tests of extroversion and scores on psi-related tasks. They found 60 studies by 17 investigators, conducted from 1945 to 1983.

**Results.** The effect size measure used for this analysis was the correlation between each subject's extroversion score and ESP score. A variety of measures had been used for both scores across studies, so various correlation coefficients were used. Nonethless, a stem and leaf diagram of the correlations showed an approximate bell shape with mean and standard deviation of 0.19 and 0.26, respectively, and with an additional outlier at $r = 0.91$. Honorton et al. reported that when weighted by degrees of freedom, the weighted mean $r$ was 0.14, with a 95% confidence interval covering 0.10 to 0.19.

**Forced-Choice versus Free-Response Results.** Because forced-choice and free-response tests differ qualitatively, Honorton et al. chose to examine their relationship to extroversion separately. They found that for free-response studies there was a significant correlation between extroversion and ESP scores, with mean $r = 0.20$ and $z = 4.46$. Further, this effect was homogeneous across both investigators and extroversion scales.

For forced-choice studies, there was a significant correlation between ESP and extroversion, but only for those studies that reported the ESP results to the subject *before* measuring extroversion. Honorton et al. speculated that the relationship was an artifact, in which extroversion scores were temporarily inflated as a result of positive feedback on ESP performance.

**Confirmation with New Data.** Following the extroversion/ESP meta-analysis, Honorton et al. attempted to confirm the relationship using the autoganzfeld data base. Extroversion scores based on the Myers-Brigg Type Indicator were available for 221 of the 241 subjects who had participated in autoganzfeld studies.

The correlation between extroversion scores and ganzfeld rating scores was $r = 0.18$, with a 95% confidence interval from 0.05 to 0.30. This is consistent with the mean correlation of $r = 0.20$ for free-response experiments, determined from the meta-analysis. These correlations indicate that extroverted subjects can produce higher scores in free-response ESP tests.

## 7. CONCLUSIONS

Parapsychologists often make a distinction between "proof-oriented research" and "process-oriented research." The former is typically conducted to test the hypothesis that psi abilities exist, while the latter is designed to answer questions about how psychic functioning works. Proof-oriented research has dominated the literature in parapsychology. Unfortunately, many of the studies used small samples and would thus be nonsignificant even if a moderate-sized effect exists.

The recent focus on meta-analysis in parapsychology has revealed that there are small but consistently nonzero effects across studies, experimenters and laboratories. The sizes of the effects in forced-choice studies appear to be comparable to those reported in some medical studies that had been heralded as breakthroughs. (See Section 5; also Honorton and Ferrari, 1989, p. 301.) Free-response studies show effect sizes of far greater magnitude.

A promising direction for future process-oriented research is to examine the causes of individual differences in psychic functioning. The ESP/extroversion meta-analysis is a step in that direction.

In keeping with the idea of individual differences, Bayes and empirical Bayes methods would appear to make more sense than the classical inference methods commonly used, since they would allow individual abilities and beliefs to be modeled. Jeffreys (1990) reported a Bayesian analysis of some of the RNG experiments and showed that conclusions were closely tied to prior beliefs even though hundreds of thousands of trials were available.

It may be that the nonzero effects observed in the meta-analyses can be explained by something other than ESP, such as shortcomings in our understanding of randomness and independence. Nonetheless, there is an anomaly that needs an explanation. As I have argued elsewhere (Utts, 1987), research in parapsychology should receive more support from the scientific community. If ESP does not exist, there is little to be lost by erring in the direction of further research, which may in fact uncover other anomalies. If ESP does exist, there is much to be lost by not doing process-oriented research, and much to be gained by discovering how to enhance and apply these abilities to important world problems.

ACKNOWLEDGMENTS

I would like to thank Deborah Delanoy, Charles Honorton, Wesley Johnson, Scott Plous and an anonymous reviewer for their helpful comments on an earlier draft of this paper, and Robert Rosenthal and Charles Honorton for discussions that helped clarify details.

REFERENCES

Atkinson, R. L., R. C. Atkinson, E. E. Smith, and D. J. Bem (1990). *Introduction to Psychology*, 10th ed. San Diego: Harcourt Brace Jovanovich.

Beloff, J. (1985). "Research Strategies for Dealing with Unstable Phenomena." In B. Shapin and L. Coly, editors. *The Repeatability Problem in Parapsychology*. New York: Parapsychology Foundation, pp. 1–21.

Blackmore, S. J. (1985). "Unrepeatability: Parapsychology's Only Finding." In B. Shapin and L. Coly, editors. *The Repeatability Problem in Parapsychology*. New York: Parapsychology Foundation, pp. 183–206.

Burdick, D. S., and E. F. Kelly (1977). "Statistical Methods in Parapsychological Research." In B. B. Wolman, editor. *Handbook of Parapsychology*. New York: Van Nostrand Reinhold, pp. 81–130.

Camp, B. H. (1937). Statement in Notes Section. *Journal of Parapsychology* 1, p. 305.

Cohen, J. (1990). "Things I Have Learned (So Far)." *American Psychologist* 34, pp. 1304–1312.

Coover, J. E. (1917). *Experiments in Psychical Research at Leland Stanford Junior University*. Stanford, Calif.

Dawes, R. M., J. Landman, and J. Williams (1984). Reply to Kurosawa. *American Psychologist* 39, pp. 74–75.

Diaconis, P. (1978). "Statistical Problems in ESP Research." *Science* 201, pp. 131–136.

Dommeyer, F. C. (1975). "Psychical Research at Stanford University." *Journal of Parapsychology* 39, pp. 173–205.

Druckman, D. and J. A. Swets, editors (1988). *Enhancing Human Performance: Issues, Theories and Techniques*. Washington, D.C.: National Academy Press.

Edgeworth, F. Y. (1886). "The Calculus of Probabilities Applied to Psychical Research." In *Proceedings of the Society for Psychical Research* 3, pp. 190–199.

——— (1885). "The Calculus of Probabilities Applied to Psychical Research, II." In *Proceedings of the Society for Psychical Research* 4, pp. 189–208.

Feller, W. K. (1940). "Statistical Aspects of ESP." *Journal of Parapsychology* 4, pp. 271–297.

——— (1968). *An Introduction to Probability Theory and Its Applications*. Vol. 1. 3rd edition. New York: Wiley.

Fisher, R. A. (1924). "A Method of Scoring Coincidences in Tests with Playing Cards." In *Proceedings of the Society for Psychical Research* 34, pp. 181–185.

——— (1929). "The Statistical Method in Psychical Research." In *Proceedings of the Society for Psychical Research* 39, pp. 189–192.

Gallup, G. J., Jr., and F. Newport (1991). "Belief in Paranormal Phenomena Among Adult Americans." *Skeptical Inquirer* 15, pp. 137–146.

Gardner, M. J., and D. G. Altman (1986). "Confidence Intervals Rather Than P-Values: Estimation Rather Than Hypothesis Testing." *British Medical Journal* 292, pp. 746–750.

Gilmore, J. B. (1989). "Randomness and the Search for Psi." *Journal of Parapsychology* 53, pp. 309–340.

——— (1990). "Anomalous Significance in Pararandom and Psi-Free Domains." *Journal of Parapsychology* 54, pp. 53–58.

Greeley, A. (1987). "Mysticism Goes Mainstream." *American Health* 7, pp. 47–49.

Greenhouse, J. B., and S. W. Greenhouse (1988). "An Aspirin a Day . . . ?" *Chance* 1, pp. 24–31.

Greenwood, J. A., and C. E. Stuart (1940). A review of Dr. Feller's critique. *Journal of Parapsychology* 4, pp. 299–319.

Hacking, I. (1988). "Telepathy: Origins of Randomization in Experimental Design." *Isis* 79, pp. 427–451.

Hansel, C. E. M. (1980). *ESP and Parapsychology: A Critical Re-evaluation*. Buffalo, N.Y.: Prometheus Books.

Harris, M. J., and R. Rosenthal (1988a). *Interpersonal Expectancy Effects and Human Performance Research*. Washington D.C.: National Academy Press.

——— (1988b). *Postscript to Interpersonal Expectancy Effects and Human Performance Research*. Washington, D.C.: National Academy Press.

Hedges, L. V., and I. Olkin (1985). *Statistical Methods for Meta-Analysis*. Orlando, Fla.: Academic.

Honorton, C. (1977). "Psi and Internal Attention States." In B. B. Wolman, editor. *Handbook of Parapsychology*. New York: Van Nostrand Reinhold, pp. 435–472.

——— (1985a). "How to Evaluate and Improve the Replicability of Parapsychological Effects." In B. Shapin and L. Coly, editors. *The Repeatability Problem in Parapsychology*. New York: Parapsychology Foundation, pp. 238–255.

——— (1985b). "Meta-analysis of Psi Ganzfeld Research: A Response to Hyman." *Journal of Parapsychology* 49, pp. 51–91.

Honorton, C., R. E. Berger, M. P. Varvoglis, M. Quant, P. Derr, E. I. Schechter, and D. C. Ferrari (1990). "Psi Communication in the Ganzfeld: Experiments with an Automated Testing System and a Comparison with a Meta-analysis of Earlier Studies." *Journal of Parapsychology* 54, pp. 99–139.

Honorton, C., and D. C. Ferrari (1989). "'Future Telling': A Meta-analysis of Forced-Choice Precognition Experiments, 1935–1987." *Journal of Parapsychology* 53, pp. 281–308.

Honorton, C., D. C. Ferrari, and D. J. Bem (1991). "Extroversion and ESP Performance: A Meta-analysis and a New Confirmation." *Research in Parapsychology 1990*. Metuchen, N.J.: Scarecrow Press.

Hyman, R. (1985a). "A Critical Overview of Parapsychology." In P. Kurtz, editor. *A Skeptic's Handbook of Parapsychology*. Buffalo, N.Y.: Prometheus Books, pp. 1–96.

——— (1985b). "The Ganzfeld Psi Experiment: A Critical Appraisal." *Journal of Parapsychology* 49, pp. 3–49.

Hyman, R., and C. Honorton (1986). "Joint Communiqué: The Psi Ganzfeld Controversy." *Journal of Parapsychology* 50, pp. 351–364.

Iversen, G. R., W. H. Longcor, F. Mosteller, J. P. Gilbert, and C. Youtz (1971). "Bias and Runs in Dice Throwing and Recording: A Few Million Throws." *Psychometrika* 36, pp. 1–19.

Jeffreys, W. H. (1990). "Bayesian Analysis of Random Event Generator Data." *Journal of Scientific Exploration* 4, pp. 153–169.

Lindley, D. V. (1957). "A Statistical Paradox." *Biometrika* 44, pp. 187–192.

Mauskopf, S. H., and M. McVaugh (1979). *The Elusive Science: Origins of Experimental Psychical Research*. Baltimore: Johns Hopkins University Press.

McVaugh, M. R., and S. H. Mauskopf (1976). "J. B. Rhine's Extrasensory Perception and Its Background in Psychical Research." *Isis* 67, pp. 161–189.

Neuliep, J. W., editor (1990). "Handbook of Replication Research in the Behavioral and Social Sciences." *Journal of Social Behavior and Personality* 5, no. 4, pp. 1–510.

Office of Technology Assessment (1989). "Report of a Workshop on Experimental Parapsychology." *Journal of the American Society for Psychical Research* 83, pp. 317–339.

Palmer, J. (1989). "A Reply to Gilmore." *Journal of Parapsychology* 53, pp. 341–344.

——— (1990). "Reply to Gilmore: Round Two." *Journal of Parapsychology* 54, pp. 59–61.

Palmer, J. A., C. Honorton, and J. Utts (1989). "Reply to the National Research Council Study on Parapsychology." *Journal of the American Society for Psychical Research* 83, pp. 31–49.

Radin, D. I., and D. C. Ferrari (1991). "Effects of Consciousness on the Fall of Dice: A Meta-analysis." *Journal of Scientific Exploration* 5, pp. 61–83.

Radin, D. I., and R. D. Nelson (1989). "Evidence for Consciousness-Related Anomalies in Random Physical Systems." *Foundations of Physics* 19, pp. 1499–1514.

Rao, K. R. (1985). "Replication in Conventional and Controversial Sciences." In B. Shapin and L. Coly, editors. *The Repeatability Problem in Parapsychology*. New York: Parapsychology Foundation, pp. 22–41.

Rhine, J. B. (1934). *Extrasensory Perception*. Boston: Boston Society for Psychic Research; reprinted by Branden Press, 1964.

——— (1977). "History of Experimental Studies." In B. B. Wolman, editor. *Handbook of Parapsychology*. New York: Van Nostrand Reinhold, pp. 25–47.

Richet, C. (1884). "La suggestion mentale et le calcul des probabilités." *Revue Philosophique* 18, pp. 608–674.

Rosenthal, R. (1984). *Meta-Analytic Procedures for Social Research.* Beverly Hills, Calif.: Sage.

——— (1986). "Meta-analytic Procedures and the Nature of Replication: The Ganzfeld Debate." *Journal of Parapsychology* 50, pp. 315–336.

——— (1990a). "How Are We Doing in Soft Psychology?" *American Psychologist* 45, pp. 775–777.

——— (1990b). "Replication in Behavioral Research." *Journal of Social Behavior and Personality* 5, pp. 1–30.

Saunders, D. R. (1985). "On Hyman's Factor Analysis." *Journal of Parapsychology* 49, pp. 86–88.

Shapin, B., and L. Coly, editors (1985). *The Repeatability Problem in Parapsychology.* New York: Parapsychology Foundation.

Spencer-Brown, G. (1957). *Probability and Scientific Inference.* London and New York: Longman, Green.

Stuart, C. E., and J. A. Greenwood (1937). "A Review of Criticisms of the Mathematical Evaluation of ESP Data." *Journal of Parapsychology* 1, pp. 295–304.

Tversky, A., and D. Kahneman (1982). "Belief in the Law of Small Numbers." In D. Kahneman, P. Slovic, and A. Tversky, editors. *Judgement Under Uncertainty: Heuristics and Biases.* Cambridge, UK: Cambridge University Press, pp. 23–31.

Utts, J. (1986). "The Ganzfeld Debate: A Statistician's Perspective." *Journal of Parapsychology* 50, pp. 395–402.

——— (1987). "Psi, Statistics, and Society." *Behavioral and Brain Sciences* 10, pp. 615–616.

——— (1988). "Successful Replication Versus Statistical Significance." *Journal of Parapsychology* 52, pp. 305–320.

——— (1989). "Randomness and Randomization Tests: A Reply to Gilmore." *Journal of Parapsychology* 53, pp. 345–351.

——— (1991). Analyzing Free-Response Data: A Progress Report." In L. Coly, editor. *Psi Research Methodology: A Re-examination.* New York: Parapsychology Foundation.

Wilks, S. S. (1965a). "Statistical Aspects of Experiments in Telepathy." *N.Y. Statistician* 16, no. 6, pp. 1–3.

——— (1965b). "Statistical Aspects of Experiments in Telepathy." *N.Y. Statistician* 16, no. 7, pp. 4–6.

# PART III

SOME PRACTICAL APPLICATIONS
OF PSI STUDIES

One of the major stumbling blocks of psychical research is that, thus far, there seem to be no practical applications of the field—or at least this is the general perception. To a large degree this is true, and a direct function of the inability to elicit consistent psi phenomena on demand, either in the laboratory or in the "real world." Certainly most people would choose a telephone over telepathy as a means to transmit precise information to a friend a thousand miles away. Psi is not consistently reliable (or to put it more bluntly, it is notoriously unreliable), it is elusive and ephemeral, and when it does occur there is often a large amount of "noise" relative to a weak "signal," and that signal itself may be transformed and distorted as it makes its way through the unconscious and subconscious to the conscious mind. This may be one reason that it has been so difficult to "train" people to use psi. However, research into altered states of consciousness that might enhance psi could prove to be a means to learn to use psi in a more concrete way (see, for instance, Tart, 1975; Honorton, 1974). Hypnosis, inducing hypnotic-like states, and hypnotic training have long been suggested as ways to enhance psi abilities (Edmunds, 1961; Rýzl, 1970) and there is research to support this contention (Honorton, 1977).

There are a few areas where practical applications of psi may be particularly useful, and have shown at least some progress toward fulfillment: healing (page 216) and remote viewing (page 232). Healing, most people would agree, is a worthy undertaking no matter what means prove effective; if we can add psi applications to the medical arsenal, so much the better. When it comes to psi and healing, there are several ways that psi may play a role (Rao, 1983). Psi may be used to help diagnose an illness. Psi may help in prescribing measures to be taken in order to promote healing. These two aspects of "psi–mediated healing" are akin to general telepathy and clairvoyance, in that previous unknown or obscure knowledge is uncovered. Psi may also cause a direct physiological effect on the person to be healed. Of course, the flip side of healing is the fear that similar techniques can be applied to hurt or kill (so-called witch doctors of "traditional" or "primitive" societies come to mind). In this section we include a paper by Dr. Larry Dossey, M.D., in which he summarizes some of the recent evidence for the direct physiological healing effects of psi. We have purposefully not included discussion in this volume of "psychic surgeons," indigenous healers, and the like (see, for instance, Puharich, 1972) given the highly controversial nature of the subject and the persistent claims of fraud against such practices (see Randi, 1982). Furthermore, even if some such practitioners are genuine, their powers may or may not derive from psi. For instance, one must always keep the "placebo effect" in mind. Indeed, it can be suggested that the placebo effect is, at least in some cases, possibly enhanced by both "belief" and self-directed psi. A patient's belief and suggestibility, whether it be about a certain pill or procedure, has the potential to influence biochemical processes in the body.

Remote viewing, which in a way is a modern term for the older concepts of clairvoyance and telepathy, may be useful when all other means fail, such as in detective work and espionage; locating mineral or fossil fuel deposits, and similar forms of prospecting, when there is limited conventional information, or the conventional information sheds no light on which of many areas to explore; or in attempting to locate lost objects, otherwise unknown archaeological sites (Puthoff and Targ, 1976; Targ, 2004; Targ and Katra, 2000; S. Schwartz, 1978, 1983, 1980/ 2000; S. Schwartz and De Mattei, 1988/2000), and the like.

Another pragmatic aspect of psi must be considered. If micro-PK is real, it could lead to ominous results if applied by the wrong persons. As we become increasingly dependent on computers and other electronic devices that rely on bits of information at the atomic and subatomic scale, imagine the havoc that might be entailed by a terrorist who can scramble computer data, navigations systems, and so forth, by PK alone. A terrorist trained in PK could conceivably board an airplane and, while quietly sitting in his or her seat, scramble the on-board computer system and bring the plane down (or, conceivably, cause the damage without even being on the airplane if micro-PK effects can be carried over a substantial distance). Indeed, given micro-PK, a person or persons with strong feelings, beliefs, or emotions might inadvertently affect sensitive electronic equipment and other technologies dependent on information storage and processing at an atomic and subatomic scale. In the future it might be important to develop methods to shield equipment from PK intrusion.

Beyond such relatively mundane and practical, although certainly important, potential uses of psi as physically healing individuals and finding objects, there may be other uses or functions that are no less important. Psi may serve important biological functions (Randall, 1971/1972, 1975) as well as psychological functions. Disturbing paranormal experiences may occur to an individual, leading her or him (or family members or friends) to consult a professional therapist. However, as Roll (1987) has pointed out, many professional therapists may dismiss paranormal experiences out of hand as impossible (or, we would add, perhaps even use the paranormal experiences "against" the patient to label her or him delusional or worse). In the absence of a reputable and sympathetic therapist, a person troubled by paranormal experiences might turn to a fortune-teller or other "occultist" for help, which might possibly exacerbate the situation if such a person is either unscrupulous and takes advantage of the situation, or is simply ill-equipped to carry out therapeutic work. Roll (1987) has called for a profession of "clinical parapsychologists" who are trained to understand and help individuals suffering from paranormal experiences. The most obvious and extreme cases include recurrent spontaneous psychokinesis (RSPK, or poltergeist activity; see the selection from Roll, page 105).

One ethical question that has been raised is that even if psi research evolves to the point where it becomes reliable, given our current Western worldview, would we want this ability to be unleashed? Rao addressed this issue, saying "Considering its potential for misuse in warfare and the possibility of creating social chaos by threatening the disruption of personal privacy, not a few among us are concerned that in unraveling the secrets of psi we might make the same but more regrettable mistake we made when we split the atom but had little control over those who would have access to its awesome power. But, then, we may wonder whether psi-missing and other self-obscuring aspects of psi, which are currently irritating because they stand in the way of psi control, may not be nature's defense against the misuse of psi after all" (Rao, 1983, p. 264).

Among psychotherapists and other psychiatrists open to the reality, or at least possible reality, of the paranormal, it has been acknowledged that psi phenomena may play an important role in psychodynamics and therapy (see collected papers in Devereux, 1953; Ehrenwald, 1977; Freud, 1922; Mayer, 2007; Ullman, 1974). In some cases psi bearing on the therapist–patient relationship may manifest itself during therapy. For instance, bits of information (referred to as "tracer elements"; Ehrenwald, 1977) from the therapist's mind unknown to the patient may be telepathically transferred to the patient and manifested in the patient's dreams, only to be recounted to the therapist during a counseling session. The psychiatrist and psychoanalyst Dr. Montague Ullman (1974, pp. 261–263) presents a case study from his own practice in which a patient had a dream that included the elements of someone building a new house and also a chromium soap dish that had been taken or stolen. Unbeknownst to the patient, Ullman had moved into a new house that had been completed for him a year and a half previously, and during the building of the house an extra chromium soap dish had been shipped to the house by mistake, but Ullman had not returned it. A week before the patient's dream, Ullman had been embarrassed when some of the original builders had been to his house to check on a picture window that was out of line due to settling of the foundation. While in the cellar, one of the builders noticed the extra chromium soap dish being stored there and embarrassed Ullman by calling attention to it and joking that he had gotten away with it (i.e., he stole it). This incident had been on the mind of Ullman during the day just before his patient had the dream. Ullman (1974, p. 262) summarizes his interpretation of the patient's dream as follows: "we see a situation in which the patient, protesting the inroads of therapy, concerns himself with vulnerable areas in the therapist's own structure."

At another level, beyond the individual or pairs and small groups of individuals where psi interactions are associated with interpersonal dynamics and bonding, psi may in some ways serve as glue that helps bind cultures, societies, and ultimately all of humanity into a single species, and also ties us more generally to life as a whole. The study of psi provides us with a new perspective; it expands our horizons and opens our consciousness—in a very literal sense. Individuals are not as isolated from one another as a traditional physical-material theory would lead us to believe. The thoughts in my head may influence the thoughts in other persons' heads (telepathy) as well as their physiology, and even the non-living material world around me (extreme examples being seen in poltergeist incidents). All of life, and perhaps the entire universe, is entangled at some level. Parapsychology and psychical research challenges the fundamental paradigms underlying much of current Western thinking.

On a higher plane still, some would suggest that through telepathy (prayer) we can communicate with "gods" (or God, if you prefer) and discarnate spirits (Myers, 1903, 1907). In this sense, psi has been put to "practical" use for millennia. It is interesting to note that even many skeptics and debunkers of parapsychology and psychical studies are also religious in a traditional sense and pray. An example is the arch-skeptic and debunker Martin Gardner (see, for instance, Gardner 1957, 1981, 1983b, 1988, 1992) who, despite his unrelenting attacks on parapsychology, is deeply religious and confirmed to parapsychologist George P. Hansen his belief in "a personal god, prayer, and life after death" (Hansen quoting a 1996 letter from Gardner, in Hansen, 2001, p. 300; Hansen's [2001, pp. 291–306] brief biography of Gardner provides fascinating insights into the mind of a debunker and is well worth reading.).

# BIOLOGY AND HEALING

It is a mistake to think that biological evolution merely adapted man's body to his environment. Adaptation goes much deeper than that. Nature can influence us from within as well as from without. We are made to "feel in our bones" convictions which serve the interests of practical life. [Tyrrell, 1946.]

If psi is real, one can argue that it must have a place in natural history. There must be a reason or purpose for psi, whether it is simply an epiphenomenon of other processes and patterns, or because it has value in an evolutionary sense for organisms, and more specifically humans.

Parapsychologist James Carpenter has developed a model of psi that he calls "first sight"; an organism extends itself into the "larger pre-sensory surroundings" where "psi processes are posited to function normally as the unconscious leading-edge of the development of all consciousness and all intention." Essentially, psi serves as a means for the organism to learn about its surroundings and initiate actions (Carpenter, 2004).

Ullman (1974, p. 263) has suggested that paranormal events are "part of an emergency response system evoked under conditions of threat to sustaining affective bonds or threat to the physical integrity of the organism." Thus, telepathy allows for the perception of danger, death, or other events occurring to individuals important to us and with whom we are bonded, and precognition and clairvoyance may bring awareness of circumstances or potential future events that could be dangerous. To have such abilities could provide a selective advantage and thus be maintained from generation to generation in a population. However, one might argue that telepathy, clairvoyance, and precognition are fairly vague and undifferentiated forms of information gathering, and are relatively "primitive" in an evolutionary context. As other forms of information gathering, through standard sensory channels (smell, sight, hearing, etc.) using increasingly complex physiological organs, were developed and refined, and logical cognitive pathways elaborated (so as to predict short-term future events based on present conditions—"the cars are traveling too fast to cross the street without being hit"), there was selective pressure to place more reliance on the refined and consistently reliable sensory data and less reliance on what is now referred to as psi or paranormally acquired data. Paranormal abilities may even be selected against and suppressed in many evolutionary contexts. Yet an underlying residuum of the paranormal may come into play sporadically, perhaps when the impulse is strong and other modes of information gathering fail. Furthermore, if psi is subject to evolutionary selection, then it is expected that there will be variation in psi abilities within a population, and indeed the cumulative data can be interpreted to indicate that not all people (or organisms) have equivalent psi abilities. All men (and women) are not created equal when it comes to the paranormal, and not all persons can develop paranormal abilities to an equal degree.

### Cortical Plasticity and Psi

Brain plasticity is a known physical reaction to changes in perceptual experience. Essentially, cortical neurons in the brain can literally be restructured depending on increasing or decreasing exposure to individual sensory experiences (sight, smell, taste, sound, tactile, balance, heat, etc.). For example, Rauschecker and Korte (1993; see also Korte and Rauschecker, 1993; Rauschecker, 1995) sutured the eyelids of newborn kittens at birth to deprive them of receiving any normal visual stimuli. After recording neuron activity in different regions of the brain, they found that the deprived cats had smaller visual areas while the auditory and somatosensory areas were expanded compared to the control group. In addition, their auditory neurons were more "sharply tuned to detect sound location" (Goldstein, 2002, p. 402).

The tactile sensory homunculus (literally meaning "little man") is a cortical representation that shows that parts of the body that experience higher tactile acuity are literally represented by larger areas in the sensory part of the human brain. Other sensory inputs to the body have similar expressions of representation on the cortex. Most research has focused on the discussion of tactile plasticity, but other research, such as the research described above with cats, has also shown that the same pattern occurs with visual and other stimuli changes. There have been experiments that show how a loss of a part of the body, such as a finger, can change the cortical map. The area of the brain that is devoted to that finger or other area of the body is no longer receiving signals, and therefore can be taken over by another area of the brain. This is true also for senses "when input from one sense is eliminated, then the brain area normally devoted to that sense can be taken over by another sense" (Goldstein, 2002, p. 456). According to Goldstein, "The sensory homunculus is not, therefore, a permanent, static map but can be changed by experience" (Goldstein, 2002, p. 456). There is also a co-occurrence hypothesis, which suggests "that stimuli that occur together will tend to be represented by activity in the same, or nearby, areas of the cortex" (Goldstein, 2002, p. 178).

The effect of losing a sense triggers the brain to regrow and adapt to this change. If there is a part of the brain that is involved with psi, could it be theoretically possible for the brain to reorganize itself if this function was not used or another sense was relied on more and therefore "took over"? Although it is not known if psi, or the part of the brain associated with psi (if it does in fact exist), is located in one area or many areas of the brain, could some sort of plasticity occur if this "sense" is underutilized or not utilized due to lack of trust, understanding, or reliability? Perhaps humans do have a very basic ability to perform psi, but since our culture has shamed it, people learn to rely on their other senses? Perhaps children begin life with psi ability, but society does not accept it and they end up relying on other senses to the point where that area of the brain no longer exists except possibly associationally with other senses. Another component of this hypothesis is that, just like other senses, some people are born with more innate ability and the performance of the sense may follow the normal bell-curve pattern with some individuals having no ability at all and others being very adept. The unusually psi-gifted individuals may be the seers, witch doctors, sorcerers, medicine men, clever men, and others who can be traced in different cultures and throughout history.

Evolutionarily before language, and when beyond both visual and auditory range, psi perhaps served as a mode of communicating danger or other critical information among humans. With the development and increased use of speech, along with the banding together of groups of humans such that individuals were generally within sight and sound of one another, possibly the necessity for psi was slowly taken over by other senses and it became a more subsidiary ability or completely ceased to be manifested. Furthermore, technological adaptations such as cell phones and computers have decreased the necessity of this potential psi mode of communication.

### Psi and Psychological Conflict

Another view of the function of psi is that it is a mechanism to relieve emotional and psychological conflict, tension, and stress in an individual, or in some cases a group of individuals (see, for instance, discussions in Devereux, 1953, and Ehrenwald, 1977, on therapeutic aspects of psi; see also the discussion above). Telepathic exchanges among individuals may, in some sense, serve the same purpose as "heart-to-heart" discussions. Apparitions initiated by a person in crisis (for instance, at the time of death; see above, page 65) may serve to help resolve emotional loose ends at the time of bodily dissolution. Poltergeist activity centered on, or emanating from, a particular individual may serve the same purpose as throwing a tantrum or physical violence using non-paranormal means. Angst and confusion, perhaps seen most commonly at various developmental stages in adolescents, may be expressed by normal means (moodiness; destructive, self-destructive, and irrational behaviors, etc.) or much more rarely by paranormal means (PK; so-called poltergeist activity: see the article by Roll, page 105).

## ARTICLE 9. DISTANCE HEALING: EVIDENCE,
*by Larry Dossey, M.D., 2007.*

[Source: Larry Dossey, "Distance Healing: Evidence," 2007. Published for the first time here.]

### Editors' Comments

Dr. Larry Dossey, M.D., is a former internist who has had a long and distinguished career since receiving his M.D. degree from Southwestern Medical School in Dallas, 1967. Dr. Dossey is a former chief of staff of Medical City Dallas Hospital, and former cochairman of the Panel on Mind/Body Interventions, Office of Alternative Medicine, National Institutes of Health. He is executive editor of the peer-reviewed journal *EXPLORE: The Journal of Science and Healing*. Dr. Dossey is best known for his studies of alternative therapies and how the mind can influence the body. The author of ten books on the role of consciousness and spirituality in healing, Dr. Dossey has brought his insights to a wide public through such works as *Healing Words: The Power of Prayer and the Practice of Medicine* (1993), *Healing Beyond the Body: Medicine and the Infinite Reach of the Mind* (2001), and *The Extraordinary Healing Power of Ordinary Things: Fourteen Natural Steps to Health and Happiness* (2006). In the concise article below, Dr. Dossey succinctly lays out evidence for the effectiveness of distance healing.

## DISTANCE HEALING: EVIDENCE, *by Larry Dossey, M.D., 2007.*

*There is increasing evidence that consciousness can manifest nonlocally, at a distance, in ways that are health-relevant. The following studies and meta- or systematic analyses examine the ability of individuals nonlocally to insert information into the environment, as it were, as in distant intentionality and intercessory prayer.*

## Human Studies

### *Positive Studies*

Achterberg, J., K. Cooke, T. Richards, L. Standish, L. Kozak, and J. Lake. "Evidence for Correlations Between Distant Intentionality and Brain Function in Recipients: A Functional Magnetic Resonance Imaging Analysis." *Journal of Alternative and Complementary Medicine* 11, no. 6 (2005), pp. 965–971.

Researcher Jeanne Achterberg and her colleagues recruited eleven healers from the island of Hawaii. Each healer selected a person they knew, with whom they felt an empathic, compassionate, bonded connection to be the recipient of their healing efforts, which the researchers called distant intentionality (DI). The healers were not casually interested in healing; they had pursued their healing tradition an average of 23 years. They described their healing efforts as sending energy, prayer, or good intentions, or thinking of the individual in the scanner and wishing for them the highest good. Each recipient was placed in an MRI scanner and was isolated from all forms of sensory contact with the healer. The healers sent forms of DI that related to their own healing practices at two-minute random intervals that were unknown to the recipient. Significant differences between the experimental (send) and control (no send) conditions were found; there was approximately one chance in 10,000 that the results could be explained by chance happenings (in the language of science, $p = 0.000127$). The areas of the brain that were activated during the "send" periods included the anterior and middle cingulate areas, precuneus, and frontal areas. This study suggests that compassionate, healing intentions can exert measurable effects on the recipient, and that an empathic connection between the healer and the recipient is a vital part of the process.

Byrd, R. "Positive Therapeutic Effects of Intercessory Prayer in a Coronary Care Unit Population." *Southern Medical Journal* 81, no. 7 (1988), pp. 826–829.

This randomized, controlled study took place at UCSF [University of California, San Francisco] School of Medicine/San Francisco General

Hospital and involved 393 patients admitted to the coronary care unit for heart attack or chest pain. Those receiving assigned prayer did better clinically on several counts. Areas of statistical significance included less need for CPR [cardiopulmonary resuscitation], less need for potent medications, and a lower incidence of pulmonary edema and pneumonia.

Harris, W., M. Gowda, J. W. Kolb, C. P. Strychacz, J. L. Vacek, P. G. Jones, A. Forker, J. H. O'Keefe, and B. D. McCallister. "A Randomized, Controlled Trial of the Effects of Remote, Intercessory Prayer on Outcomes in Patients Admitted to the Coronary Care Unit." *Archives of Internal Medicine* 159, no. 19 (1999), pp. 2273–2278.

This double-blind study took place in the coronary care unit at Mid-America Heart Institute, Kansas City, Kansas, and the University of Kansas School of Medicine. Those receiving assigned prayer had a statistically significant, overall better clinical score than the control group.

Krucoff, M. W., S. W. Crater, C. L. Green, A. C. Maas, J. E. Seskevich, J. D. Lane, K. A. Loeffler, K. Morris, T. M. Bashore, and H. G. Koenig. "Integrative Noetic Therapies as Adjuncts to Percutaneous Intervention During Unstable Coronary Syndromes: Monitoring and Actualization of Noetic Training (MANTRA) Feasibility Pilot." *American Heart Journal* 142, no. 5 (2001), pp. 760–767.

This double-blind, randomized controlled trial took place at Duke Medical Center. Prayer groups around the world prayed for people undergoing urgent cardiac catheterization and angioplasty. In this pilot study, prayer came from prayer groups around the world. The prayed-for group had 50 to 100 percent fewer complications (bleeding, arrhythmias, death, etc.) than the group not assigned prayer.

Sicher, F., E. Targ, D. Moore, and H. S. Smith. "A Randomized Double-Blind Study of the Effect of Distant Healing in a Population with Advanced AIDS—Report of a Small-Scale Study." *Western Journal of Medicine* 169, no. 6 (1998), pp. 356–363.

This double-blind study of patients with advanced AIDS took place at UCSF School of Medicine/California Pacific Medical Center. The intervention was "distant healing intentions," which often took the form of prayer. The intervention group had a lower incidence of AIDS-associated illnesses, fewer and shorter hospitalizations, fewer doctor visits, and better psychological profile scores. There was no correlation between clinical outcomes and whether the patients believed they were receiving healing intentions/prayer.

O'Laoire, S. "An Experimental Study of the Effects of Distant, Intercessory Prayer on Self-Esteem, Anxiety, and Depression." *Alternative Therapies in Health and Medicine* 3, no. 6 (1997), pp. 38–53.

In this study, directed (specific) and nondirected (nonspecific) intercessory prayer was assigned to 496 volunteers, each of whom was prayed for by three agents. Subjects improved significantly on all 11 clinical measures, while intercessors improved on 10 measures. Agents improved to a greater degree than did subjects. A significant positive correlation was found between the amount of prayer the agents did and their scores on five objective tests. Improvement on four objective measures was significantly related to subjects' belief in the power of prayer for others. Improvement on all 11 measures was significantly related to subjects' conviction concerning whether they had been assigned to a control or an experimental group.

Tloczynski, J., and S. Fritzsch. "Intercessory Prayer in Psychological Well-Being: Using a Multiple-Baseline, Across-Subjects Design." *Psychological Reports* 91, no. 3 (Part 1) (2002), pp. 731–741.

This randomized controlled trial studied the effects of intercessory prayer in undergraduates in an upper-level psychology course. Eight participants were prayed for in a Multiple Baseline Across Subjects research design, which included a 1-week minimum baseline period for all subjects followed by the sequential presentation of the independent variable so that every two weeks, two additional subjects were being prayed for until all but 2 participants, who maintained baseline, were exposed to being prayed for at 7 weeks. All participants were prayed for by one of the experimenters using a nondirective method of prayer where no specific requests were made. All subjects completed the Taylor Manifest Anxiety Scale on a daily basis for 5 weeks and the Minnesota Multiphasic Personality Inventory-2 on a weekly basis for 7 weeks. Analysis of data identified significant reductions in anxiety scores on both the tests for subjects who were prayed for but not for those who were not prayed for.

Cha, K. Y., D. P. Wirth, and R. Lobo. "Does Prayer Influence the Success of In Vitro Fertilization-Embryo Transfer? Report of a Masked, Randomized Trial." *Journal of Reproductive Medicine* 46, no. 9 (September 2001), pp. 781–787.

This triple-blind, controlled trial of off-site prayer involved women undergoing in vitro fertilization and embryo transfer in a fertility clinic in Seoul, Korea. The group receiving assigned prayer from people in the U.S., Canada, and Australia had twice the successful pregnancy rate as women in the control group, a highly significant result.

Bentwich, Z., and S. Kreitler. "Psychological Determinants of Recovery from Hernia Operations." Paper presented at Dead Sea Conference, Tiberias, Israel, June 1994.

This controlled trial of prayer involved individuals undergoing hernia surgery. The group receiving assigned prayer had a significantly better clinical course according to several pre-selected criteria.

Palmer, R. F., D. Katerndahl, and J. Morgan-Kidd. "A Randomized Trial of the Effects of Remote Intercessory Prayer: Interactions with Personal Beliefs on Problem-Specific Outcomes and Functional Status." *Journal of Alternative and Complementary Medicine* 10, no. 3 (2004), pp. 438–448.

This randomized clinical trial investigated the relevance of interpersonal belief factors as modifiers of the effectiveness of intercessory prayer. Eighty-six (86) male and female participants 18–88 years of age were randomly assigned to either treatment (n = 45) or control groups (n = 41). Several volunteers committed to daily prayer for participants in the intervention group. Intercessory prayer commenced for 1 month and were directed toward a life concern or problem disclosed by the participant at baseline. No direct intervention effect on the primary outcomes was found. A marginally significant reduction in the amount of pain was observed in the intervention group compared to controls. The amount of concern for baseline problems at follow-up was significantly lower in the intervention group when stratified by subject's baseline degree of belief that their problem could be resolved. Prayer intervention appeared to effectively reduce the subject's level of concern only if the subject initially believed that the problem could be resolved. Those in the intervention group who did not believe in a possible resolution to their problem did not differ from controls. Better physical functioning was observed in the intervention group among those with a higher belief in prayer and surprisingly, better mental health scores were observed in the control group with lower belief in prayer. The results of the current study underscore the role of interpersonal belief in prayer efficacy and are consistent with the literature showing the relevance of belief in health and well-being in general.

Leibovici, L. "Effects of Remote, Retroactive Intercessory Prayer on Outcomes in Patients with Bloodstream Infection: A Randomized Controlled Trial." *British Medical Journal* 323 (2001), pp. 1450–1451.

In this randomized, controlled, blinded experiment, prayer was offered to over 3,000 patients with sepsis four to 10 years *after* they were hospitalized. The prayed-for group had a statistically better course regarding length of stay and course of fever.

For a discussion of this unusual study, see: Olshansky, B., and L. Dossey. "Retroactive Prayer: A Preposterous Hypothesis?" *British Medical Journal* 327 (December 20, 2003), pp. 1465–1468.

For a review of twenty-four controlled trials of retro-temporal influence on biological and inanimate systems, see: Braud, W. "Wellness Implications of Retroactive Intentional Influence: Exploring an Outrageous Hypothesis." *Alternative Therapies in Health and Medicine* 6, no. 1 (2000), pp. 37–48.

## Positive Healing Studies in Nonhumans

Lesniak, K. T. "The Effect of Intercessory Prayer on Wound Healing in Nonhuman Primates." *Alternative Therapies in Health and Medicine* 12, no. 5 (2006), pp. 42–48. This study examined the effects of intercessory prayer (IP) on wound healing and related physiological and behavioral factors in 22 Garnett's greater bush babies, a monkey-like African primate. IP was employed in a randomized, double-blind study design to heal self-inflicted wounds in the animals. Animals receiving

THE PARAPSYCHOLOGY REVOLUTION

IP + tryptophan had a statistically significant wound reduction rate when compared to the tryptophan-only group. The IP group also demonstrated statistically significant increases in red blood cells, hemoglobin, and hematocrit, and a significant reduction in wound grooming and total grooming behaviors than the non-prayer group.

Bengston, W. F., and M. Moga. "Resonance, Placebo Effects, and Type II Errors: Some Implications from Healing Research for Experimental Methods." *Journal of Alternative and Complementary Medicine* 13, no. 3 (2007), pp. 317–327. In this study, a healer was able to heal mice injected with mammary cancer cells. These dramatic responses were followed by apparent immunity to mammary cancer, as re-injection of cancer cells failed to "take." See prior study:

Bengston, W. F., and D. Krinsley. "The Effect of the 'Laying on of Hands' on Transplanted Breast Cancer in Mice." *Journal of Scientific Exploration* 14, no. 3 (2000), pp. 353–364.

### Neutral or Negative Studies

Astin, J. A., J. Stone, D. I. Abrams, D. H. Moore, P. Couey, R. Buscemi, and E. Targ. "The Efficacy of Distant Healing for Human Immunodeficiency Virus—Results of a Randomized Trial." *Alternative Therapies in Health and Medicine* 12, no. 6 (2006), pp. 36–41.

This study examined the effect of distant healing or prayer on selected clinical outcomes in HIV patients who were receiving a combination antiretroviral therapy. 156 patients with a history of AIDS were divided into three arms: (1) 10 weeks of prayer/distant healing from professional healers, (2) 10 weeks of prayer/distant healing from nurses with no prior training or experience in distant healing, or (3) no distant healing. No significant treatment effects were observed for either professional healers or nurses. Subjects receiving healing intentions or prayer from either professional healers or nurses were statistically more likely to guess that they were receiving prayer or healing than patients in the control group.

A major problem with the study is that 24% of the control group and 40 percent of the professional healer or nurse groups were lost to follow-up at twelve months, resulting in a loss of 64% of the study's data. Therefore, at best this study is inconclusive and un-interpretable. No conclusions about the effectiveness of healing intentions and prayer can be drawn on the basis of this experiment.

Benson, H., J. A. Dusek, J. B. Sherwood, P. Lam, C. F. Bethea, W. Carpenter, S. Levitsky, P. C. Hill, D. W. Clem, M. K. Jain, D. Drumel, S. L. Kopecky, P. S. Mueller, D. Marek, S. Rollins, and P. L. Hibberd. "Study of the Therapeutic Effects of Intercessory Prayer (STEP) in Cardiac Bypass Patients: A Multicenter Randomized Trial of Uncertainty and Certainty of Receiving Intercessory Prayer." *American Heart Journal* 151 (2006), pp. 934–942.

This study involved 1,802 patients undergoing coronary artery bypass surgery at six U.S. hospitals. The three intervention groups included:

- 604 patients who were told they might or might not be prayed for, and were prayed for
- 597 patients who were told they might or might not be prayed for, and were not prayed for
- 601 patients who were told they would be prayed for, and were prayed for

Prayers were offered by two Catholic and one Protestant groups, who were provided brief written prayers and the first name and initial of the last name of the prayer subjects. Prayers were initiated on the eve of or day of surgery and continued for two weeks. Results:

- Among the group told they might or might not be prayed for and were: 52 percent had post-surgical complications.
- Among the group told they might or might not be prayed for, and were not: 51 percent had post-surgical complications.
- Among the group told they would be prayed for and were, 59 percent had post-surgical complications.

Mathai, J., and A. Bourne. "Pilot Study Investigating the Effect of Intercessory Prayer in the Treatment of Child Psychiatric Disorders." *Australasian Psychiatry* 12, no. 4 (2004), pp. 386–389.

This pilot study investigated whether intercessory prayer had an effect on the outcomes of a group of children with psychiatric conditions, using a triple-blind, randomized design. No additional benefits for patients receiving intercessory prayer were found, compared to those who received treatment as usual.

Krucoff, M., S. Crater, D. Gallup, J. Blankenship, M. Cuffe, M. Guarneri, R. Krieger, V. Kshettry, K. Morris, and M. Oz. "Music, Imagery, Touch, and Prayer as Adjuncts to Interventional Cardiac Care: The Monitoring and Actualization of Noetic Trainings (MANTRA II) Randomized Study." *Lancet* 366 (2005), pp. 211–217.

This double-blind, randomized controlled trial took place at Duke Medical Center and assessed the influence of distant prayer and the bedside use of music, imagery, and touch (MIT) on a total of 748 patients. No influence was found upon the immediate clinical outcome observed in patients undergoing certain heart procedures. However, six-month mortality was lower in patients assigned bedside MIT therapy. Additional "two-tiered" prayer was added following Nine-Eleven. Patients treated with two-tiered prayer had absolute six-month death and re-hospitalization rates that were about 30 percent lower than control patients, a "statistically suggestive" trend.

Walker, S. R., J. S. Tonigan, W. R. Miller, S. Corner, and L. Kahlich. "Intercessory Prayer in the Treatment of Alcohol Abuse and Dependence: A Pilot Investigation." *Alternative Therapies in Health and Medicine* 3, no. 6 (November 1997), pp. 79–86.

This study investigated the role of intercessory prayer in patients attempting recovery from alcohol abuse and dependence. The high dropout rate of subjects during the study prevents any statistical conclusions from being drawn.

Matthews, D. A., S. M. Marlowe, and F. S. MacNutt. "Effects of Intercessory Prayer on Patients with Rheumatoid Arthritis." *Southern Medical Journal* 93, no. 12 (2000), pp. 1177–1186.

This randomized clinical trial studied the effects of intercessory prayer on 40 patients with rheumatoid arthritis. All received a 3-day intervention, including 6 hours of education and 6 hours of direct-contact intercessory prayer. Nineteen randomly selected sample patients had 6 months of daily, supplemental intercessory prayer by individuals located elsewhere. Ten arthritis-specific outcome variables were measured at baseline and at 3-month intervals for 1 year. Patients receiving in-person intercessory prayer showed significant overall improvement during 1-year follow-up. No additional effects from supplemental, distant intercessory prayer were found. The investigators concluded that in-person intercessory prayer may be a useful adjunct to standard medical care for certain patients with rheumatoid arthritis, and that supplemental, distant intercessory prayer offers no additional benefits.

The add-on design of this study is puzzling. If Tylenol were used following aspirin and no additional benefit were seen, one would not conclude that Tylenol was worthless; perhaps aspirin masked its benefit. One would test Tylenol alone for its possible effects. The same logic appears to hold for intercessory prayer that is added following initial patient education and direct-contact prayer.

Matthews, W. J., J. M. Conti, and S. G. Sireci. "The Effects of Intercessory Prayer, Positive Visualization, and Expectancy on the Well-Being of Kidney Dialysis Patients." *Alternative Therapies in Health and Medicine* 7, no. 5 (2001), pp. 42–52.

Intercessory prayer and positive imagery/visualization were employed for 95 patients with end-stage renal disease undergoing renal dialysis. Intercessors were given scripted prayers and, oddly, were instructed to pray for only five minutes and were prohibited from praying for longer than 15 minutes. No significant effects were found.

Aviles, J. M., E. Whelan, D. A. Hernke, B. A. Williams, K. A. Kenny, W. M. O'Fallon, and S. L. Kopecky. "Intercessory Prayer and Cardiovascular Disease Progression in a Coronary Controlled Trial." *Mayo Clinic Proceedings* 76 (2001), pp. 1192–1198.

Intercessory prayer was offered for 799 coronary care unit patients following discharge. Prayer was offered at least once a week for 26 weeks by five intercessors per patient. Intercessory prayer was not associated with a statistically significant effect.

Harkness, E. F., N. C. Abbot, and E. Ernst. "A Randomized Trial of Distant Healing for Skin Warts." *American Journal of Medicine* 108 (2000), pp. 507–508. A total of 84 patients with skin warts were randomly assigned either to a group that received 6 weeks of distant healing by one of 10 experienced healers or to a control group that received a similar preliminary assessment but no distant healing. No statistically significant effect was found in the number or size of patients' warts.

## ANALYSES AND REVIEWS

Perhaps the most complete review of "healing studies" (remote healing; healing intentions; intercessory prayer; healing at a distance) is that of Wayne Jonas, M.D., former director of the NIH's National Center for Complementary and Alternative Medicine, and his associate Cindy C. Crawford.

Jonas, W. B., and C. C. Crawford. *Healing, Intention and Energy Medicine.* New York: Churchill Livingstone, 2003, pp. xv–xix. They say:

"We found over 2200 published reports, including books, articles, dissertations, abstracts and other writings on spiritual healing, energy medicine, and mental intention effects. This included 122 laboratory studies, 80 randomized controlled trials, 128 summaries or reviews, 95 reports of observational studies and non-randomized trials, 271 descriptive studies, case reports, and surveys, 1286 other writings including opinions, claims, anecdotes, letters to editors, commentaries, critiques and meeting reports, and 259 selected books."

The categories of this data:

Religious practice
Prayer
"Energy" healing
Qigong (laboratory research)
Qigong (clinical research)
Laboratory research on bioenergy

DMILS (EDA) [Direct Mental Interactions with Living Systems (Electrodermal Activity)]

DMILS (remote staring)

MMI (mind–matter interaction, such as RNG [Random Number Generators] studies)

MMI (group interactions with RNGs, à la Roger Nelson)

Healing in a group setting

In sorting out the quality of healing studies, using strict criteria, Jonas and Crawford give the highest grade, an "A," to mind–matter interaction studies, and a "B" to the prayer studies. The highly touted religion-and-health studies get no better than a "D," because they are epidemiological-observational studies and are not blinded and controlled.

## Further Reviews and Analyses

Abbot, Neil C. "Healing as a Therapy for Human Disease: A Systematic Review." *Journal of Alternative and Complementary Medicine* 6, no. 2 (2000), pp. 159–169.

This meta-analysis covers 59 randomized controlled studies (including 10 dissertation abstracts and 5 pilot studies) of healing in humans up to the year 2000. Of 22 fully reported trials, 10 (45%) suggested significant effects.

Astin, J. E., E. Harkness, and E. Ernst. "The Efficacy of 'Distant Healing': A Systematic Review of Randomized Trials." *Annals of Internal Medicine* 132 (2000), pp. 903–910.

Of 23 studies in distant healing, 57% showed positive results. A cautiously positive systematic review.

Benor, Daniel J. "Distant Healing." *Subtle Energies and Energy Medicine* 11, no. 3 (2002), pp. 249–264.

This is a review of 61 studies of distant healing. Significant effects are demonstrated in controlled trials in humans, animals, plants, bacteria, yeasts, cells in the laboratory, and DNA.

Braud, W., and M. Schlitz. "A Methodology for the Objective Study of Transpersonal Imagery." *Journal of Scientific Exploration* 3, no. 1 (1989), pp. 43–63.

This meta-analysis focuses on electrodermal activity (EDA), a measure of skin resistance that reflects states of tension. Healers have been able to selectively lower and raise EDA, aided by feedback from a meter attached to the healee's skin. In a series of 13 experiments by William Braud and Marilyn Schlitz involving 271 subjects and 323 sessions, the overall $P$ value was .000023. That is, such results could have occurred by chance only twenty three times in a million.

Hodge, D. R. "A Systematic Review of the Empirical Literature on Intercessory Prayer." *Research on Social Work Practice* 17, no. 2 (2007), pp. 174–187.

Many social workers appear to use intercessory prayer in direct practice settings. To help inform practitioners' use of this intervention, this article evaluates the empirical literature on the topic using the following three methods: (a) an individual assessment of each study, (b) an evaluation of intercessory prayer as an empirically supported intervention using criteria developed by Division 12 of the American Psychological Association (APA), and (c) a meta-analysis. Based on the Division 12 criteria, intercessory prayer was classified as an experimental intervention. Meta-analysis indicated small, but significant, effect sizes for the use of intercessory prayer ($g = -.171$, $p = .015$). The implications are discussed in light of the APA's Presidential Task Force on Evidence-based Practice.

Jonas, W. B. "The Middle Way: Realistic Randomized Controlled Trials for the Evaluation of Spiritual Healing. *Journal of Alternative and Complementary Medicine* 7, no. 1 (2001), pp. 5–7.

A positive meta-analysis of studies in distant mental influence on animate and inanimate systems, including distant healing and prayer.

Roberts, L., I. Ahmed, and S. Hall. "Intercessory Prayer for the Alleviation of Ill Health. *Cochrane Review* 3 (2001).

http://www.cochrane.org/cochrane/revabstr/ab000368.htm. The Cochrane Review finds the data "too inconclusive to guide those wishing to uphold or refute the effect of intercessory prayer on health care outcomes. . . . [T]he evidence presented so far is interesting enough to justify further study."

Schlitz, M., and W. Braud. "Distant Intentionality and Healing: Assessing the Evidence." *Alternative Therapies in Health and Medicine* 3, no. 6 (1997), pp. 62–73.

Analyzing 19 experiments in which one person sought to influence another person's electrodermal activity (EDA), they found highly significant effects ($p < .0000007$).

Townsend, M., V. Kladder, H. Ayele, and T. Mulligan. "Systematic Review of Clinical Trials Examining the Effects of Religion on Health." *Southern Medical Journal* 95, no. 12 (2002), pp. 1429–1434.

"Randomized controlled trials showed that intercessory prayer may improve health outcomes."

## OTHER STUDIES IN NONHUMANS

[Editors' note: Many studies have demonstrated to varying degrees the effects of intentionality on nonhuman organisms. Below Dr. Dossey provides a sampling of various studies along these lines.]

Barrington, M. R. "Bean Growth Promotion Pilot Experiment. *Proceedings of the Society for Psychical Research* 56 (1982), pp. 302–304.

Bengston, W. F., and M. Moga. "Resonance, Placebo Effects, and Type II Errors: Some Implications from Healing Research for Experimental Methods." *Journal of Alternative and Complementary Medicine* 13, no. 3 (April 2007), pp. 317–328. Available at: http://www.liebertonline.com/doi/abs/10.1089/acm.2007.6300?prevSearch=authorsfield%3A%28Bengston%2C+William+F.%29.

Bengston, W. F., and D. Krinsley. "The Effect of the 'Laying on of Hands' on Transplanted Breast Cancer in Mice." *Journal of Scientific Exploration* 14, no. 3 (2000), pp. 353–364. In this controlled study, rats injected with mammary cancer were healed through therapeutic intent in statistically significant numbers, compared to controls.

Braud, W. "Wellness Implications of Retroactive Intentional Influence: Exploring an Outrageous Hypothesis." *Alternative Therapies in Health and Medicine* 6, no. 1 (2000), pp. 37–48. Available at: http://www.integral-inquiry.com/cybrary.html# wellness.

Chauvin, R. " 'Built Upon Water' Psychokinesis and Water Cooling: An Exploratory Study." *Journal of the Society for Psychical Research* 55 (1988), pp. 10–15.

Dean, D. "An Examination of Infra-red and Ultra-violet Techniques to Test for Changes in Water Following the Laying-on-of-Hands." Doctoral dissertation, Saybrook Institute, 1983, pp. 111–115, University Microfilms International, no. 8408650.

———. "Infrared Measurements of Healer Treated Water." In W. G. Roll, J. Beloff, and R. A. White, editors. *Research in Parapsychology 1982*. Metuchen, N.J.: Scarecrow Press; 1983, pp. 100–101.

Fenwick, P., and R. Hopkins. "An Examination of the Effect of Healing on Water." *Journal of the Society for Psychical Research* 53 (1986), pp. 387–390.

Grad, B. "A Telekinetic Effect on Plant Growth." *International Journal of Parapsychology* 5 (1963), pp. 117–133.

———. "A Telekinetic Effect on Plant Growth. Part II: Experiments Involving Treatment of Saline in Stoppered Bottles." *International Journal of Parapsychology* 6 (1964), pp. 473–498.

Grad, B., and D. Dean. "Independent Confirmation of Infrared Healer Effects." In R. A. White and R. S. Broughton, editors. *Research in Parapsychology 1983*. Metuchen, N.J.: Scarecrow Press, 1984, pp. 81–83.

Haraldsson, E., and T. Thorsteinsson. "Psychokinetic Effects on Yeast: An Exploration Experiment." In W. E. Roll, R. L. Morris, and J. D. Morris, editors. *Research in Parapsychology 1972*. Metuchen, N.J.: Scarecrow Press, 1973, pp. 20–21. See also Erlendur Haraldsson, "Research on Alternative Medicine in Iceland," *MISAHA Newsletter* (Monterey Institute for the Study of Alternative Healing Arts), April–June, 1995, pp. 3–5.

Lenington, S. "Effect of Holy Water on the Growth of Radish Plants." *Psychological Reports* 45 (1979), pp. 381–382.

Lesniak, K. T. "The Effect of Intercessory Prayer on Wound Healing in Nonhuman Primates." *Alternative Therapies in Health and Medicine* 12, no. 5 (2006), pp. 42–48.

Lumsden-Cook, J. J., S. D. Edwards, and J. Thwala. "An Exploratory Study into Traditional Zulu Healing and REG Effects." *Journal of Parapsychology* 69, no. 1 (2005), pp. 129–138.

Munson, R. J. "The Effects of PK on Rye Seeds." *Journal of Parapsychology* 43 (1979), p. 43.

Pyatnitsky, L. N., and V. A. Fonkin. "Human Consciousness Influence on Water Structure." *Journal of Scientific Exploration* 9 (1995), pp. 89–105.

Radin, D., G. Hayssen, M. Emoto, and T. Kizu. "Double-Blind Test of the Effects of Distant Intention on Water Crystal Formation." *Explore: The Journal of Science and Healing* 2 (2006), pp. 408–411.

Radin, D. I., R. Taft, and G. Yount. "Possible Effects of Healing Intention on Cell Cultures and Truly Random Events." *Journal of Alternative and Complementary Medicine* 10 (2004), pp. 103–112.

Roney-Dougal, S. M., and J. Solfvin. "Field Study of Enhancement Effect on Lettuce Seeds: Their Germination Rate, Growth and Health." *Journal of the Society for Psychical Research* 66 (2004), pp. 129–142.

Saklani, A. "Follow-Up Studies of PK Effects on Plant Growth." *Journal of the Society for Psychical Research* 58 (1992), pp. 258–265.

———. "Preliminary Tests for Psi-Ability in Shamans of Garhwal Himalaya." *Journal of the Society for Psychical Research* 55 (1988), pp. 60–70.

Schwartz, S. A., R. J. DeMattei, E. G. Brame, and S. J. P. Spottiswoode. "Infrared Spectra Alteration in Water Proximate to the Palms of Therapeutic Practitioners." *Subtle Energies* 1 (1990), pp. 43–72.

Scofield, A. M., and R. D. Hodges. "Demonstration of a Healing Effect in the Laboratory Using a Simple Plant Model." *Journal of the Society for Psychical Research* 57 (1991), pp. 321–343.

Yan, X., F. Lu, H. Jiang, X. Wu, Z. Xia, H. Shen, J. Wang, M. Dao, H. Lin, and R. Zhu. "Certain Physical Manifestation and Effects of External Qi of Yan Xin Life Science Technology." *Journal of Scientific Exploration* 16 (2002), pp. 381–411.

Yan, X., H. Lin, H. Li, A. Traynor-Kaplan, Z.-Q. Xia, F. Lu, Y. Fang, and M. Dao. "Structure and Property Changes in Certain Materials Influenced by the External Qi of Qigong." *Material Research Innovations* 2, no. 6 (1999), pp. 349–359. This experiment explores the ability of a qigong master, using external *qi,* to produce significant structural changes in water and aqueous solutions, alter the phase behavior of dipalmitoyl phosphatidyl choline (DPPC) liposomes, and enable the growth of Fab protein crystals. These results demonstrate objective phenomena resulting from qigong and the potential of this ancient technology system, even in material processing. Important attributes of *qi* are summarized and the possible implications of these results from the materials perspective are discussed.

# REMOTE VIEWING

## ARTICLE 10. UNCONVENTIONAL HUMAN INTELLIGENCE SUPPORT: TRANSCENDENT AND ASYMMETRIC WARFARE IMPLICATIONS OF REMOTE VIEWING, *by L. R. Bremseth, 2001.*

[Source: Excerpts from L. R. Bremseth, "Unconventional Human Intelligence Support: Transcendent and Asymmetric Warfare Implications of Remote Viewing." 28 April 2001. Submitted in Partial Fulfillment of the Requirements for the Marine Corps War College, Marine Corps University, Marine Corps Combat Development Command, Quantico, VA 22134–5067. Available in a slightly different form from: http://www.lfr.org/LFR/csl/library/Bremseth.pdf (See: http://www.lfr.org/LFR/csl/academic/whitepapers.html). Accessed 17 August 2006.]

*Editors' Comments*

The potential practical application of parapsychological research has been studied by at least some members of the military. U.S. Navy SEAL (Sea, Air, Land) Captain (Ret) L. R. (Rick) Bremseth served in the Navy for twenty-nine and a half years (in Naval Special Warfare). In partial fulfillment of the requirements for the Marine Corps War College, Marine Corps University, Marine Corps Combat Development Command, Quantico, Virginia, Captain Bremseth wrote a thesis reviewing the experiments in remote viewing, undertaken by U.S. military and intelligence services. In his fascinating paper, portions of which we reprint here, Captain Bremseth discusses the potential practical application of a psi-mediated phenomenon, namely remote viewing, to military objectives. The story of the U.S. government's involvement in remote viewing studies is revealing on many levels, both in terms of how successful they were or were not and how they were treated by top officials, as well as for an understanding of how the U.S. government found the phenomena important enough to put resources and money into their study.

UNCONVENTIONAL HUMAN INTELLIGENCE SUPPORT: TRANSCENDENT AND ASYMMETRIC WARFARE IMPLICATIONS OF REMOTE VIEWING, *by L. R. Bremseth, 28 April 2001. (Copyright by L. R. Bremseth.)*

The views expressed in this paper are those of the author and do not reflect the official policy or position of the United States Government, Department of Defense, United States Marine Corps, Marine Corps University, or Marine Corps War College.

ABSTRACT

Concerned that a psychical (PSI) gap existed between U.S. and Soviet paranormal research efforts, the CIA [Central Intelligence Agency] sponsored discreet research into paranormal phenomena commencing in 1972. Over the succeeding twenty-three years, the U.S. military and intelligence services were actively involved in paranormal research and operations involving a process known as remote viewing. Remote viewing, which produced specialized human intelligence support, served as part of overall military and government organizations' intelligence collection efforts. In 1995, after assuming remote viewing program management responsibilities from the DIA [Defense Intelligence Agency], the CIA decided to terminate the program based on a controversial review conducted by the American Institutes for Research. Yet, remote viewing's demonstrated capacity for providing unique, non-technical intelligence support posits said program as a leading candidate for exploring currently evolving forms of warfare. Presented within is a brief history of the remote viewing program, an examination of its evolution over the course of more than twenty-three years, and a discussion of its continuing relevance to national security and emerging warfare trends.

PROLOGUE

From 1972 until 1995, United States military and intelligence organizations conducted paranormal research and operations involving a process known as remote viewing. Remote viewing is generally recognized within the scientific community as the psychic ability to access and provide accurate information, regardless of distance, shielding or time, about people, places, objects or events inaccessible through any normally recognized means (McMoneagle 220). Official confirmation of government participation in such research occurred in 1995 when a small portion of the voluminous classified research material was made publicly available via the Freedom of Information Act.[1]

Paranormal research, involving parapsychological and psychical functioning (PSI), has been perceived a controversial field by American academia and scientific communities who have met its reported results with outright dismissal, skepticism, or methodological criticism. Since both the military and the intelligence agencies pursue efforts deemed acceptable risks, their involvement with remote viewing, therefore, sparks curiosity. What made the risk of potential ridicule by association acceptable? This paper reviews remote viewing's evolution, examines why and how the United States military and intelligence agencies became involved in its controversial application as a unique human intelligence (HUMINT) support method, and explores its, heretofore, unrecognized status as an important and possibly revolutionary form of warfare with asymmetrical implications.

---

1. Archives for the remote viewing program material are in the possession of the CIA, which is currently in the process of declassifying portions of this material. The main source of information came from former program participants.

# THE SOVIETS, CENTRAL INTELLIGENCE AGENCY (CIA) AND STANFORD RESEARCH INSTITUTE (SRI)

## The PSI Gap

During the late 1960s, the United States intelligence community became concerned about a perceived disparity between U.S. and Soviet exploration and exploitation of paranormal phenomena. Intelligence information revealed that the Soviets were funding research, at an estimated level equivalent to hundreds of millions of U.S. dollars, that involved at least nine and possibly up to fourteen major research centers (DIA). Much of the U.S. concern focused on *who* was involved with the Soviet research as opposed to *what* they were actually doing, particularly when U.S. officials discovered that the KGB [Komitet Gosudarstvennoy Bezopasnosti, "Committee for State Security"] and GRU [Glavnoe Razvedyvatel'noe Upravlenie, "Main Intelligence Directorate"] were controlling the research (Swann). Their anxiety was amplified by knowledge that Soviets did not routinely invest at these levels, both monetarily and organizationally, for non-productive programs devoted to pure research.

In 1969, while participating in a scientific conference at Big Sur, California, a leading Soviet scientist presented a research paper that, when subsequently analyzed by the U.S. intelligence community, indicated the Soviets were involved in some form of "distant influencing" with mind control implications (Swann). The Soviet's organizational and funding commitment to paranormal, or psychic research, and the lack of any corresponding U.S. effort, created a perceived "PSI" gap. Further, this gap and its corresponding potential for Soviet breakthroughs were deemed to pose a national security threat that the United States could not afford to dismiss out of hand, inasmuch as the research was being funded and directed by Soviet security services. Specifically, the U.S. intelligence community was concerned that the Soviets may have developed the ability to replicate psychic phenomena and to harness its potential. This threat, in an area of research that had historically been disregarded by American academia and scientific communities, prompted American intelligence services to begin accelerating efforts for a counterpart U.S. program (Swann interview; Swann).

## CIA Involvement

Given prevailing attitudes toward psychic phenomena, the CIA did not know where to begin in measuring and/or quantifying psychical occurrences. Since most Western scientists generally regarded this whole area of endeavor as nonsense, the CIA thus began to look for a discrete research laboratory, operating outside of established academia, which could manage a quiet, classified research effort. At the time, the Stanford Research Institute (SRI), Menlo Park, California, was conducting annually funded government research, so it seemed a perfect match for the CIA's purpose (Puthoff, p. 64). In 1972 several CIA officers approached Dr. Hal Puthoff, a SRI laser research physicist and former Naval intelligence officer who had worked for the National Security Agency. Owing to Puthoff's military and scientific credentials, the agents confided to him their concerns regarding Soviet research efforts in parapsychology that the CIA had been monitoring for over a decade (Puthoff interview).

The CIA's interest in SRI and Puthoff had been piqued by a report Puthoff had drafted earlier that year regarding his observations of Ingo Swann, a New York artist and reported psychic. Puthoff invited Swann to visit SRI after they had corresponded regarding experiments to investigate the boundary between the physics of the animate and inanimate. Prior to Swann's SRI visit, and without Swann's knowledge, Puthoff arranged for access to a shielded magnetometer used in quark detection experiments by Stanford University's Physics Department. Quark experimentation required that the magnetometer be as well shielded as technologically possible to preclude outside influences (Puthoff, p. 65; Puthoff interview; Kress, p. 3).

While visiting the laboratory as part of Swann's facilities tour, Puthoff challenged Swann (who had claimed that he could perform psychokinesis) to see if he could affect the magnetometer, as it could not be affected from the outside by normal means. Intrigued by the challenge, Swann "observed" the magnetometer in a manner that eventually became known as "remote viewing" and, with pencil and paper sketched the interior of its theretofore unpublished construction. According to Puthoff, the magnetometer went "berserk" during Swann's sketching. Essentially, the output signal for the magnetometer became visibly disturbed, demonstrating a disturbance in the internal magnetic field. Astonished, Puthoff asked what Swann had done; Swann replied that he had done nothing but "look" at it. When Puthoff asked Swann for a repeat performance, the magnetometer again reacted in the same manner. Later, Puthoff reported Swann's "remote viewing" demonstration had impressed him even more than the magnetometer's reaction. Apparently the CIA was impressed as well, for several weeks later, its representatives approached Puthoff (Puthoff, p. 65; Puthoff interview; Kress, p. 3).

[. . .]

## Remote Viewing Goes Operational

### Coordinate Remote Viewing

Ingo Swann was the driving force behind the development of coordinate remote viewing, or the ability to remote view using geographic coordinates, in lieu of an outbound target person at a designated location serving as a sort of "beacon." According to Puthoff, Swann felt his abilities were not being tested or utilized to their fullest potential, especially during the early stages of the remote viewing experiments. Consequently, Swann made suggestions that helped the program develop and mature. Eventually Swann also confided that he could remote view anywhere on the planet and beyond its limits, a statement Puthoff initially considered preposterous. In response, Swann suggested an experiment was needed to determine whether someone was required at the target site during a remote viewing experiment and recommended a remote viewing of planet Jupiter prior to the upcoming NASA Pioneer 10 flyby. During this experiment, Swann described a ring around Jupiter, and at first, thought he might have remotely viewed Saturn by mistake. Astronomers and others readily dismissed Swann's description until the subsequent NASA 10 flyby revealed that the ring, in fact, existed (Puthoff, p. 68).

From this initial effort, the protocols were expanded and numerous experiments were conducted using geographic coordinates, latitude and longitude in degrees, minutes and seconds. *Scanate*, short for scanning by coordinates, was the name given to this method of remote viewing. When provided with the geographic coordinates for any given location on the planet, the remote viewer was asked to describe the location in as much detail as possible. One of the major challenges facing the SRI team with this form of remote viewing was developing protocols to preclude the possibility of a remote viewer somehow memorizing all of the world's geographic coordinates (Puthoff, p. 68).

Using Ingo Swann and Pat Price, another remote viewer, SRI conducted a long-range operational test of the *Scanate* procedures for the CIA during 1973. The purpose of the experiment was to determine remote viewing effectiveness under conditions that approximated an operational scenario (Puthoff, p. 68; Puthoff interview; Kress, pp. 4–5).

The experiment's results were profound, significantly impacting not only SRI's remote viewing program, but also the CIA support it received. The target site coordinates were for a West Virginia mountain home owned by a CIA employee; however, Swann and Price (located at SRI in Menlo Park), described a near-by facility that, in their opinion, was more interesting. The site proved to be a highly sensitive National Security Agency (NSA) facility, and both Swann and Price were accurate in their physical descriptions of the facility, as well as in their identification of its general purpose. Additionally, Price "penetrated" a secured vault and thereby obtained the facility's code name along with those of various programs, one of which was extremely sensitive. He also accessed the names of individuals who worked at the facility, but this information proved to be inaccurate (Puthoff interview: Kress, p. 5). Such was the result of the first-ever, long distance operational remote viewing test accomplished by SRI during the initial pilot program for the CIA.[2]

### A Soviet Target

During the following year, 1974, the CIA presented SRI with a long distance remote viewing experiment intended to test more fully the operational utility of this method of intelligence collection. The CIA requested that SRI, employing long distance *Scanate* procedures in a manner similar to the West Virginia site experiment, provide information about a Soviet site of ongoing operational significance. SRI employed Pat Price for the experiment. The CIA provided the map coordinates for an unidentified research facility in Semipalatinsk, USSR, a highly secret Soviet nuclear munitions site, where work was thought to involve development of particle beam weapons. Price accurately described the facility and the highly sensitive work that was being accomplished there. In particular, he sketched a giant crane-like structure that literally rolled over the tops of the buildings it straddled. Additionally, Price described ongoing work inside one of the buildings that involved problems the Soviets were experiencing in welding together thick metal gores for the construction of a sixty-foot sphere (Puthoff, pp. 69–72; Targ, pp. 82–86). According to Targ "We didn't get any feedback on this for more than three years. We discovered how accurate Price's viewings were when this sphere-fabricating activity at Semipalatinsk was eventually described in *Aviation Week* magazine, May 2, 1977" (Targ, p. 82). Unfortunately, by then Price had died.

Russell Targ observed Price during the above experiment. They were both in an electrically shielded room of SRI's Radio Physics building, located approximately ten thousand miles from Semipalatinsk. Targ knew nothing of the Semipalatinsk site so as to guard against the

---

2. Over the next five years, SRI personnel involved in the remote viewing program were subsequently investigated by numerous governmental agencies for gaining access to such a sensitive government facility.

potential for cueing or telepathy (Targ, p. 82; Kress, p. 7). Regarding this experiment, Targ stated "The accuracy of Price's drawing is the sort of thing that I, as a physicist, would never have believed, if I had not seen it for myself" (Targ, p. 82). While Price had significant success with this site, he also reported a good deal of information that proved to be inaccurate according to some of the CIA analysis (Kress, pp. 7–9). Significantly, this result was accomplished during the first-ever operational test of remote viewing for a Soviet site, and was not one of the best-ever results achieved throughout the duration of the program (Puthoff, p. 69).

Price's performance during the Semipalatinsk experiment, with its mix of accurate and inaccurate results, was fairly representative of remote viewing in general. As subsequently discovered, some early remote viewing inaccuracies may have resulted from how protocols were employed. For example, during an early SRI outbound experiment, Price proved extremely accurate in describing a San Francisco Bay area site. Two water tanks that he had reported as being at the site were not there, however, and this observation was dismissed as inaccurate. Years later, SRI researchers discovered, via an old photograph of the same site, the two missing water tanks had stood in exactly the locations described by Price, but many years prior to the actual remote viewing. As a result, the SRI team realized it was therefore crucial to specify exactly *when in time* the remote viewing experiment was to be focused (Puthoff interview).

## CIA's Reaction

As a result of the West Virginia and Semipalatinsk experiments, Dr. Kenneth A. Kress, a physicist and former CIA contract monitor for the SRI research, wrote a synopsis of the program efforts in an article entitled "Parapsychology in Intelligence: A Personal Review & Conclusions." At the time of its publication the article was classified "Top Secret" and disseminated within the intelligence community. Since then, it has been declassified and presents an even-handed remote viewing program evaluation. In his article, Kress addresses some of the CIA's and other agencies' attitudes toward SRI's research and results. He concludes that the research and experiments demonstrated paranormal abilities, but the researchers had not sufficiently explained them or achieved reproducibility. These conclusions were drawn from observations that the participating military and intelligence agencies were application oriented and thereby focused on immediate and relevant results, rather than the development and understanding of the underlying science and mechanical processes involved. Kress suggests further research, analysis, and assessment with requisite funding and an open-minded approach to better determine how paranormal phenomena could be employed for intelligence collection and related purposes (Kress, p. 14).

Additionally, Kress briefly addresses the national and political climate during the period when the CIA was providing remote viewing research support for SRI. He notes that the "Proxmire Effect"[3] was in-full force during that time and any government contracts of questionable nature were routinely being held up to ridicule and scorn (Kress 1). The CIA, in particular, was under scrutiny because of its earlier involvement with controversial areas of research, especially research with LSD reportedly connected to a death. Because the CIA was concerned that SRI research might be perceived as some form of mind altering/influencing technique and therefore linked to the earlier tainted research with LSD, the agency subsequently decided to "officially" terminate its support for SRI research in 1975 (Puthoff, p. 73; Smith interview).

Yet, the end of the CIA's support for SRI's remote viewing program did not sound the program's death knell. The Defense Intelligence Agency (DIA) had become interested in the program, as had the U.S. Air Force; both were providing programmatic funding by the time of the CIA's "official" disengagement (Smith interview).

---

3. During the 1970s Senator Proxmire gained notoriety by exposing government programs he felt wasted taxpayer money. He routinely used the media to ridicule these programs in a contemptuous manner.

## The Program Expands and Evolves

### The INSCOM Program

One result of Kress' article was its impact upon the U.S. Army intelligence community. Members of the 902 MI Group counter-intelligence division read the article and realized that if remote viewing was as effective as reported by Kress, then the 902 MI Group as well as U.S. research and development efforts, were vulnerable to its employment by potential enemies (McMoneagle interview; Smith interview).

About this same time, the 902 MI Group was being absorbed into the newly established U.S. Army Intelligence Support Command (INSCOM). INSCOM set about developing a separate program whose goal was determining the U.S. military's vulnerability to remote viewing. In July 1978 INSCOM initiated a three year remote viewing program, code named *Gondola Wish*, in which the first year would be devoted to training, the second to testing, and the third year to evaluation and reporting. Five months into the first year's training program, however, the Iran Hostage Crisis developed, the training program was consequently terminated, and INSCOM's cadre of six remote viewers immediately went operational. Since *Gondola Wish* had been the code name for the initial training program, it was renamed *Grill Flame* concurrent with the program's new operational status (McMoneagle interview).

### The Iran Hostage Crisis

With five months training under their respective belts, the *Grill Flame* remote viewers began receiving a massive influx of taskings and associated intelligence support requests from the National Security Council (NSC). One of the NSC's original obstacles encompassed identifying exactly who, among the over four hundred Americans known to be in Iran at that time, were in fact being held hostage. The *Grill Flame* remote viewers were successful in identifying all sixty-four American hostages. Further, they identified three Americans who, due to the sensitive nature of their assignments, were being held at a separate location from the main body of hostages. Had *Grill Flame* members not identified the three, thereby enabling our government to negotiate for their release along with the others (in addition to letting the Iranians know that we knew they were holding them hostage), they likely would have been tortured to death (McMoneagle interview).

Throughout the Iran Hostage Crisis *Grill Flame* members accomplished over six hundred remote viewings for the NSC. As a result of their successes, *Grill Flame* members began receiving weekly remote viewing taskings from the NSA, CIA, DIA, Secret Service, FBI and a host of federal agencies and organizations. Finally, the remote viewers identified a potential underground rescue route, discernible only to those with old Persian or Roman maps of Tehran's sewers (McMoneagle interview).

## Expected Results vs. Actual Results

During the Iran Hostage Crisis, one of the more interesting characteristics of remote viewing emerged and involves expected results, as compared to actual results that are sometimes achieved with this unique process. For example, it was imperative that the U.S. military determine suitable infiltration and exfiltration routes for conducting a hostage rescue operation. Consequently, a requisite tasking to identify such routes was given to the *Grill Flame* members. One of the resulting remote viewing products involved diagonal-like grid work with blue and orange diagonal squares, which covered an oval shaped object. Upon initial analysis, this *Grill Flame* product might have appeared to be a "miss" on the part of the remote viewer and dismissed as inaccurate (McMoneagle interview). Fortunately, someone followed up on what initially appeared to be a nonsensical result with no apparent connection to the remote viewing tasking. Located about a half mile from the U.S. embassy compound in Tehran, a market area covered by a canopy with blue and orange oblique squares, concealed an oblong shaped object that proved to be a manhole cover. U.S. personnel discovered that only Iran has these types of manhole covers (most countries use round ones to prevent people or objects from falling through). The manhole led to underground phone lines that, disappointingly, led perpendicular to the embassy. Archived area maps, however, revealed that a long forgotten sewer system dating back to pre-Persian or pre-Roman times, and unknown even to the Iranians, was physically located beneath the phone line system. The sewer system ran under the embassy compound, exiting into one of its garages, thereby providing the information requested for a potential rescue attempt (McMoneagle interview).

This phenomena, where seemingly unrelated remote viewing products actually have a direct connection with the original remote viewing tasking, may account for some of the heretofore determined "misses" or inaccuracies of past efforts. Moreover, it is reminiscent of the previously mentioned Pat Price episode in which he described two water towers that were missing at the time of his remote viewing, but had existed many years prior. Understanding these remote viewing peculiarities presented a challenge for both the viewers and tasking agencies involved. As the program evolved and corporate knowledge increased, these idiosyncrasies became better understood and utilized (McMoneagle interview).

[. . .]

## WHY WAS THE PROGRAM KILLED? WHAT LIES AHEAD?

*At every crossroad on the path that leads to the future, the warrior is forever opposed by a thousand men appointed to guard the past.*
—Paraphrased from an unknown author.

### Smokescreen or Political Correctness
[. . .]

Did the CIA terminate the remote viewing program because it feared potential ridicule by association, or did it stage a "public execution" as a means of taking the program underground? Both are legitimate questions. The first is understandable given the perception of paranormal activities by many within American society, as well as the CIA's past experiences involving controversial research efforts.

Arguably, the second question is more intriguing as it implies that the CIA recognized the value of remote viewing, yet intended to make it appear otherwise. By discrediting the program, was the CIA actually intending to continue using remote viewing but under its own supervision and for its own purposes under a newly established and more tightly controlled program? Or, was the CIA concerned that remote viewing could be used to access sensitive U.S. secrets by both U.S. and non-U.S. remote viewers, particularly if this ability was somehow to become publicly recognized and possibly regarded as intriguing or even stimulating by society at-large? What becomes of intelligence services if or when they can no longer guarantee the security of their respective nation's most sensitive secrets? Remote viewing could not be controlled and the CIA knew it. Perhaps the CIA also realized that remote viewing represented only the tip of the iceberg regarding the full spectrum of human potential and capabilities that arguably threatened its, and every other intelligence service's, status quo. . . .

## Remote Viewing and Asymmetric Warfare

For the past several years, U.S. military and government agencies have been concerned with asymmetric warfare, which in this author's view constitutes an unconventional, innovative approach that targets an adversary's vulnerabilities across a range of modalities, with the intention of achieving disproportionate results. Such concern, and the manner in which it has been promulgated, has made asymmetric warfare appear as something new with which the U.S. must now contend; however, its concept is as old as Sun Tsu [also known as Sun Tzu, fifth century B.C. Chinese military strategist who wrote *The Art of War*] and warfare itself. Historically, adversaries have sought to disrupt opponents' centers of gravity via direct or indirect methods that exploit known or suspected vulnerabilities in order to achieve maximum results. What is arguably new, however, is the amorphous context within which asymmetrical warfare is now being considered.

The U.S. anticipates that future adversaries, indirectly challenging vulnerable areas beyond traditional battlefield confines, may strike via known or as yet unrecognized means; ergo, the increased U.S. concern. Moreover, the U.S. and its allies' reliance on complex information systems has magnified their collective vulnerability to asymmetric warfare since potential attack upon these systems could elicit disproportionate consequences when compared to the corresponding effort or risk required by an opponent. Furthermore, from an asymmetric perspective, a conflict's beginning and end may be imperceptible. In fact, the very definitions and conceptualizations of the terms *"peacetime," "conflict,"* and *"war"* may already be obsolete. Remote viewing required the same deconstructing of established concepts, in concert with abstract approaches to military problems, in order to evolve and succeed, making it an interesting asymmetric model for current applications.

Unfortunately, U.S. military and government organization's promotion of asymmetric warfare as novel, serves as an indictment of the rigid thought and structure that permeates them. Nonetheless, the resulting challenge is how to develop asymmetric responses or approaches to anticipated asymmetric threats within a symmetrical society and its established institutions. Identifying, developing, and rewarding individuals capable and proficient at asymmetrical conceptualizing is probably a first step toward achieving the required national responses.

Clearly, a nation cannot expect its military and national security agencies to think and respond asymmetrically during hostilities if these institutions cannot demonstrate similar abilities during peacetime. Asymmetrical warfare's characteristics may resemble the dynamic, uncertain environments anticipated in future conflicts. Thus, individuals comfortable with uncertainty and who perform well in unconstrained environments may be potential asymmetric-minded warriors required for developing appropriate solutions.

Remote viewers provided a glimpse of asymmetrically proficient warriors who are capable of, and comfortable with, abstract/agile thinking and performing. According to McMoneagle, a peculiar discovery resulting from operational experience was that certain targets enhanced remote viewer performances. For example, McMoneagle's accuracy ranged 80–90% when tasked with nuclear targets (McMoneagle interview). If a nuclear device were being smuggled into the United States, the ability to identify its exact, or even approximate, location could prove invaluable. Employing remote viewers to preclude or counter undesired events with nuclear characteristics represents an intriguing asymmetrical approach that could obviously be extended to additional attack modalities that leverage other remote viewers' aptitudes.

A current mantra regarding asymmetrical warfare is that future military opponents will exploit vulnerable seams to avoid attacking where the U.S. is strongest. The U.S. continues to lead and excel technologically, particularly in producing the world's most advanced weaponry.

Our technological superiority is our recognized strength and is precisely what our future adversaries will seek to avoid. Hence, what is the U.S. doing to prepare for the future conflicts beyond designing and producing more technologically advanced weaponry systems? What vulnerable seams are we identifying and preparing to defend, or are we continuing to build only upon our recognized strengths? Will the U.S. rely solely on technological solutions to asymmetrical problems? To prevail, our future enemies will likely be compelled to out-think and out-conceptualize us in imaginative and abstract ways.

## Transcendent Warfare

The real challenge for the United States is not asymmetrical warfare, but rather what this writer calls *transcendent* warfare, the ability to conceptualize and subsequently actualize an entirely new form of warfare that transcends all previously known models. Said ability could enable a nation state or other entity to redefine and to advance warfare to a completely different level or dimension, possibly comprehensible by only a selected but powerful few. Granted, transcendent warfare reflects Zen-like qualities that elude definition thereby making the above challenge more difficult. *Non-linear/multi-dimensional* and *abstract/metaphysical* are tentative terms that convey this concept, however, ascribing to a pat definition may in fact signal inability to comprehend the concept altogether.

Whereas asymmetrical warfare contemplates suspected, anticipated or potentially unforeseen threats/environments, transcendent warfare appears inconceivable or impossible as it moves beyond established reality parameters. Yet, herein lies its power and its threat. Is remote viewing a form of transcendent warfare? Quite possibly, since the observed performances and results garnered from the remote viewing program challenged existing reality parameters and established scientific principles.

Case in point: the discovery of a temporal/spatial effect (of cosmic dimension) that impacts human cognitive performance and serves as an intriguing yet transcendent-based result of the remote viewing program. Local Sidereal Time (LST) reflects the relationship between the center of our galaxy (Milky Way) and the earth's horizon in relation to an individual's location at any point on the earth. When the galaxy's center is below the earth's horizon, human cognitive and anomalous performance, such as remote viewing, dramatically improves by an order of magnitude as compared to when the galaxy's center is above the earth's horizon. An analogy might be a moving telescopic lens in front of an eye. When the lens lines up perfectly with the eye, vision is extremely enhanced, but only as long as the alignment lasts. In some cases, remote viewer performance improved by over four hundred percent when LST was included in the protocols (McMoneagle, p. 223).

Utilizing a transcendent approach, LST could be factored into the planning and execution of a military or government agency operation in order to maximize human potential, thereby enhancing mission success. The benefit of incorporating LST into operational planning and execution at the training level is overwhelmingly obvious and could provide a unique venue for better understanding human performance and heretofore unrecognized influences. Such an approach, however, would necessitate educating select military and/or government agency members in substantially expanding their existing perceptions of reality prior to training.

Transcendent warfare's impact extends well beyond remote viewing, which offers a glimpse of the possible. It also holds the potential for fundamentally shifting and expanding our current understanding of reality to such an extent that manipulation of established reality parameters, such as time, becomes possible if not plausible. The first nation or group that actualizes transcendent warfare will therefore possess a strategic advantage that may prove insurmountable.

## CONCLUSIONS/RECOMMENDATIONS

*". . . There is nothing more difficult to take in hand, or more perilous to conduct, or more uncertain of success than to take the lead in the introduction of a new order of things because the innovator has for enemies all those who have done well under the old condition, and lukewarm defenders in those who may do well under the new."*

—Machiavelli, *The Prince*, 1513

### Conclusions

Between 1972 and 1995, U.S. military and governmental organizations' remote viewing research and application demonstrated its effectiveness for accessing unique HUMINT unachievable via conventional intelligence collection methods. Spanning the spectrum of conflict, remote viewers provided crucial information from peacetime engagement to the tactical, operational and strategic levels of warfare. Yet, despite its successes, the program's 1995 termination likely resulted from internal mismanagement, CIA disinterest in assuming program management, lack of sufficient political and/or corporate sponsorship, and/or government organizations' inability to assimilate, or to be associated with, long-term unconventional or controversial programs.

The remote viewing program's termination represents a missed opportunity to more fully explore, let alone comprehend, a likely aspect of transcendent warfare. Arguably, governmental organizations' failure to more fully explore and develop the underlying nature of remote viewing, and human potential in particular, was the program's greatest shortfall as it was allowed to wither and die within conventional, symmetrically-oriented institutions. At some point if not already, U.S.

inability to conceptualize transcendent warfare and to effectively develop/employ creative asymmetrical responses to dynamic environments will be recognized and exploited by our adversaries. Unless our institutions become sufficiently innovative and flexible in fostering transcendent and/or asymmetrical processes, there is little reason to believe they can develop methods or programs for effectively dealing with future transcendent or asymmetrical threats.

[. . .]

## BIBLIOGRAPHY

Defense Intelligence Agency (DIA), 1978. "Paraphysics R&D—Warsaw Pact (U)," DST-1810S–202–78, DIA Task No. PT-1810–18–76, 30 March 1978. <http://www.dia.mil>.

Graff, Dale E. *River Dreams.* Boston: Element Books, 2000.

Gruber, Elmar R. *Psychic Wars: Parapsychology in Espionage—and Beyond.* London: Blandford, 1999.

Hyman, Ray. "Evaluation of a Program on Anomalous Mental Phenomena." *Journal of Scientific Exploration* 10, no. 1. Stanford, Calif., Society for Scientific Exploration, 1996.

Kress, Kenneth A. "Parapsychology in Intelligence: A Personal Review and Conclusions." 1977. <http://www.stargate.net-hed.co.ukcia1.htm>.

May, Edwin, C. "The American Institutes for Research Review of the Department of Defense's STAR GATE Program: A Commentary." *Journal of Scientific Exploration* 10, no. 1. Stanford, Calif., Society for Scientific Exploration, 1996.

McMoneagle, Joseph. *Remote Viewing Secrets: A Handbook.* Charlottesville, Va.: Hampton Roads Publishing Company, 2000.

McMoneagle, Joseph. Personal interview.

Nelson, R. D., B. J. Dunne, Y. H. Dobyns, and R. G. Jahn. "Precognitive Remote Perception: Replication of Remote Viewing." *Journal of Scientific Exploration* 10, no. 1. Stanford, Calif., Society for Scientific Exploration, 1996.

Puthoff, Harold, E. "CIA-Initiated Remote Viewing Program at Stanford Research Institute." *Journal of Scientific Exploration* 10, no. 1. Stanford, Calif., Society for Scientific Exploration, 1996.

Puthoff, Harold, E. Personal interview. 16 November 2000.

Schnabel, Jim. *Remote Viewers: The Secret History of America's Psychic Spies.* New York: Dell, 1997.

Smith, Paul. Personal interview. 16 November 2000.

Stubblebine, Albert, Major General (Ret.). Personal interview. 13 November 2000.

Swann, Ingo. Personal interview. 14 November 2000. [Editors' note: See also Ingo Swann, "Remote Viewing: The Real Story," 1996. Available from: http://www.biomindsuperpowers.com/Pages/2.html. Accessed 18 February 2007.]

Targ, Russell. "Remote Viewing at Stanford Research Institute in the 1970s: A Memoir." *Journal of Scientific Exploration* 10, no. 1. Stanford, Calif., Society for Scientific Exploration, 1996.

Utts, Jessica. "Response to Ray Hyman's Report of September 11, 1995 'Evaluation of Program on Anomalous Mental Phenomena.'" *Journal of Scientific Exploration* 10, no. 1. Stanford, Calif., Society for Scientific Exploration, 1996.

———. "An Assessment of the Evidence for Psychic Functioning." *Journal of Scientific Exploration* 10, no. 1. Stanford, Calif., Society for Scientific Exploration, 1996.

Typed transcriptions of the interviews with Stubblebine, Swann, Puthoff and Smith are available from the author of the study. Transcriptions are not available for the McMoneagle interview.

# PART IV

OVERVIEWS AND
REFLECTIONS ON PSI

# SKEPTICS AND DEBUNKERS OF THE PARANORMAL

## ARTICLE 11. ON SOME UNFAIR PRACTICES TOWARDS CLAIMS OF THE PARANORMAL, *by Marcello Truzzi, 1998.*

[Source: Marcello Truzzi, "On Some Unfair Practices Towards Claims of the Paranormal." Published, in slightly edited form, in Edward Binkowski, editor. *Oxymoron: Annual Thematic Anthology of the Arts and Sciences.* Vol. 2: *The Fringe.* New York: Oxymoron Media, 1998. Available from: http://www.skepticalinvestigations.org/anomalistics/practices.htm. Accessed 10 July 2006.]

### Editors' Comments

The late Marcello Truzzi (1935–2003), a professor of sociology at Eastern Michigan University, was extremely interested in the sociology of claims for and against the paranormal. Truzzi was a cofounder of the Committee for the Scientific Investigation of Claims of the Paranormal (CSICOP) in 1976, and a journal he founded, called *Explorations*, was renamed *The Zetetic* and became the official publication of CSICOP (the name was later changed to the *Skeptical Inquirer*). "Zetetic" was a term that

Truzzi popularized as an alternative to skeptic, as Truzzi felt many of the so-called skeptics were actually pseudo-skeptics (see above, page 20, and Truzzi, 1987). In fact, about a year after it was established, Truzzi broke with CSICOP over the one-sidedness of the committee; Truzzi wanted to include pro-paranormal advocates within the organization and to publish research that might support a pro-paranormal position. After leaving CSICOP, Truzzi established another journal, the *Zetetic Scholar*.

Truzzi published widely and was a consultant for the Time-Life Books series *Mysteries of the Unknown* (Time-Life Books, 1987, 1988, 1989). In his short biography therein, Truzzi identified himself as a "constructive skeptic" relative to claims of the paranormal; we like the spirit of the phrase. In the perceptive article reprinted below, Marcello Truzzi describes how different standards are often applied when evaluating evidence provided by parapsychologists than would be applied to evidence among other scientific disciplines.

## ON SOME UNFAIR PRACTICES TOWARDS CLAIMS OF THE PARANORMAL, *by Marcello Truzzi, 1998.*

The reception of unconventional or extraordinary claims in science has come under increasing attention by sociologists and historians. Scientific anomalies have sparked scientific revolutions, but such claims have had to fight prejudices within science. This essay offers scattered reflections on the adjudication process confronted by protoscientists (science "wannabes") wishing admission into the scientific mainstream. My comments here are not intended in support of proponents of the paranormal (for I remain a skeptic, as defined below) but to help produce a more level playing field and a greater fairness that might help all scientists.

### EQUILIBRIUM IN SCIENCE.

Philosopher Paul Feyerabend asserted that in a free society, science is too important to be left entirely to scientists. He had a point, for institutionalized Big Science has brought with it increased vested interests, some of which may threaten scientific growth itself. Though many historians and philosophers of science remind us that science needs to remain a tentative and open system, both fallible and probabilistic, science may, as do other human institutions, develop orthodoxies and even dogmas.

Historian Thomas Kuhn spoke of the "essential tension" in science between its conservative need to accumulate a body of tested knowledge and its progressive need for innovations from theory and data that might lead to new paradigms. So, a successful scientist performs like a circus wire–walker, engaged in a balancing act with closed minded arrogance weighted at one end of the balancing pole and open minded credulity weighted at the other. If either end pulls too far, a fall may follow.

Today, I think the balance has shifted too far towards arrogance. The emergence of a new and quasi-religious dogmatism, usually termed Scientism, has been examined and criticized from diverse standpoints in recent years, particularly those of Tom Sorell, Mary Midgley and Bryan Appleyard. Though some critics of Scientism take an anti-science stance, we need not go so far to recognize some current excesses. And though some postmodernists and others question the basic epistemology of science, my concern here is only with metaphysical debates over what phenomena science should judge to be "real," especially controversial claims for the reality of anomalies (ranging from alleged processes like extra-sensory perception and psychokinesis—the claims of the parasciences—to bizarre physical things like bigfoot and UFOs—the claims of the cryptosciences). My complaints here, then, are only with scientists' violations of their own professed method; in fact, I agree with those who contend that science fundamentally IS its method rather than its tentative substantive content.

ON IMPOSSIBILITIES AND ERRORS.
In their "Introduction" to No Way: The Nature of the Impossible, mathematician Philip J. Davis and physicist David Park concluded that

although we may have conceptions of the impossible, we cannot have absolute knowledge of it, for "There is no criterion of impossibility." In line with this, philosopher Charles Sanders Peirce earlier argued that our first obligation must be to do nothing that might block inquiry. Yet, some, claiming to speak in the name of science now demand doors be closed on many subjects. Although science can only assert that extraordinary events are highly improbable, some critics speak of "laws of denial" as though we can prejudge some empirical events impossible so unnecessary to investigate. Such defenders of the *status quo* often engage in ridicule and sarcastic rhetoric that is deemed uncivil in normal scientific discourse, and sociologists of science Harry M. Collins and Trevor J. Pinch have gone so far as to characterize some such activities as scientific "vigilantism."

Such defenses of orthodoxy are not surprising, and they typically stem from an honest desire to avoid mistakenly thinking *something* special is happening when it really is not (what statisticians have termed a Type I Error). This error is embodied in the aphorism "all that glitter is not gold." However, proponents of esoteric claims are often more concerned with avoiding the mistake of thinking *nothing* special is going on when it actually is (the statistician's Type II Error). Their attitude is exemplified by the folk maxim that we "should not throw the baby out with the bath water." These contrasting types of error, and our need to follow a path avoiding both, are central to Kuhn's "essential tension" in science; and I think much of the difference between proponents and critics of extraordinary claims in science may center on which of these two types of error is designated as the more dangerous. The Chinese character for "crisis" consists of combining the symbols for "danger" and "opportunity." Such is the case with the paradigm crisis inherent in an extraordinary science claim, usually consisting of an alleged anomaly (a fact in search of theory). Conservatives in science typically view anomalies as dangers (threats to currently accepted theories) whereas progressives (proponents) of such claims see them as "opportunities" (stimulants for theory reconstruction).

## On Heresy, Scientism and Discrediting the Paranormal

As conservative science confronts the threat of anomalies, it may defend itself with excessive zeal. So much so that some organized critics of anomalies have even been characterized as a "New Inquisition" seeking to stamp out the heresies against an orthodoxy of Scientism. Ironically, since he was himself a prominent critic of many anomaly claims, Isaac Asimov distinguished between "exoheretics" (outsiders to a field) versus "endoheretics" (insiders or professional colleagues) in science. Endoheretics are usually accorded greater courtesy than are exoheretics. Thus, I have found, endoheretics are more likely to be described as "cranks" (tenacious) and as making "errors," while exoheretics are openly called "crackpots" (crazy) and are accused of "fraud." The strongest pejorative labels such as "pseudoscience" and "pathology" tend to be ascribed to the claims and methods of exoheretics.

In the effort to discredit anomaly claims, critics often characterized them as "miracles," and any connections with past religious or occult support tends to get them labelled "supernatural" or "magical." This is particularly unfortunate, because terms like "paranormal" were originally introduced to naturalize the supernatural. Protoscientific proponents of the paranormal insist that the paranormal is part of the natural order and consists of anomalies amenable to scientific investigation and possible verification. While occultists and theologians have recognized this difference between the paranormal and the supernatural, many "scientific" critics merely lump them together as "transcendental nonsense." Because of this, many critics of the paranormal mistakenly invoke David Hume's famous argument against miracles when dealing with claims of the paranormal. In fact, Hume distinguished between merely extraordinary events and miracles (which must involve divine volition and a suspension of the laws of nature). Most critics of the paranormal seem unaware of the voluminous literature distinguishing "marvels" (anomalies of nature) from "miracles." A major practical consequence of such semantic confusion is the false impression that anomalies can largely be discredited *a priori* so need no further investigation. Such rhetoric thus blocks inquiry.

As psychologist Ray Hyman has noted, many scientists may be more interested in discrediting than in disproving claims of the extraordinary. This can lead to poor scholarship and methods below normal professional standards, and it also results in *ad hominem* attacks and rhetorical tricks rather than solid falsification. Hyman noted it can also lead to the use of "hit men" (nonscientists such as journalists or even magicians) encouraged to discredit the claimants. Such nonscientists have argued about the need to "fight fire with fire" and the advantages of "horse-laughs" over arguments and evidence. Such counterattacks themselves constitute a form of pathology within science. As philosopher (and critic of the paranormal) Mario Bunge put it: "the occasional pressure to suppress it [dissent] in the name of the orthodoxy of the day is even more injurious to science than all the forms of pseudoscience put together."

## SKEPTICS OR SCOFFERS?

Perhaps the most insidious rhetorical trick has been the misappropriation of the label "skeptic" to describe what are actually *scoffers*. As sociologist Robert K. Merton pointed out, organized skepticism is a fundamental norm in science. However, the term skepticism is properly defined as *doubt,* not *denial*. It is a position of agnosticism, of nonbelief rather than disbelief. The true skeptic (a doubter) asserts no claim, so has no burden of proof. However, the scoffer (denier) asserts a *negative* claim, so the burden of proof science places on any claimant must apply. When scoffers misrepresent their position as a form of "hard-line" skepticism, they really seek escape from their burden to prove a negative position.

Perhaps the greatest confusion related to the needed distinction between skeptics and scoffers concerns their different reactions to the failure by a claimant to support an anomaly claim. The skeptics' attitude towards extraordinary claims (for example, those of parapsychology) where proponents have so far produced inadequate evidence to convince most scientists that their hypotheses about anomalies are true is characterized as a case *not proven*. A skeptic contends that "the absence of evidence is not evidence of absence." The scoffer, on the other hand, sees the failure of proponents as evidence that an anomaly claim has been *disproved*. The perspective of the scoffer, as with most dogmatists, tends to distinguish only black from white and fails to acknowledge gray areas. (Our criminal justice system may likewise be too dichotomous. Thus, similar reasoning led some citizens to conclude that the murder acquittal of O.J. Simpson meant he was judged innocent when he was merely found to be not guilty. Science might better follow the path of Scottish Law which allows for three possible judgements: guilty, not guilty or innocent, and not proven.) Scoffers use a similar foreshortening towards issues of evidence. It is common to hear statements to the effect that "there is no evidence supporting a claim" when in fact it is merely *inadequate* evidence that has been presented. Evidence is always a matter of degree, some being extremely weak; but even weak evidence can mount up (as shown by meta-analysis) to produce a stronger case. Weak evidence (most commonly anecdotal rather than systematic and experimental evidence) is often discounted, however, by assertions that it falls below some threshold of what science should consider evidence at all. This, of course, eliminates the evidential basis for most of clinical medicine and the social sciences, but that seems to hold no terror for the scoffer who invokes such criteria.

## SHIFTING GOAL POSTS AND RUBBER RULERS.

As proponents of anomalies produce stronger evidence, critics have sometimes moved the goal posts further away. This is especially clear in the case of parapsychology. To convince scientists of what had been merely supported by widespread but weak anecdotal evidence, parapsychologists moved psychical research into the laboratory. When experimental results were presented, designs were criticized. When protocols were improved, a "fraud proof" or "critical experiment" was demanded.

When those were put forward, replications were demanded. When those were produced, critics argued that new forms of error might be the cause (such as the "file drawer" error that could result from unpublished negative studies). When meta-analyses were presented to counter that issue, these were discounted as controversial, and ESP was reduced to being some present but unspecified "error some place" in the form of what Ray Hyman called the "dirty test tube argument" (claiming dirt was in the tube making the seeming psi result a mere artifact). And in one instance, when the scoffer found no counter-explanations, he described the result as a "mere anomaly" not to be taken seriously so just belonging on a puzzle page. The goal posts have now been moved into a zone where some critics hold unfalsifiable positions.

Scoffers are typically quick to demand good methodology when dealing with extraordinary claims, insisting on such things as replications, control groups, double-blind experiments, and the rule of parsimony (Ockham's Razor). They often write of the cognitive fallacies committed by paranormalists. In the process, however, they overlook the same need for rigor in many areas they defend. Thus, alternative medicine is denounced for its failure to demonstrate claims with proper experiments, ignoring the absence of experimental evidence in many areas of orthodox medicine (for example, in surgery). And scoffers denounce "psychic" counsellors but don't bother to do controlled experiments comparing them to orthodox advisors such as psychiatrists, clinical psychologists, and social workers.

Psychologists who complain about inadequate replication levels in parapsychology seem unaware of the dismal record of replication with conventional psychology. They also fail to note that what constitutes a replication is itself often a matter of controversy, and, as Harry Collins has shown, often involves social negotiation.

Astronomers who inveigh against neo-astrology seem unbothered by the nonfalsifiability of many current fashions in their own cosmological theories, and they seem to have forgotten that gravity was once rejected by Newton's fellow scientists over the assertion that there could be "action at a distance." Scoffers seem to assume a unity in science, forgetting that history reveals many disagreements among science's branches, such as physicist Lord Kelvin's (then reasonable) arguments against Darwin's theory of evolution since the sun was too young to allow the time Darwin's theory required (fusion had not yet been discovered).

The rule of parsimony asserts that the simplest adequate theory should be preferred, but, as Mario Bunge has shown in his book on the subject, the concept of simplicity is far from a simple matter. In addition, the presumption that conventional explanations adequately cover extraordinary claims is usually the very issue at hand, so invoking parsimony can sometimes beg the question.

When criticizing the paranormal, scientists who are scoffers usually fail to bring the same professional standards expected of them in their own fields. This is particularly evident when one looks at their praise for articles reporting experiments on the paranormal that obtained negative results. Some of these articles contain questionable methods and conclusions and probably would never have passed peer review had they shown positive results.

EXTRAORDINARY CLAIMS VERSUS EXTRAORDINARY PROOF.
In his famous 1748 essay *Of Miracles,* the great skeptic David Hume asserted that "A wise man . . . proportions his belief to the evidence," and he said of testimony for extraordinary claims that "the evidence, resulting from the testimony, admits of a diminution, greater or less, in proportion as the fact is more unusual." A similar statement was made by Laplace, and many other later writers. I turned it into the now popular phrase "extraordinary claims require extraordinary proof" (which Carl Sagan popularized into what is almost the war cry of some scoffers). As anomalistic psychologists Leonard Zusne and Warren H. Jones observed, this demand "may be not only used but misused to the point where no amount of evidence of a paranormal claim will avail against a skeptic who has already prejudged the issue." The central problem however lies in the fact that "extraordinary" must be relative to some things "ordinary" and as our theories change, what was once extraordinary

may become ordinary (best seen in now accepted quantum effects that earlier were viewed as "impossible"). Many now extraordinary claims may become more acceptable not when they are replicated but when theoretical contexts change to make them more welcome.

## A Catch-22 in the Burden of Proof?

In criminal law, the burden of proof is assigned to the prosecution; in the court of science, it is placed on the defender of the deviant science claim. Whereas, in our British-based legal system, the defendant is presumed innocent until proven guilty, in science the maverick scientist is presumed "guilty" (of error) until proven "innocent." This is appropriate since science must basically be conservative in its own defense against myriad would-be invaders. But it is important to remember that the proponent of the paranormal has an uphill battle from the start. The chips are stacked against him, so his assault is not so threatening to the fabric of science as scoffers often characterize it. In a sense, conservative science has "the law" on its side.

In law, we find three varieties in the weight of burden of proof:

1. proof by preponderance of evidence,
2. clear and convincing proof, and, in criminal law,
3. proof beyond a reasonable doubt.

In conventional science, we usually use (1), but when dealing with extraordinary claims, critics often seem to demand (3) since they demand all alternative explanations must be eliminated before the maverick claim is acceptable. This demand sometimes becomes unreasonable and may even make the scoffer's position unfalsifiable. Since the anomaly proponent is already saddled with a presumption of "guilt," it would seem to me that (2), clear and convincing proof, might be the best standard, though proponents may reasonably wonder why standard (1) should always be denied them.

## A Recommendation

In addition to recognizing and working through the issues I have raised above, we need scaled terms to deal with levels of evidence for the best of the extraordinary claims put forth by protoscientists. Scientists might well distinguish between extraordinary claims that are: *suggestive,* meaning interesting and worthy of attention but generally of low priority; *compelling,* meaning the evidence is strongly supportive and argues for assigning a higher scientific priority for greater investigation; and *convincing,* meaning most reasonable scientists examining the evidence would agree at least a preponderance of evidence supports the claim. Using such graded language might help us turn from our present debates, with room only for winners and losers, into dialogues between peers, all of whom should want to see science judiciously progress. We can all be winners.

# THE ELUSIVE NATURE OF PSI

## ARTICLE 12. WHAT IS BEYOND THE EDGE OF THE KNOWN WORLD? *by Jean E. Burns, 2003.*

[Source: Jean E. Burns, "What Is Beyond the Edge of the Known World?" Copyright Imprint Academic. Originally published in *Journal of Consciousness Studies* 10, nos. 6–7, pp. 7–28 (2003). Also published in *Psi Wars: Getting to Grips with the Paranormal,* edited by James Alcock, Jean Burns, and Anthony Freeman. Charlottesville, Va., and Exeter, UK: Imprint Academic, 2003, pp. 7–28.]

### Editors' Comments

Dr. Jean E. Burns is a physicist who combines her knowledge and skills in physics with a deep interest in the nature of consciousness. She is a founding associate editor of the *Journal of Consciousness Studies*. In this selection Burns summarizes much of what we know about psi, and also addresses some of the nagging issues that remain. Why is psi so elusive? What kind of physical theory can account for psi? The latter question is addressed further in the selection by Paul Stevens (p. 300).

## WHAT IS BEYOND THE EDGE OF THE KNOWN WORLD?
*by Jean E. Burns, 2003.*

### ABSTRACT
*Experiments show that psi differs from known physical processes in a variety of ways, and these differences are described herein. Because of these, psi cannot be accounted for in terms of presently known physical laws. A number of theories, of which we review a sampling, suggest ways in which known physical laws might be expanded in order to account for psi. However, there is no agreement on which of these theories, if any, will ultimately provide a general explanation. A further problem in studying psi is that it is elusive, i.e., methods are not presently known by which it can be reliably produced. However, if psi is real, its study can open the door to a new frontier of knowledge and contribute to our understanding of consciousness.*

In the early fifteenth century it was not thought possible to sail past Cape Bojador on the northwest coast of Africa. Maps of the time showed Jerusalem at the centre of the world, with the continents of Europe, Africa and Asia arranged symmetrically around it. Surrounding them was an ocean called the "Great Outer Sea of Boundless Extent."

However, in previous years there had been improvements in both ship-building and navigation, with the compass coming into common use. So Prince Henry of Portugal became determined to send an expedition around Cape Bojador. Many expeditions failed, each time for a different reason, but finally one succeeded. Soon thereafter Portuguese sailors travelled around the southern tip of Africa and then to

India. A few years after that Columbus set sail across the Atlantic. The attempts to travel past the edge of the known world were successful (Spar, 2001).

The present search by parapsychologists to understand psi in many ways resembles the search for a way to travel past Cape Bojador. As then, there are no maps to provide guidance. Present-day technology and experimental methodologies can help make the search. But is there only boundless ocean (no psi phenomena) beyond present knowledge? Is there any land (phenomena) at all? If psi exists and we can come to understand it, the rewards of new knowledge could be great. So far parapsychology has had some encouraging views of what may be land, and indications of what that land is like (if it's there), as we will see below. But, in this analogy, parapsychologists have yet to round Cape Bojador.

More specifically, and as we will see in further detail in the following sections, present knowledge of psi (or what appears to be psi) is as follows. Experiments show that it differs from known physical processes in a variety of ways. On the other hand, correlations of psi with some physical variables are known (e.g., local sidereal time), although the reasons for these correlations are not known. There are a number of theoretical models for psi (we will review a sampling), but there is no generally accepted theory of it. Finally, psi is elusive, in that the psychological conditions which produce it are not well understood and it cannot reliably be produced at any given time. Indeed, some major efforts to replicate experiments have failed to produce a detectable amount of psi, as we will see. In order to be considered an established phenomenon, it would seem that either a theory should be known which explains the differences between psi and presently known physics and gives testable predictions, or at least it should be possible to reliably produce it. But neither is the case at present.

We should note that there are two types of psi usually studied in parapsychology experiments: extrasensory perception (ESP) and psychokinesis (PK). ESP refers to the transfer of information without using any known physical mechanism, and PK refers to the action of mental intention on matter without using any known physical mechanism.

## Ways in Which Psi Differs from Presently Known Physical Principles

Psi appears to follow principles which are very different from the presently known laws governing the physical world. For one thing, a variety of experiments have shown that the distance between source/sender and effect/receiver makes no difference to results (Jahn and Dunne, 1987; Rao, 2001). In presently known physics nearly all influences decrease inversely as the square of the distance involved. The only exception, quantum non-locality, can only influence correlations between random sequences—it cannot transfer any information (Eberhard, 1978) and so cannot account for psi effects. (We will examine this point in more detail in the section on Theories of Psi. For now we need only note that unless conventional physics is modified in some way, quantum non-locality cannot explain the transfer of information by psi.)

Another difference is that in presently known physics all transfer of information involves a signal (which can travel no faster than the velocity of light). The transmission of information by psi is presumably not instantaneous, because that possibility is contrary to special relativity.[1] However, no physical signal has ever been found. Electromagnetic signals, which would be the obvious thing to look for, have been ruled out because numerous experiments have shown that psi results can be obtained even when the receiver is shielded by a Faraday cage (Stokes, 1997).[2]

Another distinction between psi and physical effects is the way they depend on surrounding conditions. A physical result depends on various conditions, at varying distances and locations, as specified by physical laws. But a person who responds via psi to some distant event does not respond to the totality of conditions which could produce a physical effect, but only to some particular event which has meaning to him or

---

1. An instantaneous signal can define an absolute time, the same in all inertial frames, and special relativity does not permit this.

2. The possibility that psi is carried by extremely low frequency (ELF) electromagnetic waves has been explored, as these could penetrate some Faraday cages. However, such waves can be ruled out because their capacity for carrying information is very low (Puthoff and Targ, 1979).

her. No explanation is known of how this selective response can be produced.

## Classical and quantum randomness

In order to understand the relationship of psi to randomness, we should first understand the way randomness appears in presently known physics. First we should make a distinction between (a) events that merely follow a random pattern because they are determined by a large number of independent causes and (b) events that are quantum random. The first type of events can be described in terms of classical (deterministic) physics, and we will refer to these as "classically random." An example would be the flipping of a coin, because the results of each coin flip depends on random air currents, the way it is thrown, etc. On the other hand, quantum random events are inherently unpredictable, i.e., it is not possible to completely describe them in terms of specific causes. An example of a quantum random event is the location where a photon arrives on photographic film in the double slit experiment (a well-known experiment in physics). The pattern the photons make when many have arrived can be predicted—it is a series of bright lines. Furthermore, any individual photon must arrive at a place where a bright line, not a dark one, will be when the full pattern is made. However, aside from that, the location where any individual photon arrives is quantum random—inherently unpredictable. The process is like assembling a jigsaw puzzle, with the pieces being added in random order. You always get the same picture at the end, and the randomness only has to do with which piece is added next.

Quantum randomness is associated with a phenomenon called collapse of the wave function. However, the phenomenon of collapse is not well understood. The problem is that although the equations of quantum mechanics can be used to make detailed predictions about physics experiments, collapse is not described by these equations, but is separate from them.[3] So physicists do not agree on what collapse is and

---

3. This distinction is explained in detail by Penrose (1989).

when or whether it occurs. A minority of physicists say there is no such thing as collapse (e.g. Bohm and Riley, 1993; Etter and Noyes, 1999). However, most physicists consider collapse to be an objective physical event. Some say it occurs regardless of whether an observer is present, but others say it can only occur in the presence of a conscious observer. (For examples of interpretations of collapse, see Freeman (2003) and Herbert (1985).)

Does quantum randomness affect our daily lives? Most physicists agree that collapse occurs when measuring instruments are used which are designed to detect quantum events, although the latter group would require a conscious observer also. For instance, in the double slit experiment, most physicists who say that no conscious observer is needed would say that collapse occurs when each photon reaches the film. But the group who says an observer is needed would say that collapse occurs when a conscious observer views the film. However, events in people's lives do not usually depend on the results of such experiments. Most physicists would probably also agree that collapse takes place in nature even without the presence of scientific measuring instruments, although why, when or how it takes place is not understood. Many physicists in the first group (no conscious observer needed) would probably agree that collapse takes place at the molecular level. But events in people's lives do not ordinarily depend on events at the molecular level and so would not depend on quantum randomness. Most physicists in the second group (conscious observer needed) would probably feel that collapse takes place at the macroscopic level. Even so, probably most events in people's lives would be viewed as determined by classical physics, but some events might depend on quantum randomness. So we can answer the above question by saying that in some interpretations of quantum mechanics quantum randomness might sometimes affect our daily lives. We will leave the possibility open.

We should note, however, that experiments in parapsychology laboratories make use of microscopic events involving quantum randomness, such as radioactive decay or quantum tunnelling. So the random sequences produced in these experiments can depend on quantum randomness. Let us now go on to see how randomness is involved with precognition and psychokinesis, and the issues each raises with respect to presently known physics.

## Precognition

The way random processes play a part in precognition experiments is that targets are usually chosen randomly after the subject's guesses have been recorded. Sometimes this process uses mechanical shufflers or the like and is obviously classically random. Sometimes a quantum random process is used. For instance, a subject might try to predict the time when an electron from radioactive decay is detected by a Geiger counter (Schmidt, 1969). The reader is probably asking at this point, given that quantum processes are inherently unpredictable, does precognition work for these? No formal study has been done which compares precognition results for targets selected in a classical random process with those for targets selected in a quantum random process. However, no obvious differences in the two types of experiment have been noted, and it appears that precognition works about as well for quantum randomness as it does for classical randomness. No explanation is known for how this can be.

One way to learn how precognition works is to model various possibilities and see which model(s) the data fit best. One possibility is that a person learns about present conditions through clairvoyance (ESP in present time) and then makes a rough extrapolation into the future. In this way the future could be known roughly, but not accurately. In another possibility we can assume that the macroscopic events of the future are entirely pre-specified and can be displayed in a Great Cosmic Record in the Sky. In order to know a future event a person would simply have to find the relevant place in the Record, presumably an easier task than in the former case. But we should also allow for the possibility of a future that changes. We will allow for the possibility that quantum randomness can affect the course of some daily events. Also, views differ on whether we have free will, but if we do, this also would affect the future. We can describe the third model as the Great

Cosmic Website in the Sky, connected to everything and constantly updated.[4]

According to the first model, precognition involves not only knowledge of present conditions, but also extrapolation of these conditions into the future. Not all of the conditions which affect the future might be taken into account, or the projections might be inaccurate, so this method would presumably be less successful than clairvoyance. In the second model, precognition and clairvoyance would be equally successful. In the third model, precognition would be about as successful in some circumstances, but not in others, depending on the possibilities for change. A meta-analysis which compared the results of precognition and clairvoyance experiments done up to that time shows that these were approximately equally successful (Steinkamp et al., 1998). This study would seem to support Models 2 or 3, but not Model 1.

Further light can be shed on comparisons of the models by some recent experiments which have determined the precognitive target in more complex ways. Specifically, the precognitive target was determined from the closing price of a specific stock, together with the temperature of a world city, on a certain date (Steinkamp, 2000). Because weather is sensitive to a large number of conditions and stock prices involve many individual decisions, the target would depend on a complex array of factors. One experiment showed significant results for the clairvoyance target, but chance results for the precognition target

---

4. This model could work in the following way. The Cosmic Website could track all present physical conditions and project the future according to the mathematical laws of physics. The specific outcome of a quantum random event is inherently non-computable, as we have seen, but each time one occurs the Website updates. Because all physical conditions are tracked, the patterns in people's brains which describe their present intentions are also tracked and the effects of these intentions are included in the display of the future. If free will exists, then by its nature it cannot be described by a mathematical formula (otherwise it would not be free). (For an analysis of the physics involved, see Mohrhoff (1999).) However, each time a free-will decision is made which produces physical action or simply affects intentions in the brain, the Website updates. For the most part free-will decisions are conditioned by the brain, and any changes to the future are small, but sometimes a more substantial change is made.

(Steinkamp, 2000). This finding would support Model 1 and Model 3 (the latter because of the dependence on volition and perhaps quantum randomness), but not Model 2. However, follow-up studies have not shown significant results in either category, although with near significance for precognition in some cases (Steinkamp, 2001), so results are inconclusive.

We can distinguish between the models in another way. According to Model 1 there would be a decrease in accuracy as the period between prediction and the actual event increases because of the increased difficulty in making an estimate. In Model 2 the time period probably would not matter, and in Model 3 it might matter somewhat, depending on conditions. Time intervals described in anecdotal accounts range from minutes or hours to years. (Anecdotal cases in which the time period is a year or more are usually dreams (Stokes, 1997).) Analyses of several collections of anecdotal accounts show that the number of accounts reported decreases with increasing time interval, but the accuracy and number of details stays about the same (Stokes, 1997). However, anecdotal accounts can be subject to selective reporting, so these results are inconclusive. Time intervals involved in laboratory experiments on precognition vary from seconds to several days or longer. A meta-analysis of precognition experiments which explored whether success depends on the period between prediction and actual event was also inconclusive (Honorton and Ferrari, 1989),[5] so this question remains open.

Probably our best conclusion as regards the models is that not enough is known to decide which ones fit the data better, and further experimental work is needed. However, given that precognition is (by definition) the

---

5. The data of the meta-analysis shows a decrease in results with increasing time periods. However, this result is not consistent among different subgroups of subjects, and Honorton and Ferrari (1989) suggest that the difference in results between subgroups might be accounted for by differences in motivational factors. Therefore, as Stokes (1997) points out, the overall results may depend on these factors rather than precognitive attrition. Stokes (1997) also reviews other experimental findings, but does not find conclusive evidence for precognitive attrition.

ability of a person to predict a future event which is determined by factors not known to that person by any presently known physical means, we can conclude that precognition is not explained by presently known physical laws.

## Psychokinesis

Experiments on PK can be generally described as follows. Because it is a small effect, experiments to investigate it are usually designed to produce a random sequence of events, with the goal of influencing this sequence to be non-random. Statistical analysis can then be made to detect PK. Tumbling cubes (dice) and devices called random event generators (REGs), which produce binary bit sequences (0's and 1's) from a random source such as electronic noise, are often used in experiments (Radin, 1997).

A random sequence has on average an equal number of 0's and 1's, and an operator (person attempting to use PK) tries to produce more 0's in half her target sequences and more 1's in the other half. Meta-analysis shows that operators can successfully produce these desired shifts (Radin, 1997). The distribution of bits in a random sequence has the shape of a Gaussian curve with a mid-point at zero. The distribution of bits in a set of PK trials will have the same shape, but the mid-point will be slightly shifted towards more 1's when the goal is 1's and slightly shifted towards more 0's when the goal is 0's (Jahn and Dunne, 1987). In each case the curve as a whole is shifted, and this can be interpreted to mean that the effect of the intention of the operator is to alter the probability of each event from 50/50 to a slight bias favouring the desired result (Jahn and Dunne, 1987). In this respect PK seems able to produce an ordering of random physical processes, with the direction of ordering associated with the intention of the operator. It is not known how this can occur.

In addition to trials in which the operator holds an intention, two other types of trials can be made. First, all experiments include control runs (also called calibration runs), which simply ensure that the random sequences being produced continue to be random when no operator is present. Also, some laboratories include runs, called baseline runs, in which the operator is present but is instructed to hold no intention. Baseline runs typically show no shift in the Gaussian curve, as would be expected. But curiously, a very large number of trials shows the consistent result that in this case the width of the curve (a measure of a statistical quantity called the variance) is narrower than in the control runs (Jahn and Dunne, 1987). It is as if the operator, in an effort to have no intention, decreases the variation normally present in a random sequence in some sort of unconscious process.

It has recently been found, in separate investigations by Pallikari (2003; Pallikari and Boller, 1999) and Schmidt (2000a, 2000b), that in the PK datasets they analysed, sequences of bits cluster more than they would in a random sequence. In other words, in a random sequence there will be two consecutive 1's or two consecutive 0's a certain proportion of the time, three consecutive 1's or three consecutive 0's a smaller proportion of the time, and so forth. But in the above datasets, analysis using a statistical measure of correlations within a sequence showed that the same bit appeared consecutively, or nearby, more often than random.[6] This is called the "gluing effect" by Pallikari (2003) and "bunching" by Schmidt (2000a, 2000b). Pallikari (2003) did not find the gluing effect in a baseline run she analysed. However, aside from that, little is presently known about this effect, e.g. whether it occurs consistently in PK runs or is sporadic,[7] whether an anti-correlation effect is sometimes produced, and similar questions.

PK results (shifting of the mean) appear to be independent of physical parameters involved in producing a random sequence when comparisons are made between parameters which are not markedly different. For instance, in experiments using tumbling cubes results do not seem to depend on whether only a few or up to ninety-six cubes are used at a

---

6. Pallikari and Boller (1999) used a Hurst exponent for their analysis, and Schmidt (2000a) used a new measure which he developed.

7. Stanford (1977) summarizes several early experiments which looked for clustering (which he also called "stringing") of PK hits and misses. These experiments did not find such an effect, which implies that it does not always occur.

time (Stanford, 1977). In a similar vein, when operators were presented with interspersed trials from two REGs, with results from one depending on one binary bit and results from the other depending on one hundred binary bits, results from the two machines were not significantly different (Schmidt, 1974).[8] However, in a scaled-up version of the latter experiment, with results depending on two hundred and two million bits, respectively, results were significantly better for the machine which presented the *larger* number of bits (Ibison, 1998). Further experiments would need to be done in order to confirm this result. However, assuming it is confirmed, no explanation is known of why PK results would be better when a larger number of bits must be acted on.

It has also been found that if two unrelated people both hold the intention to influence an REG, the result is somewhat better than if only one does it (Dunne, 1993). If the two people have a close relationship, results are about four times better than those of a single operator (Dunne, 1993). Experiments also show that if a large number of people hold a common focus of interest, REGs can be affected during the time this focus is held. For instance, during an Academy Award ceremony, which had a worldwide television audience of about one billion people, REGs showed non-random results during times of high interest, such as opening an envelope to give an award, but normal random behaviour at other times. Similarly, during the Opening Ceremonies of the 1996 Olympic Games, watched by about three billion people, REGs became non-random, but operated normally before and after (Radin, 1997).

### Time-displaced PK, the experimenter-psi effect, and the complexity of psi targets

Experiments show that if a random sequence is entirely specified—for instance, by a mathematical algorithm—no PK results can be produced

---

8. In an earlier experiment Schmidt (1973) found that if binary trials were presented at two different rates, operators did better at the lower rate. However, because of the rate difference the operators had conscious knowledge of which machine they were using in each trial, and this could have predisposed them towards a preference for the lower rate.

on that sequence (Jahn and Dunne, 1987), a finding which is not at all surprising. (The latter type of sequence is called pseudorandom.) But then what are we to make of the following experiment (Schmidt, 1976), which has shown the same basic result in many replications over the past twenty-five years? The experimenter records a series of random sequences, which are physically random (e.g., from radioactive decay), not pseudorandom. He does not look at the results, but makes a copy (by automated means) to present to the operator, and places the master copy in a safe place. The operator then plays the recorded copy and attempts to influence the sequences, just as though he were experiencing them in real time. Common sense would say that the operator cannot possibly affect them because they have already been recorded. However, when the data is examined, it shows PK results in accordance with the intention the operator was instructed to hold. (The copy of the data the operator acted on is identical to the master copy, so the data itself was presumably not changed.) This effect is called "time–displaced PK." (The name derives from some of the proposed explanations for the effect.)

Three explanations for this phenomenon have been considered in parapsychology. The first is called the "experimenter-psi effect." This explanation notes that more than one person can affect the outcome of a PK experiment, and the persons who affect it are not necessarily aware of their effect. So PK results can be produced by the experimenter and/or any other persons involved in the experiment, not only the so–called operator. In early versions of the above experiment (Schmidt, 1976) the operator was instructed by the experimenter as to what intention (target) to hold, so the experimenter could have produced the PK. In later experiments, sometimes a third person specified the targets after the data had been recorded (Schmidt, 1993). In that case the experimenter might foresee by precognition the targets the third person will choose and produce these by PK. Alternatively, the third person could use ESP at an unconscious level (with this faculty perhaps augmented by linkage to the experimenter and others involved in the experiment). By this means he or she could learn the pattern present in the recorded sequence and then choose targets that best fit this pattern.

Another explanation, proposed by Helmut Schmidt, the originator of these experiments, is that PK can only occur when a conscious observer collapses the quantum mechanical wave function (Schmidt, 1982). Because nobody has observed the data until the operator acts on it, the operator in that case would be able to produce PK results. (Presumably the master copy and the operator's copy would collapse simultaneously.) Schmidt tested this hypothesis by giving a group of operators sequences of randomly interspersed pre-observed and non-pre-observed data. However, the results were inconclusive (Schmidt and Stapp, 1993), and the question of whether pre-observation has any effect is unresolved.

A third, rather exotic, possibility is that psi signals can travel backwards in time (theories reviewed by Stokes, 1987; 1997; see also Shoup, 2002). In that case the operator would hold the intention to affect the data, and the psi signal would then travel backwards in time to affect what had happened earlier.

Although the experimenter-psi effect would seem to provide a simple explanation for the above experiments, a possible problem for this explanation is that in later experiments the specification of the PK targets has become more complex. For instance, in a set of experiments done by Helmut Schmidt with various third parties, the pre-recorded data was divided into consecutive blocks. (No one saw the data before target assignment; it was simply identified by blocks.) The third party assigned the targets by obtaining a copy of a pre-specified newspaper and then deriving a 6-digit seed number from the last digits in a pre-specified weather column. This number was used to determine an entry point into a random number table, and the random sequence generated by that entry point then determined the targets for the consecutive blocks of data (Schmidt, 1993; Schmidt and Stapp, 1993). Obviously, all the targets were determined by the seed number obtained from the weather readings.

The experiments using the above procedure cumulatively showed a significant deviation from the mean (Schmidt, 1993). This result can be explained by experimenter-psi if the experimenter (with his efforts perhaps augmented by unconscious linkage to others involved in each experiment) knew the 6-digit seed numbers by precognition, accessed the random number table by ESP, and then produced data by PK which conformed to the targets.[9] However, this process is obviously very complex.

Can psi use a process that is this complex? We saw earlier that PK results appear to be improved when they depend on a larger number of bits. On the other hand, it is inconclusive as to whether precognition results can be obtained in a process as complex as this. Whether time-displaced PK can be explained in terms of the experimenter-psi effect depends on the limitations, presently unknown, as to what psi can do.

Although PK itself is not explained by presently-known physics, the time-displaced aspect of the above experiments is not actually that far from it. If the explanation is experimenter-psi, there is no time displacement. Although the explanation for collapse of the wave function is not considered established in contemporary physics, collapse by a conscious observer is among the hypotheses considered. Because the dynamical equations of physics fulfil a condition called "time reversibility," the possibility of a signal travelling backwards in time is allowed by these equations (Shoup, 2002).

## CORRELATIONS OF PSI WITH PHYSICAL EFFECTS

When information reaches a person via psi, in whatever way this may occur, this information evidently has to be processed by the brain before the person can use it. One reason for this conclusion is that event-related potentials (negative slow wave at 150–500 msec) are associated with the presentation of psi targets (McDonough et al., 2002).

Another reason for this conclusion comes from comparison with the way the brain processes sensory data—it is sensitive to differences in physical quantities, such as light intensity or sound intensity, and processes

---

9. An alternative, more exotic, possibility is that the experimenter, linked with others in the experiment, affected the weather readings by PK to produce targets which fit fluctuations in the data sequences.

these differences, rather than absolute levels. In a similar vein, although there is some scatter in the data, several parapsychology experiments suggest that pictures which have a greater change in the variation of light intensity when different parts of the picture are compared (indicating a more complex picture at the sensory level) produce better psi results than those which have less change in the variation of light intensity (May et al., 1994; 2000).[10] This suggests that the brain processes incoming psi information at a basic sensory level.

Additionally, Millay (1999) has shown that colours and shapes transmit better than the conceptual understanding of what these represent, which also suggests that incoming psi data enters the brain at a basic sensory level.

Incoming psi data can also produce physiological effects. For instance, experiments have shown that if one person attempts to influence another by psi, the recipient shows physiological effects such as changes in skin conductivity (Braud and Schlitz, 1991; Radin, 1997; Schlitz and LaBerge, 1997). Physiological effects can also occur precognitively. When emotionally provocative pictures are shown, skin conductance, heart rate and blood volume are affected not only during the presentation, but also two seconds before. Pictures with a calming or neutral theme, randomly interspersed with the others, do not show this effect (Radin, 1997).

Correlations of psi with several physical conditions are also known. Analysis of a large number of ESP experiments has shown that fluctuations in the earth's magnetic field[11] have a negative correlation with psi results (Spottiswoode, 1997a). A possible interpretation of this result is that the magnetic field fluctuations produce some sort of low-level interference with brain processing, so that processing of a weak effect such as psi is interfered with.

---

10. A picture having a greater variation of light intensity across it is more technically described as having a greater Shannon entropy. The pictures which produce better psi results have a greater change (gradient) in Shannon entropy when each part of the picture is compared to adjacent parts and these changes are averaged.

11. The correlation is with the ap geomagnetic index [Editors' note: This is a measure of geomagnetic activity around the globe for any particular day.].

It has also been shown that ESP results are correlated with local sidereal time (LST). (The latter describes the relative position of the stars for a given observer.) More specifically, at 13:30 LST, plus or minus about an hour, ESP scores increase three-fold over their average value (May, 2001; Spottiswoode, 1997b). Nearly all the ESP data was collected at northern latitudes, and for these latitudes the central part of the galaxy is below the horizon at 13:30 LST (May, 2001). A possible interpretation is that some sort of radiation, or perhaps fluctuations in radiation, comes from the central part of the galaxy and interferes with brain processing of weak effects. When the central part of the galaxy is below the horizon at 13:30 LST, its effect is shielded by the earth, and brain processing of weak effects would be thereby improved. It is unknown what sort of radiation might produce such an effect, however.

## THEORIES OF PSI

As we have seen in the preceding section, it does not appear that psi is governed by laws which are similar to presently known physical principles. On the other hand, assuming it does follow laws, these must necessarily be *compatible* with known physical principles because these are experimentally verified. So it seems likely that there would be points of commonality between the laws of psi, whatever these may be, and known physical principles, and most theories of psi start from an assumed commonality.

Herein we will simply consider a sampling of theories that show the sort of ideas being considered in the field. Before doing that we will examine quantum non-locality, to see why conventional physics must be modified if this phenomenon is to be invoked to explain the distance independence of psi. We will then examine some general theories of psi which include explanations for its independence of distance.[12] Finally

---

12. Experiments have shown that when an operator is at a distance from the PK apparatus, comparable results are obtained to when the operator is nearby (Jahn *et al.*, 1997). This finding suggests that PK is independent of distance although the possibility that these results can be accounted for by experimenter-psi has not been ruled out.

we will consider a few of the more detailed models of PK. For an extensive bibliography of theories, see Stokes (1987, 1997).

## Quantum non-locality

The reason the concept of quantum non-locality must be modified from conventional physics when used in a theory of psi is that psi effects involve the transfer of information, whereas quantum non-locality permits correlations, but does not permit transfer of information. It is important to understand this distinction, and we will take it up in some detail. But first, let's see what the phenomenon is. Quantum non-locality permits a correlation between two sequences of measurements, one sequence at location A and one sequence at location B, with this correlation independent of distance. We saw earlier (in the section on Randomness) that if a sequence of measurements has a range of possible results, then the over-all results must fulfil some pattern (the probability distribution), which is determined by the laws of quantum mechanics. However, if the two sequences are linked by quantum non-locality, they are constrained in a further way—in that case each measurement at A has a correspondence, to the extent of the correlation, with a measurement at B. For instance, suppose both measurements can be represented by binary sequences. Let's suppose the correlation links 0s with 0s and 1s with 1s, with a correlation of 75%. Then 75% of the time, when there is a 0 at A, a 0 occurs at B and similarly, when there is a 1 at A, a 1 occurs at B. This correlation occurs independently of the distance between A and B.

If the sequence at A could be controlled, it would be possible to send a message to B. (If the correlation is less than 100%, the message would have some inaccuracies, but nevertheless a message could be sent.) But the order in which each result appears is random, i.e., it is inherently unpredictable and uncontrollable. For instance, in the above example there is no way to control the order of 0s and 1s. There is no way to impose a message on the sequence, so no message can be sent in this way.

There is more to know about non-locality which at first glance appears to be a promising way to send a message, so let's go on. The pre-determined overall patterns at A and B can vary according to different knob settings (parameters) on the measurement apparatus. The degree of correlation is also specified by the laws of quantum mechanics and depends on the knob settings. So we ask, couldn't we use the knob settings at A as a code? For instance, if there are three knob settings, A1, A2 and A3, these could be used for a three-element code. Measurements at A could be made for a while using knob A1. The person at B could choose some knob setting, say B2, produce the corresponding sequence, and check it with the known probability distributions and correlations which correspond to each combination of B2 with the knobs at A. It would seem that he could determine by this means which knob was used at A. Unfortunately, the laws of quantum mechanics and special relativity, taken together, imply that the probability distributions and correlations combine in a way which prohibits the person at B from learning which knob A used. In fact, these laws taken together prohibit the transfer of information via non-locality by any method at all (Eberhard, 1978).[13] (This finding is known as Eberhard's Theorem.) So even though a correlation exists between the sequences at A and B, it is not possible for a person at A to transfer any information to B.

## Theories involving quantum non-locality

For the above reason theories of psi which invoke quantum non-locality propose a modification, in one way or another, to presently known physics. For instance, Josephson and Pallikari-Viras (1991) propose that living organisms can detect patterns in sequences that by scientific standards would be considered random. They point out that randomness is determined scientifically by taking an average over many sequences, and they suggest that living organisms may be able to discriminate information in individual sequences even though the overall pattern of many

---

13. Eberhard (1978) points out that signals could be sent via non-locality if an alternate to special relativity could be used in which the order of all events was determined in an absolute way in some preferred frame of reference.

sequences appears random. In that case the information in the sequences could be transmitted non-locally.

Von Lucadou (1995) takes a different approach. Physical laws involve both abstract principles and properties, such as mass and distance, which the principles apply to. Von Lucadou proposes that the principles involved in quantum mechanics can apply unchanged to systems which can be described in terms of properties that are analogous to mass, distance and the other quantities used in conventional physics. He further proposes that psychological variables can be used in such an analogous system, which could thereby describe the action of psi. Because this proposed system would use the same laws as conventional physics, there would be no way to transfer information non-locally—there would only be correlations between random sequences. However, von Lucadou proposes that ESP and PK both occur via correlations only.

Atmanspacher, Römer and Walach (2002) make a different proposal regarding non-locality. They list the mathematical conditions which underlie the structure of quantum mechanics, and ask how these might be varied or weakened in order to be applied to other fields. They suggest that a weakened version of quantum theory could be applied to a model in which persons are linked by a collective unconscious, with non-local transfer of mental states possible between those who are linked.

## Theories involving hyperspace

Alternatively, it has been proposed that ESP is independent of ordinary three-dimensional space because of connections in additional dimensions. For instance, Rauscher and colleagues have proposed extending Minkowski space (the four-dimensional space used in special relativity) to the complex plane and have shown that events separated by space or time in ordinary space can coincide in this extended space (Rauscher, 1993; Rauscher and Targ, 2001).

In another hyperspace theory Sirag (1993a, 1993b; 1996) considers the ten-dimensional space which forms the basis of string theory (and thereby forms the basis of all physical laws). He points out that a generalization of this space can be shown mathematically to intersect with another space, with different properties.

Because the first space incorporates all the principles of the physical world, the second space must be something different, and Sirag proposes that this other space describes the properties of universal mind.[14] The intersection of these spaces would describe the way consciousness and the physical world interact, and therefore would account for the properties of psi. In particular, the properties of the intersection include time, but not physical space (Sirag, 1993a), so the lack of dependence of psi on space could be explained in this way.

## Theories of psychokinesis

Now let's examine some theories of PK. As we have seen in the examples of time-delayed PK, in many experiments it is difficult to know whether psi results should be ascribed to psychokinesis or precognition, and May and co-workers have explored the possibility that results that appear to be due to PK could actually be due to precognition (May, Utts, et al., 1995). They point out in their theory, called Decision Augmentation Theory or DAT, that in many experimental situations the process which produces binary bits is ongoing, and the beginning of a sequence to be affected is decided by the initiative of an operator, by a button push or some similar action. Therefore, if an operator knows by precognition what sequence is about to be produced by random noise or radioactive decay, it is not really necessary for her to affect this process by PK. Instead, she can simply push the button when a favourable sequence is coming up. They show that the z-score (a statistical measure) has a different dependence on the number of bits affected, depending on

---

14. The first space is based on a finite subgroup of $SU_2$ and the second space is a Lie algebra. The mathematical properties of the first space have a known correspondence to properties of the physical world. However, it is not known what properties of mind correspond to the properties of the Lie algebra.

whether PK or precognitive selection is operating, and in this way the two processes can be distinguished experimentally. This test has been applied to sets of experimental data that included sequences with different numbers of bits. However, conclusions on whether PK or DAT was operating depend on details of the analysis, and there has not been agreement about this (Dobyns and Nelson, 1998; May et al., 1995). Additional experimental considerations to distinguish DAT from PK have been proposed by Ibison (2000).

Several PK theories—Schmidt (1982) and Walker (1975, 1979)—have proposed that PK occurs via collapse of the wave function by a conscious observer. These theories have also proposed modifications to the equations of quantum mechanics which would allow for PK (non-random transitions) to occur. In these theories a system can be affected by PK until it is viewed by a conscious observer. Therefore, according to these theories, PK results can be found in sequences which are *not* pre-observed, but not in sequences which are. As discussed above (in the section on time-displaced PK), Schmidt compared results for the two kinds of sequences in an experiment, but results were inconclusive (Schmidt and Stapp, 1993).

Walker (1975) has also proposed that PK can only produce changes within the limits of the uncertainty principle. Such changes would be extremely small. However, Walker (1975) has shown that for cases in which an effect of such a change can be magnified exponentially, the final change can be macroscopic. Specifically, he showed that if a travelling cube (used in many early PK experiments) undergoes a small change in orientation at the beginning of the trajectory, then after the cube travels a certain minimum distance, it undergoes a macroscopic change in endpoint which increases as the cube travels forward.[15] According to this theory the wave function would reflect this possible change in endpoint, and wave function collapse at the end of the trajectory would make the PK deviation manifest.

---

15. A more detailed analysis of the dynamics of the cube has recently been done (Burns, 2002b, 2002c). The results differ from Walker's in some particulars, but confirm the above conclusions.

Burns (2002a) also proposes that PK can only make changes within the limits of the uncertainty principle, but in a different context. The action of vacuum radiation produces constant fluctuations in matter particles within the limits of the uncertainty principle. The effect of these fluctuations is magnified as molecules interact with each other, with the result that the direction of travel of molecules is randomized after only a few interactions (Burns, 1998). As a result the action of vacuum radiation can account for entropy increase at the microscopic level (Burns, 1998; 2002d). Burns (2002a) proposes that PK occurs through the ordering of these random motions in particles. She shows that the impact of about $10^5$ ordered air molecules could change the initial position of a travelling cube sufficiently to produce a sideways deviation of several centimetres after 50 cm of forward travel (Burns, 2002b, 2002c).

Pallikari (2003) makes a different sort of proposal. As we saw earlier, experimental data shows that the action of PK on a random binary sequence not only produces a shifting of the mean, but also a bunching or gluing effect, in that both 0's and 1's tend to be adjacent to or near each other more often than would be found in a random sequence. Pallikari proposes that this gluing is the only physical effect PK produces. In that case, a shift in the mean can occur in relatively short sequences because the gluing would leave an imbalance in the number of 0's and 1's, but no shift in the mean would be found in long sequences. She points out that if gluing is the only effect of PK, any effect of mean-shifting would be sufficiently small that its lack of observation in scientific experiments could be explained.

## PSYCHOLOGICAL FACTORS ASSOCIATED WITH THE PRODUCTION OF PSI

Having considered physical aspects of psi, both experimental and theoretical, let us now turn to psychological variables which may influence the production and reception of psi. A few personality traits have consistently been associated with increased reception of ESP. For instance, those who believe that ESP will occur in a testing session score better on the average than those who do not; this result is called the "sheep-goat effect" (Palmer, 1971, 1972, 1978).[16] Extroverts obtain higher ESP scores on the average than introverts (Honorton et al., 1998; Palmer and Carpenter, 1998). Less defensive subjects (as measured on the Defense Mechanism Test) tend to score better on ESP tests (Haraldsson and Houtkooper, 1995). Also, those with creative ability tend to score better (Dalton, 1997). Little is known about the most favourable traits for senders of ESP, however (Bem and Honorton, 1994).

Some findings seem related to the comfort and relaxation of the subject. For instance, experimental studies have shown that relaxation of the subject increases ESP scores (Rao, 2001). Also, it is generally thought that psi results are better when the laboratory personnel the subject interacts with are supportive of obtaining those results (Dalton, 1997; Delanoy, 1997). This view is supported by a study in which two parallel sets of experiments were run, with conditions the same except that in one the subjects were informed of experimental procedures by a psi proponent and in the other by a sceptic. The experiment with the psi proponent showed statistically significant results, but the one with the sceptic did not (Wiseman and Schlitz, 1997). Additionally, if there is a sender, results are better if the sender and receiver are emotionally or biologically close (Dalton, 1997).

Sometimes instead of matching a target, a subject will produce psi results which miss the target to a statistically significant amount. This phenomenon is called "psi missing." This phenomenon seems to occur more often when the subject is uncomfortable with the experiment or some conditions in it, or is sceptical that psi exists (Rao, 2001). In a probably related phenomenon if a subject is asked to switch back and forth between contrasting targets during an experiment, he may have a

---

16. This correlation has been found for a belief that ESP will take place in the testing session, and is not found as strongly for simply a belief in ESP in the abstract (Palmer, 1978; Rao, 2001). In a similar vein persons who report having previous psi experiences are found to score better in ganzfeld experiments (Dalton, 1997).

positive score on one and a negative score (psi missing) on the other (Rao, 2001). The latter is called the "differential effect."

It seems likely that ESP scores are better when interest in the target and/or the experiment is heightened, and this is often considered to be the explanation for the "decline effect" which has been found in a broad array of ESP and PK experiments. In this effect psi scores are better in the first test unit, decrease in the second, revert to random or near random at about the third, and then gradually return to the previous scores. This effect occurs at all levels, e.g. at the trial level (the third trial of a run reverts to near random) and run level (the third run of a series reverts to near random), and even occurs across sets of experiments done by the same laboratory (Dunne et al., 1994). The effect of series position on results is also known in conventional psychology (Dunne et al., 1994), which supports the idea that the decline is caused by flagging interest at the mid-point of a series. However, the actual cause is unknown.[17]

The characteristics of ESP targets presumably contribute to the participants' interest. Some experiments have shown better results for dynamic ESP targets, such as film clips, than for static targets, such as photos, although this has not been a consistent finding (Rao, 2001). A review of ESP experiments suggests that multisensory targets (e.g., music with pictures, sound with videos) are preferable to targets that are solely visual (Delanoy, 1988).

In order to help the subject become aware of the target, it is generally thought that an environment of uniform low-level visual and audio fields, as is provided in ganzfeld experiments (see description by Palmer, 2003), is helpful, because psi appears to be processed in the brain like a

---

17. We should note that although there is considerable scatter in the magnitude of results from different laboratories for any given type of psi experiment, a polynomial regression plot shows a decline to near random and subsequent recovery across laboratories and across decades for various types of experiments (Bierman, 2001, Figures 4, 7, 8). (A few categories are fit by a steadily declining line.) Bierman (2001) proposes that these effects are due to the relationship of psi to the physical/ontological nature of reality, rather than being a psychological effect.

weak sensory signal (Broughton, 1991; Rao, 2001). However, whether sensory reduction actually does help scores has apparently not been specifically tested.

Besides all the above considerations, it appears to be helpful in producing psi if the subject has a heightened focus and holds certain attitudes. With respect to heightened focus, several psi experimenters suggest that a subject should only do one session per day, which should be the highlight of the day (Delanoy, 1997; Targ and Katra, 1997). Stanford (1977), in reviewing descriptions in the literature of attitudes which may help produce PK, cited "intention without effort to make things happen" and "release of effort." In the first attitude the goal can be treated as a game and approached in a playful way. In the second the intention to make something happen is first held and then let go. In a phenomenological study Heath (2000) described components common to the experiences of eight people who had produced PK events. These components included a sense of connection to the target and/or other people, a feeling of dissociation from the usual ego identity, the presence of playfulness and/or peak levels of emotion, and release of effort.

## REPLICABILITY OF PSI EFFECTS

A large number of experiments have now been done on phenomena which appear to be psi, those described in this article and others, such as those on psi in the dream state (Sherwood and Roe, 2003) and remote viewing (Hyman, 1996; Radin, 1997; Utts, 1996). We will not review the statistical analysis of these experiments here (see Radin, 1997). However, this analysis strongly supports the view that some sort of anomalous process is affecting data which would otherwise be random. But is this process psi? Let us remind ourselves that by psi we mean information transfer (ESP) and/or physical change (PK) involving the presence of consciousness, using no presently known physical mechanism, which occurs independently of distance and to some extent across time. Given the various effects on the data (such as described herein), the process appears to be psi. But alternative hypotheses are always possible. The most that can be said is that an anomaly is demonstrably present, but it conceivably could be a garden-variety anomaly of unknown nature.

Nevertheless, although the existence of psi is not proved, there is sufficient evidence for it that if psi were any ordinary phenomenon, it would probably be provisionally accepted and non-controversial. That this is not the case appears to be due to (1) its elusive nature (as we will discuss next), (2) its major differences from known physical principles (as we have seen herein), and (3) the lack of any generally accepted theory which can account for those differences.

Even though some factors important to producing psi are known, methods to produce it reliably in the laboratory remain unknown, as all parapsychologists are aware. It is the practice in parapsychology to publish all studies intended to study psi, whether it appears or not (this is done because the inclusion of null results is needed for a proper statistical analysis).[18] And it is commonplace to see papers which say in essence, "This experiment was intended to study X attribute of psi. Unfortunately, we didn't detect any psi." It may be possible to learn specifically what psychological states are needed to produce psi, such that one can reliably produce it. But without such knowledge psi is elusive.

One of the most frustrating aspects of this elusiveness is the failure to replicate large studies which in cumulative effect had given highly significant statistical evidence for psi. The ganzfeld experiments give one example. A meta-analysis of experiments in 1985 showed a $p$-value of $2.2 \times 10^{-11}$ (where the smaller the p-value is compared to 1, the less likely it is that results were obtained by chance) (Honorton, 1985; $p$-value from Milton, 1999). In other words the analysis strongly suggested that an anomalous phenomenon was present. At this point parapsychologist Charles Honorton and sceptic Ray Hyman jointly published guidelines for replication of the experiments (Hyman and Honorton,

---

18. The omission of null results is called the "file drawer" problem.

1986). Eleven further studies, which met these guidelines, were then done by Honorton's laboratory, and these were also statistically significant ($p$-value of $3.3 \times 10^{-4}$) (Bem and Honorton, 1994; $p$-value from Milton, 1999). By 1997 thirty additional experiments had been published from other laboratories. If this effect is to be considered replicable, it is reasonable to expect that a sufficient number of these experiments would produce significant effects that the cumulative total of this data would also reach statistical significance. However, although some of these experiments showed statistical significance (i.e., evidence that psi was produced), not all did, and a meta-analysis did not show statistical significance (Milton, 1999; Milton and Wiseman, 1999). As Palmer (2003) has discussed, after ten more studies were published and added, results went back into significance ($p$-value of $4.8 \times 10^{-3}$). However, meta-analyses which go in and out of significance as more studies are added cannot be said to give robust evidence for a phenomenon. If by "replicable" phenomenon we mean that researchers can be given a list of instructions on how to produce it, and most (not necessarily all) will then be able to produce it, then a more definitive specification of how to produce results is needed.

A similar problem is seen in the attempt to replicate the results of the extensive PK database of the PEAR (Princeton Engineering Anomalies Research) laboratory. Results for the first set of experiments were compiled over a period of twelve years. The shift in the mean value of the data was small (about $10^{-4}$ bits deviation for every bit processed [Editors' note: That is, only about 1 bit out of every 10,000 seemed to be influenced by PK.]), but the database was so huge that the resulting $p$-value was $3.5 \times 10^{-13}$ (Jahn et al., 1997). In 1996 a consortium of three laboratories (at Freiberg and Giessen in Germany, plus the original PEAR lab) was formed in order to replicate these results. Physically random sequences were generated using the same type of equipment as in the first project. Experimental protocols and data analysis procedures were essentially the same. But no shift in the mean was found, not even in the portion of the data generated by the PEAR laboratory. Although the experimenters raised various possibilities that might be involved in this difference in result, they were unable to specify any definite reason for it (Jahn et al., 2000).

## CONCLUSION

In spite of this elusiveness, if there were some theoretical structure which could make predictions about the dependence of psi on physical parameters, such that when psi does appear it would follow these predictions, probably psi would be accepted, at least as a subject of study. But, as we have seen, there is no generally accepted theory of psi—only some competing proposals. It would seem that psi needs either a recipe for reliably producing it or an experimentally verifiable theory of its relationship to known physics before it will be considered an established phenomenon.

On the other hand, psi should not be written off as having negligible chance of existing simply because it is not consonant with presently known physical laws. Or at least, something else should first be taken into account. Not everyone believes that free will exists. However, as we have seen, presently known physical laws encompass only determinism and randomness. So if free will exists, and if by this concept we mean something free and intended, not determined or random, then free will is not described by these laws (Burns, 1999). Furthermore, the only difference between free will and PK is that free will initiates action by affecting neural processes within the brain, whereas PK can act outside the body. So if PK is written off because it is not consonant with contemporary physical laws, then free will must be written off also.

For that matter the concept of consciousness does not appear in any presently known physical laws. Furthermore, the description of consciousness is very different from that of physical matter, in that consciousness does not appear to occupy physical space and characteristics such as qualia [Editors' note: Introspective mental sense data, such as qualities and feelings like red-ness and sour-ness.] appear to be different from known physical quantities. So regardless of the ontological status of consciousness—emergent physicalism, dualism or anything else—it seems likely that the principles which govern it will differ from known physical laws. Psi phenomena may be giving us an advance view of some of these principles.

In summary, we have likened the signs that psi exists to the signs of land past Cape Bojador seen in the fifteenth century. Are these signs only akin to a tangled mass of seaweed, drifting aimlessly in the current, which merely appears to be land? Or is there a huge continent of further findings, with all that this implies? Time will tell. In the meantime, although you—the reader—may not want to join a voyage to the edge of what may be boundless ocean, you may want to be informed of the reports from people who do voyage there. It is the purpose of this Special Issue [Editors' note: Here Burns refers to the issue of the *Journal of Consciousness Studies* in which this article first appeared.] to inform you of the present state of these explorations.

## Acknowledgments
My thanks for helpful comments on the draft manuscript to James Alcock, Geoffrey Dean, Anthony Freeman, Fotini Pallikari, Adrian Parker, Helmut Schmidt, Stefan Schmidt and Harald Walach.

## References
Atmanspacher, R., R. Römer, and R. Walach (2002). "Weak Quantum Theory: Complementarity and Entanglement in Physics and Beyond." *Foundations of Physics* 32, pp. 379–406.

Bem, D. J., and C. Ronorton (1994). "Does Psi, Exist? Replicable Evidence for an Anomalous Process of Information Transfer." *Psychological Bulletin* 115, pp. 4–18.

Bierman, D. J. (2001). "On the Nature of Anomalous Phenomena." In P. van Loocke, editor. *The Physical Nature of Consciousness.* New York: Benjamins, pp. 269–292.

Bohm, D., and B. J. Riley (1993). *The Undivided Universe.* New York: Routledge.

Braud, W. G., and M. J. Schlitz (1991). "Consciousness Interactions with Remote Biological Systems: Anomalous Intentionality Effects." *Subtle Energies* 2, no. 1, pp. 1–46.

Broughton, R. S. (1991). *Parapsychology: The Controversial Science.* New York: Ballantine.

Burns, J. E. (1998). "Entropy and Vacuum Radiation." *Foundations of Physics* 28, pp. 1191–1207.

—— (1999). "Volition and Physical Laws." *Journal of Consciousness Studies* 6, no. 10, pp. 27–47.

—— (2002a). "Quantum Fluctuations and the Action of the Mind." *Noetic Journal* 3, no. 4, pp. 312–317.

—— (2002b). "The Tumbling Cube and the Action of the Mind." *Noetic Journal* 3, no. 4, pp. 318–329.

—— (2002c). "The Effect of Ordered Air Molecules on a Tumbling Cube." *Noetic Journal* 3, no. 4, pp. 330–339.

—— (2002d). "Vacuum Radiation, Entropy and the Arrow of Time." In R. L. Amoroso, G. Hunter, M. Kafatos, and J.-P. Vigier, editors. *Gravitation and Cosmology: From the Hubble Radius to the Planck Scale.* Dordrecht: Kluwer, pp. 491–498.

Dalton, K. (1997). "Is There a Formula to Success in the Ganzfeld? Observations on Predictors of Psi-Ganzfeld Performance." *European Journal of Parapsychology* 13, pp. 71–82.

Delanoy, D. L. (1988). "Characteristics of Successful Free-Response Targets: Experimental Findings and Observations." *Proceedings of the 31st Parapsychological Association Annual Convention,* pp. 230–246.

—— (1997). "Important Psi-Conducive Practices and Issues: Impressions from Six Parapsychological Laboratories." *European Journal of Parapsychology* 13, pp. 63–70.

Dobyns, Y. R., and R. D. Nelson (1998). "Empirical Evidence Against Decision Augmentation Theory." *Journal of Scientific Exploration* 12, no. 2, pp. 231–257.

Dunne, B. J. (1993). "Co-operator Experiments with an REG Device." In K. R. Rao, editor. *Cultivating Consciousness.* Westport, Conn.: Praeger, pp. 149–163.

Dunne, B. J., Y. R. Dobyns, R. G. Jahn, and R. D. Nelson (1994). "Series Position Effects in Random Event Generator Experiments, with Appendix by Angela Thompson." *Journal of Scientific Exploration* 8, no. 2, pp. 197–215.

Eberhard, P. (1978). "Bell's Theorem and the Different Concepts of Locality." *Nuovo Cimento* 46(B), pp. 392–419.

Etter, T., and R. P. Noyes (1999). "Process, System, Causality, and Quantum Mechanics: A Psychoanalysis of Animal Faith." *Physics Essays* 12, no. 4.

Freeman, A. (2003). *Consciousness: A Guide to the Debates.* Santa Barbara, Calif.: ABC-CLIO.

Haraldsson, E., and J. M. Routkooper (1995). "Meta-analyses of 10 Experiments on Perceptual Defensiveness and ESP." *Journal of Parapsychology* 59, no. 3, pp. 251–271.

Heath, P. R. (2000). "The PK Zone: A Phenomenological Study." *Journal of Parapsychology* 64, no. 1, pp. 53–71.

Herbert, N. (1985). *Quantum Reality*. New York: Doubleday.

Honorton, C. (1985). "Meta-analysis of Psi Ganzfeld Research: A Response to Hyman." *Journal of Parapsychology* 49, pp. 51–91.

Honorton, C., and D. C. Ferrari (1989). "Meta-analysis of Forced-Choice Precognition Experiments." *Journal of Parapsychology* 53, pp. 281–308.

Honorton, C., D. C. Ferrari, and D. J. Bem (1998). "Extraversion and ESP Performance: A Meta-analysis and New Confirmation." *Journal of Parapsychology* 62, no. 3, pp. 255–276.

Hyman, R. (1996). "Evaluation of a Program on Anomalous Mental Phenomena." *Journal of Scientific Exploration* 10, no. 1, pp. 31–58.

Hyman, R., and C. Honorton (1986). "A Joint Communique: The Psi Ganzfeld Controversy." *Journal of Parapsychology* 50, pp. 350–364.

Ibison, M. (1998). "Evidence That Anomalous Statistical Influence Depends on the Details of the Random Process." *Journal of Scientific Exploration* 12, no. 3, pp. 407–423.

——— (2000). "An Acceptance-Rejection Theory of Statistical Psychokinesis." *Journal of Parapsychology* 64, no. 2, pp. 165–179.

Jahn, R. G., and B. J. Dunne (1987). *Margins of Reality*. New York: Harcourt Brace Jovanovich.

Jahn, R. G., B. J. Dunne, R. D. Nelson, Y. H. Dobyns, and G. J. Bradish (1997). "Correlations of Random Binary Sequences with Pre-stated Operator Intention: A Review of a 12-Year Program." *Journal of Scientific Exploration* 11, no. 3, pp. 345–367.

Jahn, R., J. Mischo, D. Vaitl et al. (2000). "Mind/Machine Interaction Consortium: PortREG Replication Experiments." *Journal of Scientific Exploration* 14, no. 4, pp. 499–555.

Josephson, B. D., and F. Pallikari-Viras (1991). "Biological Utilization of Quantum Nonlocality." *Foundations of Physics* 21, pp. 197–207.

May, E. C. (2001). "Towards the Physics of Psi: Correlation with Physical Variables." *European Journal of Parapsychology* 16, pp. 42–52.

May, E. C., S. J. P. Spottiswoode, and L. V. Faith (2000). "The Correlation of the Gradient of Shannon Entropy and Anomalous Cognition." *Journal of Scientific Exploration* 14, no. 1, pp. 53–72.

May, E. C., S. J. P. Spottiswoode, and C. L. James (1994). "Shannon Entropy: A Possible Intrinsic Target Property." *Journal of Parapsychology* 58, no. 4, pp. 384–401.

May, E. C., S. J. P. Spottiswoode, J. M. Utts, and C. L. James (1995). "Applications of Decision Augmentation Theory." *Journal of Parapsychology* 59, no. 3, pp. 221–250.

May, E. C., J. M. Utts, and S. J. P. Spottiswoode (1995). "Decision Augmentation Theory." *Journal of Parapsychology* 59, no. 3, pp. 195–220.

McDonough, B. E., N. S. Don, and C. A. Warren (2002). "Differential Event-Related Potentials to Targets and Decoys in a Guessing Task." *Journal of Scientific Exploration* 16, no. 2, pp. 187–206.

Millay, J. (1999). *Multidimensional Mind: Remote Viewing in Hyperspace.* Berkeley, Calif.: North Atlantic Books.

———. (1999). "Should Ganzfeld Research Continue to Be Crucial in the Search for a Replicable Psi Effect?" Part I. *Journal of Parapsychology* 63, no. 4, pp. 309–333.

Milton, J., and R. Wiseman (1999). "Does Psi Exist? Lack of Replication of an Anomalous Process of Information Transfer." *Psychological Bulletin* 125, pp. 387–391.

Mohrhoff, U. (1999). "The Physics of Interactionism." *Journal of Consciousness Studies* 6, nos. 8–9, pp. 165–184.

Pallikari, F. (2003). "Must the Magic of Psychokinesis Hinder Precise Scientific Measurement?" *Journal of Consciousness Studies* 10, nos. 6–7, pp. 199–219.

Pallikari, F., and E. Boller (1999). "A Rescaled Range Analysis of Random Events." *Journal of Scientific Exploration* 13, no. 1, pp. 25–40.

Palmer, J. (1971). "Scoring in ESP Tests as a Function of Belief in ESP. Part I: The Sheep-Goat Effect." *Journal of the American Society for Psychical Research* 65, pp. 363–408.

——— (1972). "Scoring in ESP Tests as a Function of Belief in ESP. Part II: Beyond the Sheep-Goat Effect." *Journal of the American Society for Psychical Research* 66, pp. 1–25.

——— (1978). "Extrasensory Perception: Research Findings." In S. Krippner, editor. *Advances in Parapsychological Research II: Extrasensory Perception.* New York: Plenum.

——— (2003). "ESP in the Ganzfeld: Analysis of a Debate." *Journal of Consciousness Studies* 10, nos. 6–7, pp. 51–68.

Palmer, J., and J. C. Carpenter (1998). "Comments on the Extraversion-ESP Meta-analysis by Honorton, Ferrari and Bem." *Journal of Parapsychology* 62, no. 3, pp. 277–282.

Penrose, R. (1989). *The Emperor's New Mind.* New York: Oxford.

Puthoff, H. E., and R. Targ (1979). "A Perceptual Channel for Information Transfer Over Kilometer Distances." In C. T. Tart, H. E. Puthoff, and R. Targ, editors. *Mind at Large.* New York: Praeger, pp. 13–76.

Radin, D. (1997). *The Conscious Universe.* New York: HarperCollins.

Rao, K. R. (2001). *Basic Research in Parapsychology.* 3rd edition. Jefferson, N.C.: McFarland.

Rauscher, E. A. (1993). "A Theoretical Model of the Remote-Perception Phenomenon." In B. Kane, J. Millay, and D. Brown, editors. *Silver Threads: 25 Years of Parapsychology Research.* Westport, Conn.: Praeger, pp. 141–155.

Rauscher, E. A., and R. Targ (2001). "The Speed of Thought: Investigation of a Complex Space-Time Metric to Describe Psychic Phenomena." *Journal of Scientific Exploration* 15, no. 3, pp. 331–354.

Schlitz, M. J., and S. LaBerge (1997). "Covert Observation Increases Skin Conductance in Subjects Unaware of When They Are Being Observed: A Replication." *Journal of Parapsychology* 61, no. 3, pp. 185–196.

Schmidt, H. (1969). "Precognition of a Quantum Process." *Journal of Parapsychology* 33, pp. 99–108.

———— (1973). "PK Tests with a High-Speed Random Number Generator." *Journal of Parapsychology* 37, p. 105.

———— (1974). "Comparison of PK Action on Two Different Random Number Generators." *Journal of Parapsychology* 38, p. 47.

———— (1976). "PK Effect on Pre-recorded Targets." *Journal of the American Society for Psychical Research* 70, pp. 267–292.

———— (1982). "Collapse of the State Vector and Psychokinetic Effect." *Foundations of Physics* 12, pp. 565–581.

———— (1993). "Observation of a Psychokinetic Effect Under Highly Controlled Conditions." *Journal of Parapsychology* 57, no. 4, pp. 351–372.

———— (2000a). "A Proposed Measure for Psi-Induced Bunching of Randomly Spaced Events." *Journal of Parapsychology* 64, no. 3, pp. 301–316.

———— (2000b). "PK Tests in a Pre-sleep State." *Journal of Parapsychology* 64, no. 3, pp. 317–331.

Schmidt, H., and H. Stapp (1993). "PK with Prerecorded Random Events and the Effects of Pre-observation." *Journal of Parapsychology* 57, no. 4, pp. 331–349.

Sherwood, S. J., and C. A. Roe (2003). "A Review of Dream ESP Studies Conducted Since the Maimonides Dream ESP Studies." *Journal of Consciousness Studies* 10, nos. 6–7, pp. 85–109.

Shoup, R. (2002). "Anomalies and Constraints: Can Clairvoyance, Precognition, and Psychokinesis Be Accommodated Within Known Physics?" *Journal of Scientific Exploration* 16, no. 1, pp. 3–18.

Sirag, S.-P. (1993a). "Consciousness: A Hyperspace View." Appendix to J. Mishlove, *Roots of Consciousness.* 3rd edition. Tulsa, Okla.: Council Oak Books, pp. 327–365.

——— (1993b). "Hyperspace Reflections." In B. Kane, J. Millay, and D. Brown, editors. *Silver Threads: 25 Years of Parapsychology Research*. Westport, Conn.: Praeger, pp. 156–165.

——— (1996). "A Mathematical Strategy for a Theory of Consciousness." In S. R. Hameroff, A. W. Kaszniak, and A. C. Scott, editors. *Toward a Science of Consciousness*. Cambridge, Mass.: MIT Press, pp. 579–588.

Spar, D. L. (2001). *Ruling the Waves*. New York: Harcourt.

Spottiswoode, S. J. P. (1997a). "Geomagnetic Fluctuations and Free-Response Anomalous Cognition." *Journal of Parapsychology* 61, no. 1, pp. 3–12.

——— (1997b). "Apparent Association Between Effect Size in Free-Response Anomalous Cognition and Local Sidereal Time." *Journal of Scientific Exploration* 11, pp. 109–122.

Stanford, R. G. (1977). "Experimental Psychokinesis: A Review from Diverse Perspectives." In B. Wolman, editor. *Handbook of Parapsychology*. New York: Van Nostrand, pp. 324–381.

Steinkamp, F. (2000). "Does Precognition Foresee the Future? A Postal Experiment to Assess the Possibility of True Precognition." *Journal of Parapsychology* 64, no. 1, pp. 3–18.

——— (2001). "Does Precognition Foresee the Future? Series 2: A Laboratory Replication, and Series 3: A Worldwide Web Replication." *Journal of Parapsychology* 65, no. 1, pp. 17–40.

Steinkamp, F., J. Milton, and R. L. Morris (1998). "A Meta-analysis of Forced-Choice Experiments Comparing Clairvoyance and Precognition." *Journal of Parapsychology* 62, no. 3, pp. 193–218.

Stokes, D. M. (1987). "Theoretical Parapsychology." in S. Krippner, editor. *Advances in Parapsychological Research*. Jefferson, N.C.: McFarland, pp. 77–189.

——— (1997). *The Nature of Mind: Parapsychology and the Role of Consciousness in the Physical World*. Jefferson, N.C.: McFarland.

Targ, R., and J. Katra (1997). "Psi-Conducive Protocols." *European Journal of Parapsychology* 13, p. 95.

Utts, J. (1996). "An Assessment of the Evidence for Psychic Functioning." *Journal of Scientific Exploration* 10, no. 1, pp. 3–30.

von Lucadou, W. (1995). "The Model of Pragmatic Information (MPI)." *European Journal of Parapsychology* 11, pp. 58–75.

Walker, E. H. (1975). "Foundations of Paraphysical and Parapsychological Phenomena." In L. Oteri, editor. *Quantum Physics and Parapsychology*. New York: Parapsychology Foundation.

——— (1979). "The Quantum Theory of Psi Phenomena." *Psychoenergetic Systems* 3, pp. 259–299.

Wiseman, R., and M. Schlitz (1997). "Experimenter Effects and the Remote Detection of Staring." *Journal of Parapsychology* 61, no. 3, pp. 197–207.

# THEORIES OF PSI

One reason that many scientists have rejected paranormal studies outright is due to lack of an underlying theoretical mechanism that might explain psi phenomena. Analogously, the movement of continents through geologic time (so-called continental drift, more properly plate tectonics), now accepted by all geologists, was rejected for decades due in large part to the lack of a theoretical mechanism to account for such continental movement. At present there is no theory of psi that is accepted by the majority of researchers in the field. However, there are plenty of theories being developed and proposed to fill the void. Some of these have already been touched on in the previous selection by Burns (page 265). Hypotheses presented concerning the theoretical basis for psi do not necessarily have to be currently verifiable to prove useful. A scientific hypothesis can be introduced in a nascent form that offers only limited possibilities for testing, but may, as more research and attention is focused on it, yield fruitful ideas and evidence in the future. The following selection reviews various physical theories of psi.

**ARTICLE 13.** THEORIES ON THE PHYSICAL BASIS OF PSI,
*by Paul Stevens, 1997.*

---

[Source: Paul Stevens, "Current Psi Theories." Chapter 2 in *A Biophysical Approach to Psi Effects and Experience.* Ph.D. thesis, University of Edinburgh, 1997. Copyright Paul Stevens. (Formerly posted on the Website of the Koestler Parapsychology Unit, University of Edinburgh, as "Theories on the Physical Basis of Psi." Formerly available from: http://moebius.psy.ed.ac.uk/Physical_H.php3. Accessed 10 July 2006.)]

### Editors' Comments

Dr. Paul Stevens received his Ph.D. from the University of Edinburgh, through the Koestler Parapsychology Unit (KPU), based on his thesis titled *A Biophysical Approach to Psi Effects and Experience*. During his Ph.D. work, he received a Summer Fellowship at the University of Nevada, Las Vegas. After completing his Ph.D., Stevens stayed on at KPU as a research fellow. Much of Stevens's research has focused on the effects that weak, low-frequency magnetic fields may have on human behavior and psi experiences (see, for instance, Stevens 2000, 2005). Dr. Stevens is currently the editor of the *European Journal of Parapsychology* and a Senior Lecturer at Bournemouth University.

The Koestler Parapsychology Unit is named after its benefactors, the late writer Arthur Koestler (1905–1983; see Koestler, 1967, 1972) and his third wife Cynthia Koestler (who jointly committed suicide with her husband in 1983). In their wills the Koestlers left funds to endow a Chair of Parapsychology at a British University to promote research into ". . . the capacity attributed to some individuals to interact with their environment by means other than the recognised sensory and motor channels" (Lamont, Stevens, and Watt, for Koestler Parapsychology Unit, 2006). In 1984 the endowment was awarded to the University of Edinburgh, which, through the late parapsychologist John Beloff, already had a history of teaching and research in parapsychology.

In this selection, formerly posted on the KPU Website, some of the basic physical theories of psi are succinctly reviewed by Dr. Stevens.

## THEORIES ON THE PHYSICAL BASIS OF PSI,
*by Paul Stevens, 1997.*

The following are summaries of some of the attempts to look for theories which might help explain how psi operates. These are written for a non-technical audience—interested parties should look at the references provided for a better idea of the specifics.

## Teleological Model of Psi (TM)

Helmudt Schmidt proposed a teleological (goal-seeking) model that postulated psi as representing a modification of the probabilities for different world histories. That is, the psi agent need concentrate only on the desired outcome of an event. Psi would act to skew the probability of that event happening, or having happened in the case of retrospective psychokinesis (retro-PK). As such, this theory was not a theory of a psi mechanism but rather one which looked at the way psi was experienced by the psi agent. It was one of the first parapsychological theories to include a unified psi: PK, ESP, precognition—all were aspects of one common psi principle wherein reality was altered to match expectation. This theory also meant that psi would be independent of space and time as when and where in the world history psi occurred would be irrelevant, and that psi is independent of task complexity as the psi agent aims only for the desired end-point. As most human actions are essentially teleological—when we want to pick something up, we do not consider in detail which muscles we wish to move, and so on—this brought psi more into the realms of human experience. Feedback was considered to be vital: the psi agent can have an effect only if it is coupled to its environment in such a way that it may receive a stimulus. There was also what was called a "divergence problem." That is, all future psi agents could so have an effect on the present world history. In effect, this meant that for any experiment, the psi agent was not only the experimental participant but all future readers of the experimental paper!

Schmidt, H. (1975). "Towards a Mathematical Theory of Psi." *The Journal of the American Society for Psychical Research* 69, no. 4, pp. 301–320.

## Quantum Mechanical Theory of Psi (QMTP)

Evan Harris Walker identified consciousness with quantum-mechanical hidden variables. In quantum theory, any system may be described in terms of a wave-function—a complex superposition of waves, the squared amplitude of each being related to the probability of an individual event occurring. The complete wave-function describes all possible outcomes of that system. Thus the wave-function of a coin-toss will describe the outcomes of heads or tails, with the amplitude of each being equal to the square-root of the 50% probability of getting a head or a tail. The problem is that this wave-function describes all the outcomes at once, whereas conscious experience tells us that we will observe only one outcome. This naturally led to the idea that conscious observation somehow affects the system, causing the wave-function to collapse into one specific state—the one we experience. If this is indeed the case, then perhaps the consciousness can actually choose, to some extent, which outcome actually occurs—a process which sounds very much like the concept of psychokinesis.

Walker developed this theory by pointing out that the brain itself is also a physical system, and so it too develops probabilistically into a number of superposed potential states. That is, the collapse doesn't take place due to the physical act of observation, but is linked to an act of mind, consciousness taking on the role of a "hidden variable" of the wave-function which describes the physical system. Schmidt also explicitly stated that PK was related to the collapse of the wave-function in an extension to his original teleological model. An important feature of this theory is the unity of psi. PK, ESP and precognition are all aspects of the observation process. In fact, the basic process may be seen as similar to the idea of retro-psychokinesis in that the observation of the system would appear to affect the outcome of the system, no matter at what time that outcome would be said to have been determined in a classical sense. For example, the collection of random number data at time $t=0$ could be affected at any subsequent time as long as it was not observed at $t=0$. ESP then becomes the selection of the system to correspond to the prediction. Psi is also seen as being independent of space and time. A requirement of hidden variables is that they must, according to a well-known tenet of quantum theory called Bell's Theorem, be non-local in nature. In real-terms this would mean that the space-time location of the system to be affected is not important: only the feedback to the observer is. Psi is also independent of task complexity. Again, the important feature is the act of observation, so it is only the feedback which is important. This does mean that some form of true feedback to the oberver is vital. However, this again brings up the divergence problem although in this model, while future psi agents can also have an effect, it is argued that they can act only to increase the variance of experimental results rather than change what has already been observed.

Walker, E. H. (1975). "Foundations of Paraphysical and Parapsychological Phenomena." In L. Oteri, editor. *Quantum Physics and Parapsychology.* Parapsychology Foundation.

Walker, E. H. (1984). "A Review of Criticisms of the Quantum Mechanical Theory of Psi Phenomena." *Journal of Parapsychology* 48, pp. 277–332.

Schmidt, H. (1984). "Comparison of a Teleological Model with a Quantum Collapse Model of Psi." *Journal of Parapsychology* 48, no. 4, pp. 261–276.

## Thermal Fluctuation Model

Richard Mattuck presents an interesting variation of the QMTP based on the idea that the mind somehow utilises the thermal energy of molecules to alter the outcome of an event. It is well known that there is a degree of uncertainty associated with any measurement, with the actual measured values showing small fluctuations around a mean value. These fluctuations are partially due to the agitation of the measured system by the random thermal energies of particles in the system (remember that an atom at a given temperature is equivalent to that atom having a certain kinetic energy in a random direction. The hotter the material, the more its atoms are "jiggling" about), and have been shown to be related to the uncertainty principle in quantum theory. Mattuck relates a PK effect to the processing of information at a certain rate, and offers a detailed analysis of the rate of information change associated with a theoretical PK effect on various components of an example target system.

Mattuck, R. D. (1982). "Some Possible Thermal Quantum Fluctuation Models for Psychokinetic Influence on Light." *Psychoenergetics* 4, pp. 211–225.

## THE MODEL OF PRAGMATIC INFORMATION (MPI)

Walter von Lucadou utilises a system-theoretic approach to psi rather than a quantum-level approach. It does however assume that the description of any system will have a similar form to the axioms of quantum theory. Von Lucadou formulates a basic descriptive equation for the "pragmatic information," I, contained within a system, denoting the information which is meaningful to the observing organism, such that: $I = R \star A = B \star E = n \star i$. The first term states that the pragmatic information will be determined by the reliability, R, of the system (a change in the structure of the system) coupled with the autonomy, A (a change in the function of the system). The second term states that the pragmatic information will also be determined by the novelty, E, of the information in the system coupled with the confirmatory value, B of that information. The final term puts forward the idea that there is a minimum amount of pragmatic information, i (analogous to the idea of quanta in quantum theory). He then goes on to show how quantum theory axioms may, by analogy, be used to show the dynamics of inter-relationships between these concepts.

Von Lucadou also uses the system-theoretic concept of organisational closure, an organisationally closed system defined as being one which dynamically defines its boundaries by the interaction of its constituent parts. Such a system will also be seen as a unified body when viewed from outside the system. A physical example would be an atom, which exists only through the interaction between a nucleus and its electron, but which has properties that exist only because of this interaction. A psychological example would be a social group whose membership share some common belief structure that is an amalgam of the individual beliefs, these individual beliefs also being influenced by the group belief. In a psi experiment, organisational closure is related to the interaction between the psi agent and the target system, and is described by the internal pragmatic information of the system. The experimenter is outside of this closure but wants to get external pragmatic information in the form of experimental results. A psi effect is then defined as a meaningful correlation between the psi agent and the target system, although this correlation is non-local—a property where the properties of one system are dependent on that of another, distant system but where there is assumed to be no causal connection.

von Lucadou, W. (1987). "The Model of Pragmatic Information." Proceedings of the 30th Parapsychological Association Convention, pp. 236–254.
von Lucadou, W. (1994). "The Endo- Exo- Perspective—Heaven and Hell of Parapsychology." Proceedings of the 37th Parapsychological Association Convention, pp. 242–252.

## Psi-Mediated Instrumental Response (PMIR) & Conformance Behaviour Model

Another use of the systems theory approach to psi phenomena is that of Rex Stanford who proposed a general model wherein an organism uses psi, as well as sensory means, to scan its environment for information related to its needs. This is often, but need not necessarily be, an unconscious process. In this model, cybernetic PK is viewed as being an instrumental response to this scanning. As the model is seen as an active scanning process by the organism, the use of psi would be governed by a variety of factors, both situational and psychological.

In this approach, PK and ESP are seen as being separate processes, although telepathy can be seen as involving both extrasensory scanning for information about another organism and mental/behavioural influence of that organism by PK. Psi events occur in relation to the needs of the organism, and depend on the closeness in time of the relevant object or event. One of the most interesting aspects of this model is that psi can occur without the need for conscious perception of the need-relevant circumstance, making this one of the few theories that does not explicitly imply a link between consciousness and psi. It also allows that explicit feedback is not necessary as ESP provides relevant information. Although the author only states that this role is fulfilled by ESP, it at least allows for the more subtle forms of feedback due to the extended interaction between the target system and its environment mentioned earlier.

Stanford later modified the theory into one of conformational behaviour, removing the scanning component and saying that the organism merely reacted to relevant psi-mediated stimuli in its environment. That is, conformance behaviour deals with "changes in the ordering of a relatively unordered system in relationship to a relatively ordered system," which allowed simpler organisms who would not normally be thought of as being capable of scanning their environment, to utilise psi.

Stanford, R. G. (1990). "An Experimentally Testable Model for Spontaneous Psi Events." In S. Krippner, editor. *Advances in Parapsychological Research*, McFarland, pp. 54–167.

Stanford, R. G., Z. Zenhausern, A. Taylor, and M. Dwyer (1975). "Psychokinesis as Psi-Mediated Instrumental Response." *Journal of the American Society for Psychical Research* 69, no. 2, pp. 127–134.

## Decision Augmentation Theory (DAT)

In an approach diametrically opposed to the OTs [Observational Theories], this theory, which developed out of the Intuitive Data Sorting theory, posits that humans may have the ability to make decisions, based on information gained precognitively. Thus, rather than causing the desired outcome, they take advantage of natural fluctuations in the target system, selecting times and situations that will produce an outcome close to that which was desired. For example, in a "score high" PK protocol, the Random Event Generator (REG) might produce a binary data-stream of:

0101001000**1011101011**0110100110101**0001101011**0101110010100

If the data collection for a 10-bit sample was as for the first bold block (A), then the PK score would be 0.7 (seven 1s and 3 zeros). For the second bold block (B) it would be 0.5 (five 1s and five 0s). Sample A would then have given an above chance PK score, whereas sample B would be at chance-level. DAT says that the psi agent could have received some sort of precognitive cue that would have enabled them to start data-collection at the point where A begins rather than where B begins. If this biased selection process were continued, then we might conclude that the psi-agent had influenced the data stream to be non random when in fact it was still completely random overall. A further result of this process is that the final PK score will be inversely related to the sample length, and related to the number of decision points available to the psi agent.

This model, being precognition-based, requires psi to be time independent to some extent although there is some debate as to whether it is an actual future which is precognitively "perceived," or just a probabilistic future associated with a specific desired outcome. The main advantage of this approach according to the authors is that it removes the need to explain the two disparate active (PK) and passive (ESP) psi processes. It also allows for a PK effect in pseudo-random (and therefore deterministic) data, which would be difficult to explain by a causal influence model.

May, E. C, J. M. Utts, and S. J. P. Spottiswoode (1995). "Decision Augmentation Theory: Towards a Model of Anomalous Phenomena." *Journal of Parapsychology* 59, no. 3, pp. 195–220.

May, E. C., S. J. P. Spottiswoode, J. M. Utts, and C. L. James (1995). "Applications of Decision Augmentation Theory." *Journal of Parapsychology* 59, no. 3, pp. 221–250.

Dobyns, Y. H. (1993). "Selection Versus Influence in Remote REG Anomalies." *Journal of Scientific Exploration* 7, no. 3, pp. 259–269.

Dobyns, Y. H. (1996). "Selection ·Versus Influence Revisited: New Methods and Conclusions." *Journal of Scientific Exploration* 10, no. 2, pp. 253–268.

## ELECTROMAGNETIC THEORIES

The main electromagnetic-based theories tend to be split into two categories. The first is that there is a psi signal which is electromagnetic in nature, similar in nature to a radio signal. Advantages to this idea are that we know that organisms use electrical signals as part of their normal physiology, and we do indeed emit electromagnetic radiation which relates to physiological activity, and we understand the principles by which information may be encoded onto electromagnetic waves (this principle, called modulation, is how audio and video signals are transmitted by radio waves). The second category is that originally advocated by Michael Persinger. He proposed that psi involves the naturally occurring radiation that makes up the Earth's electromagnetic field. He proposed a simple synchronisation effect wherein the conditions of this field affected two people simultaneously, causing both to have similar experience. When the two later compared notes, they might conclude that they had experienced a case of psi, erroneously supposing the experience was due to the transfer of a signal between them. This approach is essentially a classical case of a "hidden variable." While this could possibly explain some simple experiences, it could not account for more complex experiences, or those where there did indeed appear to be a transfer of information. For such cases, Persinger goes on to propose that the naturally occurring wave might be used as a carrier wave in the same way as with the mental radio model, with the weak electromagnetic field of the psi agent imposing the desired information onto this stronger wave.

Becker, R. O. (1992). "Electromagnetism and Psi Phenomena." *Journal of the American Society for Psychical Research* 86, no. 1, pp. 1–17.

Persinger, M. A. (1989). "Psi Phenomena and Temporal Lobe Activity: The Geomagnetic Factor." *Research in Parapsychology*. Scarecrow Press, pp. 121–156.

Persinger, M. A., and S. Krippner (1989). "Dream ESP Experiences and Geomagnetic Activity." *Journal of the American Society for Psychical Research* 83, pp. 101–116.

# PSI, SCIENCE, AND SOCIETY

**ARTICLE 14.** SOME THOUGHTS INSPIRED BY THE ESSAY TITLE: "HOW THE SCIENTIFIC ESTABLISHMENT'S ACCEPTANCE OF ESP AND PK WOULD INFLUENCE CONTEMPORARY SOCIETY," *by Serena Roney-Dougal, 1992.*

[Source: Serena Roney-Dougal. "Some Thoughts Inspired by the Essay Title: 'How the Scientific Establishment's Acceptance of ESP and PK Would Influence Contemporary Society.'" *Exceptional Human Experience* 10, no. 1, pp. 16–22 (1992).]

*Editors' Comments*

Dr. Serena Roney-Dougal is a British parapsychologist who received her Ph.D. from Surrey University. For over thirty years she has been studying and teaching in the realms of parapsychology, spirituality, psychic healing, altered states of consciousness, mental development, yogas, ancient myths and legends of Britain bearing on the "fairy [faery] faith" (see also Čiča, 2002), dowsing, divination, traditional and indigenous faiths, sacred sites, and related topics. In the following selection, the final one of this volume, Roney-Dougal makes connections between psi and, among other topics, spirituality, religion, occultism, morality, conscience, mythology, traditional "sacred sites," and past and future societies. Psi phenomena have met with wide acceptance in some ancient and traditional societies. If contemporary establishment science were to accept, or even embrace, psi, there would be far-ranging implications for all aspects of modern society.

## SOME THOUGHTS INSPIRED BY THE ESSAY TITLE: "HOW THE SCIENTIFIC ESTABLISHMENT'S ACCEPTANCE OF ESP AND PK WOULD INFLUENCE CONTEMPORARY SOCIETY,"
*by Serena Roney-Dougal, 1992.*

This essay has been inspired by the competition title[1], enabling me to express some deeply felt thoughts that I would not normally write

---

1. This essay was submitted to the Imich Essay Contest, which was initiated by Dr. Alexander Imich in 1987 to stimulate interest in the question of "How the Scientific Establishment's Acceptance of ESP and PK Would Influence Contemporary Society," hence the title of this paper, which otherwise might better be called something like "The Spiritualization of the Occult" or "Magic and Conscience." The essay is especially notable because although the author has a doctorate in psychology, this paper is based not on her academic training but is written from the heart. Because EHE [the journal *Exceptional Human Experience*] is founded on the idea that Western scientific rationality cannot do justice to exceptional human experiences and that we need to go further within ourselves to find a deeper fulcrum to begin our studies, we welcome Dr. Roney-Dougal's attempt to do just that.—Ed. [Editor of the journal *Exceptional Human Experience*]

down. I have taken the opportunity to write my thoughts, ideas, ideals, and dreams in a totally nonanalytic, nonscientific, nonrationalist, and nonlogical manner. In fact, it is the total opposite of the type of article, paper, or lecture that I am accustomed to write. I have felt a deep need to write this essay, and it feels very good to have written it, as I do sincerely feel that I am raising ethical and moral issues that every parapsychologist must confront. Quite possibly many of them have confronted these issues already, but if so, they are remarkably silent about it.

Psi, in itself, is a talent, a force, a power that can be used for good or evil, as is so well exemplified in our mythical and fairy tale literature. Taking this theoretical assumption as potential fact, I would be downright scared if the present-day materialist establishment scientist accepted ESP and PK. After all, look what they did with the discovery of atomic physics; they, together with the politicians, promptly turned it into the ever-present threat of world destruction that has so profoundly affected every aspect of our lives ever since. I would not trust the present-day scientific and political establishment to put psi to good use because its major impetus in essence is life destructive. It is essential that the establishment scientists maintain their disinterest and disbelief until the whole worldview (i.e. a paradigm so pervasive that it is accepted by the whole of society without question and without people even realizing that it is a worldview) of our society has shifted to a more spiritually oriented philosophy that does not immediately seek to use every discovery to gain control over others, especially for purposes of warfare, such as remote viewing for spying or the dreaded "thought police" of science fiction.

I do in fact see this attitude beginning to change in the corridors of power and within the ivory towers, and this essay is written looking towards the positive. I hope it will help to create what I see as a possible future outcome of psi research, together with the whole shift in worldview that accompanies the deep level knowing and living from the "clairvoyant reality" (LeShan, 1974).

## Assumptions

There are two assumptions in the title: ESP and PK are valid phenomena and the scientific establishment influences contemporary society. I have recently come across some amusing examples that would seem to bear out the second assumption; however, as far as I can see, in most instances our society is influenced first and foremost by the media, and it is only the underlying worldview that is influenced by the academic establishment. This influence percolates through in various formats until eventually, with a time delay of several decades, it affects society. As far as acceptance of psi goes, it seems as though the academic community is totally out of synch with a large proportion of contemporary society, which is presently enthusiastically espousing all matter psychic and spiritual. There are hundreds of new spiritual groups, a new pagan resurgence, diverse occult societies, and dozens of growth therapies and personal development groups; trancing, channeling, crystal therapies, healing groups, rebirthing, Reiki, EST, and all the other cults and movements of the past two decades far too numerous to mention.

From this point of view, it appears that the scientific establishment will be about the last to change, and so its influence on contemporary society is more in the way of confirmation of changes that have already happened, thus forming what was once new into the accepted and the established, which then becomes the worldview. The establishment, by its very nature, has an inertial, restraining force on new ideas. It holds onto the old ways longest, but once it does incorporate new ideas, then they in turn are held onto tenaciously for a very long time.

It is necessary, therefore, in order to see what sort of influence the scientists of that time would have on society, to picture exactly what sort of establishment there would be that did accept psi (ESP and PK). Not only the attitude towards psi would have changed. A whole lifestyle and the philosophy that engendered it would have changed as well, and if it had not, would not the planet be in *very* serious trouble?

## THE EMERGING PHILOSOPHY:
## A POTENTIAL CHANGE IN WORLDVIEW

What is a society like that accepts psi as part and parcel of its being? In this essay we must disregard all the vast array of prior cultures as possible prototypes, because we now live in a global village as a result of our technological achievements, and so there is an ever increasing blending together of all the cultures within our planet. Psi within society has a very different meaning when you can pick up the telephone and speak with a friend on the other side of the world! Thus, the "New Age" or "Aquarian" culture, which has grown up within our technologically sophisticated world, is probably the best indicator we have of a future psi-oriented society. The dissidents of one generation are the establishment of the next.

The first thing that strikes me about this subculture is that they use all the technology but firmly reject the materialistic philosophy and value systems of the society that created the technology. They are highly spiritual in a nonreligious sense; that is, there is a recognition and a respect for the spiritual aspect of life, but there is as yet no clear *form*: each individual finds his or her own way through the plethora of spiritual teachings. People seem to be trying out various old systems, such as Buddhism, Paganism, Hinduism, Sufism, and they are blending them together into a mystical framework very akin to the "perennial philosophy" described by Huxley (1946, 1974). It seems that people are no longer looking to a God to tell them what to do, or to help them when they are in trouble, or to punish them when they are naughty, or to forgive them, but are actually looking within themselves for *all* these things. They are finding the divinity within their own selves and are becoming self-responsible. It is as though when humanity was very young, in the Neolithic and through the Bronze Ages, people looked to an all-beneficent Mother and worshipped Her, much as babies and toddlers idolize their mothers. As humanity grew up, needs changed and patriarchy emerged with people looking to a stern Father to discipline them and keep them on the right path. During the so-called Age of Reason, humanity, like all other adolescents, rebelled and rejected both Mother and Father. But now humanity is reaching the age of adulthood, and we must become Father and Mother within ourselves. We must accept total responsibility for the power of our very thoughts to create our own reality, which includes our gods. We must accept total responsibility for the care of our planet and all upon it, as did the Mother in matriarchal times, and we must discipline and guide, as did the Father in patriarchal times, both within ourselves and within society. We can no longer do wrong and look to a Father to forgive us and put it all right; we must shoulder the responsibility ourselves.

This philosophy is of necessity more abstract than that of religions of the past because an adult can work with a greater degree of abstraction than can children who need concrete examples (myths and parables) in order to understand what they are being told. Nor do adults need the bribery and blackmail implicit in the Christian teachings of fear of hell-fire or the rewards of heaven, as did adolescent humanity. Rather, we can now appreciate and work for the mutual good and benefit not only of our own selves but for that of the whole planet. This is no longer a selfish philosophy emphasizing enlightenment or heavenly reward of the individual: it is a collective philosophy concerned with the evolution of consciousness of humanity as a whole, but one by which each individual stands to gain.

This emerging philosophy sees the universe and all life as an intercon-nected whole, with every action and every thought affecting every part of the universe. This philosophy sees spirit in every aspect of life: water, earth, air and fire. The Fairy Faith of the Celtic peoples is in some ways being renewed and, as Evans-Wentz (1911, 1977) pointed out, belief in psi is an integral part of that old faith—a faith that was very close to na-ture. This new philosophy sees our species as going through an evolution-ary shift that is greater than each of us individually—a shift inspired and in some way generated by Mother Nature (Planet Earth or Gaia are the latest fashionable words). Thus, at a practical level, this philosophy says that we are wholly part of the Universe (as in holography), and especially so of the planet, so we *must* learn to live in harmony with it. The realization that all is interwoven and interlinked must surely create a change in practical life attitudes, such as appreciating the need to recycle everything: no more trash cans, no more garbage dumps. Electricity from renewable sources together with energy conservation would lead to less acid rain, less nuclear waste and radioactive discharge. Energy can be conserved even in such simple ways as using wash lines rather than tumble dryers and solar- or wind-powered cars that reduce the noxious fumes that kill our trees. And an end must be put to the present debt-driven economy that is slowly murdering the planet because all countries are in debt and have to overproduce in order to pay back the interest rates charged. At the individual level, for example, this in turn forces farmers to use pesticides and fertilizers on their land in order to make sufficient profit to pay the banks, and in other ways, every one who has some form of debt or loan is contributing to the overuse of the planet's resources. These and many more examples of attitude change are inspired by the question, "How is the way in which I live my life affecting the rest of the planet?" and they are having a radical effect on the way we actually live our lives. This change will accelerate once the Establishment acknowledges the psychic-spiritual realm as the *equal* corollary of the material.

The United States is seen by most people in the world as the worst offender in this respect, because it is the affluence of our American life style that is crippling the rest of the world, particularly South and Central America. Under the emerging philosophy it is up to each individual to change their life style in accord with the planet's needs. There is great emphasis on each individual living their belief every day at every moment, living a spiritual awareness of the interconnectedness of everything at every level. If the scientific establishment accepts the existence of psi, then they are going to be affected in some way by this holistic mystical philosophy because psi is a logical, necessary aspect of it. As Krippner (1982) has remarked, "If the brain is a hologram interpreting a holographic universe, ESP and PK are necessary components of that universe. Indeed, holographic theorists would have to hypothesize the existence of ESP and PK had not the parapsychologists carefully documented their existence over the years" (pp. 124–125).

## The New Physics

Many of the aspects of the change in worldview that would accompany the scientific establishment's acceptance of ESP and PK are already occurring in the "New Physics." If Newton had not made his discoveries, the philosophy of the clockwork universe would never have been promulgated nor accepted so enthusiastically, though doubtless sooner or later someone would have proposed it because it grew out of the spirit of the time. We have a similar evolution occurring in our time with quantum physics, which has taken 50 years to emerge from the laboratory into a position of influence in the way that people view the world. Books like the *Tao of Physics* (Capra, 1975) have deeply affected contemporary society, whatever the scientific establishment may think about them. *The Holographic Paradigm* (Wilber, 1982) and *The Implicate Order* (Bohm, 1980) offer a new worldview that is closely linked with the perennial philosophy held by mystics of all ages, at a time when there is very deep dissatisfaction with the old materialistic reductionist worldview. The journal *Nature* might consider Sheldrake's *A New Science of Life* (1981) a candidate for burning, but the people loved it.

All these new ideas from various scientists are being enthusiastically accepted by a wide range of people. If there had been no Einstein or no quantum physics, then this new/old philosophy could not have inspired and taken root in contemporary society in the same way. This is the way the scientific establishment influences society despite itself! There is obviously an enormous *need* for this new philosophy for it to have been so eagerly and rapidly absorbed and embraced by so many. In accepting psi there wouldn't be quite the radical shift that is being required in the change from a Newtonian to an Einsteinian world. In fact, this present shift is in many ways preparing the establishment for the acceptance of psi, and I feel that *only* when the "New Physics" philosophy is well grounded will the psi worldview come into its own, for a psi worldview is essentially the same as that promulgated in the *Holographic Paradigm* and other books of a similar nature, of which there are so many at present.

## The Changing Face of the Occult

In the process of the scientific establishment's coming to accept psi, many of the present fears connected with the occult, witchcraft in particular, have to be faced, for it is part of the history of the white race that profoundly affects our present attitudes. The trauma engendered throughout a whole continent by the horrors of the Inquisition and the so-called Witch Trials in which an estimated 9 million women were tortured and murdered, together with a small number of men, is still manifest today, and is probably the single most important factor behind present-day skepticism towards psi—and also present-day parapsychologists' unwillingness to be associated with occultism. We must not forget that the Roman Catholic Church, under penalty of excommunication, forbade the practice of any psychical arts, even healing, and the Church ruled over most of Europe for nearly 900 years, right up to the Protestant Reformation. Today we may laugh at the idea of excommunication, but in those times it was the equivalent of being a leper.

It is difficult to explain the extent to which the Inquisition still affects us today except by an analogy such as the following. In the reign of William of Orange and Mary in Britain (1689–1702), a clan in Scotland called Campbell visited their neighbors, the Macdonalds, bearing a note from William of Orange stating that the Macdonalds should be punished for being tardy in accepting his authority over them. The Campbells did not act openly and were invited in by the Macdonalds as guests and treated with all hospitality and courtesy. The next morning the Campbells blocked both ends of the pass of Glencoe and murdered every single Macdonald: men, women, children, and babes. The horror of this massacre still echoes today, and anyone named Campbell living in Scotland will bear witness to this. If such a small localized event can cause such ripples over the centuries, consider the effect of the sustained murders by the Inquisition and the Witch Trials over a whole continent for nearly three centuries. The Inquisition led directly to the Protestant movement and the intense hatred of Papists in Britain to the extent of importing a German monarch to rule the country rather than having the rightful heir who was a Catholic. The Witch Trials, which continued under the Protestants, initiated the folklore of the wicked witch or evil step-mother that exist today in our children's stories, and led later to a denial that psi even existed. It is very feasible that a large part of the "fear of psi" discussed by Tart (1984) is a relic of these times.

In my research into occultism, I found that occultism is a relic of various pre-Christian religions; esoteric Judaic, Egyptian, and pagan European. In all these religions, psi plays a central role in one's interaction with spiritual reality, in whatever form it may be seen by that religion. There are good and bad groups involved with the occult, even as there are in every other aspect of life, and the good and responsible members of the occult groups and societies all seem to be promoting the positive aspects of the New Age philosophy outlined above. Surely, this can only be for the good of the planet, and therefore all of us.

## Witchcraft, the Fairy Faith and Earth Mysteries

Witchcraft, often called the Craft of the Wise or Wicca, is the old religion of Britain and much of Europe, and it is found everywhere there was a belief in fairies. Both of these faiths, the Wiccan and the Fairy Faith (Evans-Wentz, 1911, 1977), are connected with a belief in "second sight," seers being practitioners of the Craft, or blessed by fairies. The practice of the Craft is at best the application of psi for healing, for seeing into the future, for making the Earth fertile so that crops grow well, cows bear milk, hens lay. Naturally this craft has a negative side, and it is this which is most emphasized when the ignorant think of witchcraft. There is a clear historical reason for this negative emphasis on practical applications of psi, as discussed above. It was only by emphasizing the negative and creating a fear of evil witches that the Church could extinguish the ancient pagan religion.

The new occultism that is emerging today emphasizes the spiritual, the good, the caring aspect of psi because it is very important that this feeling that psi is evil be eradicated. To this end, it is probably very important that we adopt the yogic philosophy that it is *the spiritual* development of the person that is most important, with the psychic abilities, or siddhis, being merely markers along the path of personal self-development and not goals to be pursued for their own sake, else one become a fakir (faker) rather than a yogi (one united with the divine).

A central aspect of the new occultism, which is linked with the Fairy Faith and the Craft, is the growing discipline of Earth Mysteries. There has been a vast quantity of research over the past 60 years into ley lines and ancient stone circles, dolmens, menhirs, tumuli, and barrows that has been totally ignored by most scientists, including parapsychologists, and yet it is very relevant to our understanding of the social implications of psi from an anthropological and historical perspective. This research into ancient monuments has found that tumuli and barrows are often called fairy mounds and are reputed to be the places where "fairy folk" live. Tumuli, stone circles, and ley lines tend to be places where there are geomagnetic anomalies (Deverux, 1982), which ties in with Persinger's (1987) research into the correlation between geomagnetism and reported instances of psi. There is sufficient material now available to be able to propose the hypothesis that these ancient sacred sites are places where psi ability can be enhanced. The folklore that the builders of these incredible monuments were scientists of the psychic arts no longer seems so fanciful in the light of this research. Earth Mysteries researchers (Evans, 1984; Michell, 1967) have also suggested that the modern UFO sightings are equivalent in many ways to our ancestors' sightings of fairies, the mythology of both being very similar. These hypotheses need to be tested before they can be considered anything more than anecdote and folklore. That is the tour de force of parapsychology and the scientific method in general: that it can turn the nebulous and nefarious into confirmed and proven phenomena.

Parapsychologists, in particular, should remember that our subject matter is the technology, the tool, of the occultist. We *should* therefore be working as closely with the occultist as we are being urged to work with the conjuring magician, putting to the test and verifying that which is correct in their lore, and weeding out what is incorrect, for their good and for ours. What right have we scientists to look down our noses and say "the occult is very popular, and we won't touch that stuff because it is only superstition, and we are much too superior; nor do we want our precious image to be tarnished by contact with them." What right have we to be so superior, so distant, so cold, so clinical? What if the people are right? There is a need for mystery and magic, and the stronger that need is stamped upon the more it will emerge in disturbed psychotic ways. Jung (1977, 1987) equates spirit with the collective unconscious, and the symbols and phenomena of the occult are typical archetypes. By denying these archetypes we deny a very deep part of ourselves that then emerges in various distorted forms such as Nazism, fascism, and the present-day hatred of nature that is so rapidly destroying the ecosystem necessary to sustain life. For, having destroyed the Spirit by denying its existence, now the destructive force is turning to the material aspect of life. Once one accepts that there is a fundamental spiritual *need* in a person's life, then it will be given a fair chance of being expressed in a positive manner that will help the person to develop mentally and spiritually, rather than repressing it so that it harms them by making them neurotic, unfulfilled, dissatisfied, greedy, and all the other characteristics of our materialistic world. I feel that this is an integral part of the change that will occur once psi is accepted by establishment scientists.

## Some Thoughts Regarding Spirit

Consider for a moment the strange aberration of our society (or at least some of the academic elite of our society), in its refusal to accept the existence of Spirit or spirits (other than the alcoholic variety). The evidence of archaeology and anthropology shows that all cultures from the beginning of recorded history and probably before and in every part of the globe have believed in spirits. It is only in the last three centuries that there has been a growing lack of belief, but even in the last 50 years, which has probably been the most materialistic epoch this globe has ever known, many people still believe in Spirit or spirits in some form or other. Even in our avowedly antispiritual culture, the materialistic philosophy is actually confined primarily to the academic establishment and to city dwellers.

So the really intriguing question is why do these materialists hold their totally aberrant belief that there are no spirits? They have never *proven* that spirits do not exist; they have just reasoned them away! Is it not strange? Is it not very strange that the intense technological change of our century should coincide with the only period in the whole of human history when certain influential thinkers have doubted the existence of spirits? Why, I ask myself, should there have been such a universal belief if there were no reason for it? And I do mean reason, not proof! And would not the quality of life be improved if we did recognize and honor the existence of spirits—the Spirit of the Earth, the bubbling brook, the old oak tree, the Spirit of the Age? By recognizing and respecting the spirit of a thing, we can more readily care for it and love it and nurture it, and no society who so recognizes the spirit aspect of the world could mistreat planet Earth and all upon her as we moderns have done.

In the previous passage, I am not talking about ghosts and things that go bump in the night, but about a more abstract conception of spirit that is more in line with Jung, or with the idea expressed colloquially in phrases such as "spirit of the time." Jung viewed the soul as being the personal unconscious. He also considered that the soul of a living person becomes their spirit when they die. Thus he saw two quite distinct aspects of spirit, for spirit as the collective unconscious is the archetypal numinous aspect of all humanity. The Fairy Faith of Europe is probably a relic of the ancient animistic religion, but that is at present manifesting in the form of UFOs (Evans, 1984). The language of the collective unconscious is the language of symbols as used so extensively in religions, and its medium is dreams and other altered states of consciousness that permit access to primary process mentation. Psi events are frequently manifestations of the collective unconscious, which stirs us very deeply at a nonlogical, nonanalytical, nonintellectual level. For we are not just a bundle of thoughts, we have feelings, emotions, sensations, and intuitions as well, and probably most of our days are actually lived at these levels: feeling good, feeling bad, feeling like going for a walk, and so on. The recent trend in meditation and other techniques for expanding awareness has emphasized how much can be missed if we equate mind solely with logical, verbal thought.

## The Energy-Matter Equation

It occurred to me some years ago when I was trying to explain some aspects of the new physics to a lay audience, that Einstein's famous equation, $E = mc^2$, can be seen as a symbol of the shift that is occurring from a materialistic worldview to a spiritual one. Since Newton the Western world has focused almost exclusively on the matter side of the equation, on the material side of life, and now the shift towards focusing on the energy side of the equation is beginning and is reflected in the language of the young, as in such phrases as "good vibes." Thus, one can conceive of the spirit of a thing as being the energy aspect of that thing, which is directly related to its matter aspect but which has totally different laws governing its behavior, as is found in particle physics (e.g., the wave/particle aspect of light itself).

The energy engendered by emotion is probably the strongest energy of our body/minds, with the emotional energy engendered by religious beliefs possibly the most powerful, for good or ill (as seen in the various religious wars around the world, e.g., Northern Ireland, Iran). When we concentrate our attention on the energy side of humanity, we start to concentrate on the spiritual aspect of life, an aspect that is so furiously denied by the materialists, who concentrate their attention solely on the matter side of the equation. Thus, establishment scientists' response to parapsychology is primarily an emotional one, though they might dress it up with logic and analysis, and they reject parapsychology for exactly the same reason that they reject the spiritual aspect of life. Those who advocate parapsychology also must recognize that there is an emotional component to their behavior, for if they work without heart then they are soulless machines, and no good will come of their work. We are dealing here with issues that encompass more than the rational or the purely intellectual. There is always an emotional component, however much it may be dressed up in impersonal terminology and logical rationalism. By asserting that there are psychic events occurring in our own and others' lives we open up a Pandora's box in which all the spiritual aspects of life were shut up and locked away during the "Age of Reason." This locking up of our spiritual awareness and the spiritual aspect of life has led directly to the material problems confronting our generation.

The negative spiritual aspect of the mind has often been conceptualized as demonic, and we disregard demons at our peril, for they are reappearing as mass psychosis in our prisons and mental hospitals, which are overflowing with violent, aggressive, crazy people—mainly men. It is interesting to note, that men have been the perpetrators of the worst horrors in the name of materialism. The people who are polluting the air and the seas and threatening the whole planet with destruction *must* find their souls, their hearts, their spiritual beings. At present they appear to be soulless automatons; only heartless creatures could so destroy our beautiful planet.

### The Religious Impulse

Many psychical researchers, particularly the founders of the psychical research societies, were openly religious; for instance, William James wrote *The Varieties of Religious Experience* (1903), and more recently, Sir Alister Hardy set up the Religious Experience Research Unit at Oxford University. So not all parapsychologists have been ashamed of the religious connotations of parapsychology, although parapsychology is the materialistic, mechanistic aspect of psi research. An indication of this is that there is not one reference to the above book by James in the *Handbook of Parapsychology* (Wolman, 1977). If parapsychology continues to resist its spiritual implications there is a possibility that if and when the scientific establishment accepts the existence of psi, it will use and abuse psi in much the same way that the findings of nuclear physics have been abused. If however, the philosophies discussed in this paper are an integral part of accepting the existence of psi, including by parapsychologists themselves, then psi will be less likely to be exploited for personal greed and gain.

Let us not, therefore, deny the motive force of religion, but rather let us admit openly that our society *needs* this aspect of life as much as it needs the material aspect. "Men, women and children do not live by bread alone." Through parapsychology we can perhaps find the language to re-state the eternal truths of all the religions—a language that is of necessity a scientific language, because this is the language with the most influence over a large proportion of influential people at this time. The mystical philosophy encompasses the basic truths of all the religions from prehistoric times to the present day, from pagan times to Zen. Having a near-death experience or an out-of-body experience, seeing a ghost or "knowing" that a loved one far away is in trouble, can often be a direct manifestation of the spiritual world of the person having the psi experience. Therefore, if and when the scientific establishment accepts ESP and PK, its worldview must encompass a philosophy that is aware of the energy aspect (i.e., spirit) as well as the matter aspect. So we must not ignore the spirit hypothesis. Philosophically and intellectually, I do not know if it is provable; but within my heart, I know that we ignore that aspect of life at our peril and at the peril of the planet and all forms of life upon it.

The founders of psychical research were interested in proving the existence of spirits to help stem the then rising tide of materialism. However, they also felt it necessary to distance themselves from spiritualism and from occultism, both of which were flourishing in Victorian times. By openly expressing their disgust with physical mediumship and rejecting, or at least shelving, a spirit hypothesis, it is possible that parapsychologists have thrown the baby out with the bathwater. Despite rampant spiritualism, mediumship, and occultism, the overall prevailing spirit of Victorian times was a reductionist and materialistic one—but oh! What a dark spirit to follow, one that even led to people losing their minds during the peak of behaviorism.

Through psychic phenomena we actually have to contemplate the possibility of what have always been considered to be attributes of divinity, such as omniscience, for telepathy, clairvoyance, and precognition make it at least theoretically possible to know everything; and omnipotence, for that is the logical conclusion to which the concept of PK leads. In other words, psi is the manifestation of what have always been considered to be divine forces, so let us recognize the potential divinity of our natures, realize that we can create reality in a very literal sense, and let that reality we create recognize the existence of spirit, rather than creating a reality that denies the existence of spirit, or questions it in inappropriate ways, as we presently do, which is nearly as bad. Let us be high-spirited in our lives, but not spiritless!

## Ethics and Morality

As I mentioned earlier, it is possible that part of the fear of the occult shown by so many parapsychologists is because the occult represents the remnants of various ancient persecuted religions. These religions emphasized the spiritual side of Nature and life, and psi was used as a "spiritual technology." Without a rigorous ethics and morality this leads to a disgusting abuse of mental power. The blackest magicians of our present society are those who are destroying our planet in the name of progress and profit (in the past they were called greed and avarice). To acknowledge that energy is interchangeable with matter and that there is an energy aspect to be considered as well as a material one is to re-evaluate the *whole* of one's life, in much the same way as the New Age worldview leads to a re-evaluation. When we add psi to this we have to ask questions such as "Do I pollute the world with negative thoughts, including the guilt trip for having the negative thoughts?" For surely every thought one has has the potential for affecting everything else. And, "Am I aware of and in control of all my negative emotions?" for my negative emotions can play havoc with those around me, let alone the potential effect that they have on the general world atmosphere. In other words, we have to embrace what has always been called a religious or spiritual philosophy very akin to Buddhism.

If, in potential, I can astral travel in the true sense of the words, and thus can mentally link with any place in the universe, then I begin to realize the awesome potential of my mind and how careful I must be with my thoughts, because my thoughts not only link me with all of creation but can also materialize into physical reality. Then the Buddhist creed of "Right Thought" strikes home in a very dramatic and immediate manner. Full activation of our psi potential brings considerable responsibility and a dreadful need for a truly spiritual state of being: a realization of the divinity within each of us.

I have always seen parapsychology as the "earthing" of the spiritual. In our experiments we explore the psychic in a very logical, rational, exoteric manner. We assign clearly demonstrable proof ratings to the different variables. In such a manner we have inadvertently confirmed many spiritual teachings, for example, that one's attitude or belief about something may actually affect the occurrence of that particular matter. Faith, it used to be called, although now it is "the sheep-goat effect," was said to be able to move mountains. Jesus spoke quite extensively on the incredible effect of faith, which has now become transmuted to attitude, and the Hindus have a spiritual path centered around faith called Bhakti Yoga. Our modern terms are more applicable to our present society, but underneath the change in terminology the concept lives on.

Another example of the "earthing of a religious concept" occurs when doing a ganzfeld or other free-response experiment. The first thing the participant is taught to do is to become aware of the content of their mind. This action is what the Christians call contemplation and the Buddhists call mindfulness, and it is the first step in meditation, the first step in learning how to develop one's mind. The state of consciousness that the ganzfeld induces is to be found in quite a number of different religions as well, albeit induced by radically different methods, such as getting up and chanting at 3 A.M. The point in common with all of the methods is the aim to create a state of consciousness whereby the conscious mind is stopped, thus allowing one to access material from the collective unconscious.

## Science with a Conscience

It is no wonder, then, that so many academic scientists are so skeptical of, and derisive about, parapsychology. Whether we like it or not we are advocating a return to a spiritual way of life, one that puts spirit energy back into the materialist equation, and this threatens the whole power base of the materialist science that is presently in power. They also find it threatening because it means that they have to look into their own consciences once again. (I even had to look up the spelling of "conscience," it is so long since I used the word; con-science, with knowledge.) Inglis (1986) calls today's science "scientism," and when I see advertisements on television no longer using sex or affluence to sell their products but rather a "scientist" in a white coat, then I know that scientists are verily the most influential symbol of today, the high priests of the latest religion. This makes it even more important for scientists to regain their conscience, their morality, their judgment of what is right and wrong. It makes it even more important for scientists to admit publicly that matter has spirit as its counterpart, just as light has dark as its counterpart, for then the whole of our city-based society will do likewise, rather than just the few dissidents and country people as at present. If an advertisement can sell washing powder through "scientific" approval then we can sell anything! It is important to note here that it is society's view of establishment science that is selling the washing powder. With psi we have the strange situation of phenomena that a majority of people, according to the polls, believe in, but that are rejected by establishment science. If the establishment were to accept psi, then the belief system of the whole society would change accordingly.

As mentioned briefly earlier, scientists must learn to follow their hearts as well as their minds, for psi is a very emotional method of communication, a feeling more often than a thought. The aspect of bringing heart back into science and society is possibly one of the more important influences that must occur with the acceptance of psi by the establishment.

Just as a healer can affect the rate of growth of a seedling or the healing of a wound, so we can affect the healing of Planet Earth. I am not suggesting that with the acceptance of psi there will be a return to superstition, because superstition is belief without any foundation, without confirmation. The method of science is a sure way to a clear understanding of the matter in question, and so makes a firm foundation for a belief. However, I do feel that the present philosophy associated with science will change along with the establishment science's acceptance of psi. Then we will have a science with a conscience, a science that not only examines the *tools* of magic, but one that also looks at the purpose for which the tools are intended once they are ready for the marketplace.

# REFERENCES

Bohm, D. (1980). *Wholeness and the Implicate Order*. London: Routledge and Kegan Paul.

Capra, F. (1975). *The Tao of Physics*. London: Fontana.

Devereux, P. (1982). *Earth Lights: Towards an Understanding of the Unidentified Flying Object Enigma*. Wellingborough, Northamptonshire, UK: Turnstone Press.

Evans, H. (1984). *Visions, Apparitions, Alien Visitors*. Wellingborough, Northamptonshire, UK: Aquarian Press.

Evans-Wentz, W. Y. (1977). *The Fairy-Faith in Celtic Countries*. Gerrards Cross, UK: Colin Smythe. (Originally published in 1911.)

Huxley, A. (1974). *The Perennial Philosophy*. London: Chatto and Windus. (Originally published in 1946.)

Inglis, B. (1986). *The Hidden Power*. London: Jonathan Cape.

James, W. (1903). *The Varieties of Religious Experience: A Study in Human Nature*. London: Longman, Green.

Jung, C. G. (1987). *Psychology and the Occult*. Princeton, N.J.: Princeton University Press. (Originally published in 1977.)

Krippner, S. (1982). "Holonomy and Parapsychology." In K. Wilber, editor. *The Holographic Paradigm and Other Paradoxes: Exploring the Leading Edge of Science*. Boulder, Colo.: Shambhala, pp. 124–125.

LeShan, L. (1974). *The Medium, the Mystic, and the Physicist: Toward a General Theory of the Paranormal*. New York: Viking.

Michell, J. F. (1967). *The Flying Saucer Vision: The Holy Grail Restored*. London: Sidgwick and Jackson.

Persinger, M. A. (1987). "Spontaneous Telepathic Experiences from *Phantasms of the Living* and Low Global Geomagnetic Activity." *Journal of the American Society for Psychical Research* 81, pp. 23–36.

Sheldrake, R. (1981). *A New Science of Life: The Hypothesis of Formative Causation*. London: Blond and Briggs.

Tart, C. T. (1984). "Acknowledging and Dealing with the Fear of Psi." *Journal of the American Society for Psychical Research* 78, pp. 133–143.

Wilber, K., editor (1982). *The Holographic Paradigm and Other Paradoxes: Exploring the Leading Edge of Science*. Boulder, Colo.: Shambhala.

Wolman, B. B., editor (1977). *Handbook of Parapsychology*. New York: Van Nostrand Reinhold.

# CONCLUDING REMARKS

THINKING CLEARLY ABOUT THE PARANORMAL. WHERE DO WE, THE COMPILERS, STAND? THE FUTURE OF PARAPSYCHOLOGY, AND THE FUTURE OF THE PLANET.

*I profess no overwhelming certainty as to the true explanation of the phenomena un-*
*der review. I am, however, certain of two things. The first is that we are here con-*
*fronted with a great range of unsolved problems and unexplained phenomena, all of*
*which are potentially of great psychological and philosophical interest. The second is*
*that these issues are not of merely academic concern. They are important to anyone*
*who thinks and feels about the human situation.*

—ALAN GAULD *(Mediumship and Survival: A Century of Investigations, 1983, p. 16)*

*No one, I imagine, in recent years, has had the aprioristic temerity of a Helmhotz*
*[Hermann von Helmholtz, German physicist, 1821–1894], who told Sir William*
*Barrett that neither the testimony of all the Fellows of the Royal Society nor the ev-*
*idence of his own senses would make him believe in thought-transference [that is,*
*telepathy], since this phenomenon was impossible! Nor would it be easy to find a*
*contemporary parallel to the eminent biologist who told William James that even if*
*telepathy were an established fact, scholars should conspire to suppress or hide it,*
*since such facts would upset the uniformity of nature.*

—THEODORE BESTERMAN *(Collected Papers on the Paranormal, 1968, p. 85)*

## Thinking Clearly About the Paranormal

In this volume we have presented an overview of some of the key aspects of the study of the paranormal. What does one make of all the data and analyses, all the opinions and theories, concerning this most perplexing subject?

The late John Beloff (1990, pp. 15–27, in an essay first presented as a public lecture in 1963) outlined five major approaches, positions, or guiding principles relative to psychical and paranormal phenomena. Here we review his classification, commenting and elaborating upon it further.

§ 1. **Total Disbelief** (our term) in the paranormal. This is essentially the position of the extreme skeptics, the institutionalized Skepticism. No paranormal phenomena exist, and all the reputed evidence for paranormal phenomena can be explained away by some combination of scientific naïveté on the part of the "believer" in the paranormal, human credulity, self-deception and wishful thinking, and downright purposeful deception and fraud, either on the part of researchers in the field, on the part of the subjects, or both. In the most basic form of this position, paranormal phenomena are explained away as not existing because they cannot exist; after all they would be paranormal, and paranormal phenomena have no place in "real science." We personally find this to be an extremely dogmatic and untenable position. Even if there should be no undoubted documented cases of the paranormal thus far recorded, in our conception of "true skepticism" one must regard with a healthy skepticism and critical faculty not only any claims for the paranormal, but also any claims that paranormal phenomena are flatly impossible and therefore all such evidence should be dismissed wholesale.

§ 2. **Paranormal Insignificance** (our term). Beloff (1990, p. 16) summarizes the second position as follows:

> According to this line of argument there are phenomena that are genuinely paranormal but they have absolutely no other significance.

They are, in fact, the exceptions in an otherwise well-ordered universe. They occur from time to time and we may take note of the fact but nothing whatsoever follows from their existence. The laws of nature still stand, everything goes on as before, only maybe a few scientists feel chastened at the discovery that their theories have not quite the universal application which, in a more self-confident mood, they might have claimed for them.

Beloff traces this idea back to the work of William James in the early twentieth century, who, somewhat similarly to Rupert Sheldrake (1981, 1988) more recently, suggested that possibly the laws of nature themselves evolved, and are still evolving, and thus are not as monolithic and absolute as most scientists believe. There may be occasional, perhaps spontaneous and totally unpredictable, exceptions to the rules that we observe and these instances are classified as paranormal. And indeed, by this conception they would not be normal, but in a way they are so totally anomalous that no larger theory can be developed from them and there is no way to systematically elicit paranormal effects (such as in a laboratory setting) or predict when they might occur, and for all practical purposes they have no utility and are best ignored. Beloff (1990, p. 16) suggests that James only suggested this theory "half playfully" and never took it very seriously, but Beloff does cite philosopher Antony Flew (1953) as someone who adopts a similar position of not absolutely denying all evidence for the paranormal, but downplaying it by regarding it as nothing more than weak or minor anomalies that lack any further scientific or philosophical implications.

We find this position, of acknowledging paranormal phenomena but then dismissing them as insignificant, shallow and perhaps self-serving to some parties. In our assessment, if paranormal phenomena of any kind (no matter how seemingly obscure, trivial, or rare) are genuine, this has profound philosophical implications. The very concept of the inviolability of natural law is a cornerstone of much of modern Western science. To acknowledge paranormal effects, but to then trivialize them and deny them any significance, is perhaps a classic example of having one's cake and eating it too. With such a position one does not need to either attempt to rationally argue paranormal phenomena away or upset one's own belief system. One simply and completely ignores paranormal phenomena.

§ 3. **Scientific Monism** (Beloff's term, 1990, p. 19). The third position summarized by Beloff (1990) is a very common one today. Despite mistakes made, and acknowledged cases of deception and fraud, there is a mass of empirical evidence for at least some genuine paranormal phenomena. Such phenomena are labeled "paranormal" because they do not fit within the bounds, framework, and theories of much of what we might call traditional science as generally conceived. Well, if this is the case, then it is not paranormal phenomena that must be explained away, but traditional science must be extended, perhaps rethought and retooled, to incorporate the paranormal phenomena (at which point they might be considered more "normal" although even when finally fit snuggly into a larger scientific framework the label paranormal may remain as a historical artifact). If the members of Skepticism ever admitted to the reality of any paranormal phenomena, they might adopt an attitude similar to this, with the possible additional comment to the effect that "well, we actually knew that all along" or "psychical researchers were right for the wrong reasons," thus still belittling scholars of the paranormal.

§ 4. **Substantial Dualism** (Beloff's term, 1990, p. 19). One can accept the reality of paranormal phenomena, including those demonstrated empirically using standard scientific methodology, yet from this fact not necessarily conclude that science, or at least physical science (in particular physics and chemistry), per se as currently formulated, must be extended, but rather conclude that there is a different order of reality, involving the mental, psychic, or conscious (including unconscious, subconscious, and super-conscious) aspects of humans and potentially other living beings. In a sense this position can be seen as postulating two parallel realms, both of which can be studied with scientific methodologies. The two realms are complementary and intersect and interact at places, but ultimately are separate and distinct and one may not necessarily depend on the other. Potentially, we might postulate, there could be a universe composed of only one or the other, rather than both. Perhaps we just happen to live in a universe that encompasses both realms.

Even if this hypothesis is accepted, that there are two distinct realms (the material-energy realm of physical science and the psychic realm), an "ultimate theory of everything" might be conceived that would unite the two realms into one at a higher level. This ultimately might lead back to something comparable to the third position (scientific monism) in the sense of an extended science, rather than paranormal phenomena being truly beyond science. This also brings up the philosophical problem of Descartes' mind–body dualism (see Burnham and Fieser, 2006; Calef, 2006; Descartes, 1641, 1901). If there is a physical universe "body" that operates according to certain principles, and a "mind" universe that operates according to its own laws, how do they operate in conjunction with one another?

Perhaps related to certain concepts of substantial dualism, psychologist and parapsychologist Lawrence L. LeShan has suggested that there are at least two basic ways to view and relate to the world, which he refers to as the "world of multiplicity" and the "world of the One" (LeShan, 1974b; see also LeShan, 1969, 1974a, 1984). In LeShan's conception, each of these represents "an altered state of consciousness" and "a different metaphysical system" (LeShan, 1974b, p. 574) "within which human beings can operate effectively in terms of the processes permitted in those systems" (p. 574). The world of multiplicity is the commonsense or everyday state of consciousness and reality, where objects and events are discrete and separate from each other, although they can certainly influence each other in cause-and-effect relationships. In the world of the One, attained or entered by many serious mystics, there are no separate and discrete entities, but everything is interacting with everything else in a larger field. According to LeShan, "Each metaphysical system permits certain types of events to occur and does not permit others. We can legitimately state that what is 'normal' (permissible) in one metaphysical

system is 'paranormal' (non-permissible) in another" (p. 573). Referring
to the world of the One, LeShan continues:

> In a universe in which matter is conceptualized as continuous and in
> which all objects, entities, and events "flow" into each other; in which
> boundaries and dividing lines are illusionary; and in which pastness, pre-
> sentness, and futurity are illusions, neither space nor time can act as pre-
> venting information exchange with the great One, which comprises the
> cosmos. Telepathy, precognition, clairvoyance, and the like are expected
> and normal processes with this system. [LeShan, 1974b, p. 575.]

§ 5. **Theory of Synchronicity** (Jung as cited by Beloff, 1990,
p. 19). The final position that Beloff (1990) discusses is a very old concept, but one he takes from Carl Jung (1952; see also Main, 1997, and
von Franz, 1980), namely synchronicity. This concept is essentially the
very ancient notion that there can be acausal, but nonetheless genuine,
links between disparate phenomena without any exchange of material or
energy between the linked phenomena. This can be labeled a principle
of sympathy, and described in terms of links between the microcosm and
the macrocosm, the inner world and the outer world. It can be viewed as
an underlying principle of both classical astrology and alchemy. The
modern thinker might argue against astrology by asserting that there is no
causal mechanism by which the positions of stars and planets can influence the fortunes of an individual human's life, but this is to misunder-
stand the very basis of astrology and the concept of sympathy and
synchronicity, "as above, so below." Likewise, alchemy (which Jung took
an interest in) was more about the transformation of the human soul and
psyche than turning base metal into gold. Applied to psi phenomena,
two persons having the same thought, or being able to call cards in a
deck above the level of chance, is not a matter of causal relationship, but
just is. Synchronicity. Or, another way to think about it in a Jungian sense
is that "absolute knowledge," or "knowledge of the unconscious," is
accessed (von Franz, 1980; see quotes from von Franz earlier in this

work, pages 34 and 44). The parapsychologist Theo K. de Graaf has "surmise[d] the existence of a probability space of which the space–time dimensions undergo a local constriction under the influence of an intentional information field. . . . Because of its conduciveness to generating synchronistic events, this local constriction of probability space was christened a synchronitron" (de Graaf and Houtkooper, 2004).

Beloff (1990, p. 23) argues against the acausal aspect of the Theory of Synchronicity, stating that: "Logically, an event A may be regarded as the cause of an event B provided it can be shown that an event of class A is sufficient condition for the occurrence of an event of class B. It is immaterial whether this implies action at a distance, action across a time interval or whether A is a mental event and B a physical event." In our opinion, however, this may simply devolve into a semantic argument if there is no known mechanism, or perhaps we should say no theory hypothesized, to link two events in a cause-and-effect relationship. If an event of class A is consistently correlated with an event of class B, then it may be that A is causal to B, or B is causal to A, or they are simply correlated in line with the old adage that "correlation does not necessarily imply causation."

## *Where Do We, the Compilers, Stand?*

A legitimate question to ask is, where do we, as commentators and compilers of the papers reprinted herein, stand on the issue of psi, psychical phenomena, parapsychology, and the paranormal? We have attempted to approach the subject of psychic phenomena from the perspective of genuine constructive skepticism (to use Truzzi's phrase, which captures the spirit of our intent; see above, page 256). That is, we did not come to this subject as "true believers" in psychic phenomena nor as ardent debunkers intent on proving that the very concept of psi studies is rubbish and unworthy of serious scientific attention. We will discuss the topics that we believe have the most "promise" within the field, and then some of the questions that remain even after performing a substantial review of the history and the study of parapsychology.

Of all the reputed psychical and parapsychological phenomena that have been reported and catalogued, telepathy is the category that we personally find there is the most compelling experimental and spontaneous evidence in support of. As has been pointed out many times before, telepathy is "perhaps the best attested of all psychical phenomena" (Beloff, 1990, p. 24). Much of the nineteenth-century work of the Society for Psychical Research was focused on telepathy, initially referred to variously as "thought-reading" and "thought-transference." Since the 1880s research on telepathy has been a mainstay of psychical researchers and parapsychologists. It seems to us that a strong case can be made for some form of telepathic communication from one mind to another in both experimental and spontaneous settings. However, we must stress that we are not obdurate "believers" in telepathy; we simply regard the evidence in favor of its occurrence as worthy of serious consideration.

Telepathy, like many purported instances of psi, as commonly experienced seems to be an elusive and even evasive phenomenon, one that cannot necessarily be produced "on command." It is unclear if all persons possess at least some limited telepathic ability. The evidence suggests to us strongly that certainly not everyone manifests telepathy in equal quantity. Some persons may display it prominently, at least at times, while others may live their entire lives without any known or acknowledged telepathic experiences (which does not necessarily mean they are not theoretically capable of such, but functionally any telepathic faculties may be suppressed by cultural and/or evolutionary processes). It also appears that certain pairs or small groups of individuals can share stronger telepathic connections than can other pairs or groups. Two people may possibly share a stronger than normal telepathic connection due to what we might term compatible brain/mind configurations or "resonance" and/or due to shared experiences together (for instance, living together for a period of time or possible sharing in a strong telepathy-inducing incident, such as a very traumatic or emotional event).

There is research that deals with some of the psychophysiological aspects of psi. By measuring such factors as heart rate, blood pressure, electroencephalographic readings, and electrodermal activity, researchers have been able to monitor the ways people respond on an emotional and instinctual level to stimuli. It is known that physiological responses of individuals may correlate, become "in sync," or resonate under certain circumstances, for instance if individuals are dancing or involved in athletic activity together, participating in religious or ritualistic ceremonies, or even watching a movie together, their heart rates, sweating, and so forth may occur in unison. They are said to be in entrainment (Mayer, 2007, pp. 234–235). Entrainment appears to be related to social bonding, and under typical circumstances there is nothing paranormal about it.

There is also evidence that entrainment may occur paranormally. Several studies have found significant physiologic correlations between emotionally or psychologically connected pairs of individuals even when the individuals were isolated from each other. In a typical study, individuals of such a pair might be isolated from each other in shielded rooms ten to twenty meters apart, and one member of the pair is shown images that serve as stimuli. By conventional thinking, the second member of the pair (isolated from the first such that no normal sensory communication is possible) should show no response. However, even when isolated from each other, statistically significant correlations were found between the pairs in the physiologic parameters monitored in a series of experiments (Radin, 2004; Standish et al., 2004). Is this a form of telepathy expressed at the basic level of essentially involuntary physiological responses? Is it what might be referred to colloquially as "entanglement" between individuals (analogous to the concept of quantum entanglement or quantum non-locality, where measurements or actions on a particle influence or affect another particle or particles with which it is "entangled," even across a considerable spatial separation)?

Not only do physiological responses among some individuals appear to be able to correlate paranormally, but also in some cases it appears that individuals may respond to stimuli up to several seconds before the stimuli actually occur (see Spottiswoode and May, 2003). In a paper titled "Unconscious Perception of Future Emotions: An Experiment in

Presentiment," parapsychologist Dean Radin presented "calm" targets (like landscapes and cheerful people) and "extreme" targets (like violent and erotic photos) to participants and tested their psychophysiological responses (heart rate, blood volume, and electrodermal activity) before, during, and after presentation of the different targets:

> Extreme targets were expected to produce classical orienting responses after the targets were displayed, and a "presentiment" (future feeling) effect was predicted to produce orienting pre-sponses before the pictures were displayed. Calm targets were expected to cause no unusual responses before or after the target was displayed. Four experiments, involving 31 participants who viewed a total of 1,060 target photos, showed the expected orienting response after the target photo was displayed. In accordance with a presentiment hypothesis, there was a clear orienting pre-sponse that peaked with a four standard error difference in physiological measures between extreme and calm targets one second before the target photo was displayed. [Radin, 1997b.]

Recently Radin (2006b) has summarized further studies along these same lines:

> Under double-blind conditions, skin conductance levels of individuals were recorded before, during and after exposure to randomly selected calm or emotional pictures. Pre-stimulus skin conductance levels prior to calm and emotional trials showed a significant differential response (N = 131 participants, 4,569 trials, p = 0.00003), in accordance with the hypothesis that the autonomic nervous system responds in accordance with the emotionality of an upcoming random stimulus. Numerous conventional explanations for these effects have been examined and rejected as implausible. This experiment has been successfully replicated by independent investigators, and new designs examining pre-stimulus changes in heart rate and slow cortical potentials, and using audio tones and light flashes as stimuli, confirm the effect. These studies challenge the notion that human psychophysiology can be modeled solely by unidirectional processes.

This type of research provides more evidence for a lower or basic cognitive psi ability, perhaps related to Carpenter's (2004) concept of "first sight" (see page 212) and the apparent ability of plants and single cells to remotely respond to consciousness and emotions (see above, page 50; Backster, 2003; Swanson, 2003; Vogel, 1974).

Unlike many human endeavors, where practice can improve one's skill and chances of success, in many situations the opposite appears to be the case with telepathic phenomena. Even in the 1880s members of the Society for Psychical Research noted the "decline effect" where an initially high-scoring individual in experimental tests would lose their telepathic ability over time. This, in turn, might lead to fraud on the part of the percipient. She or he may feel frustrated and want to continue to please the experimenters, who show such an interest in the phenomena and therefore the percipient, thus leading to attempts to compensate for the declining true telepathic abilities by committing crude or sophisticated fraud, which in turn is caught and taints the entire body of work with the particular percipient, or even an entire series of experiments with not only that percipient but with others as well. Thus any genuine telepathic signal may be lost amidst the confusion. Furthermore, if telepathy does in fact exist, we believe it to reside on a primarily unconscious level; rarely does the effect seem to register in conscious awareness, let alone be sustained enough to channel consistently or perform repeated studies. Telepathy may be a more latent process in humans and perhaps in certain other animals. However, some of the remote viewing work by McMoneagle seems to show some evidence of practice leading to better results (McMoneagle, 1997, 2002).

In Rhine types of experimental settings, such as card guessing, one can establish that a certain percipient statistically scores higher than expected by chance, but for any one particular correct call of a card, was it due to chance in that instance or by telepathic (or clairvoyant) transference of information? Evidently, it is difficult for the experimenter or the experimentee to distinguish which individual case of high scoring was due to psi or chance (or, as Horne, 1996, has suggested, is it just that the odds are changed by psi and no particular event is directly due to psi?). Because the individual does not seem to be able to control psi at a conscious level, this may be more evidence for psi on the subliminal or unconscious level of awareness. At the very beginning of its existence, the Society for Psychical Research spent considerable effort on experimental studies of telepathy (thought-transference), many showing remarkable results, such as the reproduction of simple drawings by the percipient that were focused upon by the agent, but in hindsight some of these studies are tainted (see discussion on page 26; also see Beloff, 1990, 1993).

More convincing to us among the early (1880s) studies of the Society for Psychical Research are the cases of spontaneous telepathy collected and catalogued by members of the society. The first report based on these spontaneous cases was presented to the second general meeting of the Society for Psychical Research on December 9, 1882, and subsequently published in the *Proceedings* (Barrett et al., 1883). It was in this report that the word "telepathy" was first coined (Barrett et al., 1883, p. 147; the word was the creation of F. W. H. Myers). This work of compilation and attendant theorizing on the nature of telepathy continued to be reported in the *Proceedings* of the SPR in subsequent years, and the massive two-volume work *Phantasms of the Living* by Edmund Gurney, Frederic W. H. Myers, and Frank Podmore was published under the auspices of the SPR in 1886 (an abridged and revised edition came out in 1918, and it has been reprinted since).

Although telepathy is traditionally classified as a paranormal phenomenon, at least as the term paranormal has been used historically, that does not mean it is a non-natural phenomenon. Indeed, if telepathy really does occur, we view it as a fully natural phenomenon, although currently very poorly understood, one that has as yet eluded both a cogent theoretical causal explanation (although some theories have been proposed, none have found widespread acceptance) and consistent replication in laboratory settings to a degree that has been found convincing to the most die-hard modern skeptics. Laboratory replicability with 75 to 100% consistent results, however, is not the only criterion by which to judge if something is real, natural, and should be included within the context of modern science. If such were the case, then much of astronomy, geology, and meteorology would at best be relegated to the realm of para-science. Indeed, in these three fields many of the most critical observations and data cannot be found or replicated in a laboratory. Rather, they must be observed from spontaneous cases in nature, just as with the study of telepathy and various other psi phenomena more generally. Furthermore, all of these fields have struggled long and hard, and continue to struggle, to formulate and revise cogent explanatory theories for the phenomena they study. It is exactly the same case in parapsychology and the study of psi phenomena.

Here we want to make clear that even if telepathic phenomena are real, they are (in our opinion) naturalistic phenomena that must be taken as just that, and not extended to satisfy other agendas, such as to vindicate personal religious beliefs (pro- or con-) or the concept that there is life after death. All too often, it seems to us, certain persons have assumed that admission or vindication of telepathy implies much more. Thus in an anthology titled *Science and Religion: Are They Compatible?*, the professional skeptic Paul Kurtz (2003, p. 218) defines paranatural phenomena as a "range of events . . . that deal with still other dimensions of reality: classical mystical or supernatural claims that allegedly intrude into our universe from without." Kurtz continues, "I am here referring primarily to a theistic order of reality and to phenomena including discarnate souls, intelligent design, and 'creation science.' Visitations from extraterrestrials beyond this world may be considered to be both paranormal and paranatural." Kurtz goes on to state that paranormal phenomena (including, by his definition, telepathy) and paranatural phenomena "stand between the natural and supernatural realms" (p. 218). Having lumped telepathy with a hodgepodge of other supposed phenomena, Kurtz feels he can then dismiss the whole lot. Conversely, it appears to us, a skeptic like Kurtz has boxed himself in and if he were to admit to the possible reality of telepathy, then he would be faced with the prospect of having to reevaluate his position on many other reputed phenomena. Indeed, there is no link between the reality or non-reality of telepathic phenomena and, for instance, the reality or non-reality of "visitations from extraterrestrials" or life after death (the main focus of Kurtz, 2003, is to argue against a concept of life after death).

To give a similar example, the anthology titled *Science and the Paranormal* (Abell and Singer, 1983) is subtitled *Probing the Existence of the Supernatural*. Immediately the average reader might equate "science" with "probing" and "paranormal" with "supernatural" (in fact this is misleading as paranormal and supernatural are two distinct concepts). In the forward, by Paul Kurtz (p. vii), telepathy is lumped with other "bizarre beliefs" in "'psychic' forces" that include "clairvoyance, precognition, telepathy, psychokinesis, psychic surgery, psychic healing, astral projection, levitation, plant ESP, life after life, hauntings, and apparitions." In four hundred pages of text the contributors to this anthology deal with, and systematically dismiss, such diverse topics as astrology, Big Foot, Yeti, the Loch Ness monster, the Bermuda triangle, Atlantis, ancient astronauts, and UFOs. In no substantive way do the authors ever deal with paranormal phenomena as studied by serious psychical researchers and parapsychologists. In the one chapter that makes any pretense to deal with parapsychology directly, "Parapsychology and Quantum Mechanics," the author Martin Gardner never actually addresses the body of evidence for telepathy or any other psi phenomena, but confines himself to primarily discussing and criticizing one particular theory involving quantum mechanics, that of physicist Evan Harris Walker (see Walker, 1975, 1984, 2000; Walker in Long, 1977), that has been proposed to explain psi. Having, to his satisfaction, dismissed Walker's theory, Gardner simply calls for replicable experiments that will demonstrate psi to "unbelievers" (Gardner's term, 1983a, p. 68). An anonymous (presumably by the editors Abell and Singer) introduction to Gardner's chapter states, without references, that "Relatively few research psychologists believe there is any convincing evidence that ESP or PK even exists, and most physicists regard the physical theories of ESP and PK as nonsense." Thus we see how telepathy is treated, or more accurately ignored, by professional skeptics even in a book that ostensibly is focused on the paranormal.

As early as the 1880s various members of the Society for Psychical Research, and particularly F. W. H. Myers, were hypothesizing that telepathy could explain naturalistically various cases of genuine (as opposed to purposeful deception and fraud) so-called spirit phenomena, apparitions, clairvoyance, and the like. Over a century later, we continue to find this idea enticing. Some mediums, for instance, assuming that they are not frauds and conjurers, may pick up telepathic impressions from the people around them rather than actually channeling any discarnate entity or spirit. Clairvoyance, in the sense of "seeing" things from a distance, may not be so much an issue of seeing material phenomena, but of picking up telepathic impressions from other people, or animals such as pets. For instance, if a percipient is requested by an agent to "travel" to a distant spot and relate what is "seen" there, such as the home of the agent some miles away from the experiment (assuming the percipient has never been there physically), might not the percipient simply pick up telepathically impressions from the agent directly? Or, if the spot is unknown to the agent, might not the percipient pick up telepathically information about the location from persons who are there or have been there? Or, if as some believe, telepathy does not necessarily respect the bounds of space and time in a conventional manner, perhaps the percipient can even receive information telepathically from the agent or another person (perhaps the percipient himself or herself) who will be there in the future.

An important question concerns whether or not telepathic impressions can be received from what we regard as the future, the present, and the past. If telepathy is independent of time, at least to some extent, this has major implications. The strongest case seems to be for telepathic phenomena in the present. If telepathy extends into the past, this might explain some phenomena that are commonly thought of as reincarnation, and if it extends into the future this could explain various instances of so-called clairvoyance, remote viewing, and supposed non-telepathic extrasensory perception (ESP). For instance, if a percipient calls the order of cards in a randomly shuffled deck that is not viewed by any person until after the calls are made with a greater than chance accuracy, this might be taken as classic clairvoyance. However, to check the calls, someone must look through the deck and record the cards after the fact.

If the telepathic faculty can receive information from the future, then the information about the cards may not have been received directly from the cards (that is, clairvoyantly as clairvoyance is here defined), but telepathically from the person going through the deck to check the cards. (In some cases, according to this hypothesis, the percipient and the agent may even be the same person, but acting in different roles at different times, for instance when one does an experiment consisting of randomly shuffling a deck of cards, calling them in sequence, and then checking one's own calls after the fact.)

It is often hypothesized that telepathy is independent of space or distance. That is, that it can occur between individuals at any distance. Certainly there appears to be both experimental and spontaneous evidence that telepathy can occur over thousands of miles, but this does not demonstrate that it is independent of distance. The strength of the telepathic signal and the receptivity of the persons involved are at this stage of our knowledge virtually impossible to control or even take into account. Another factor may be the targeting of the percipient by the agent, or vice versa, the focusing of the percipient on the agent, or both simultaneously. It has also been pointed out that one must distinguish between what can be called "intensity" and "intelligibility" (Vasiliev, 2002, pp. 128–129). The way we currently measure or detect a telepathic signal is by the information content it transmits; yet this does not necessarily give any information about the signal's strength. To analogize with light, the intensity or strength of light energy follows an inverse square law (as does gravitational force and many other forces and "influences" in nature), thus the light intensity is reduced by the square of the distance from the source. If, however, a flashing light is used to send an information-bearing signal from the agent to the recipient, as long as the recipient can see the light, the information will be transmitted in full, independent of the intensity of the light, and thus independent of distance. We hypothesize that if one could control signal strength, agent/percipient receptivity, and targeting, then it may be found that telepathy weakens or attenuates over distance. The distance involved to detect appreciable attenuation of the telepathic signal, however, may be on the same order as the size of Earth or greater, and thus we may be limited empirically in testing this hypothesis. Indeed, in analyzing a number of reputable studies of ESP, parapsychologist Karlis Osis (1976, p. 196) concluded, "In a careful analysis of the relevant experimental data, it was noted that ESP scores seem to decrease quite uniformly with increased distances." Perhaps, one could also suggest, this is because of the perception of distance, meaning that if you consciously know the location of an object or person you may have the perception that it is easier to transmit data over a short distance, rather than a long distance, even though this may or may not be true.

Likewise, assuming for the moment that telepathic information can be received from not only the present, but also from the past and the future (see Eisenbud, 1982), we hypothesize that the signal quickly weakens as we move away from the present in either direction. Perhaps this occurs for psychological reasons, the present and immediate past (and immediate future) have more significance (in most cases) for individuals and history tends to become more obscure and of less personal significance as one goes back in time. Furthermore, it may be more difficult to contextualize increasingly removed future events based on knowledge in the present. Thus it would be expected that most cases of spontaneous telepathy would be more or less temporally simultaneous between the individuals involved, and in fact this seems to be the case in the recorded examples (unless there has been a bias toward recording only such examples), but retro-cognition and pre-cognition are also possible (and documented cases exist), but progressively scarcer as one moves away from the present. One may receive more readily a telepathic premonition about the future of a day or two hence than about the future years from the present. Likewise any telepathic impressions received from the past are more likely to be from the relatively recent past. (Of course, holding original telepathic signal strength and receptivity of the percipient constant. Another complicating factor is that a telepathic impression may be received in the present, but held latent or dormant by the recipient, only to be brought to the conscious level at some point after being received.)

In a study of 148 cases of spontaneous precognition, British clinical psychologist J. E. Orme (1974; see also discussion in Zohar, 1982, pp. 73–75) found that 57 occurred within 24 hours before the event, another 14 within 24 to 48 hours before the event, and in general the incidence of spontaneous precognitions declined dramatically as the temporal separation between the precognition and the event increased. Likewise, in a literature review of 520 precognitive dreams, parapsychologists Theo K. de Graaf and Joop M. Houtkooper observed "an exponential decline of the time periods that has elapsed between the precognitive events and their fulfillment" (de Graaf and Houtkooper, 2004; see also J. W. Dunne, 1952). (It has been suggested that a strong emotional signal, as from a violent event, may leave a stronger trace in time and thus penetrate time "further" than a weaker signal. Similarly, it has been suggested that occurrences such as major battles and murders may remain "imprinted" on the locations where they occurred.)

Some of the strongest evidence for reincarnation-types of phenomena, such as that documented by the late Dr. Ian Stevenson, appear to involve relatively recent deaths and transfer of information, in some cases under circumstances that may send a strong signal (such as a violent death), and the transfer of information is generally over a relatively short distance (for instance, from one village to the next over at most a few hundred miles; see Stevenson 1960a, 1960b, 1966, 1975, 1977, 1980, 1983b, 1987, 1997a, 1997b, and page 123 above). This would fit with our telepathy hypothesis. It is not reincarnation per se in the classical sense, but simply telepathic transfer of information. So-called "walk-ins," where a person near death or in a coma supposedly is entered by another spirit or entity, may also be explained by our telepathic hypothesis as simply the transfer of some information or a telepathic signal (possibly more or less randomly) from one person or mind (perhaps someone who is under stress, such as a person who is dying) to another who is particularly receptive (a person in a coma, for instance).

A way to experimentally test the temporal attenuation of telepathic phenomena (versus classical clairvoyance) might be for a presumed clairvoyant to call the cards in a series of different randomly shuffled decks, then check the calls right away on some of the decks (the decks to be picked randomly relative to the order they were called to compensate for any decline effect), but put away the other decks and not check them for many years or decades later. If the clairvoyant produced positive (statistically significant) results initially (with the decks checked almost immediately) but produced appreciably lesser or insignificant results with the decks checked years later, this could lend credence to the concept that the supposed clairvoyance is actually telepathy (admittedly, reception of telepathic information from the future) as well as the hypothesis that the telepathic signal attenuates with time.

What is the information that is passed on telepathically? Is it sensory, emotional, or cognitive? Does it pass from the consciousness of one mind to the subconscious of another, and then arise into consciousness? Can it be passed from the subconscious or even unconscious of one mind to the sub- or unconscious of another mind? How is it passed on? These remain open questions, but similar issues plague even the hard sciences. Take the subject of gravity: Well, what is gravity and how does gravity work? Yet we know it works, even if we are not sure how. There are competing theories as to what causes gravity (A warping of space-time? The interaction of particles or waves?) and even how fast it propagates (At the speed of light? Or instantaneously? Is it finite in speed?). It is now "understood" that all entities with mass have a gravitational attraction for all other entities, even if in many cases gravity does not manifest itself as measurable under "normal" conditions. Thus the two candlesticks on my shelf are "known" to have a gravitational attraction for each other, are "actively" attracting each other, yet this has no manifestation or affect that I can personally perceive or measure. If I pick up one candlestick and drop it, then its gravitational attraction to Earth (but still not to the other candlestick) is clearly manifested. Somewhat analogously, is the telepathic signal, or psi phenomena more generally, also prone to manifestation, perception, and measurement only under certain conditions, even though actually present all of the time, but currently we do not understand what precisely those conditions are to make psi manifest?

Besides telepathy, the other paranormal phenomenon that we find there is some solid experimental evidence to substantiate is what is commonly referred to as psychokinesis or telekinesis; that is, the effects of mind on matter, or more specifically mind or mental processes alone affecting material systems without any currently known intervening agency. Classically, this is the stuff of mediums and conjurers, and invokes levitation of objects and people at séances and similar venues, most or all of which may be fraudulent. We want to stress that at this time we are very leery of any displays of so-call macro-psychokineses; the best cases supporting the genuineness of some instances of macro-PK may be well documented and thoroughly investigated poltergeist incidents (recurrent spontaneous psychokinesis; see page 105). At the other end of the spectrum, namely minute statistical changes in subatomic particles such as electrons, there also appears to be viable evidence for psychokinesis. From 1979 to 2007, researchers at the Princeton Engineering Anomalies Research laboratories of Princeton University ran credible experiments on the interactions of consciousness with matter at a microlevel (see above, page 144). Sophisticated, highly sensitive, and finely calibrated electronic random event generators (REGs) have picked up anomalous non-random trends that apparently correlate with, or document, the effects of consciousness on matter, or psychokinesis.

The DMILS (Direct Mental Interactions with Living Systems; see Delanoy, 2001) research also may provide a different avenue for the manifestation of PK on a micro level. It would seem logical to assert that distinct types of matter would differentially be influenced by PK. Collections of molecules in a gaseous state may behave differently under psi influences than solid materials like crystalline rock, and PK may influence living biological matter differently than nonliving matter. We suggest that PK and telepathy may be much more apparent when involving more fluid/changing systems.

Here we should point out that the REG psychokinesis experiments are very different, in our opinion, from such studies as the effects of intercessory prayer on people. Intercessory prayer, if it works, may be a telepathic effect from one mind to another, the receiving mind (that is the sick patient who is benefited, for instance) then may self-divert, consciously or unconsciously, the "telepathic energy" or "telepathic suggestion" into healing or in the case of maleficent prayer, the "energy" may cause harm (either way, possibly via self-directed PK). Thus, theoretically such effects of consciousness on other living systems or entities may be more akin to classical telepathy than psychokinesis.

Ultimately we believe that the scientific study of parapsychology should not be dismissed by science because there has yet to be an agreed upon theoretical framework to describe it. There are anomalies that remain unexplained. These anomalies offer a tantalizing hint at another existing level of reality that interacts with our known reality but that we do not yet have the tools to understand or control. This is much like the state of electricity in the eighteenth century; although electricity existed and could be manifested by rubbing amber with cat fur, little was known about its operating principles and no technological applications had yet been developed. It is arrogant to assume that just because little theoretical progress has been made as to the cause and nature of psi that there is nothing of value within parapsychology.

## The Future of Parapsychology, and the Future of the Planet

*If we are indeed witnessing . . . an emergence involving psi and spiritual self-development in humanity, then many disastrous predictions concerning both the planet and humanity could be reviewed. Such an evolutionary possibility would make sense in terms of the survival of our species and Earth. The dangers facing the human species, the quick extinction of thousands of human cultures, as well as animal and flora species, the ecological disaster looming over our planet—all of them mostly due to crass ignorance of ecological interconnected dynamics, and to a lack of a planetary consciousness—all this could trigger the frantic search for a solution by the collective unconscious, or Gaia consciousness.*

—CHRISTINE HARDY *(Parapsychology in the Twenty-First Century, 2005, p. 236)*

Given the very real problems in the world today, it is easy to conclude that there are more pressing matters that we should be pursuing than parapsychology. But look again. The lessons of parapsychology may be crucial to addressing the current and future evolution of humanity. Of the fundamental issues of parapsychological studies, perhaps the most important is the question of the nature and limits of human potential. Reports of psi have been found in many cultures throughout history. Are we beings that can create or co-create our own realities? Is there a real link between mind and matter? Do our "private" thoughts actually affect, even if in most cases only subtly, other persons and non-living matter? Are we really able to communicate with one another, perhaps primarily at an unconscious level, without the use of the conventional sense organs? What implications do these concepts have for medicine? For interpersonal relationships and group dynamics? For therapeutic applications? For cultural identities in an ever more global economy and interconnected world dynamic?

The elucidation of the psi faculty is another building block as we continue to learn what it truly means to be human. The commonalities that connect all people, and indeed our species with the rest of life, overshadow and dwarf our petty differences. Not only do all of us (whether "us" refers to all of humanity, or all of life) share the same basic genetic material, and depend on the same global environment for our sustenance, but additionally parapsychology suggests that all humans, and possibly all of life, share in, and are embedded in, what might be referred to as a common psychical environment. This concept is profound and leads to a worldview very different from the materialistic technology-based mind-set that has dominated much of modern Western thinking. The worldview that informs future human thought will determine the direction civilization takes and thus will impact the future of the entire planet in coming centuries and millennia.

So, where does the immediate future of parapsychology lie? Certainly more must be done to understand the nature of, and elucidate the manifestations and mechanisms of, psi. Despite much theoretical work, parapsychology still lacks a single, generally agreed upon, overarching theoretical explanation for the existence and functioning of psi. Furthermore, there is a general scarcity of funding for parapsychology, and consequently few new faces are entering the field. This, in our opinion, is a sad state of affairs given the potential importance and implications of parapsychological research.

Despite the paucity of resources, and the conceptual and logistical difficulties of studying psi, which appears to be elusive by its very nature, great strides have been made since the founding of the Society for Psychical Research in 1882. Parapsychology and psychical research has documented its subject in field settings through the study of spontaneous cases of psi, captured psi in the laboratory (even if inconsistently, and sometimes fleetingly), subjected the data to rigorous analyses, and developed a vocabulary to present its findings. The paranormal has been brought into the fold of serious scientific research. The parapsychology revolution has begun, but it is an unfinished revolution. In the near future we hope that progress will be made on two fronts: (1) Research on psi must continue, further documenting and elucidating the nature of genuinely paranormal phenomena. (2) The research community must do more to publicly disseminate what it has learned about the paranormal, so that this information can be used in a positive, constructive manner.

# ACKNOWLEDGMENTS

Fist and foremost, we thank our wonderful and understanding editor, Mitch Horowitz, for his support, encouragement, help, and patience with this project. We could not have completed this book without him, and he also came up with the title, *The Parapsychology Revolution,* based on the quotation from Bernstein (1965, pp. 310–311; see above, page 12). We also thank Dr. Schoch's literary agent, Sarah Jane Freymann. She has been supportive of all of Dr. Schoch's endeavors for many years now, and this is the fourth book that she has handled for him.

We thank William G. Roll, Sally Rhine Feather (Rhine Research Center), Robert G. Jahn, Jessica Utts, Elyse Gustafson (Institute of Mathematical Statistics), Larry Dossey, L. R. Bremseth, Edward Binkowski, Jean E. Burns, Anthony Freeman (Imprint Academic), Paul Stevens, Serena Roney-Dougal, and Caroline Watt for permission to reprint material or for help in acquiring such permissions.

*Robert Schoch's acknowledgments:* I must thank Mitch Horowitz for his insight, helpful comments, and the wonderful discussions he and I have had concerning topics related to this book. Mitch brought various references to my attention, including an article by Robert Galbreath (1971) on modern occultism, the comments by Henry Steel Olcott (1875) on the cheating of mediums, and the comments of Elizabeth Lloyd Mayer (2007) concerning the *Skeptical Inquirer.* My collaborator on this project, Logan Yonavjak, has been a wonderful, and often very patient, student, field assistant (on research trips to Egypt and Peru), and now colleague. I thank her for all of her help. I thank Linda

Parker for sharing with me her spider dream (see page 88) and other instances of possible telepathy. More than anyone else, however, I owe a debt of gratitude to my colleague and friend Dr. Colette M. Dowell. She has been incredibly supportive of all my research projects over the years. She has traveled with me on trips to Peru, Bosnia, and Egypt. When it comes to the paranormal, Colette has played a very special role for me. She has provided me with numerous firsthand instances of telepathy (sometimes I was on the "sending" end and sometimes I was on the "receiving" end), and she even made it possible (apparently inadvertently) for me to observe a minor "poltergeist" incident (mentioned on pages 103–104).

*Logan Yonavjak's acknowledgments:* I would like to express my sincere gratitude first and foremost to Dr. Schoch, who has been my mentor for more than three years and who had the idea to embark on this project back in 2003. He has taken the time to give me amazing opportunities to travel and perform research, which have all had a tremendous impact in shaping me as a person. I would not be who I am today without his mentorship and friendship. I would also like to thank my mother, Liane Salgado, who spent many hours patiently listening and guiding me in many aspects of this project and who was the original inspiration. She gave me a book called *The Field,* by Lynne McTaggart, which I subsequently gave to Dr. Schoch, and that book helped spark both of our curiosities in the topic. My father, Donald Yonavjak, has also been a source of insight and gave me the Leadbeater quote (page ix), which in my mind tied together the material in this anthology. My boyfriend, Taylor Garbutt, was always willing to listen if I was feeling overwhelmed, and allowed me to bounce many random ideas off him at all hours of the day and night. I would also like to express my gratitude to Noah Chatham, a long-time family friend who constantly encourages and inspires me with his inner strength. Many of the individuals at the Rhine Research Center (RRC) also contributed to my studies, and without their library I do not think I would have been able to do much of the research! Dr. Sally Rhine Feather, the daughter of J. B. and Louisa Rhine, kept me informed concerning presentations and other opportunities at the RRC and was very supportive of this project, and Dr. Christine Simmonds, who is a successful parapsychologist and a wonderful friend, provided many insightful comments and interesting ideas for this work.

# PERMISSIONS

# SOURCES AND READINGS

The literature relevant to parapsychology and psychical research is vast. Here we list the works we cited in our commentaries (we tried to keep citations to a minimum, so as not to disrupt the flow of the reader) along with various references that we found especially useful and that we believe the interested reader might find particularly helpful. Many of the selections included in this anthology have their own bibliographies, which we kept intact in the forms given in the original articles. The interested reader will want to pursue those sources as well.

For general introductions to the science of parapsychology, see especially J. White with Mitchell (1974), Wolman (1977), Edge et al. (1986), and Irwin (2004). More technical and detailed reviews of various topics in parapsychology can be found in the excellent multi-volume series edited by Krippner titled *Advances in Parapsychological Research* (1977–1997). Rao (1984) compiled an interesting anthology of what he considered the "Basic Experiments in Parapsychology," and indeed his volume does reprint some of the more important technical papers describing various experiments that had been carried out by the early 1980s, but unfortunately it is marred by inclusion of a paper by Kanthamani and Kelly (1974a) describing work with the subject Bill Delamore, who has been accused of using sleight of hand and other tricks to produce supposed "paranormal phenomena" (see Hansen, 1990; Diaconis, 1978, 1979; Kelly, 1979). An excellent short history of parapsychology and its predecessors is provided by Beloff (1993), and Haynes (1982) has told the story of the first hundred years of the Society for Psychical Research.

If you are interested in learning more about topics related to parapsychology, such as near-death experiences, out-of-body experiences, and anomalous healing experiences, an excellent place to start is Cardeña, et al. (2000). For an incredibly insightful, entertaining, and personal look at parapsychology by a major contributor to the field, we recommend Hansen (2001).

Some major institutions and organizations, along with their primary journal publications (where applicable) in the field of parapsychology and psychical research include:

**Society for Psychical Research** (http://www.spr.ac.uk/)
*Proceedings of the Society for Psychical Research*
*Journal of the Society for Psychical Research*

**American Society for Psychical Research** (http://www.aspr.com/)
*Journal of the American Society for Psychical Research*

**Rhine Research Center, An Institute for the Study of Consciousness**
(http://www.rhine.org/)
*Journal of Parapsychology*

**Parapsychological Association** (http://www.parapsych.org/)

**European Journal of Parapsychology** (http://ejp.org.uk/)
*European Journal of Parapsychology*

**Society for Scientific Exploration** (http://www.scientificexploration.org/)
*Journal of Scientific Exploration* (this journal includes many parapsychological and related articles, but is not devoted exclusively to parapsychology)

*A note on the order of the entries in this bibliography*: We have listed entries alphabetically by author surnames; where there are multiple authors, the entries are listed by the first author after single author works by the same person. Where we list more than one work by the same author or authors, the works are listed chronologically from oldest to youngest. We believe that such chronological ordering per author will make it easier to locate any particular work, and it also gives a "synopsis history" of the development of an author's works.

*A note on the Internet and World Wide Web*: Daily more and more material is being posted and published on the Internet, including much that is relevant to parapsychology and psychical research. Also, much psi-based research is currently taking place online (Radin, 2002c). Rupert Sheldrake, for instance, has conducted several online experiments (see www.sheldrake.org). We have listed some online articles, but unfortunately online sources can change. For online sources, we have given the Internet/World Wide Web addresses (URLs: uniform resource locators) and the dates when we successfully accessed the material. Unfortunately, some of these sites and pages may have changed; they may no longer be active, or the URLs may have changed. In such cases, it may be possible for the interested reader to find the applicable or comparable material through one of the many search engines that are available for navigating the Internet/WWW.

Abell, George O., and Barry Singer, editors. *Science and the Paranormal: Probing the Existence of the Supernatural.* New York: Scribner, 1983.

Aickin, Mikel. Reviewer comment on Rupert Sheldrake and Aimée Morgana, "Testing a Language-Using Parrot for Telepathy." *Journal of Scientific Exploration* 17, pp. 615–616 (2003).

Alcock, James E. *Parapsychology: Science or Magic? A Psychological Perspective.* Oxford: Pergamon Press, 1981.

———. "Give the Null Hypothesis a Chance: Reasons to Remain Doubtful about the Existence of Psi." *Journal of Consciousness Studies* 10, pp. 29–50 (2003). Also published in *Psi Wars: Getting to Grips with the Paranormal,* edited by James Alcock, Jean Burns, and Anthony Freeman. Charlottesville, Va., and Exeter, UK: Imprint Academic, 2003, pp. 29–50.

Alcock, James, Jean Burns, and Anthony Freeman, editors. *Psi Wars: Getting to Grips with the Paranormal.* Charlottesville, Va., and Exeter, UK: Imprint Academic, 2003.

Alvarado, Carlos S. "Out-of-Body Experiences." In Etzel Cardeña, Steven Jay Lynn, and Stanley Krippner, editors. *Varieties of Anomalous Experience: Examining the Scientific Evidence.* Washington, D.C.: American Psychological Association, 2000, pp. 183–218.

———. "Thoughts on the Study of Spontaneous Cases—an Editorial." Originally published in *Journal of Parapsychology,* June 2002. Available from FindArticles.com: http://www.findarticles.com/p/articles/mi_m2320/is_2_66/ai_90532943. Accessed 25 August 2006.

————. "Reflections on Being a Parapsychologist." *Journal of Parapsychology* 67, pp. 211–248 (2003). Available from: http://www.survivalafterdeath.org/articles/ alvarado/parapsychologist.htm. Accessed 8 July 2006.

American Psychiatric Association. *Diagnostic and Statistical Manual of Mental Disorders, Fourth Edition (DSM–IV)*. Washington, D.C.: American Psychiatric Association, 1994.

Angoff, Allan, editor. *The Psychic Force: Essays in Modern Psychical Research from the International Journal of Parapsychology*. New York: Putnam, 1970.

Angoff, Allan, and Diana Barth, editors. *Parapsychology and Anthropology: Proceedings of an International Conference Held in London, England, August 29–31, 1973*. New York: Parapsychology Foundation, 1974.

Anonymous. *Parapsychology and the Rhine Research Center*. Durham, N.C.: Parapsychology Press, 2001.

————. *The Varieties of Healing Experience: Exploring Psychic Phenomena in Healing*. Transcript of the Interdisciplinary Symposium of October 30, 1971. Denver, Colo.: Academy of Parapsychology and Medicine, 1972.

————. See Epes Sargent (1869).

Arvey, Michael. *ESP*. San Diego, Calif.: Greenhaven Press, 1989. Book for children.

Ashby, Robert H. *The Guidebook for the Study of Psychical Research*. New York: Samuel Weiser, 1972.

Backster, Cleve. *Primary Perception: Biocommunication with Plants, Living Foods, and Human Cells*. Anza, Calif.: White Rose Millennium Press, 2003.

Backster Website. "Definitions of Biocommunication and Primary Perception." Available from: http://www.primaryperception.com. Accessed 11 June 2007.

Baggally, W. W. "Report on Sittings with Charles Bailey, the Australian Apport Medium." *Journal of the Society for Psychical Research* 15, pp. 194–208 (1912).

Barker, William J. See Bernstein (1965).

Barnard, Guy Christian. "Mediumship and Its Investigation." Excerpt from *The Supernormal*. London, Rider and Co., 1933. Available from: http://www.survival afterdeath.org/articles/barnard/mediumship.htm. Accessed 4 September 2006.

Barrett, W. F. "On Some Phenomena Associated with Abnormal Conditions of Mind." *Proceedings of the Society for Psychical Research* 1, pp. 238–244 (1883). Paper first read before the British Association in 1876.

————. "Poltergeists: Old and New." *Journal of the Society for Psychical Research* 15, pp. 36–40 (1911).

Barrett, Sir William, and Theodore Besterman. *The Divining-Rod: An Experimental and Psychological Investigation*. London: Methuen and Co., 1926.

Barrett, W. F., Edmund Gurney, and Frederic W. H. Myers. "Thought-Reading." *The Nineteenth Century*, pp. 890–900 (June 1882).

Barrett, W. F., C. C. Massey, W. Stainton Moses, Frank Podmore, Edmund Gurney, and Frederic W. H. Myers. "Report of the Literary Committee." *Proceedings of the Society for Psychical Research* 1, pp. 116–155 (1883).

Batcheldor, Kenneth J. "Contributions to the Theory of PK Induction from Sitter-Group Work." Paper presented at a symposium on the Batcheldor Approach. In William G. Roll, John Beloff, and Rhea A. White, editors. *Research in Parapsychology, 1982: Jubilee Centenary Issue*. Metuchen, N.J.: Scarecrow Press, 1983, pp. 45–48.

———. "Contributions to the Theory of PK Induction from Sitter-Group Work." *Journal of the American Society for Psychical Research* 78, pp. 105–122 (1984).

———. "Notes on the Elusiveness Problem in Relation to a Radical View of Para-normality." Compiled, edited, and with a preface and notes by Patric V. Giesler. *Journal of the American Society for Psychical Research* 88, pp. 90–116 (1994).

Bauer, Eberhard. "Criticism and Controversy in Parapsychology—An Overview." *European Journal of Parapsychology* 5, pp. 141–166 (1984).

Bauer, Henry H. "Science in the 21st Century: Knowledge Monopolies and Re-search Cartels." *Journal of Scientific Exploration* 18, pp. 643–660 (2004).

Besant, Annie. *The Ancient Wisdom: An Outline of Theosophical Teachings*. New York: Theosophical Publishing, 1897.

Beichler, James E. "The Search for Spock: Developing the Theoretical Basis of Psi." *YGGDRASIL: The Journal of Paraphysics*, 1998. Available from: http://members.aol.com/jebco1st/Paraphysics/search1.htm. Accessed 17 August 2006.

Bellavite, Paolo, and Andrea Signorini. *The Emerging Science of Homeopathy: Complex-ity, Biodynamics, and Nanopharmacology*. Revised and expanded edition. Berkeley, Calif.: North Atlantic Books, 2002.

Beloff, John. *The Relentless Question: Reflections on the Paranormal*. Jefferson, N.C.: Mc-Farland, 1990.

———. *Parapsychology: A Concise History*. London: Athlone Press, 1993.

Bernstein, Morey. *The Search for Bridey Murphy*. New York: Doubleday, 1956.

———. *The Search for Bridey Murphy, with New Material by William J. Barker*. Garden City, N.Y.: Doubleday, 1965.

Besterman, Theodore. *Crystal-Gazing; A Study in the History, Distribution, Theory and Practice of Scrying*. London: Rider, 1924.

———. *Collected Papers on the Paranormal*. New York: Garrett Publications, 1968.

Black, J. "The Spirit-Photograph Fraud: The Evidence of Trickery, and a Demonstra-tion of the Tricks Employed." *Scientific American* 127, pp. 224–225, 286 (1922).

Blackmore, Susan. "Do We Need a New Psychical Research?" *Journal of the Society for Psychical Research* 55, pp. 49–59 (1988). Text of a lecture delivered to the Society on 12 March 1987. Available from: http://www.susanblackmore.co.uk/Articles/JSPR1988.htm. Accessed 4 June 2005.

———. *Dying to Live: Near-Death Experiences.* Buffalo, N.Y.: Prometheus Books, 1993.

———. "The Adventures of a Psi-Inhibitory Experimenter." In Paul Kurtz, editor. *A Skeptic's Handbook of Parapsychology.* Buffalo, N.Y.: Prometheus Books, 1985, pp. 425–448.

Blavatsky, H. P. *Isis Unveiled: A Master-Key to the Mysteries of Ancient and Modern Science and Theology.* 2 vols. New York: J. W. Bouton, 1877. Reprint, two volumes bound as one. Los Angeles: Theosophy Co., 1931.

———. *The Secret Doctrine: The Synthesis of Science, Religion, and Philosophy.* 2 vols. London: Theosophical Publishing, 1888. Reprint, two volumes bound as one. Los Angeles: Theosophy Co., 1925.

Bockris, John O'M. *The New Paradigm: A Confrontation Between Physics and the Paranormal Phenomena.* College Station, Tex.: D&M Enterprises Publisher, 2004.

Bozzano, Ernesto. *Übersinnliche Erscheinungen bei Naturvölkern.* Bern, Switz.: A. Francke A.G. Verlage, 1948.

Bradley, H. Dennis. *An Indictment of the Present Administration of the Society for Psychical Research.* London, privately published undated pamphlet, 32 pages, circa 1931.

Braud, William G. "Lability and Inertia in Conformance Behavior." *Journal of the American Society for Psychical Research* 74, pp. 297–318 (1980).

———. "Lability and Inertia in Psychic Functioning." In Betty Shapin and Lisette Coly, editors. *Concepts and Theories of Parapsychology: Proceedings of an International Conference Held in New York, New York, December 6, 1980.* New York: Parapsychology Foundation, 1981, pp. 1–28.

Braude, Stephen E. *ESP and Psychokinesis: A Philosophical Examination.* Revised edition. Parkland, Fla.: Brown Walker Press, 2002.

Bremseth, L. R. "Unconventional Human Intelligence Support: Transcendent and Asymmetric Warfare Implications of Remote Viewing," 2001. Available from: http://www.lfr.org/LFR/csl/library/Bremseth.pdf. See: http://www.lfr.org/LFR/csl/academic/whitepapers.html. Accessed 17 August 2006.

Brian, Denis. *The Enchanted Voyager: The Life of J.B. Rhine: An Authorized Biography.* Englewood Cliffs, N.J.: Prentice-Hall, 1982.

Broad, C. D. *Lectures on Psychical Research, Incorporating the Perrott Lectures Given in Cambridge University in 1959 and 1960.* New York: Humanities Press, 1962.

Brookes-Smith, C. "Review of *The World of Ted Serios* by J. Eisenbud." *Journal of the Society for Psychical Research* 44, pp. 260–265 (1968).

Brophy, Thomas. *The Mechanism Demands A Mysticism.* Blue Hill, Maine: Medicine Bear Publishing, 1999.

Brown, G. S. "Statistical Significance in Psychical Research." *Nature* 172, pp. 154–156 (1953).

Bruce, Alexandra. *Beyond the Bleep: The Definitive Unauthorized Guide to What the Bleep Do We Know?* St. Paul, Minn.: The Disinformation Company, 2005.

Buchanan, Joseph R., editor and publisher. *Buchanan's Journal of Man.* Vol. IV: 1853. Cincinnati: J. R. Buchanan, 1854.

———. *Manual of Psychometry: The Dawn of a New Civilization.* Third edition. Boston: Cupples, Wilson and Co., 1889.

Bucke, Richard Maurice. *Cosmic Consciousness.* New York: Penguin Compass, 1991.

Burnham, Douglas, and James Fieser. "René Descartes (1596–1650)." *Internet Encyclopedia of Philosophy* (2006). Available from: http://www.iep.utm.edu/d/descarte.htm. Accessed 30 May 2007.

Burns, Jean E. "What Is Beyond the Edge of the Known World?" *Journal of Consciousness Studies* 10, nos. 6–7, pp. 7–28 (2003). Also published in *Psi Wars: Getting to Grips with the Paranormal*, edited by James Alcock, Jean Burns, and Anthony Freeman. Charlottesville, Va., and Exeter, UK: Imprint Academic, 2003, pp. 7–28.

Calef, Scott. "Dualism and Mind." *Internet Encyclopedia of Philosophy* (2006). Available from: http://www.iep.utm.edu/d/dualism.htm. Accessed 30 May 2007.

Cannon, Alexander. *The Power Within: The Re-examination of Certain Psychological and Philosophical Concepts in the Light of Recent Investigations and Discoveries.* New York: Dutton, 1953.

Cardeña, Etzel, Steven Jay Lynn, and Stanley Krippner, editors. *Varieties of Anomalous Experience: Examining the Scientific Evidence.* Washington, D.C.: American Psychological Association, 2000.

———. "Introduction: Anomalous Experiences in Perspective." In Etzel Cardeña, Steven Jay Lynn, and Stanley Krippner, editors. *Varieties of Anomalous Experience: Examining the Scientific Evidence.* Washington, D.C.: American Psychological Association, 2000, pp. 3–21.

Carey, Benedict. "A Princeton Lab on ESP Plans to Close Its Doors." *The New York Times.* 10 February 2007. Available from: http://www.nytimes.com/2007/02/10/science/10princeton.html?ex=1171774800&en=0918a35671868d65&ei=5070&emc=eta1. Accessed 10 February 2007.

Carpenter, James C. "First Sight: Part One, a Model of Psi and the Mind." *Journal of Parapsychology*. Fall 2004. Available from FindArticles.com: http://www.find articles.com/p/articles/mi_m2320/is_2_68/ai_n16107398. Accessed 23 August 2006.

Castaneda, Carlos. *The Teachings of Don Juan: A Yaqui Way of Knowledge*. Berkeley: University of California Press, 1968.

———. *A Separate Reality; Further Conversations with Don Juan*. New York: Simon & Schuster, 1971.

———. *Journey to Ixtlan: The Lessons of Don Juan*. New York: Simon & Schuster, 1972.

———. *The Power of Silence: Further Lessons of Don Juan*. New York: Simon & Schuster, 1987.

Cerullo, John J. *The Secularization of the Soul: Psychical Research in Modern Britain*. Philadelphia: Institute for the Study of Human Issues, 1982.

Charpak, Georges, and Henri Broch. Translated by Bart K. Holland. *Debunked! ESP, Telekinesis and Other Pseudoscience*. Baltimore: Johns Hopkins University Press, 2004.

Chéroux, Clément, Andreas Fischer, Pierre Apraxine, Denis Canguilhem, and Sophie Schmit. *The Perfect Medium: Photography and the Occult*. New Haven, Conn.: Yale University Press, 2005.

Christopher, M. *Panorama of Magic*. New York: Dover, 1962.

———. *Search for the Soul*. New York: Thomas Y. Crowell, 1979.

Child, Irvin L. "Psychology and Anomalous Observations: The Question of ESP in Dreams." *American Psychologist* 40, pp. 1219–1230 (1985).

Čiča, Zoran. "Vilenica and Vilenjak: Bearers of an Extinct Fairy Cult." *Narodna umjetnost—Hrvatski časopis za etnologiju i folkloristiku* (*Croatian Journal of Ethnology and Folklore Research*) 39, pp. 31–63 (2002).

Cognitive Sciences Laboratories (CSL). "Primary Definitions." Available from: http://www.lfr.org/LFR/csl/foundation/definitions.html. Accessed 1 June 2007 but dated 1999–2001.

Coover, John Edgar. *Experiments in Psychical Research at Leland Stanford Junior University*. Stanford, Calif.: Leland Stanford Junior University Publications, Psychical Research Monograph no. 1 (665 pages and errata sheet), 1917. Reprinted New York: Arno Press, 1975.

Coover, John E. "Metapsychics and the Incredulity of Psychologists." In Carl Murchison, editor. *The Case For and Against Psychical Belief*. Worcester, Mass.: Clark University, 1927, pp. 229–264.

Cox, W. E. "Precognition: An Analysis." *Journal of the American Society for Psychical Research* 50, pp. 47–58 (1956).

———. "Precognition: An Analysis, II." *Journal of the American Society for Psychical Research* 50, pp. 99–109 (1956).

Crandon, L. R. G. "The Margery Mediumship." In Carl Murchison, editor. *The Case For and Against Psychical Belief.* Worcester, Mass.: Clark University, 1927, pp. 65–109.

Crookes, William. *Psychic Force and Modern Spiritualism: A Reply to the "Quarterly Review" and Other Critics.* London: Longman, Green, 1872. Pamphlet, 24 pages.

———. "Sir William Crookes on Psychical Research." In *Annual Report of the Board of Regents of the Smithsonian Institution, Showing the Operations, Expenditures, and Conditions of the Institution for the Year Ending June 30, 1899.* Washington, D.C.: Government Printing Office, 1901, pp. 185–205.

———. *Researches into the Phenomena of Modern Spiritualism.* Third edition. Los Angeles: Austin Publishing, 1913. Copy formerly in the possession of J. E. Coover. See above under Coover, 1917.

Cutten, George Barton. *Three Thousand Years of Mental Healing.* New York: Scribner, 1911.

Dale, L. A. "The Psychokinetic Effect: The First A.S.P.R. Experiment." *Journal of the American Society for Psychical Research* 40, pp. 123–151 (1946).

Darby, John (pseudonym of James Edmund Garretson). *Nineteenth Century Sense: The Paradox of Spiritualism.* Philadelphia: Lippincott, 1887.

De Beauregard, O. Costa. "The Paranormal Is Not Excluded from Physics." *Journal of Scientific Exploration* 12, pp. 315–320 (1998).

De Mille, Richard. *Castaneda's Journey: The Power and the Allegory.* Santa Barbara, Calif.: Capra Press, 1976. Reprinted 1977.

De Mille, Richard, editor. *The Don Juan Papers: Further Castaneda Controversies.* Santa Barbara, Calif.: Ross-Erikson Publishers, 1980.

Delanoy, Deborah L. "Anomalous Psychophysiological Responses to Remote Cognition: The DMILS Studies." *European Journal of Parapsychology* 16, pp. 30–41 (2001).

Dalkvist, Jan. "The Ganzfeld Method: Its Current Status." *European Journal of Parapsychology* 16, pp. 19–22 (2001).

Dean, E. Douglas. "Plethysmograph Recordings as ESP Responses." *International Journal of Neuropsychiatry* 2, pp. 439–446 (1966).

De Graaf, Theo K., and Joop M. Houtkooper. "Anticipatory Awareness of Emotionally Charged Targets by Individuals with Histories of Emotional Trauma." Originally published in *Journal of Parapsychology*, Spring 2004. Available from FindArticles.com: http://findarticles.com/p/articles/mi_m2320/is_1_68/ai_n13699201. Accessed 23 March 2007.

Denton, William, and Elizabeth M. F. Denton. *The Soul of Things; or Psychometric Researches and Discoveries*. Boston: Walker, Wise and Co., 1863. Reprinted, with a new introduction by Colin Wilson. Wellingborough, Northamptonshire, UK: Aquarian Press, 1988.

Descartes, René. *Meditations on First Philosophy*. Originally published in Latin, 1641. Translated by John Veitch, 1901. Available from: http://www.filepedia.org/node/3. Accessed 30 May 2007.

d'Espérance, E. *Shadow Land; or, Light from the Other Side*. London: George Redway, 1897. Copy consulted formerly in the collection of the International Institute for Psychic Investigation.

Dessoir, M. "Die Parapsychologie." *Sphinx* 7, pp. 341–344 (1889).

Devereux, George, editor. *Psychoanalysis and the Occult*. New York: International Universities Press, 1953.

De Vesme, C. *Histoire du Spiritualisme Expérimental*. Paris: Jean Meyer, 1928.

———. *Lo maravilloso en los juegos de azar: Lotería, carreras, bolsa, naipes, ruleta, etc.* Madrid: Aguilar, 1929.

———. *A History of Experimental Spiritualism*. Vol. 1: *Primitive Man*. Translated from the French by Stanley de Brath. London: Rider, 1931 [1931a].

———. *A History of Experimental Spiritualism*. Vol. 2: *Peoples of Antiquity*. Translated from the French by Fred Rothwell. London: Rider, 1931 [1931b].

———. *Le ordalie*. Milan: Spartaco Giovine, 1945. Reprinted as *Ordalie, roghi e torture*. Genova: Fratelli Melita Editori, 1987.

De Vesme. See also Von Vesme.

Diaconis, P. "Statistical problems in ESP research." *Science* 201, pp. 131–136 (1978).

———. "Rejoinder to Edward F. Kelly." *Zetetic Scholar* 5, pp. 29–31 (1979).

Dingwall, E. J. *Ghosts and Spirits in the Ancient World*. London: Kegan Paul, Trench, Trubner and Co., 1930.

Dobyns, Y. H., B. J. Dunne, R. G. Jahn, and R. D. Nelson. "The MegaREG Experiment: Replication and Interpretation." *Journal of Scientific Exploration* 18, pp. 369–397 (2004).

Dodds, E. R. "Supernormal Phenomena in Classical Antiquity." *Proceedings of the Society for Psychical Research* 55, pp. 189–237 (1971).

Dossey, Larry. *Healing Words: The Power of Prayer and the Practice of Medicine*. New York: HarperCollins, 1993.

———. *Healing Beyond the Body: Medicine and the Infinite Reach of the Mind.* Boston and London: Shambhala, 2001.

———. *The Extraordinary Healing Power of Ordinary Things: Fourteen Natural Steps to Health and Happiness.* New York: Harmony, 2006.

———. "Distance Healing: Evidence" (2007). Published in this volume.

Drewes, Athena A. "Dr. Louisa Rhine's Letters Revisited: The Children." *Journal of Parapsychology.* December 2002. Available from FindArticles.com: http://www.find articles.com/p/articles/mi_m2320/is_4_66/ai_97754937. Accessed 4 September 2006.

Dubrov, A. P., and V. N. Pushkin. *Parapsychology and Contemporary Science.* Translated from the Russian. New York: Consultants Bureau, 1982.

Dunne, B. J. "Co-operator Experiments with an REG Device." In K. R. Rao, editor. *Cultivating Consciousness: Enhancing Human Potential, Wellness, and Healing.* Westport, Conn.: Praeger, 1993, pp. 149–163.

Dunne, Brenda J., and Robert G. Jahn. "Experiments in Remote Human/Machine Interaction." *Journal of Scientific Exploration* 6, no. 4, pp. 311–332 (1992).

———. "Consciousness and Anomalous Physical Phenomena." Princeton Engineering Anomalies Research, School of Engineering/Applied Science, Princeton University, *PEAR Technical Note* 95004, May 1995 (32 pages).

Dunne, Brenda J., and Robert G. Jahn. "Information and Uncertainty in Remote Perception Research." *Journal of Scientific Exploration* 17, no. 2, pp. 207–241 (2003).

Dunne, J. W. *An Experiment with Time.* London: Faber and Faber, 1952 edition.

Dürr, H. P., and F. T. Gottwald, editors. *Rupert Sheldrake in der Diskussion: Das Wagnis einer neuen Wissenschaft des Lebens.* Bern, Switz.: Scherz, 1997.

Edge, Hoyt, editor. "Deception in Psychic Photography." *Quarterly Transactions of the British College of Psychic Science* 14, pp. 154–159 (1935).

Edge, Hoyt L., Robert L. Morris, Joseph H. Rush, and John Palmer. *Foundations of Parapsychology: Exploring the Boundaries of Human Capability.* Foreword by T. X. Barber. Boston: Rutledge and Kegan Paul, 1986.

Edge, Hoyt, Luh Ketut Suryani, Niko Tiliopoulos, and Robert Morris. "Two Cognitive DMILS Studies in Bali." *Journal of Parapsychology.* Fall 2004. Available from FindArticles.com: http://www.findarticles.com/p/articles/mi_m2320/is_2_68/ai_n16107400. Accessed 23 August 2006.

Edmunds, Simeon. *Hypnotism and the Supernormal.* London: Aquarian Press, 1961.

Ehrenwald, J. "Therapeutic Applications," In S. Krippner, R. A. White, M. Ullman, and R. O. Becker, editors. *Advances in Parapsychological Research*, Vol. 1: *Psychokinesis.* New York: Plenum Press, 1977, pp. 133–148.

Einstein, Albert. See Sinclair (1930, 1971).

Eisenberg, Howard. *Inner Spaces: Parapsychological Explorations of the Mind.* Don Mills, Ontario, Canada: Musson Book Co., 1977.

Eisenbud, J. "Psychic Photography and Thoughtography." In John White, editor. *Psychic Exploration: A Challenge for Science.* Introduction by Edgar D. Mitchell. New York: Perigee/Putnam, 1974, pp. 314–331.

———. "On Ted Serios' Alleged 'Confession.' " *Journal of the American Society for Psychical Research* 69, pp. 94–96 (1975).

———. "Observations on a Possible New Thoughtographic Talent." *Journal of the American Society for Psychical Research* 71, pp. 299–304 (1977) [1977a].

———. "Paranormal Photography." In B. B. Wolman, editor. *Handbook of Parapsychology.* New York: Van Nostrand Reinhold, 1977, pp. 414–432 [1977b].

———. "Cutting the Deck with Susie Cottrell." *Skeptical Inquirer* 5, no. 3, pp. 68–70 (1981).

———. *Paranormal Foreknowledge: Problems and Perplexities.* New York: Human Sciences Press, 1982.

———. *Parapsychology and the Unconscious.* Berkeley, Calif.: North Atlantic Books, 1983.

Eisendrath, D. B., Jr. "An Amazing Weekend with the Amazing Ted Serios: Part II." *Popular Photography* 67, no. 4, pp. 85–87, 131–133, 136 (October 1967).

Ennemoser, Joseph. *History of Magic. To which is added an appendix of the most remarkable and best authenticated stories of Apparitions, Dreams, Second Sight, Somnambulism, Predictions, Divination, Witchcraft, Vampires, Fairies, Table-Turning, and Spirit-Rapping Selected by Mary Howitt.* Translated from the German by William Howitt. 2 vols. London: Henry G. Bohn, 1854.

Feather, Sally Rhine, and Michael Schmicker. *The Gift: ESP, the Extraordinary Experiences of Ordinary People.* New York: St. Martin's Press, 2005.

Flammarion, Camille. *The Unknown.* New York: Harper and Bros., 1902.

———. *Mysterious Psychic Forces.* Boston: Small, Maynard and Co., 1907.

———. *Death and Its Mystery: Before Death.* Translated by E. S. Brooks. New York: The Century Co., 1922 [1922a].

———. *Death and Its Mystery: At the Moment of Death.* Translated by Latrobe Carroll. New York: The Century Co., 1922 [1922b].

———. *Death and Its Mystery: After Death.* Translated by Latrobe Carroll. New York: The Century Co., 1923.

———. *Haunted Houses.* New York: D. Appleton Co., 1924.

Flew, Antony. *A New Approach to Psychical Research.* London: Watts and Co., 1953.

Fodor, Nandor. *Encyclopedia of Psychic Science.* With a preface by Sir Oliver Lodge. London: Arthurs Press Limited, circa 1934. Reprinted, with a new foreword by Leslie Shepard, University Books, 1966.

———. "The Poltergeist Psychoanalyzed." *Psychiatric Quarterly* 22, pp. 195–203 (1948).

———. *On the Trail of the Poltergeist.* New York: Citadel Press, 1958.

———. *The Haunted Mind.* New York: Garrett Publications, 1959.

———. *Between Two Worlds.* West Nyack, N.Y.: Parker Publishing, 1964.

Fontana, David. "Survival Research: Opposition and Future Developments." *Journal of the Society for Psychical Research* 68, pp. 193–209 (2004).

Freedman, Morris, Stanley Jeffers, Karen Saeger, Malcolm Binns, and Sandra Black. "Effects of Frontal Lobe Lesions on Intentionality and Random Physical Phenomena." *Journal of Scientific Exploration* 17, pp. 651–668 (2003).

Freud, Sigmund. *Dreams and Telepathy.* Paper read before the Vienna Psychoanalytical Society. Originally published in German as "Traüm und Telepathie" in *Imago* 8, pp. 1–22 (1922). Translated by C. J. M. Hubback. English translation appears as "Dreams and Telepathy." In G. Devereux, editor. *Psychoanalysis and the Occult.* New York: International Universities Press, 1953, pp. 69–86. The same English translation also appears in Philip Rieff, editor. *Freud: Studies in Parapsychology.* New York: Collier Books, 1963, pp. 63–88.

Fukurai, T. *Proeven van Gedachte-Grafie met Japansche Mediums.* Amsterdam: Druk C. A. Spin and Zoon, circa 1930s.

Galbreath, Robert. "The History of Modern Occultism: A Bibliographic Survey." *Journal of Popular Culture* 5, no. 3, pp. 726–754 (1971).

Gardner, M. *Fads and Fallacies in the Name of Science.* New York: Dover Publications, 1957.

———. *Science: Good, Bad, and Bogus.* Buffalo, N.Y.: Prometheus Books, 1981.

———. "Parapsychology and Quantum Mechanics." In George O. Abell and Barry Singer, editors. *Science and the Paranormal: Probing the Existence of the Supernatural.* New York: Scribner, 1983, pp. 56–69 [1983a]. Originally published in 1981.

———. *The Whys of a Philosophical Scrivener.* New York: Quill, 1983 [1983b].

———. *The New Age: Notes of a Fringe Watcher.* Buffalo, N.Y.: Prometheus Books, 1988.

———. *On the Wild Side.* Buffalo, N.Y.: Prometheus Books, 1992.

Garrett, Eileen J. *Adventures in the Supernormal.* New York: Helix Press, 2002.

Gauld, Alan. *The Founders of Psychical Research.* New York: Schocken Books, 1968.

———. *Mediumship and Survival: A Century of Investigations.* London: Paladin Books, 1983.

Gibson, Edmond P., Lottie H. Gibson, and J. B. Rhine. "The PK Effect: Mechanical Throwing of Three Dice." *Journal of Parapsychology* 8, pp. 95–109 (1944).

Goldstein, Bruce E. *Sensation and Perception*. Sixth edition. Pacific Grove, Calif.: Wadsworth Group, 2002.

Green, Celia, and Charles McCreery. *Apparitions*. Oxford, UK: Institute of Psychophysical Research, 1975.

Gregory, A. "Investigating Macro-physical Phenomena." *Parapsychology Review* 13, no. 5, pp. 13–18 (1982).

Greyson, Bruce. "A Typology of Near-Death Experiences." *American Journal of Psychiatry* 142, pp. 967–969 (1985).

———. "Can Science Explain the Near-Death Experience?" *Journal of Near-Death Studies* 8, pp. 77–92 (1989).

———. "Biological Aspects of Near-Death Experiences." *Perspectives in Biology and Medicine* 42, pp. 14–32 (1998).

———. "Near-Death Experiences." In Etzel Cardeña, Steven Jay Lynn, and Stanley Krippner, editors. *Varieties of Anomalous Experience: Examining the Scientific Evidence*. Washington, D.C.: American Psychological Association, 2000, pp. 315–352.

Greyson, Bruce, and Charles P. Flynn, editors. *The Near-Death Experience: Problems, Prospects, Perspectives*. Springfield, Ill.: Charles C. Thomas, 1984.

Gris, Henry, and William Dick. *The New Soviet Psychic Discoveries*. Englewood Cliffs, N.J.: Prentice-Hall, 1978.

Gruber, Elmar R. "PK Effects on Pre-Recorded Group Behavior of Living Systems." *European Journal of Parapsychology* 3, pp. 167–175 (1980).

Gudas, Fabian, editor. *ExtraSensory Perception*. New York: Scribner, 1961.

Guglielmi, Michel, and Stefania Serafin. "Consciousness Reframed 2004: Cyber-Angel." Available from: http://www.mgdesign.dk/publi-conf/paper_bejiing.pdf. Accessed 4 September 2006.

Guiley, Rosemary Ellen. *Encyclopedia of the Strange, Mystical, and Unexplained*. Introduction by Marion Zimmer Bradley. New York: Gramercy Books, 2001. Originally published in 1991.

Gurney, Edmund. "Letters on Phantasms: A Reply." *The Nineteenth Century*, October 1887, pp. 522–533.

Gurney, Edmund, Frederic W. H. Myers, and Frank Podmore. *Phantasms of the Living*. 2 vols. London: Rooms of the Society for Psychical Research and Trübner and Co., 1886. Two-volume facsimile reproduction, with an introduction by Leonard R. N. Ashley, Gainesville, Fla.: Scholars' Facsimiles and Reprints, 1970.

————. *Phantasms of the Living.* Abridged edition prepared by Mrs. Henry Sidgwick. London: Kegan Paul, Trench, Trubner and Co.; New York: Dutton, 1918. Reprinted along with Mrs. Henry Sidgwick (Eleanor Mildred Sidgwick), "Phantasms of the Living: An Examination and Analysis of Cases of Telepathy Between Living Persons Printed in the 'Journal' of the Society for Psychical Research Since the Publication of the Book 'Phantasms of the Living,' by Gurney, Myers, and Podmore, in 1886." *Proceedings of the Society for Psychical Research* 86 (October 1922), and Mrs. Henry Sidgwick, "On Hindrances and Complications in Telepathic Communication" (1924), with a new foreword by Gardner Murphy. New Hyde Park, N.Y.: University Books, 1962.

Haddock, Joseph W. *Somnolism and Psycheism; or, the Science of the Soul and the Phenomena of Nervation, as Revealed by Vital Magnetism or Mesmerism, Considered Physiologically and Philosophically: With Notes of Mesmeric and Psychical Experience.* Second edition. London: James S. Hodson, 1851.

Hammons, Steve. "Navy SEAL Officer's Report on 'Remote Viewing' Urges 'Transcendent' Intelligence." Article dated 26 December 2006. Available from: http://www.americanchronicle.com/articles/viewArticle.asp?articleID=18354. Accessed 25 May 2007.

Hansel, C. E. M. *ESP: A Scientific Evaluation.* New York: Scribner, 1966.

————. *ESP and Parapsychology: A Critical Reevaluation.* Buffalo, N.Y.: Prometheus Books, 1980.

Hansen, George P. "Deception by Subjects in Psi Research." *The Journal of the American Society for Psychical Research* 84, no. 1, pp. 25–80 (January 1990). Available from: http://www.tricksterbook.com/ArticlesOnline/DeceptionFraudTrickery Parapsychology.html. Accessed 26 August 2006.

————. *The Trickster and the Paranormal.* Xlibris Corporation, 2001.

Hansen, George P., Jessica Utts, and Betty Markwick. "Critique of the PEAR Remote-Viewing Experiments." *Journal of Parapsychology* 56, pp. 97–113 (1992).

Haraldsson, E., and K. Osis. "The Appearance and Disappearance of Objects in the Presence of Sri Sathya Sai Baba." *Journal of the American Society for Psychical Research* 71, pp. 33–43 (1977).

Hardy, Christine. "Tackling the Mind-Matter Problem from a Consciousness Perspective." In Michael A. Thalbourne and Lance Storm, editors. *Parapsychology in the Twenty-First Century: Essays on the Future of Psychical Research.* Foreword by Brian D. Josephson. Jefferson, N.C.: McFarland, 2005, pp. 230–241.

Hart, Hornell Norris. *Toward a New Philosophical Basis for Parapsychological Phenomena.* New York: Parapsychology Foundation, 1965. Parapsychological Monographs, no. 6.

Haynes, Renée. *The Hidden Springs: An Inquiry into Extra-Sensory Perception*. New York: Devin-Adair Co., 1961.

———. *The Society for Psychical Research, 1882–1982, A History*. London: Macdonald, 1982.

Heath, Pamela Rae. *The PK Zone: A Cross-Cultural Review of Psychokinesis (PK)*. Lincoln, Neb.: iUniverse, 2003.

Hess, David J. *Science in the New Age: The Paranormal, Its Defenders and Debunkers, and American Culture*. Madison: University of Wisconsin Press, 1993.

Heywood, Rosalind. *Beyond the Reach of Sense: An Inquiry into Extra-Sensory Perception*. With an introduction by J. B. Rhine. New York: Dutton, 1974. Originally published in 1959.

Hodgson, R. "Indian Magic and the Testimony of Conjurers." *Proceedings of the Society for Psychical Research* 9, pp. 354–366 (1894).

Holms, A. Campbell. *The Facts of Psychic Science and Philosophy Collated and Discussed*. London: Kegan Paul, Trench, Trubner and Co., 1925. Reprinted with a new foreword by Leslie Shepard. New Hyde Park, N.Y.: University Books, 1969.

Holroyd, Stuart. *Psi and the Consciousness Explosion*. New York: Taplinger Publishing, 1977.

Honorton, Charles. "Psi-Conducive States of Awareness." In John White, editor. *Psychic Exploration: A Challenge for Science*. Introduction by Edgar D. Mitchell. New York: Perigee/Putnam, 1974, pp. 616–638.

———. "Psi and Internal Attention States." In B. B. Wolman, editor. *Handbook of Parapsychology*. New York: Van Nostrand Reinhold, 1977, pp. 435–472.

———. "Rhetoric over Substance: The Impoverished State of Skepticism." In K. Ramakrishna Rao, editor. *Charles Honorton and the Impoverished State of Skepticism*. Jefferson, N.C.: McFarland, 1994, pp. 191–214. Originally published in *Scienza & Paranormale* 1, no. 3, June 1993.

Horgan, John. *Rational Mysticism: Dispatches from the Border Between Science and Spirituality*. Boston: Houghton Mifflin, 2003.

Horne, James R. "Morality and Parapsychology." In Michael Stoeber and Hugo Meynell, editors. *Critical Reflections on the Paranormal*. Albany: State University of New York Press, 1996, pp. 197–215.

Hufford, David J. *The Terror That Comes in the Night: An Experience-Centered Study of Supernatural Assault Traditions*. Philadelphia: University of Pennsylvania Press, 1982.

Hulme, A. J. Howard, and Frederic H. Wood. *Ancient Egypt Speaks: A Miracle of "Tongues."* London: Rider and Co., circa 1936–1938.

Hyman, Ray. *The Elusive Quarry: A Scientific Appraisal of Psychical Research*. Buffalo, N.Y.: Prometheus Books, 1989.

————. "How Not to Test Mediums: Critiquing the Afterlife Experiments." *Skeptical Inquirer* 27, no. 1, pp. 20–30 (January–February 2003).

————. "Hyman's Reply to Schwartz's 'How Not to Review Mediumship Research'." *Skeptical Inquirer* (March 2003). Available from: http://www.csicop.org/si/2003–05/follow-up-hyman.html. Accessed 4 September 2006.

Inglis, Brian. *Natural and Supernatural: A History of the Paranormal from Earliest Times to 1914*. Revised edition. Dorset, UK: Prism, 1992.

Innes, A. Taylor. "Where are the Letters? A Cross-Examination of Certain Phantasms." *The Nineteenth Century*, pp. 174–194 (August 1887).

Irwin, Harvey J. *An Introduction to Parapsychology*. Fourth edition. Jefferson, N.C.: McFarland, 2004.

Jahn, Robert G., editor. *The Role of Consciousness in the Physical World*. AAAS Selected Symposium no. 57. Boulder, Colo.: Westview Press, 1981.

————. "The Persistent Paradox of Psychic Phenomena: An Engineering Perspective." *Proceedings IEEE* (Institute of Electrical and Electronics Engineers) 70, no. 2, pp.136–170 (1982).

————. "Anomalies: Analysis and Aesthetics." *Journal of Scientific Exploration* 3, no. 1, pp.15–26 (1989).

————. "The Complementarity of Consciousness." Princeton Engineering Anomalies Research, School of Engineering/Applied Science, Princeton University, *PEAR Technical Note* 91006, December 1991 (13 pages).

————. "Information, Consciousness, and Health." *Alternative Therapies* 2, no. 3, pp. 32–38 (1996). Available from: http://www.princeton.edu/~pear/pdfs/JahnAT pages.pdf. Accessed 12 June 2007.

————. "20th and 21st Century Science: Reflections and Projections." *Journal of Scientific Exploration* 15, pp. 21–31 (2001).

————. "The Challenge of Consciousness." *Journal of Scientific Exploration* 15, pp. 443–457 (2001).

Jahn, Robert G., Paul Devereux, and Michael Ibison. "Acoustical Resonances of Assorted Ancient Structures." Princeton Engineering Anomalies Research, School of Engineering/Applied Science, Princeton University, *PEAR Technical Note* 95002, March 1995 (60 pages).

Jahn, Robert G., and Brenda J. Dunne. *Margins of Reality: The Role of Consciousness in the Physical World*. San Diego, Calif.: Harcourt Brace Jovanovich, 1987.

————. "Science of the Subjective." *Journal of Scientific Exploration* 11, pp. 201–224 (1997).

————. "A Modular Model of Mind/Matter Manifestations (M5)." *Journal of Scientific Exploration* 15, pp. 299–329 (2001).

————. "Sensors, Filters, and the Source of Reality." *Journal of Scientific Exploration* 18, pp. 547–570 (2004).

Jahn, R. G., B. J. Dunne, and R. D. Nelson. "Engineering Anomalies Research." *Journal of Scientific Exploration* 1, no. 1, pp. 21–50 (1987).

James, William. "On Trance Phenomena of Mrs. Piper." *Proceedings of the Society for Psychical Research* 6, pp. 651–659 (1890).

————. *The Will to Believe and Other Essays in Popular Philosophy*. New York: Longman, Green, 1897.

————. *The Varieties of Religious Experience*. New York: Longman, Green, 1902.

————. *William James on Psychical Research*. Compiled and edited by Gardner Murphy and Robert O. Ballou. New York: Viking, 1969.

Jaynes, Julian. *The Origin of Consciousness in the Breakdown of the Bicameral Mind*. Boston: Houghton Mifflin, 2000. Originally published in 1976; revised and reissued in 1982 and 1990.

Jeffers, Stanley. "Physics and Claims for Anomalous Effects Related to Consciousness." In James Alcock, Jean Burns, and Anthony Freeman, editors. *Psi Wars: Getting to Grips with the Paranormal*. Charlottesville, Va., and Exeter, UK: Imprint Academic, 2003, pp. 135–152. Originally published in *Journal of Consciousness Studies* 10, nos. 6–7, 2003.

————. "The PEAR Proposition: Fact or Fallacy?" *Skeptical Inquirer*, May 2006. Available from: http://www.csicop.org/si/2006–03/pear.html. Accessed 27 August 2006.

Johnson, Martin. "A New Technique of Testing ESP in a Real-Life, High-Motivated Context." *Journal of Parapsychology* 37, pp. 210–217 (1973).

Johnson, R. C. *Psychical Research*. New York: Philosophical Library, 1956.

Jung, C. G. "Synchronicity: An Acausal Connection Principle." Part I of C. G. Jung and W. Pauli, *The Interpretation of Nature and the Psyche*, translated by R. F. C. Hull. London: Routledge and Kegan Paul, 1952.

Kanthamani, H., and Kelly, E. F. "Awareness of Success in an Exceptional Subject." *Journal of Parapsychology* 38, pp. 355–382 (1974) [1974a].

————. "Card Experiments with a Special Subject. I. Single-Card Clairvoyance." *Journal of Parapsychology* 38, pp. 16–26 (1974) [1974b].

————. "Card Experiments with a Special Subject II. The Shuffle Method." *Journal of Parapsychology* 39, pp. 206–221 (1975).

Kelly, E. F. "Reply to Persi Diaconis." *Zetetic Scholar* 5, pp. 20–28 (1979).

Kennedy, J. E. "The Role of Task Complexity in PK: A Review." *Journal of Parapsychology* 42, pp. 89–122 (1978).

————. "Redundancy in Psi Information: Implications for the Goal-Oriented Hypothesis and the Application of Psi." *Journal of Parapsychology* 43, pp. 290–314 (1979).

————. "Why Is Psi So Elusive? A Review and Proposed Model." *Journal of Parapsychology* 65, pp. 219–246 (2001).

————. "The Capricious, Actively Evasive, Unsustainable Nature of Psi: A Summary and Hypothesis." *The Journal of Parapsychology* 67, pp. 53–74 (2003).

Kennedy, J. E., and Taddonio, J. L. "Experimenter Effects in Parapsychological Research." *Journal of Parapsychology* 40, pp. 1–33 (1976).

Klarreich, Erica. "Stamp Booklet Has Physicists Licked." *Nature* 413, p. 339 (2001). Available from: http://www.tcm.phy.cam.ac.uk/~bdj10/stamps/nature.html. Accessed 28 August 2006.

Koestler, Arthur. *The Ghost in the Machine.* New York: Macmillian, 1967; London: Hutchinson, 1967.

————. *The Roots of Coincidence.* Postscript by Renée Hayes. London: Hutchinson and Co., 1972.

Koestler Parapsychology Unit, University of Edinburgh. Peter Lamont, Paul Stevens, and Caroline Watt. "Introduction and History of the KPU." Available from: http://moebius.psy.ed.ac.uk/. Last updated 13 July 2006. Accessed 25 May 2007.

Korte M., and J. P. Rauschecker. "Auditory Spatial Tuning of Cortical Neurons Is Sharpened in Cats with Early Blindness." *Journal of Neurophysiology* 70, pp. 1717–1721 (1993).

Kozyrev, N.A. "Possibility of Experimental Study of the Properties of Time," Joint Publications Research Service 45238, May 2, 1968. U.S. Department of Commerce, joint publication service, Washington D.C., 1968.

Kress, Kenneth A. "Parapsychology and Intelligence: A Personal Review and Conclusions." *Journal of Scientific Exploration* 13, pp. 69–85 (1999).

Krippner, S. "Introduction." In S. Krippner, R. A. White, M. Ullman, and R. O. Becker. *Advances in Parapsychological Research.* Vol. 1: *Psychokinesis.* New York: Plenum, 1977, pp. 1–14.

————. *Human Possibilities: Mind Exploration in the USSR and Eastern Europe.* Garden City, N.Y.: Anchor/Doubleday, 1980.

Krippner, Stanley, Rhea White, Montague Ullman, and Robert O. Becker, editors. *Advances in Parapsychological Research.* Vol. 1. New York: Plenum, 1977.

Krippner, Stanley, Mary Lou Carlson, Montague Ullman, and Robert O. Becker, editors. *Advances in Parapsychological Research.* Vol. 2. New York: Plenum, 1978.

————. *Advances in Parapsychological Research.* Vol. 3. New York: Plenum, 1982.

————. *Advances in Parapsychological Research.* Vol. 4. Jefferson, N.C.: McFarland, 1984.

————. *Advances in Parapsychological Research.* Vol. 5. Jefferson, N.C.: McFarland, 1987.

————. *Advances in Parapsychological Research.* Vol. 6. Jefferson, N.C.: McFarland, 1990.

Krippner, Stanley, Mary Lou Carlson, Steven Hart, Elizabeth Schneck, Montague Ullman, and Robert O. Becker, editors. *Advances in Parapsychological Research.* Vol. 7. Jefferson, N.C.: McFarland, 1994.

Krippner, Stanley, Steven Hart, Elizabeth Schneck, Montague Ullman, and Robert O. Becker, editors. *Advances in Parapsychological Research.* Vol. 8. Jefferson, N.C.: McFarland, 1997.

Kurtz, Paul, editor. *A Skeptic's Handbook of Parapsychology.* Buffalo, N.Y.: Prometheus Books, 1985.

————, editor. *Skeptical Odysseys: Personal Accounts by the World's Leading Paranormal Inquirers.* Amherst, N.Y.: Prometheus Books, 2001.

————. "Explaining Claims of the 'Paranatural': Life After Death." In Paul Kurtz, with the assistance of Barry Karr and Ranjit Sandhu, editors. *Science and Religion: Are They Compatible?* Amherst, N.Y.: Prometheus Books, 2003, pp. 217–227.

Lamont, Peter, Paul Stevens, and Caroline Watt. See Koestler Parapsychology Unit, University of Edinburgh, 2006.

Lang, Andrew. *Cock Lane and Common-Sense.* London: Longman, Green, 1894. Published in 1894 by Longman, Green both as a "large paper" (printed on larger paper with wider margins) edition of 60 copies, copy no. 23 being consulted for this work, and a general small-paper edition.

————. *The Book of Dreams and Ghosts.* London: Longman, Green, 1897.

————. *The Making of Religion.* London: Longman, Green, 1898. Second edition: Longman, Green, 1900. Third edition: Longman, Green, 1909. 1968 reprint of 1898 first edition, New York: AMS Press.

Lane, Michael, editor. *Introduction to Structuralism.* New York: Basic Books, 1970.

Laszlo, Ervin. *You Can Change the World: The Global Citizen's Handbook for Living on Planet Earth.* Introduction by Mikhail Gorbachev and postscript by Paulo Coelho. Contribution by Masami Saionji. New York: SelectBooks, 2003.

————. *The Connectivity Hypothesis: Foundations of an Integral Science of Quantum, Cosmos, Life, and Consciousness.* New York: State University of New York Press, 2003.

————. *Science and the Akashic Field: An Integral Theory of Everything.* Rochester, Vt.: Inner Traditions, 2004.

Laubscher, B. J. F. *Sex, Custom and Psychopathology: A Study of South African Pagan Natives.* London: George Routledge and Sons, 1937; New York: Robert M. McBride, 1938.

Layard, J. "Psi Phenomena and Poltergeists." *Proceedings of the Society for Psychical Research* 47, pp. 237–247 (1944).

Leadbeater, C. W. *Man Visible and Invisible: Examples of Different Types of Men as Seen by Trained Clairvoyance*. Second revised edition. London: Theosophical Publishing Society, 1907.

———. *The Chakras: A Monograph*. Chicago: The Theosophical Press, 1927; Adyar, Madras, India: Theosophical Publishing House, 1927.

Leeds, Morton, and Gardner Murphy. *The Paranormal and the Normal: A Historical, Philosophical and Theoretical Perspective*. Metuchen, N.J.: Scarecrow Press, 1980.

LeShan, Lawrence L. *Toward a General Theory of the Paranormal: A Report of Work in Progress*. With an introduction by Henry Margenau. New York: Parapsychology Foundation, 1969. Parapsychological Monographs, no. 9.

———. *The Medium, The Mystic, and the Physicist: Toward a General Theory of the Paranormal*. New York: Viking, 1974 [1974a].

———. "Psychic Phenomena and Mystical Experience." In John White, editor. *Psychic Exploration: A Challenge for Science*. Introduction by Edgar D. Mitchell. New York: Perigee/Putnam, 1974, pp. 571–576 [1974b].

———. *From Newton to ESP: Parapsychology and the Challenge of Modern Science*. Wellingborough, Northhamptonshire, UK: Turnstone Press, 1984.

Levy, Walter J. "The Effect of the Test Situation on Precognition in Mice and Jirds: A Confirmation Study." *Journal of Parapsychology* 36, pp. 46–55 (1972). Editors' note: Walter Levy was caught committing experimental fraud and consequently any of the studies he was involved in should be questioned. See Rhine, 1974.

Levy, W. J., and Anita McRae. "Precognition in Mice and Jirds." *Journal of Parapsychology* 35, pp. 120–131 (1971). Editors' note: Walter Levy was caught committing experimental fraud and consequently any of the studies he was involved in should be questioned. See Rhine, 1974.

Lodge, Sir Oliver. Abstract of a paper on automatism and possession. *Journal of the Society for Psychical Research* 13, pp. 180–186 (1908).

Loehr, Frank. *The Power of Prayer on Plants*. With a new introduction. New York: Signet Books, New American Library, 1969. Originally published in 1959.

Lobach, Eva, and Dick J. Bierman. "Who's Calling at This Hour? Local Sidereal Time and Telephone Telepathy." *The Parapsychological Association Convention 2004, Proceedings of Papers*, pp. 91–97 (2004).

Long, Joseph K., editor. *Extrasensory Ecology: Parapsychology and Anthropology*. Metuchen, N.J.: Scarecrow Press, 1977.

Long, Max Freedom. *Recovering the Ancient Magic*. London: Rider, 1936.

McConnell, R. A. *ESP: Curriculum Guide*. New York: Simon & Schuster, 1971.

———, editor. *Encounters with Parapsychology*. Pittsburgh: McConnell, 1982.

————, editor. *Parapsychology and Self-Deception in Science.* Pittsburgh: McConnell, 1982.

————, editor. *An Introduction to Parapsychology in the Context of Science.* Pittsburgh: McConnell, 1983.

————. *Parapsychology in Retrospect: My Search for the Unicorn.* Pittsburgh: McConnell, 1987.

McKenna, Paul, with Giles O'Bryen. *The Paranormal World of Paul McKenna.* London: Faber and Faber, 1997.

McKie, Robin. "*Royal Mail's* Nobel Guru in Telepathy Row." *The Observer,* September 30, 2001. Available from: http://observer.guardian.co.uk/uk_news/story/0,6903,560604,00.html. Accessed 28 August 2006.

McMoneagle, Joseph. *Mind Trek: Exploring Consciousness, Time, and Space Through Remote Viewing.* Charlottesville, Va.: Hampton Roads Publishing, 1997.

————. *The Stargate Chronicles: Memoirs of a Psychic Spy.* Charlottesville, Va.: Hampton Roads Publishing, 2002.

McMullen, George. *One White Crow.* With the research papers of J. N. Emerson on Psychic Archaeology, foreword by Raymond W. Worring, introduction by Stephan A. Schwartz. Norfolk, Va.: Hampton Roads Publishing, 1994.

McTaggart, Lynne. *The Field: The Quest for the Secret Force of the Universe.* New York: Quill, 2002.

Main, Roderick, editor. *Jung on Synchronicity and the Paranormal.* Princeton, N.J.: Princeton University Press, 1997.

Mangan, Gordon L. *A Review of Published Research on the Relationship of Some Personality Variables to ESP Scoring Level.* New York: Parapsychology Foundation, 1958. Parapsychological Monographs, no. 1.

Manning, M. "The subject's report." *Proceedings of the Society for Psychical Research* 56, pp. 353–361 (1982).

Markwick, Betty. "The Soal-Goldney Experiments with Basil Shackleton: New Evidence of Data Manipulation." *Proceedings of the Society for Psychical Research* 56, pp. 250–277 (1978).

Matlock, James G. "Cat's Paw: Margery and the Rhines, 1926." In Debra H. Weiner and Robert Morris, editors. *Research in Parapsychology, 1987.* Metuchen, N.J.: Scarecrow Press, 1988, pp. 162–165.

Mattuck, R. D. "Random Fluctuation Theory of Psychokinesis: Thermal Noise Model." In J. D. Morris, W. G. Roll, and R. L. Morris, editors. *Research in Parapsychology, 1976.* Metuchen, N.J.: Scarecrow Press, 1977, pp. 191–195.

————. "Thermal Noise Theory of Psychokinesis: Modified Walker Model with Pulsed Information Rate." *Psychoenergetic Systems* 3, pp. 301–325 (1979).

Mattuck, Richard D., and Evan Harris Walker. "The Action of Consciousness on Matter: A Quantum Mechanical Theory of Psychokinesis." In Andrija Puharich, editor. *The Iceland Papers: Select Papers on Experimental and Theoretical Research on the Physics of Consciousness: Frontiers of Physics Conferences, Reykjavik, Iceland, November 1977.* Amherst, Wisc.: Essentia Research Associates, 1979, pp. 111–159.

Mauskopf, Seymour H., and Michael R. McVaugh. *The Elusive Science: Origins of Experimental Psychical Research.* Afterword by J. B. and L. E. Rhine. Baltimore: Johns Hopkins University Press, 1980.

May, Edwin C. "Towards the Physics of Psi: Correlations with Physical Variables." *European Journal of Parapsychology* 16, pp. 42–52 (2001).

Mayer, Elizabeth Lloyd. *Extraordinary Knowing: Science, Skepticism, and the Inexplicable Powers of the Human Mind.* With forewords by Freeman Dyson and Carol Gilligan. New York: Bantam, 2007.

Millay, Jean. *Multidimensional Mind: Remote Viewing in Hyperspace.* Foreword by Stanley Krippner. Berkeley, Calif.: North Atlantic Books, 1999.

Milton, Julie. "A Critical Review of the Displacement Effect." In Debra H. Weiner and Robert Morris, editors. *Research in Parapsychology, 1987.* Metuchen, N.J.: Scarecrow Press, 1988, pp. 125–127.

Milton, Julie, and Richard Wiseman. "Does Psi Exist? Lack of Replication of an Anomalous Process of Information Transfer." *Psychological Bulletin* 125, pp. 387–391 (1999).

Mishlove, Jeffery. "Repeatability, Fraud and *A Priori* Objections." Excerpt from *Psi Development Systems.* Published by Ballantine in 1988. Available from: http:// jeff.zaadz.com/blog/2006/5/objections_to_esp. Accessed 26 August 2006.

———. *Psi Development Systems.* Jefferson, N.C.: McFarland, 1983.

Mitchell, Edgar D. "An ESP Test from Apollo 14." *Journal of Parapsychology* 35, pp. 89–107 (1971).

Mitchell, Edgar D. See J. White (1974).

Moehringer, J. R. "A Hushed Death for Mystic Author Carlos Castaneda." Obituary dated 1998. Available from: http://www.angelfire.com/electronic/awakening101/ obituary.html. Accessed 21 February 2007.

Morris, Robert L. "Parapsychology, Biology, and ANPSI." In B. B. Wolman, editor. *Handbook of Parapsychology.* New York: Van Nostrand Reinhold, 1977, pp. 687–715.

Moss, Thelma. *The Probability of the Impossible: Scientific Discoveries and Explorations in the Psychic World.* New York: New American Library, 1974.

Murphy, Gardner. "Telepathy as an Experimental Problem." In Carl Murchison, editor. *The Case For and Against Psychical Belief.* Worcester, Mass.: Clark University, 1927, pp. 265–278.

Murphy, Gardner, and Robert O. Ballou, editors. *William James on Psychical Research.* With an introduction and concluding remarks by Gardner Murphy. New York: Viking, 1969.

Myers, Frederic W. H. *Human Personality and Its Survival of Bodily Death.* 2 vols. London: Longman, Green, 1903.

Myers, Frederic W. H. *Human Personality and Its Survival of Bodily Death.* Edited and abridged by the author's son Leopold Hamilton Myers. New York: Longman, Green, 1907.

Nash, Carroll B. *Science of Psi: ESP and PK.* Springfield, Ill.: Charles C. Thomas, 1978.

Nelson, Roger D. "FieldREG Measurements in Egypt: Resonant Consciousness at Sacred Sites." Princeton Engineering Anomalies Research, School of Engineering/Applied Science, Princeton University, *PEAR Technical Note* 97002, July 1997 (36 pages).

———. "The Physical Basis of Intentional Healing Systems." Princeton Engineering Anomalies Research, School of Engineering/Applied Science, Princeton University, *PEAR Technical Note* 99001, January 1999 (28 pages).

———. "Gathering of Global Mind." No date. Available from: http://noosphere.princeton.edu/story.html. Accessed 4 September 2006.

Nelson, R. D., G. J. Bradish, Y. H. Dobyns, B. J. Dunne, and R. G. Jahn. "FieldREG I: Anomalies in Group Situations." *Journal of Scientific Exploration* 10, pp. 111–141 (1996).

Nelson, R. D., B. J. Dunne, Y. H. Dobyns, and R. G. Jahn. "Precognitive Remote Perception: Replication of Remote Viewing." *Journal of Scientific Exploration* 10, pp. 109–110 (1996).

Nelson, R. D., R. G. Jahn, B. J. Dunne, Y. H. Dobyns, and G. J. Bradish. "FieldREG II: Consciousness Field Effects: Replications and Explorations." *Journal of Scientific Exploration* 12, pp. 425–454 (1998).

Nickell, Joe, Barry Karr, and Tom Genoni. *The Outer Edge: Classic Investigations of the Paranormal.* With an introduction by Carl Sagan. Amherst, N.Y.: Committee for the Scientific Investigation of Claims of the Paranormal (CSICOP), 1996.

North, Anthony. *The Paranormal: A Guide to the Unexplained.* London: Blandford, 1996. Reprint, 1997.

———. *The Supernatural: A Guide to Mysticism and the Occult.* London: Blandford, 1998.

Olcott, Henry S. *People from the Other World.* Hartford, Conn.: American Publishing Co., 1875.

Oppenheim, Janet. *The Other World: Spiritualism and Psychical Research in England, 1850–1914.* Cambridge, UK: Cambridge University Press, 1985.

Orme, J. E. "Precognition and Time." *Journal of the Society for Psychical Research* 47, pp. 351–365 (1974).

Ortiz, D. *Gambling Scams: How They Work, How to Detect Them, How to Protect Yourself.* New York: Dodd, Mead, 1984.

Osis, Karlis. "A Test of the Relationship Between ESP and PK." *Journal of Parapsychology* 17, pp. 298–309 (1953).

———. "Precognition Over Time Intervals of One to Thirty-three Days." *Journal of the American Society for Psychical Research* 12, pp. 82–91 (1955).

———. "ESP Over Distance: A Survey of Experiments Published in English." In Rhea A. White, editor. *Surveys in Parapsychology: Reviews of the Literature with Updated Bibliographies.* Metuchen, N.J.: Scarecrow Press, 1976, pp. 180–202. Originally published in the *Journal of the American Society for Psychical Research* 59, pp. 22–42 (1965).

Osis, Karlis, and J. Fahler. "Space and Time in ESP." *Journal of the American Society for Psychical Research* 59, pp. 130–145 (1965).

Ostrander, Sheila, and Lynn Schroeder. *Psychic Discoveries Behind the Iron Curtain.* Englewood Cliffs, N.J.: Prentice-Hall, 1970.

———. *Handbook of Psi Discoveries.* New York: Berkley/Putnam, 1974.

———. *Supermemory: The Revolution.* New York: Carroll and Graf, 1991.

———. *Psychic Discoveries.* New York: Marlowe and Co., 1997.

Osty, Eugene. *La Connaissance Supra-normale: Étude Expérimentale.* Paris: Librairie Félix Alcan, 1923. Second edition, 1925.

———. *Supernormal Faculties in Man.* Translated by Stanley De Brath. New York: Dutton, circa 1923.

Owen, Dale. *Footfalls on the Boundary of Another World.* Philadelphia: Lippincott, 1860.

Palmer, John. "Extrasensory Perception: Research Findings." In Stanley Krippner, Mary Lou Carlson, Montague Ullman, and Robert O. Becker, editors. *Advances in Parapsychological Research.* Vol. 2: *Extrasensory Perception.* New York: Plenum, 1978, pp. 59–243.

———. "Progressive Skepticism: A Critical Approach to the Psi Controversy." *Journal of Parapsychology* 50, pp. 31–44 (1986).

Parker, Adrian, and Göran Brusewitz. "A Compendium of the Evidence for Psi." *European Journal of Parapsychology* 18, pp. 29–48 (2003).

PEAR [Princeton Engineering Anomalies Research laboratory]. "Princeton's PEAR laboratory to close." Press release dated 10 February 2007. Available from: http://www.princeton.edu/%7Epear/press_release_closing.html. Accessed 25 May 2007.

Perot, Rene. "An Experimental Study of Psychokinesis." *Revue Metapsychique* 6, pp. 75–83 (1967).

Perry, Michael C. *The Easter Enigma: An Essay on the Resurrection, with Special Reference to the Data of Psychical Research.* With an introduction by Austin Farrer. London: Faber and Faber, 1959.

Persinger, M. A. "Spontaneous Telepathic Experiences from Phantasms of the Living and Low Global Geomagnetic Activity." *Journal of the American Society for Psychical Research* 83, pp. 23–36 (1987).

Persinger, M. A., and G. B. Schaut. "Geomagnetic Factors in Spontaneous Telepathic, Precognitive, and Postmortem Experiences." In D. H. Weiner and R. D. Nelson, editors. *Research in Parapsychology, 1986.* Metuchen, N.J.: Scarecrow Press, 1987, pp. 88–90.

Pierce, John Robinson. *Symbols, Signals, and Noise: The Nature and Process of Communication.* New York: Harper and Bros., 1961.

Podmore, Frank. *Apparitions and Thought-Transference: An Examination of the Evidence for Telepathy.* London: Walter Scott, 1894.

———. *Studies in Psychical Research.* London: Kegan Paul, Trench, Trübner and Co., 1897.

———. *Modern Spiritualism: A History and a Criticism.* 2 volumes. London: Methuen and Co., 1902. Reprinted, with a new introduction by E. J. Dingwall, as *Mediums of the 19th Century.* New Hyde Park, N.Y.: University Books, 1963.

———. *Mesmerism and Christian Science.* Philadelphia: George W. Jacobs and Co., circa 1909.

Pratt, J. Gaither. *ESP Research Today: A Study of Developments in Parapsychology Since 1960.* Metuchen, N.J.: Scarecrow Press, 1973.

Pratt, J. G. "A Decade of Research with a Selected ESP Subject: An Overview and Reappraisal of the Work with Pavel Stepanek." *Proceedings of the American Society for Psychical Research* 30, pp. i–vi, 1–78 (1973).

Pratt, J. G., and H. H. J. Keil. "Firsthand Observations of Nina S. Kulagina Suggestive of PK Upon Static Objects." *Journal of the American Society for Psychical Research* 67, pp. 381–390 (1973).

Pratt, J. G., J. B. Rhine, B. M. Smith, C. E. Stuart, and J. A. Greenwood. *Extra-Sensory Perception After Sixty Years.* New York: Holt, 1940.

Price, G. R. "Science and the Supernatural." *Science* 122, pp. 359–367 (1955).

———. "Apology to Rhine and Soal." *Science* 175, p. 359 (1972).

Price, H. "Psychic Photography: Some Scientific Aids to Spurious Phenomena—I." *Journal of the American Society for Psychical Research* 19, pp. 570–587 (1925) [1925a].

―――. "Psychic Photography: Some Scientific Aids to Spurious Phenomena—II." *Journal of the American Society for Psychical Research* 19, pp. 617–636 (1925) [1925b].

―――. "Regurgitation and the Duncan Mediumship." *Bulletin of the National Laboratory of Psychical Research* 1, 1931.

―――. *Leaves From a Psychist's Case-Book.* London: Gollancz, 1933.

―――. *Confessions of a Ghost-Hunter.* London: Putnam, 1936.

―――. *Fifty Years of Psychical Research: A Critical Survey.* London: Longman, Green, 1939.

―――. *Poltergeist Over England: Three Centuries of Mischievous Ghosts.* London: Country Life, 1945.

Price, Margaret M., and J. B. Rhine. "The Subject-Experimenter Relation in the PK Test." *Journal of Parapsychology* 8, pp. 177–186 (1944).

Prince, W. F. "My Doubts About Spirit Photographs." *Scientific American* 133, pp. 370–371 (1925).

―――. *The Enchanted Boundary: Being a Survey of the Negative Reactions to Claims of Psychic Phenomena, 1820–1930.* Boston: Boston Society for Psychic Research, 1930.

―――. "The Sinclair Experiments Demonstrating Telepathy." *Bulletin of the Boston Society for Psychic Research* 16, pp. 1–138 (1932).

Puharich, Andrija [Henry]. *Beyond Telepathy.* With an introduction by Ira Einhorn. Garden City, N.Y.: Anchor/Doubleday, 1973. Originally published in 1962.

Puharich, Henry K. "The Work of the Brazilian Healer Arigó." In *The Varieties of Healing Experience: Exploring Psychic Phenomena in Healing. Transcript of the Interdisciplinary Symposium of October 30, 1971.* Los Altos, Calif.: Academy of Parapsychology and Medicine, 1972, pp. 45–54.

Puthoff, H. E., and R. Targ. "A Perceptual Channel for Information Transfer Over Kilometer Distances: Historical Perspective and Recent Research." *Proceedings of the Institute of Electrical and Electronic Engineers* 64, pp. 329–354 (1976).

Radin, Dean. *The Conscious Universe: The Scientific Truth of Psychic Phenomena.* San Francisco: HarperEdge, 1997 [1997a].

―――. "Unconscious Perception of Future Emotions: An Experiment in Presentiment." *Journal of Scientific Exploration* 11, pp. 163–180 (1997) [1997b].

―――. "Exploring Relationships Between Random Physical Events and Mass Human Attention: Asking for Whom the Bell Tolls." *Journal of Scientific Exploration* 16, pp. 533–547 (2002) [2002a].

―――. "A Dog That Seems to Know When His Owner Is Coming Home: Effect of Environmental Variables." *Journal of Scientific Exploration* 16, pp. 579–592 (2002) [2002b].

————. "Preliminary Analysis of a Suite of Informal Web-Based Psi Experiments." (2002) [2002c]. Available from: http://www.boundaryinstitute.org/articles/ GotPsi-public.pdf. Accessed 13 September 2006.

————. "Event-Related Electroencephalographic Correlations Between Isolated Human Subjects." *Journal of Alternative and Complementary Medicine* 10, no. 2, pp. 315–323 (2004).

————. *Entangled Minds: Extrasensory Experiences in Quantum Reality*. New York: Paraview Pocket Books, 2006 [2006a].

————. "Psychophysiological Tests of Possible Retrocausal Effects in Humans." *Proceedings of the American Association for the Advancement of Science, Pacific Division* 25, part 1, p. 88 (June 18, 2006) [2006b].

Radin, Dean and Roger D. Nelson. "Evidence for Consciousness-Related Anomalies in Random Physical Systems." *Foundations of Physics* 19, pp. 1499–1514 (1989).

————. "Meta-analysis of Mind-Matter Interaction Experiments: 1959–2000." Available from: http://www.boundaryinstitute.org/experimental.htm. Paper cited there as "2000." Accessed 17 August 2006.

Rahmani, Levy. *Soviet Psychology: Philosophical, Theoretical, and Experimental Issues*. New York: International Universities Press, 1973.

Rammohan, V. Gouri, editor. *New Frontiers of Human Science: A Festschrift for K. Ramakrishna Rao*. Jefferson, N.C.: McFarland, 2002.

Randall, J. L. "Recent Experiments in Animal Parapsychology." *Journal of the Society for Psychical Research* 46, pp. 124–135 (1971–1972).

————. "Psi Phenomena and Biological Theory." *Journal of the Society for Psychical Research* 46, pp. 151–165 (1971–1972). Reprinted in Rhea A. White, editor. *Surveys in Parapsychology: Reviews of the Literature with Updated Bibliographies*. Metuchen, N.J.: Scarecrow Press, 1976, pp. 333–349.

————. *Parapsychology and the Nature of Life*. New York: Harper and Row, 1975.

Randi, James. *Flim-Flam! Psychics, ESP, Unicorns, and Other Delusions*. Introduction by Isaac Asimov. Amherst, N.Y.: Prometheus Books, 1982.

————. "More Card Tricks from Susie Cottrell." *Skeptical Inquirer* 5, no. 3, pp. 70–71 (1981).

Ransom, C. "Recent Criticisms of Parapsychology: A Review." *Journal of the American Society for Psychical Research* 65, pp. 289–307 (1971).

Rao, K. Ramakrishna, editor. *J. B. Rhine: On the Frontiers of Science*. Jefferson, N.C.: McFarland, 1982.

————. "On the Question of Application." Roundtable discussion on applications of Psi. In William G. Roll, John Beloff, and Rhea A. White, editors. *Research in*

*Parapsychology, 1982: Jubilee Centenary Issue.* Metuchen, N.J.: Scarecrow Press, 1983, pp. 263–264.

———, editor. *The Basic Experiments in Parapsychology.* Jefferson, N.C., and London: McFarland, 1984.

———. "Louisa E. Rhine: 1891–1983." In K. R. Rao, editor. *Case Studies in Parapsychology: In Honor of Dr. Louisa E. Rhine.* Jefferson, N.C.: McFarland, 1986, pp. 1–4.

———, editor. *Charles Honorton and the Impoverished State of Skepticism: Essays on a Parapsychological Pioneer.* Jefferson, N.C.: McFarland, 1994.

———, editor. *Basic Research in Parapsychology.* Second edition. Jefferson, N.C.: McFarland, 2001.

———. *Consciousness Studies: Cross-Cultural Perspectives.* Jefferson, N.C.: McFarland, 2002.

Rauschecker, Josef P. "Compensatory Plasticity and Sensory Substitution in the Cerebral Cortex." *Trends in Neuroscience* 18, pp. 36–43 (1995).

Rauschecker, Josef P., and Martin Korte. "Auditory Compensation for Early Blindness in Cat Cerebral Cortex." *Journal of Neuroscience* 13, pp. 4538–4548 (1993).

Rauscher, Elizabeth A., and Russell Targ. "The Speed of Thought: Investigation of a Complex Space-Time Metric to Describe Psychic Phenomena." *Journal of Scientific Exploration* 15, pp. 331–354 (2001).

Regush, Nicholas M., editor. *Frontiers of Healing: New Dimensions in Parapsychology.* New York: Avon Books, 1977.

Reynolds, C. "An Amazing Weekend with the Amazing Ted Serios. Part I." *Popular Photography* 67, no. 4, pp. 81–84, 136–140, 158 (1967).

Rhine, J. B. *Extra-Sensory Perception.* With a foreword by William McDougall and an introduction by Walter Franklin Prince. Boston: Boston Society for Psychic Research, 1934; London: Faber and Faber, 1935. Faber edition with an additional preface and appendix by J. B. Rhine.

———. *New Frontiers of the Mind: The Story of the Duke Experiments.* New York: Farrar and Rinehart, 1937.

———. *New World of the Mind.* William Sloane Associates, 1953.

———. "Psi and Psychology: Conflict and Solution." *Journal of Parapsychology* 32, pp. 101–128 (1968).

———, editor. *Progress in Parapsychology.* Durham, N.C.: Parapsychology Press, 1971.

———, "A New Case of Experimenter Unreliability." *Journal of Parapsychology* 38, pp. 215–225 (1974).

——— and associates. *Parapsychology from Duke to FRNM.* Durham, N.C.: Parapsychology Press, 1965.

Rhine, L. E. "Conviction and Associated Conditions in Spontaneous Cases." *Journal of Parapsychology* 15, pp. 164–191 (1951).

———. "Subjective Forms of Spontaneous Psi Experiences." *Journal of Parapsychology* 17, pp. 77–114 (1953).

———. "Psychological Processes in ESP Experiences. Part I: Waking Experiences." *Journal of Parapsychology* 26, pp. 88–111 (1962).

———. "Dr. L. E. Rhine's Reply to Dr. Stevenson." Letter to the editor. *Journal of Parapsychology* 34, pp. 149–164 (1970).

———. *Mind Over Matter: Psychokinesis.* London: Collier/Macmillan, 1970.

———. *Psi: What Is It? An Introduction to Parapsychology.* New York: Harper and Row, 1975.

———. *The Invisible Picture: A Study of Psychic Experiences.* Jefferson, N.C.: McFarland, 1981.

———. *Something Hidden.* Jefferson, N.C.: McFarland, 1983.

Rhine, Louisa E., and J. B. Rhine. "The Psychokinetic Effect: I. The First Experiment." *Journal of Parapsychology* 7, pp. 20–43 (1943).

Rhine Research Center. "The History of the Rhine Research Center." No date. Available from: http://www.rhine.org/f_hist.htm. Accessed 9 September 2006.

Richet, Charles. *Thirty Years of Psychical Research: Being a Treatise on Metapsychics.* Translated by Stanley De Brath. New York: Macmillan, 1923.

Richmond, Cora L. V. *My Experiences While Out of My Body and My Return After Many Days.* Boston: Christopher Press, 1915.

Roberts, F. S. "Time Perception and Precognition." *Journal of the Society for Psychical Research* 59, pp.141–148 (1993).

Roll, William G. "The Problem of Precognition." In Rhea A. White, editor. *Surveys in Parapsychology.* Metuchen, N.J.: Scarecrow Press, 1976, pp. 3–17.

———, editor. *Research in Parapsychology: Abstracts and Papers from the Twenty-first Annual Convention of the Parapsychological Association, 1978.* Metuchen, N.J., and London: Scarecrow Press, 1979.

———. "Notes on Clinical Parapsychology." In D. H. Weiner and R. D. Nelson, editors. *Research in Parapsychology, 1986.* Metuchen, N.J.: Scarecrow Press, 1987, pp. 161–162.

———. "Poltergeists, Electromagnetism and Consciousness." *Journal of Scientific Exploration* 17, no. 1, pp. 75–86 (2003).

Roll, W. G., and L. Gearhart. "Geomagnetic Perturbations and RSPK." In W. G. Roll, R. L. Morris, and J. Morris, editors. *Research in Parapsychology, 1973.* Metuchen, N.J.: Scarecrow Press, 1974, pp. 44–46.

Roney-Dougal, Serena. "Some Thoughts Inspired by the Essay Title 'How the Scientific Establishment's Acceptance of ESP and PK would Influence Contemporary Society.' " *Exceptional Human Experience* 10, no. 1, pp. 16–22 (1992).

Rose, Ronald. *Living Magic: The Realities Underlying the Psychical Practices and Beliefs of Australian Aborigines.* Foreword by J. B. Rhine. New York: Rand McNally, 1956.

———. *South Seas Magic.* London: Robert Hale, 1959.

Rose, Lyndon, and Ronald Rose. "Psi Experiments with Australian Aborigines." *Journal of Parapsychology* 15, pp. 122–131 (1951).

———. "Experiments in PK with Aboriginal Subjects." *Journal of Parapsychology* 16, pp. 219–220 (1952).

Rosenthal, Robert. *Experimenter Effects in Behavioral Research.* New York: Appleton-Century-Crofts, 1966.

Rossner, John. *Toward a Parapsychology of Religion.* 2 vols. Book 1: *From Ancient Magic to Future Technology.* Book 2: *From Ancient Religion to Future Science.* Washington, D.C.: University Press of America, 1979.

Rubik, Beverly. *Life at the Edge of Science: An Anthology of Papers by Beverly Rubik.* Philadelphia: Institute for Frontier Science, 1996.

Rush, J. H. "Problems and Methods in Psychokinesis Research." In S. Krippner, R. A. White, M. Ullman, and R. O. Becker, editors. *Advances in Parapsychological Research.* Vol. 1: *Psychokinesis.* New York: Plenum, 1977, pp. 15–78.

———. "Spontaneous Psi Phenomena: Case Studies and Field Investigations." In Hoyt L. Edge, Robert L. Morris, Joseph H. Rush, and John Palmer, editors. *Foundations of Parapsychology: Exploring the Boundaries of Human Capability.* Foreword by T. X. Barber. Boston: Rutledge and Kegan Paul, 1986, pp. 47–69.

Rushton, W. A. H. "Serios-Photos: If Contrary to Natural Law, Which Law?" *Journal of the Society for Psychical Research* 44, pp. 289–293 (1968).

Rýzl, Milan. *Parapsychology: A Scientific Approach.* New York: Hawthorn Books, 1970.

Sanders, Pete A., Jr. *You Are Psychic! The Free Soul Method.* New York: Fawcett/Columbine, 1989.

Sargent, Epes [Anonymous]. *Planchette; or the Despair of Science. Being a Full Account of Modern Spiritualism, Its Phenomena, and the Various Theories Regarding It. With a Survey of French Spiritism.* Boston: Roberts Bros., 1869.

Scargle, Jeffrey. "Was There Evidence of Global Consciousness on September 11, 2001?" *Journal of Scientific Exploration* 16, pp. 571–577 (2002).

———. "Reviewer Comment on Rupert Sheldrake and Aimée Morgana, 'Testing a Language-Using Parrot for Telepathy.' " *Journal of Scientific Exploration* 17, p. 615 (2003).

Schlitz, M. J., and C. Honorton. "Ganzfeld Psi Performance Within an Artistically Gifted Population." *Journal of the American Society for Psychical Research* 86, pp. 83–98 (1992).

Schmeidler, Gertrude Raffel. *ESP in Relation to Rorschach Test Evaluation*. New York: Parapsychology Foundation, 1960. Parapsychological Monographs, no. 2.

———. "Psi-Conducive Experimenters and Psi-Permissive Ones." *European Journal of Parapsychology* 13, pp. 83–94 (1997).

Schmeidler, Gertrude Raffel, and R. A. McConnell. *ESP and Personality Patterns*. With an introduction by Gardner Murphy. New Haven, Conn.: Yale University Press, 1958.

Schmidt, Helmut. "Precognition of a Quantum Process." *Journal of Parapsychology* 33, pp. 99–108 (1969).

———. "Comparison of PK Action on Two Different Random Number Generators." *Journal of Parapsychology* 38, pp. 47–55 (1974).

———. "Toward a Mathematical Model of Psi." *Journal of the American Society for Psychical Research* 69, pp. 301–319 (1975).

———. "PK Effect on Pre-Recorded Targets." *Journal of the American Society for Psychical Research* 70, pp. 267–291 (1976).

———. "Collapse of the State Vector and Psychokinetic Effect." *Foundations of Physics* 12, pp. 565–581 (1982).

Schmidt, Helmut, R. Morris, and L. Rudolph. "Channeling Evidence for a PK Effect to Independent Observers." *Journal of Parapsychology* 50, pp. 1–15 (1986).

Schmidt, Helmut, and Henry Stapp. "PK with Prerecorded Random Events and the Effects of Preobservers." *Journal of Parapsychology* 57, pp. 331–349 (1993).

Schoch, Robert M. "Religion and Paranormal Phenomena." Unpublished paper based on a lecture titled "Ancient Religious Beliefs and Paranormal Phenomena" presented by Schoch at the Rhine Research Center, Durham, N.C., 13 January 2006.

———. *DVD of Robert M. Schoch's Presentation at CPAK 2006*. Conference on Precession and Ancient Knowledge, 14 October 2006, University of California, Irvine. Published and distributed by VW Tapes / Von Wiegandt Productions, www.vwtapes.com.

Schoch, Robert M., with Robert Aquinas McNally. *Voices of the Rocks: A Scientist Looks at Catastrophes and Ancient Civilizations*. New York: Harmony Books, 1999.

———. *Voyages of the Pyramid Builders: The True Origins of the Pyramids from Lost Egypt to Ancient America*. New York: Tarcher/Putnam, 2003.

———. *Pyramid Quest: Secrets of the Great Pyramid and the Dawn of Civilization*. New York: Tarcher/Penguin, 2005.

Schouten, Sybo Ao, and Edward F. Kelly. "On the Experiment of Brugmans, Heymans, and Weinberg." *European Journal of Parapsychology* 2, pp. 255–298 (1977–1979).

Schrenck-Notzing, A. von. *Therapeutic Suggestion in Pychopathia Sexualis (Pathological Manifestations of the Sexual Sense) with Especial Reference to Contrary Sexual Instinct.* Translated from the German by Charles Gilbert Chaddock. Philadelphia: F. A. Davis Co., 1895.

———. *Phenomena of Materialisation: A Contribution to the Investigation of Mediumistic Teleplastics.* London: Kegan Paul, Trench, Trubner and Co., 1923 [1923a].

———. *Materialisations-Phaenomene: Ein Beitrag zur Erforschung der Mediumistischen Teleplastie.* München: Ernst Reinhardt, 1923 [1923b].

Schrödinger, Erwin. *What is Life? And Other Scientific Essays.* Garden City, N.Y.: Doubleday, 1956.

Schwartz, Gary E. "How *Not* To Review Mediumship Research: Understanding the Ultimate Reviewer's Mistake." 2003. Available from: http://www.csicop.org/si/2003-09/alternative-medicine.html. Accessed 4 September 2006.

Schwartz, Gary E. R., and Linda G. S. Russek. *The Living Energy Universe.* Charlottesville, Va.: Hampton Roads, 1999.

Schwartz, Gary E., with William L. Simon. *The Afterlife Experiments: Breakthrough Scientific Evidence of Life After Death.* Foreword by Deepak Chopra. New York: Pocket Books, 2002.

Schwartz, Stephan A. *The Secret Vaults of Time: Psychic Archaeology and the Quest for Man's Beginnings.* New York: Grosset and Dunlap, 1978.

———. *The Alexandria Project.* New York: Delacorte/Eleanor Friede, 1983.

———. "The Location and Reconstruction of a Byzantine Structure in Marea, Egypt, Including a Comparison of Electronic Remote Sensing and Remote Viewing." 1980 and 2000. Available from: http://www.stephanaschwartz.com/home.htm. Accessed 2 September 2006.

———. See also McMullen (1994).

Schwartz, Stephan A., and Randall J. De Mattei. "The Discovery of an American Brig: Fieldwork Involving Applied Remote Viewing Including a Comparison with Electronic Remote Sensing." 1988 and 2000. Available from: http://www.stephanaschwartz.com/home.htm. Accessed 2 September 2006.

Schwarz, B. E. "K: A Presumed Case of Telekinesis." *International Journal of Psychosomatics* 32, pp. 3–21 (1985) [1985a].

———. "K: A Presumed Case of Telekinesis." *Pursuit* 8, pp. 50–61 (1985) [1985b].

Scott, C., and P. Haskell. "Fresh Light on the Shackleton Experiments." *Proceedings of the Society for Psychical Research* 56, pp. 43–72 (1974).

Seligmann, Kurt. *The History of Magic and the Occult*. New York: Gramercy Books, 1997. Originally published in 1948.

Sermonti, G. "The Impossible Exists: About the 'Seven Experiments' Suggested by Rupert Sheldrake." *Biology Forum* 89, pp. 479–482 (1996).

Shapin, Betty, and Lisette Coly, editors. *Communication and Parapsychology: Proceedings of an International Conference Held in Vancouver, Canada, August 9–10, 1979*. New York: Parapsychology Foundation, 1980.

Sheldrake, Rupert. *A New Science of Life: The Hypothesis of Formative Causation*. Los Angeles: Tarcher, 1981.

———. *The Presence of the Past: Morphic Resonance and the Habits of Nature*. London: Collins, 1988.

———. *Seven Experiments That Could Change the World*. London: Fourth Estate, 1994.

———. "Impossible . . . for the Current Physics: Reply to the Open Letter by Giuseppe Sermonti." *Biology Forum* 89, pp. 483–486 (1996).

———. *Dogs That Know When Their Owners Are Coming Home, and Other Unexplained Powers of Animals*. New York: Crown, 1999.

———. "Listen to the Animals: Why Did So Many Animals Escape December's Tsunami?" *The Ecologist*. March 2005. Available from: http://www.sheldrake.org/papers/Animals/animals_tsunami.html. Accessed 28 August 2006.

Sheldrake, Rupert, Catherine Lawlor, and Jane Turney. "Perceptive Pets: A Survey in London." *Biology Forum* 91, pp. 57–74 (1998). Available from: http://www.sheldrake.org/papers/Animals/perceptivelondon.html. Accessed 28 August 2006.

Sheldrake, Rupert, and Aimée Morgana. "Testing a Language-Using Parrot for Telepathy." *Journal of Scientific Exploration* 17, pp. 601–615 (2003). Available from: http://sheldrake.org/papers/Animals/parrot_telepathy.html. Accessed 28 August 2006.

Sheldrake, R., and P. Smart. "A Dog That Seems to Know When Its Owner Is Returning: Preliminary Investigations." *Journal of the Society for Psychical Research* 62, pp. 220–232 (1998).

———. "A Dog That Seems to Know When His Owner Is Coming Home: Videotaped Experiments and Observations." *Journal of Scientific Exploration* 14, no. 2, pp. 233–255 (2000) [2000a].

———. "Testing a Return-Anticipating Dog, Kane." *Anthrozoös* 13, no. 4, pp. 203–212 (2000) [2000b].

Shepard, Leslie A., editor. *Encyclopedia of Occultism and Parapsychology*. 2 vols. Compiled and edited from *Encyclopedia of the Occult* by Lewis Spence (1920) and *Encyclopedia of Psychic Science* by Nandor Fodor (1934), with additional material edited by Leslie A. Shepard. New York: Avon Books, 1980.

Sidgwick, Henry, Alice Johnson, Frederic W. H. Myers, Frank Podmore, and Elenor Mildred Sidgwick. "Report on the Census of Hallucinations." *Proceedings of the Society for Psychical Research* 10, part 26, pp. 25–422 (1894).

Sinclair, Upton. *Mental Radio: Does It Work, and How?* With an introduction by William McDougall. London: T. Werner Laurie, 1930. Pasadena, Calif.: Upton Sinclair, 1930. Preface by Albert Einstein, translated from the original German, published in the Collier Books edition in 1971.

Smyth, Charles Piazzi. *Our Inheritance in the Great Pyramid*. London: Alexander Strahan and Co., 1864.

———. *Our Inheritance in the Great Pyramid*. Fourth edition. London: Daldy, Isbister and Co., 1880.

Soal, S.G., and F. Bateman. *Modern Experiments in Telepathy*. London: Faber and Faber, 1954; New Haven, Conn.: Yale University Press, 1954. Yale edition includes an introductory note by G. E. Hutchinson.

Spottiswoode, James, and Ed May. "Skin Conductance Prestimulus Response: Analyses, Artifacts and a Pilot Study." *Journal of Scientific Exploration* 17, no. 4, pp. 617–641 (2003).

Standish, Leanna J., Leila Kozak, L. Clark Johnson, and Todd Richards. "Electroencephalographic Evidence of Correlated Event-Related Signals Between the Brains of Spatially and Sensory Isolated Human Subjects." *Journal of Alternative and Complementary Medicine* 10, no. 2, pp. 307–314 (2004).

Stanford, Rex G. "Toward Reinterpreting Psi Events." *Journal of the American Society for Psychical Research* 72, pp. 197–214 (1978).

———. "Research Strategies for Enhancing Conceptual Development and Replicability." *Journal of Parapsychology* 67, pp. 17–51 (2003).

Stanford, Rex G., Robert Zenhausern, Adelle Taylor, and Mary Ann Dwyer. "Psychokinesis as Psi-Mediated Instrumental Response." *Journal of the American Society for Psychical Research* 69, pp. 127–133 (1975).

Stearn, Jess. *Edgar Cayce: The Sleeping Prophet*. New York: Bantam, 1967.

Stevens, Paul. "Current Psi Theories." Chapter 2 in *A Biophysical Approach to Psi Effects and Experience*. Ph.D. thesis, University of Edinburgh, 1997. Formerly posted on the Website of the Koestler Parapsychology Unit, University of Edinburgh, as "Theories on the Physical Basis of Psi." Available from: http://moebius.psy.ed.ac.uk/Physical_H.php3. Accessed 10 July 2006.

———. "Noise, Physics and Psi: New Ideas for Research." *International Journal of Parapsychology* 11, pp. 63–72 (2000).

———. "The Effect of Weak Magnetic Fields on a Random Event Generator: Reconsidering the Role of Geomagnetic Fluctuations in MicroPK Studies." *European Journal of Parapsychology* 20, pp. 135–149 (2005).

———. "My Career in Parapsychology." Available from: http://pflyceum.org/ 128.html. Accessed 3 June 2007.

Stevenson, Ian. "The Evidence for Survival from Claimed Memories of Former Incarnations. Part I. Review of the Data." *Journal of the American Society for Psychical Research* 54, no. 2, pp. 51–71 (April 1960) [1960a].

———. "The Evidence for Survival from Claimed Memories of Former Incarnations. Part II. Analysis of the Data and Suggestions for Further Investigations." *Journal of the American Society for Psychical Research* 54, no. 3, pp. 95–117 (July 1960) [1960b].

———. *Twenty Cases Suggestive of Reincarnation.* New York: American Society for Psychical Research, 1966.

———. "Telepathic Impressions." *Proceedings of the American Society for Psychical Research* 29, pp. i–viii, 1–198 (1970). Also published as *Telepathic Impressions.* Charlottesville: University Press of Virginia, 1970.

———. "Xenoglossy: A Review and Report of a Case." *Proceedings of the American Society for Psychical Research* 31, pp. i–vii, 1–268 (1974). Also published as *Xenoglossy: A Review and Report of a Case.* Charlottesville: University Press of Virginia, 1974.

———. *Cases of the Reincarnation Type.* Vol. 1: *Ten Cases in India.* Charlottesville: University Press of Virginia, 1975.

———. *Cases of the Reincarnation Type.* Vol. 2: *Ten Cases in Sri Lanka.* Charlottesville: University Press of Virginia, 1977.

———. "Some Comments on Automatic Writing." *Journal of the American Society for Psychical Research* 72, pp. 315–332 (1978).

———. *Cases of the Reincarnation Type.* Vol. 3: *Twelve Cases in Lebanon and Turkey.* Charlottesville: University Press of Virginia, 1980.

———. "Cryptomnesia and Parapsychology." *Journal of the Society for Psychical Research* 52, pp. 1–30 (1983).

———. *Cases of the Reincarnation Type.* Vol. 4: *Twelve Cases in Thailand and Burma.* Charlottesville: University Press of Virginia, 1983.

———. *Children Who Remember Previous Lives.* Charlottesville: University Press of Virginia, 1987.

———. "Guest Editorial: Was the Attempt to Identify Parapsychology as a Separate Field of Science Misguided?" *Journal of the American Society for Psychical Research* 82, pp. 309–317 (1988).

————. "Thoughts on the Decline of Major Paranormal Phenomena." *Proceedings of the Society for Psychical Research* 57, pp. 149–162 (1990).

————. *Where Reincarnation and Biology Intersect*. Westport, Conn.: Praeger, 1997 [1997a].

————. *Reincarnation and Biology: A Contribution to the Etiology of Birthmarks and Birth Defects*. Westport, Conn.: Praeger, 1997 [1997b].

Stevenson, I., and Pratt, J. G. "Exploratory Investigations of the Psychic Photography of Ted Serios." *Journal of the American Society for Psychical Research* 62, pp. 103–129 (1968).

Stewart, J. L., W. G. Roll, and S. Baumann. "Hypnotic Suggestion and RSPK." *Proceedings of Presented Papers: The 29th Annual Convention of the Parapsychological Association*, pp. 205–224 (1986).

Stober, Michael, and Hugo Meynell, editors. *Critical Reflections on the Paranormal*. Albany: State University of New York Press, 1996.

Stokes, Douglas M. "Theories of Anomalous Temporal Phenomena." *Parapsychology Review* 16, pp. 12–15 (1985).

————. "Spontaneous Psi Phenomena." In Stanley Krippner, Steven Hart, Elizabeth Schenck, Montague Ullman, and Robert O. Becker, editors. *Advances in Parapsychological Research* 8. Jefferson, N.C.: McFarland, 1997, pp. 6–87.

Stone, Robert B. *The Secret Life of Your Cells*. Atglen/West Chester, Penn.: Whitford Press/Schiffer Publishing, 1989.

Storm, Lance, and Michael A. Thalbourne. "A Paradigm Shift Away from the ESP-PK Dichotomy: The Theory of Psychopraxia." *Journal of Parapsychology* 64, pp. 279–300 (2000).

Stuart, C. E., and J. G. Pratt, editors. *A Handbook for Testing Extra-Sensory Perception, as Developed in the Duke University Parapsychology Laboratory*. With a foreword by J. B. Rhine. New York: Farrar and Rinehart, 1937. The book was variously sold with a "Record Pad for Testing Extra-Sensory Perception" and a set of "ESP Cards for Testing Extra Sensory [*sic*] Perception," referred to popularly as "Zener Cards," which included cards displaying a square, a circle, a star, a plus sign, or wavy lines, five for each symbol.

Swanson, Claude. *The Synchronized Universe: New Science of the Paranormal*. Tucson, Ariz.: Poseidia Press, 2003. Second printing, 2005.

Talbot, Michael. *Mysticism and the New Physics*. New York: Bantam, 1981.

————. *The Holographic Universe*. New York: HarperCollins, 1991.

Tannen, Louis. *Catalog of Magic No. 3*. New York: Tannen, 1985.

Targ, Russell. *Limitless Mind: A Guide to Remote Viewing and Transformation of Consciousness*. Novato, Calif.: New World Library, 2004.

Targ, Russell, and Jane E. Katra. "Remote Viewing in a Group Setting." *Journal of Scientific Exploration* 14, pp. 107–114 (2000).

Targ, Russell, and Harold E. Puthoff. *Mind-Reach: Scientists Look at Psychic Abilities.* Introduction by Margeret Mead, foreword by Richard Bach, preface by Harold E. Puthoff. Charlotesville, Va.: Hampton Roads, 2004. Originally published in 1977.

Targ, Elisabeth, Marilyn Schlitz, and Harvey J. Irwin. "Psi-Related Experiences." In Etzel Cardeña, Steven Jay Lynn, and Stanley Krippner, editors. *Varieties of Anomalous Experience: Examining the Scientific Evidence.* Washington, D.C.: American Psychological Association, 2000, pp. 219–252.

Tart, Charles T. *States of Consciousness.* New York: Dutton, 1975.

———. "Acknowledging and Dealing with the Fear of Psi." *Journal of the American Society for Psychical Research* 78, pp. 133–143 (1984).

———. "Science Versus Opinion on the Paranormal." Available from: http://www.paradigm-sys.com/ctt_articles2.cfm?id=26. Accessed 19 August 2006. First published in 1997 in *Journal of Consciousness Studies–Online.*

Taylor, John. *The Great Pyramid. Why Was It Built? And Who Built It?* London: Longman, Green, 1859. Although dated 1859 on the title page, actually published in 1860.

Tenhaeff, W. H. C. *Telepathy and Clairvoyance: Views of some little investigated capabilities of Man.* With a foreword by Berthold Eric Schwartz, M.D. Springfield, Ill.: Charles C. Thomas, 1972.

Thalbourne, Michael A. *A Glossary of Terms Used in Parapsychology.* With a preface by John Beloff. Charlottesville, Va.: Puente Publications, 2003.

Thalbourne, Michael A., and Lance Storm, editors. *Parapsychology in the Twenty-first Century: Essays on the Future of Psychical Research.* With a foreword by Brian D. Josephson. Jefferson, N.C.: McFarland, 2005.

Thomas, Northcote W. *Crystal Gazing: Its History and Practices, with a Discussion of the Evidence for Telepathic Scrying.* With an introduction by Andrew Lang. New York: Dodge Publishing Co., 1905.

Thouless, R. H. "The Present Position of Experimental Research into Telepathy and Related Phenomena." *Proceedings of the Society for Psychical Research* 47, pp. 1–19 (1942).

———. "Some Experiments on PK Effects in Coin Spinning." *Journal of Parapsychology* 9, pp. 169–175 (1945).

———. "A Report on an Experiment on Psychokinesis with Dice and a Discussion of Psychological Factors Favoring Success." *Proceedings of the Society for Psychical Research* 49, pp. 116–117 (1949–1952).

———. *From Anecdote to Experiment in Psychical Research.* London: Routledge and Kegan Paul, 1972.

Thouless, R. H., and B. P. Wiesner. "On the Nature of Psi Phenomena." *Journal of Parapsychology* 10, pp. 107–119 (1946).

———. "The Psi Processes in Normal and 'Paranormal' Psychology." *Proceedings of the Society for Psychical Research* 48, pp. 177–196 (1947).

Time-Life editors. *Psychic Voyages.* Mysteries of the Unknown series. Amsterdam: Time-Life Books, 1987.

———. *Mind Over Matter.* Mysteries of the Unknown series. Amsterdam: Time-Life Books, 1988.

———. *Psychic Powers.* Mysteries of the Unknown series. Amsterdam: Time-Life Books, 1989.

Tompkins, Peter, and Christopher Bird. *The Secret Life of Plants.* New York: Harper and Row, 1973.

Tromp, Marlene. *Altered States: Sex, Nation, Drugs, and Self-Transformation in Victorian Spiritualism.* Albany: State University of New York Press, 2006.

Truzzi, Marcello. "On Pseudo-Skepticism." Originally published in the *Zetetic Scholar* (1987). Available from: http://www.anomalist.com/commentaries/pseudo.html. Accessed 21 May 2007.

———. "On Some Unfair Practices Towards Claims of the Paranormal." Article was published in slightly edited form in: Edward Binkowski, editor. *Oxymoron: Annual Thematic Anthology of the Arts and Sciences.* Vol. 2: *The Fringe.* New York: Oxymoron Media, 1998. Available from: http://www.skeptical-investigations.org/anomalistics/practices.htm. Accessed 10 July 2006.

Tymn, Michael. "Mediumship: Direct Connection to a Level of the Afterlife, Telepathy or Fraud?" (2002). Available from: http://www.survivalafterdeath.org/articles/other/tymn.htm. Accessed 7 July 2006.

Tyrrell, G. N. M. "The Significance of the Whole." In *The Personality of Man: New Facts and Their Significance.* Middlesex, UK: Penguin, 1946. Available from: http://www.survivalafterdeath.org/articles/tyrrell/significance.htm. Accessed 4 September 2006.

———. *Science and Psychical Phenomena, Apparitions.* New Hyde Park, N.Y.: University Books, 1961. Originally published in 1953.

Tyson, Neil deGrasse. "The Beginning of Science." *Natural History,* March 2001. Available from: http://research.amnh.org/~tyson/18magazines_beginning.php. Accessed 28 May 2007.

Ullman, Montague. "Psi and Psychiatry." In John White, editor. *Psychic Exploration: A Challenge for Science.* Introduction by Edgar D. Mitchell. New York: Perigee/Putnam, 1974, pp. 247–267.

Ullman, Montague, and Stanley Krippner, with Alan Vaughan. *Dream Telepathy.* New York: Macmillan, 1973.

Utts, Jessica. "Replication and Meta-Analysis in Parapsychology." *Statistical Science* 6, no. 4, pp. 363–403 (1991). Available from: http://anson.ucdavis.edu/~utts/91rmp.html. Accessed 21 June 2006.

———. "The Significance of Statistics in Mind-Matter Research." *Journal of Scientific Exploration* 13, pp. 615–638 (1999). Available from: http://anson.ucdavis.edu/%7Eutts/JSE1999.pdf. Accessed 25 May 2007.

Utts, Jessica, and Brian Josephson. "The Paranormal: The Evidence and its Implications for Consciousness." [London] *Times* Higher Education Supplement, April 5, 1996, p. v. Available from: http://anson.ucdavis.edu/%7Eutts/azpsi.html. Accessed 25 May 2007.

Van de Castle, Robert L. "Anthropology and Psychic Research." In John White, editor. *Psychic Exploration: A Challenge for Science.* Introduction by Edgar D. Mitchell. New York: Perigee/Putnam, 1974, pp. 269–287.

Van Over, Raymond, editor. *Psychology and Extrasensory Perception.* New York: New American Library, 1972.

Vasilescu, Eugen, and Elena Vasilescu. "The Mechanism of Telepathy." *Journal of the Society for Psychical Research* 61, pp. 211–220 (1996).

———. "Experimental Study on Precognition." *Journal of Scientific Exploration* 15, pp. 369–377 (2001).

Vasiliev, L. L. *Experiments in Mental Suggestion.* Charlottesville, Va.: Hampton Roads, 2002. English translation of 1962 Russian publication. First English translation published by the Institute for the Study of Mental Images, Church Crookham, Hampshire, England, in 1963.

———. *Experiments in Distant Influence.* New York: Dutton, 1976.

Vilanskaya, Larissa, compiler. *Parapsychology in the USSR.* Part I: *Psychoregulation and Psychic Healing.* Part II: *The Biofield: Its Nature, Influences, and Interactions.* San Francisco: Washington Research Center, 1981.

Vogel, Marcel. "Man-Plant Communication." In John White, editor. *Psychic Exploration: A Challenge for Science.* Introduction by Edgar D. Mitchell. New York: Perigee/Putnam, 1974, pp. 289–312.

Von Franz, Marie-Louise. *On Divination and Synchronicity: The Psychology of Meaningful Chance.* Studies in Jungian psychology by Jungian analysts, no. 3. Toronto: Inner City Books, 1980. Based on transcripts of a series of lectures delivered by von Franz at the C. G. Jung Institute, Zürich, in 1969.

Von Vesme, Caesar. *Geschichte des Spiritismus. Einzig autorisierte Übersetzung aus dem Italienischen und mit Anmerkungen versehen von Feilgenhauer.* 3 vols. Vol. 1: *Das Altertum* (1898). Vol. 2: *Mittelalter und Neuzeit* (1898). Vol. 3: *Die Neuzeit* (1900). Leipzig: Verlag von Oswald Mutze, 1898–1900.

Von Vesme. See also De Vesme.

Walker, Evan Harris. "The Nature of Consciousness." *Mathematical Biosciences* 7, pp. 131–178 (1970).

———. "Consciousness as a Hidden Variable." *Physics Today* 24, no. 4, p. 39 (1971).

———. "Application of the Quantum Theory of Consciousness to the Problem of Psi Phenomena." In W. G. Roll, R. L. Morris, and J. D. Morris, editors. *Research in Parapsychology, 1972.* Metuchen, N.J.: Scarecrow Press, 1973, pp. 51–53.

———. "Foundations of Paraphysical and Parapsychological Phenomena." In Laura Oteri, editor. *Quantum Physics and Parapsychology: Proceedings of an International Conference Held in Geneva, Switzerland, August 26–27, 1974.* New York: Parapsychology Foundation, 1975, pp. 1–44.

———. "Comparison of Some Theoretical Predictions of Schmidt's Mathematical Theory and Walker's Quantum Mechanical Theory of Psi." *Journal of Research in Psi Phenomena* 2, no. 1, pp. 54–70 (1977).

———. "Quantum Mechanical Tunneling in Synaptic and Ephaptic Transmission." *International Journal of Quantum Chemistry* 11, pp. 103–127 (1977).

———. "The Compleat Quantum Mechanical Anthropologist." In Joseph K. Long, editor. *Extrasensory Ecology: Parapsychology and Anthropology.* Metuchen, N.J.: Scarecrow Press, 1977, pp. 53–95.

———. "A Review of Criticisms of the Quantum Mechanical Theory of Psi Phenomena." *Journal of Parapsychology* 48, pp. 277–332 (1984).

———. *The Physics of Consciousness: Quantum Minds and the Meaning of Life.* Cambridge, Mass.: Perseus Books, 2000.

Warcollier, René. *La Télépathie: Recherches Expérimentales.* Paris: F. Alcan, 1921.

———. *Experimental Telepathy.* Edited and abridged by Gardner Murphy from *La Télépathie*, Articles in the *Revue Metaphysique*, and recent unpublished studies. Translated by Josephine B. Gridley, with the cooperation of Maud King Murphy. Boston: Boston Society for Psychic Research, 1938.

———. *Mind to Mind.* New York: Creative Age Press, 1948.

Watkins, Alfred. *Early British Trackways, Moats, Mounds, Camps, and Sites.* Hereford, UK: Watkins Meter Co., and London: Simpkin, Marshall, Hamilton, Kent, and Co., 1922.

Weiner, Debra H. "Thoughts on the Role of Meaning in Psi Research." In D. H. Weiner and R. D. Nelson. *Research in Parapsychology, 1986.* Metuchen, N.J.: Scarecrow Press, 1987, pp. 203–223.

Wendlandt, O. J. "Fake Photography, Remarkable Demonstration at Shefield." *Quarterly Transactions of the British College of Psychic Science* 13, pp. 320–321 (1935).

West, Donald J. "A Critical Survey of the American PK Research." *Proceedings of the Society for Psychical Research* 47, pp. 281–290 (1942–1945).

West, D. J., and G. W. Fisk. "A Dual ESP Experiment with Clock Cards." *Journal of the Society for Psychical Research* 37, pp. 185–197 (1953).

White, John, editor, with Edgar D. Mitchell. *Psychic Exploration: A Challenge for Science.* New York: Perigee/Putnam, 1974.

White, Michael. *Weird Science: An Expert Explains Ghosts, Voodoo, the UFO Conspiracy, and Other Paranormal Phenomena.* New York: Avon, 1999.

White, Rhea A. "A Comparison of Old and New Methods of Response to Targets in ESP Experiments." *Journal of the American Society for Psychical Research* 58, pp. 21–56 (1964).

———. "The Limits of Experimenter Influence on Psi Test Results: Can Any be Set?" *Journal of the American Society for Psychical Research* 70, pp. 333–369 (1976).

———. *Surveys in Parapsychology: Reviews of the Literature with Updated Bibliographies.* Metuchen, N.J.: Scarecrow Press, 1976.

———. *Parapsychology: New Sources of Information, 1973–1989.* Metuchen, N.J.: Scarecrow Press, 1990.

White, Rhea A., and Laura A. Dale, editors. *Parapsychology: Sources of Information.* Compiled under the auspices of the American Society for Psychical Research. Metuchen, N.J.: Scarecrow Press, 1975.

Wigner, Eugene P. "Remarks on the Mind-Body Question." In Irving John Good, Alan James Mayne, and John Maynard Smith, editors. *The Scientist Speculates: An Anthology of Partly-Baked Ideas.* New York: Basic Books, 1962, pp. 284–302.

Wiklund, Nils. "On the Assessment of Evidence for Psi." *European Journal of Parapsychology* 5, pp. 256–271 (1983–1985).

Wilkinson, H. P., and Alan Gauld. "Geomagnetism and Anomalous Experiences, 1868–1980." *Proceedings of the Society for Psychical Research* 57, pp. 275–310 (1993).

Wiseman, Richard, and Emma Greening. "'It's still bending': Verbal Suggestion and Alleged Psychokinetic Ability." *British Journal of Psychology* 96, pp. 115–127 (2005).

Wiseman, R., and C. Watt. "Experimenter Differences in Cognitive Correlates of Paranormal Belief and Psi." *Journal of Parapsychology* 66, pp. 371–385 (2002).

Wiseman, Richard, and Marilyn Schlitz. "Experimenter Effects and the Remote Detection of Staring." *Journal of Parapsychology* 61, pp. 197–208 (1997).

Wood, Frederic H., and A. J. Howard Hulme. "The Nona-Rosemary Language Tests in Ancient Egyptian." Pamphlet published by the International Institute for Psychical Research, London. Reprint of an article in *Psychic Science* (1936).

Wolman, Benjamin J., editor. *Handbook of Parapsychology*. New York: Van Nostrand Reinhold, 1977.

Wright, George E. *Practical Views on Psychic Phenomena*. New York: Harcourt, Brace and Howe, 1920.

Wyld, George. "Clairvoyance." *Proceedings of the Society for Psychical Research* 1, pp. 156–157 (1883).

Wynn, Charles M., and Arthur W. Wiggins. *Quantum Leaps in the Wrong Direction: Where Real Science Ends and Pseudoscience Begins*. With cartoons by Sidney Harris. Washington, D.C.: Joseph Henry Press, 2001.

Youngson, R. M. *Scientific Blunders: A Brief History of How Wrong Scientists Can Sometimes Be*. New York: Carroll and Graf, 1998.

Zammit, Victor. "A Lawyer Presents the Case for the Afterlife: Irrefutable Objective Evidence" (2002). Available from: http://www.victorzammit.com/book/index.html#download. Accessed 14 May 2005.

Zohar, Danah. *Through the Time Barrier: A Study of Precognition and Modern Physics*. London: Heinemann, 1982.

Zollschan, George K., John F. Schumaker, and Greg F. Walsh, editors. *Exploring the Paranormal: Perspectives on Belief and Experience*. Dorset, UK: Prism, 1989.

# INDEX

# ABOUT THE COMPILERS

**Robert M. Schoch** earned his Ph.D. in geology and geophysics from Yale University (May 1983). He also holds two undergraduate degrees (B.A. in anthropology and B.S in geology from George Washington University) and two earned master's degrees (M.S. and M. Phil., both in geology and geophysics from Yale University). Since 1984, Dr. Schoch has been a full-time faculty member at the College of General Studies at Boston University. Dr. Schoch is known internationally for his work in Egypt; he has been quoted extensively in the media with reference to the Great Sphinx and ancient civilizations; and he has been featured in a number of documentaries, including the Emmy Award–winning *The Mystery of the Sphinx*. He is the author, with R. A. McNally, of a series of books detailing his studies: *Voices of the Rocks: A Scientist Looks at Catastrophes and Ancient Civilizations* (1999); *Voyages of the Pyramid Builders: The True Origins of the Pyramids from Lost Egypt to Ancient America* (2003); and *Pyramid Quest: Secrets of the Great Pyramid and the Dawn of Civilization* (2005).

Dr. Schoch's research has helped spur renewed attention to the interrelationships between geological phenomena, natural catastrophes, and the early history of civilization. His studies of the Great Pyramid and Great Sphinx in Egypt, as well as other ancient ruins around the globe, tie directly in with current research involving ancient mysticism, paranormal phenomena, and the basis of religious beliefs.

**Logan Yonavjak** is a former student of Dr. Schoch's at Boston University, and in 2003 and 2005 she served as his field assistant on research-related expeditions to Egypt, the Sinai, and Peru. Since 2004, Yonavjak has been actively involved with the Rhine Research Center (Durham, North Carolina) through volunteer work, participating in studies and attending classes and lectures. In the spring of 2005, Yonavjak was appointed as an international work scholar in the Perrott-Warrick Project directed by Dr. Rupert Sheldrake that dealt with an online telepathy study. Yonavjak is a graduate of the University of North Carolina at Chapel Hill, where she earned her B.A. degree in geography, with a Geographic Information Systems (GIS) concentration.

JEREMY P. TARCHER/PENGUIN

a member of Penguin Group (USA) Inc.

*New York*

# THE

## PARAPSYCHOLOGY

## REVOLUTION